CW01095164

Walter Legge
Words and Music

Walter Legge
Words and Music

edited by
Alan Sanders

Duckworth

First published in 1998 by
Gerald Duckworth & Co. Ltd.
The Old Piano Factory
48 Hoxton Square, London N1 6PB
Tel: 0171 729 5986
Fax: 0171 729 0015

A catalogue record for this book is available
from the British Library

ISBN 0 7156 2774 0

Typeset by Ray Davies
Printed in Great Britain by
Redwood Books Ltd, Trowbridge

Contents

Introduction   *Alan Sanders*   1

1. Formative Years and Early Career   *Marie Tobin*   5

2. The Reviewer   17

3. Pre-War Associations   68
   I. Jean Sibelius   68
  II. Gerhard Hüsch and Herbert Janssen   84
 III. Arnold Bax   92

4. Wartime Activities   94
    I. Sir Thomas Beecham   94
   II. Sir Henry Wood   99
  III. Leopold Stokowski   101
  IV. Constant Lambert   103
   V. Leslie Heward   110
  VI. British Composers   113
 VII. Gerald Moore   115

5. The Philharmonia Orchestra   121
   I. Dennis Brain   121
  II. Two Clarinet Players: Frederick Thurston and Bernard
      Walton   125
 III. Running an Orchestra   127

6. Wilhelm Furtwängler   131

7. Post-War EMI Affiliations   167
   I. Herbert von Karajan   167
  II. 'Those Whom the Gods Love...'   175
 III. The Maharaja of Mysore   186
 IV. Albert Schweitzer   192
  V. EMI Colleagues   197

Contents

VI.	Two Composers: Sibelius and Britten	202
VII.	Nicolai Gedda	204
VIII.	Two Operatic Recordings	205
IX.	Otto Klemperer	209
X.	Carlo Maria Giulini	211
XI.	George Szell	214

8. Artists and Friends — 218

I.	Fritz Kreisler	218
II.	David Oistrakh	219
III.	De Sabata and Cantelli	226
IV.	Four Singers: Hilde Konetzni, Rosa Ponselle, Lauritz Melchior, Maria Callas	230
V.	More English Friends and Colleagues	237
VI.	Wieland Wagner	246
VII.	Wolfgang Sawallisch	251

9. Sir William Walton — 255

Postscript   *Dame Elisabeth Legge-Schwarzkopf* — 277

Index of Names — 278

Plates between pp. 122 and 123

Introduction

Alan Sanders

The idea of collecting an anthology of Walter Legge's writings first arose when I was compiling a discography of recordings made by his wife, Dame Elisabeth Schwarzkopf. This work eventually formed the second part of *Elisabeth Schwarzkopf: A Career on Record,* published in the autumn of 1995: part one comprises John Steane's richly illuminating essay on the experience of listening to Dame Elisabeth's recordings in company with the singer herself. Before the format of that book was agreed various notions as to the most advantageous context for publication of the discography were mooted and then discarded. These included plans to republish some of Walter Legge's writings.

I had long been familiar with Mr Legge's articles for the magazine *Gramophone*, and had admired their style and content. As a by-product of work on Dame Elisabeth's recordings my research revealed a rich legacy of further articles, a wealth of correspondence with some of the greatest musical figures of the twentieth century, and many evocative, penetrating reviews of pre-war concert and opera performances, originally written by Mr Legge for the *Manchester Guardian*. Some of this material had already appeared in Dame Elisabeth's memoir of her late husband, *On and Off the Record*, published in 1982 by Scribners in the USA and by Faber in the UK. But there were many more papers of importance which had not been used in that book, and it should be emphasised that the present volume contains nothing which was published in the earlier collection. At length it was agreed by all concerned that the 'new' Legge material could stand very well on its own as a separate volume.

Two factors have, I believe, made Walter Legge's writings an invaluable addition to our knowledge of the man and the world of music in which he lived. The first is the simple fact that he tended to keep papers relating to all aspects of his life and work. So often we read of important documents which have been discarded or destroyed, but Legge was concerned with capturing and preserving great performances through the medium of sound recording, and no doubt he also saw the value of preserving the written word in similar fashion. The second factor is that he was a man of strong convictions and feelings, and he conveyed his thoughts to paper in a direct, uncompromising manner. With him there was no mask, no holding back, no ambiguity of expression. We know that he made at least one attempt at an autobiography. It would have been a fascinating document, but there is some compensation in the fact that in the written material which does exist he reveals clearly the different facets of his own personality, his enthusiasms and aversions, his joys and his fears: many of his experiences are vividly and pithily recalled.

I have arranged the material in such a way that correspondence with individuals is often collected in its entirety at the point where it commenced. This means that some of the longer-lived exchanges continue outside the time span indicated by the scope of the chapter concerned, but it seemed to me preferable in many cases to trace the history of a relationship as a whole rather than to present the material in pieces according to date and other contexts.

It will be as frustrating to the reader as it has been to me that some of the correspondence is obviously incomplete, but in these instances all extant material has been presented. There are also cases where allusions to events or individuals can no longer be explained: every effort has been made to trace as many references as possible. In order to keep the content of this volume within sensible bounds I have also had to omit a large number of existing letters and a few articles.

It is my hope that this collection will serve to increase our knowledge of a remarkable figure in twentieth-century musical life, and shed light on his friends and associates.

Acknowledgements

This book owes everything to the support of Dame Elisabeth Legge-Schwarzkopf, who has facilitated work on the project in all manner of ways, who has given me access to a wealth of written matter in her possession, and who has allowed a rich collection of material to be reproduced in these pages. Copyright in relation to the writings of the late Ernest Newman also belongs to Dame Elisabeth, and I am grateful to her for permission to reproduce several of Mr Newman's letters.

I am also indebted to a number of other individuals and institutions for permission to use copyright material belonging to several writers. Concert and opera reviews taken from 1930s issues of the *Manchester Guardian* are reproduced with the permission of Guardian and Observer News Services (© *The Manchester Guardian*). Gramophone Publications Ltd have generously allowed me to reproduce Marie Tobin's essay on her brother, originally published in *International Classical Record Collector*, and articles by Mr Legge on Maria Cebotari, Dennis Brain, Leslie Heward, Ginette Neveu, Dinu Lipatti and Gerald Moore, originally published in the magazine which was then called *The Gramophone*. Letters, articles and memoranda belonging to EMI, and letters from the late Maria Callas are reproduced by permission of Mr Charles Rodier of EMI Classics. Letters from Sir Thomas Beecham are reproduced with the permission of Shirley, Lady Beecham. I am indebted to Dr Elio de Sabata for permission to use a letter from Victor de Sabata, to Lady Susana Walton for permission to reproduce a number of letters from Sir William Walton, to the Britten Estate Ltd for permission to use letters from Lord Britten, to Dr Percy M. Young for permission to use a letter from Miss Harriet Cohen, to Dr Werner Kupper of Kupper and Lehner, Zürich, for permission to use letters from Herbert von Karajan, to the late Sir Michael Tippett, OM, for permission to use a letter from him, to Dr Peter Curzon for permission to use letters from Sir Clifford Curzon, to Mrs Yvonne Brain for permission to use a letter from her late husband Dennis Brain, to Ms Rhena Schweitzer Miller for permission to use letters from her father Dr Albert Schweitzer, to Miss Lotte Klemperer for permission to use letters and other documents from her father Dr Otto Klemperer, to Mrs Wendy Pyatt for permission to use letters from Gerald Moore, to the Royal Academy of Music for permission to use letters from Sir Henry Wood, to the John Ireland Trust for permission to use letters from John Ireland, to Frau Elisabeth Furtwängler for permission to use letters from her late husband Dr Wilhelm Furtwängler, to Sr Carlo Maria Giulini for permission to use letters from him, to Lewis Foreman for having obtained permission to reproduce a letter from Sir Arnold Bax, to Frau Gertrud Wagner for permission to use letters from her late husband Wieland Wagner, to Herr Wolfgang Sawallisch for permission to use letters from him, to the Board of Legal Successors of Jean Sibelius for permission to use letters from Sibelius, to Mr Ib Melchior for permission to use a letter from his late father Lauritz Melchior and to Mr John Teltsch of the Estate of George Szell for permission to reproduce letters from Mr Szell. Every effort has been made to trace all other copyright holders, and apologies are offered to any whose permission has inadvertently not been obtained. I am also indebted to Richard Osborne for information relating to the Karajan letters, to Tony Locantro for background information on EMI staff members, and to Lyndon Jenkins for various other facts and figures.

March 1998   Alan Sanders

1

Formative Years and Early Career

Marie Tobin

We commence by placing the subject of this book in context. No person knew Walter Legge more closely and continuously over the first four decades of his life than his younger sister Marie. Her account of his background and earlier life was originally published in the Autumn 1995 edition of *International Classical Record Collector*.

Walter Legge was born on 1 June 1906 in Keith Grove, near Ravenscourt Park, on the outskirts of London. He was named Harry Walter after his father, but eventually, to avoid confusion, he became known as Walter. His parents, then both aged 35, were born in 1871 and had known each other since their early teens. They came from a modest Victorian background with no claim on either side to an artistic heritage.

What singled out Walter Legge's father from the rest of his 12 brothers and sisters was the infirmity which struck him when he was three years old. He contracted poliomyelitis, which left him partially paralysed. He was of course unable to take part in the usual games and sporting activities of young people, but he was compensated by having an intelligence well above the ordinary. Soon noticed by the teachers at his school near Notting Hill Gate, he was given every possible encouragement to make progress with his studies and received a good basic education until the then minimum statutory age of 14.

Harry's father, a heating engineer, then arranged an apprenticeship for his son with a successful tailor friend, who owned a business in a house on Shepherd's Bush Green. This was an occupation deemed particularly suitable for disabled people in those days. In due course Harry rented a house near Ravenscourt Park and set up his own business, which through his dedication to perfection became very successful.

Reading and sketching were two of the young Harry Legge's favourite occupations, but the real, in every way inexplicable passion of his life was a love of music. Once having taught himself the rudiments, he soon learnt to read and sing tonic sol-fa at sight; he was fortunate enough to possess perfect pitch. When he had saved sufficient capital he bought himself a piano so that he could put his knowledge to satisfying use.

1. *Formative Years and Early Career*

By the time Harry Legge was married in 1905, the cylinder phonograph had been invented, and a year later, when Walter was some six weeks old, his father arrived home one day with an unexpected present, 'for the boy', he said. Much to his wife's astonishment it turned out to be a phonograph. This was soon superseded by a gramophone, which Walter's father purchased when models became readily available. This machine was to have an unanticipated but powerful influence on his son's development. Legge senior began to build up a record collection, and over the years it became representative of the types of music which were available on pre-electric 78s.

Until the early 1920s, when radio began to capture the public interest, it was only by means of gramophone records that most people were able to hear the world-famous voices of the time. Now Walter Legge's father began to purchase records of operatic arias sung by such vocal immortals as Caruso, Tetrazzini, Chaliapin, Martinelli, Galli-Curci and Alma Gluck. One of the most popular recorded singers then was the Australian bass-baritone Peter Dawson, whose renderings of popular ballads such as *On the Road to Mandalay* and *Roses of Picardy* found their place in the elder Legge's collection.

A sudden expansion occurred when he acquired a classical record collection from a local doctor, along with a handmade gramophone in a handsome cherry-wood cabinet. The doctor favoured instrumental music, and the glorious sounds of Kreisler and Elman opened up new vistas for Walter and his father, as did a first acquaintance with chamber music such as the Debussy String Quartet, and piano recordings by such household names as Pachmann, Paderewski and Moiseiwitsch, who much later was to play at concerts organised by Walter. The collection did however contain one piece sufficiently avant-garde to evoke contrasting reactions from father and son. This was Scriabin's *Poem of Ecstasy*. Walter's father immediately disapproved, but in spite of the primitive orchestral reproduction Walter found it exciting and rewarding. One could say that this was the point where Walter first began to rely on his own artistic judgement.

Walter's mother had a more cosmopolitan outlook on life than might be expected from one who had been brought up in strict Victorian surroundings. Before her marriage, Walter's maternal grandmother had spent some years abroad as lady's maid to the Countess Szecheni, whose husband knew Liszt and was associated with the movement for the unification of Italy. The years abroad obviously affected her outlook, and she acquired a taste for the French style of cooking. Several of her recipes and hints for introducing special flavours into family repasts were passed on to her daughter. Legge senior found his wife's culinary expertise very much to his taste, and Walter was accustomed to having good food, well prepared, but without any undue extravagance. This must surely have laid the foundation of his later distinction as a connoisseur of fine food and wine. Poetry, particularly that of Pope and Byron, and drama, which of course meant

Shakespeare, were the main interests of Walter's mother, and they equalled in intensity his father's love of music. It is no wonder, therefore, that these two strong influences had a deep and subtle effect on the young Walter, who, as he reached his teens, had already decided that music, in some as yet undefined way, would be the centre of his life.

There were several obstacles to the realisation of his aim: first, he had very poor eyesight, and as soon as he began to read it became apparent that he would always have to wear spectacles. For one who was to become an avid book collector and constant reader of books on many subjects as well as music, this must have been a terrible trial. Specialist opticians provided him with ever stronger spectacles, and thus he was able to continue reading and writing to the very end of his life.

The first problem led to the second: Walter's father, soon realising his son's handicap, thought he had found an ideal solution that would also fulfil his own ambition for his son. He planned that on leaving school (Latymer High School in Hammersmith), Walter should join the family business and eventually inherit it. So it was that Walter, with what despair we can only surmise, was enrolled at the erstwhile Regent Street Polytechnic to study the tailoring trade. This may well have been the most bitter experience of his youth, but it would have been foolhardy to expect, so soon after the end of the First World War, that he could hope to break into the world of music without any kind of specialist training.

We now know that Walter continued to harbour a secret ambition that he would break out of the shackles of the family business, and find a foothold in some musical organisation, whatever it might be. During any free time at his disposal, he continued to study every aspect of musical history and theory, and concentrated on the writings of respected contemporary writers. The public library was the source of all the information he was able to acquire, and later in life he gave full credit to a service which many now take for granted. At the age of 15, following a suggestion from his mother, Walter decided to attend one of the Celebrity Concerts held every Sunday afternoon at the Royal Albert Hall in London. Almost for the first time, freed from the artificial sound of music conveyed through a gramophone horn, he was able to hear most of the world-famous artists of the day who graced the platform of that impressive hall each Sunday. Walter became an *habitué*, and artists whose names had previously been known to him only from a record label or catalogue, became an exciting and impressive reality. There were singers such as Feodor Chaliapin, Mattia Battistini, Beniamino Gigli, Giovanni Martinelli, Luisa Tetrazzini, Amelita Galli-Curci, and the baritone, Titta Ruffo, who became Walter's idol. There were also such famous instrumentalists as Fritz Kreisler, Mischa Elman, Benno Moiseiwitsch, Vladimir de Pachmann and Ignaz Jan Paderewski, plus others too numerous to mention. Walter was mesmerised. Later, after attending these concerts for some years, he became more critical and occasionally infuriated his father by his adverse comments on the performance of established stars.

On the other side of Hyde Park, a smaller concert hall, the Queen's Hall, accommodated some 2,000 people and provided equally exciting musical fare. There he could hear the Monday orchestral concerts given by the London Symphony Orchestra. Walter attended many of this orchestra's concerts, as well as those of other ensembles who appeared there, and developed an ability to discriminate between the good, the less good, and the downright bad. He became familiar with the standard orchestral repertoire of the time, and he also heard less run-of-the-mill works that adventurous conductors introduced into their programmes. In 1932, for instance, he attended the first British performance of Mahler's Second, *Resurrection* Symphony under Bruno Walter, in a concert which also included Beethoven's *Choral Fantasia* with Schnabel playing the piano part. At the Queen's Hall he also heard star singers of international reputation: Elisabeth Schumann, Maria Olczewska, Conchita Supervia, and Walter's idea of a 'very great singer', Frieda Hempel.

Walter's first experience of opera had been when, as a boy of 7, his father had taken him to a performance of *The Bohemian Girl* by Balfe at the King's Theatre in West London, where a travelling opera company, the Carl Rosa, made regular visits. It was opera in English, of course, and Walter heard other popular operas there with his father. One in particular which he always remembered was Verdi's *Il trovatore*.

These experiences hardly prepared him for his first visit to Covent Garden in 1924, when he was 18 years old. The repertoire for the International Opera Season that year included *The Ring*, *Tristan und Isolde*, *Der Rosenkavalier* and *Salome*, all with casts of top-flight singers. Walter's conversion to German opera was immediate and complete. A new world seemed to open before him. Each year he looked forward keenly to the six weeks of the International Season, becoming totally absorbed with unrestrained enthusiasm in an ever-widening range of repertoire. Walter later realised that an appreciation of Verdi opera, which had given him so much pleasure in the past, could take its place side by side with a growing involvement with German operatic masterpieces; but at 18 he became a convinced Wagnerian, and a thoroughly emotionally involved admirer of Richard Strauss.

At the age of 20 Walter was introduced to the manager of the HMV record shop in London's Oxford Street, a Cornishman named C. Maxwell Tregurtha. This was the first such shop wholly devoted to the sale of gramophone records, and had been officially opened in July 1921 by Sir Edward Elgar. The introduction was probably not a matter of chance. There was in fact a kind of magic in the very title 'His Master's Voice', which had captured Walter's imagination since the days when he first heard and saw the collection of records his father so treasured. So it would be quite in order to assume that Walter in some way set up the introduction. There is no doubt that Tregurtha was impressed by the young man's knowledge and enthusiasm, and soon engineered a niche for him within The Gramophone Company – that of Lecturer, which entailed Walter travelling around the provinces to visit HMV outlets and give recitals and talks about the records manufactured by the Company to audiences of invited customers. It was good for business and sales increased. Unfortunately, after a few months, Walter made himself unpopular by criticising company policy, and soon found himself unemployed.

Walter's father's reaction to this event can be imagined. He must have felt that his original fears had been realised – that Walter was too audacious in venturing into a famous record company, and that his career prospects were finished. But Walter was not easily daunted, and his ambition was strong enough to enable him to overcome any embarrassment a less determined young man might have felt in the circumstances. Shortly afterwards he came to hear that another vacancy was to be created in the company, and he quickly put his name forward. This time a totally different kind of appointment was in view. As a test of his ability he was required to submit an analysis of Beethoven's *Archduke* Trio, which had just been recorded by Cortot, Thibaud and Casals in November and December 1928, and was to be released on HMV's red label in May 1929. The analysis would be printed inside the cover of the record set's album. Walter borrowed an old typewriter from a friend, shut himself away with the records and a miniature score, and set about a task which he knew would mean success or failure as far as any future position in HMV was concerned. He sweated for days over this challenge to prove himself, not just as a bright young hopeful, but as a capable and knowledgeable writer on a specialised musical subject. Never afterwards did he suffer such uncertainty as to whether his style and understanding of the subject would meet with the approval of The Gramophone Company management. It did – and the result of this pivotal point in Walter's career can be seen in the album notes attached to this famous recording.

Having secured his new appointment Walter was put to the task of writing album notes, sales copy for a bi-monthly new record release circular, plus more analytical notes. It was all grist to the mill of experience he was accumulating. And after about a year he assumed fresh responsibilities.

The Voice magazine was The Gramophone Company's 'official organ', published for the benefit of HMV's appointed dealers and company employees. From mid-1930 it became Walter's task to edit the magazine, and the job gave him full scope to use his initiative in making the publication attractive to its readers. Some of the articles he wrote himself, others he commissioned from well-known critics. C. Maxwell Tregurtha wrote several articles on the techniques of selling, window display and design. There were also technical articles on the elements of 'Radio, Amps and Ohms' by P.P. Eckersley, Chief Engineer of the BBC. Always on the cover was a picture of a famous artist or group of artists. This was all valuable experience for Walter in giving him, as he wrote many years later, 'a solid grounding in such matters as typefaces, printing processes and layout'.

And years afterwards, too, when he had his own orchestra, the experience thus gained helped him in preparing programmes and publicity material.

His work as Editor of *The Voice* also took him into the recording department of HMV, and he soon became friendly with the recording manager whom he was to succeed some years later – Fred Gaisberg. A man without any guile or malice in his makeup, Gaisberg readily allowed Walter to turn up at any sessions of special interest, such as the historic recording of Elgar's Violin Concerto in July 1932, with the young Yehudi Menuhin as soloist and Elgar himself conducting.

For some time Walter had been exercising his mind over a problem which had a special application at the time – the need for HMV to expand its catalogue in times of depression to include the kind of works that so far were regarded as almost unsaleable. Saleability: that is what really matters to any manufacturer of any product. In the record business it was bad news for music lovers, whose tastes were unlikely to be catered for because the sales potential of their kind of music was too small to justify the cost. The particular reason for Walter approaching this problem so seriously related to one of many visits he had made to the public library during his teenage years. There, searching among the shelves for books of special musical interest, he chanced upon the biography of the then almost unknown Austrian composer, Hugo Wolf. The author was Ernest Newman, the highly-esteemed critic of the *Observer* and later, the *Sunday Times*.

Newman was not merely a talented journalist, but a great writer of English prose on a wide range of subjects. But it was his books devoted to musical topics, particularly his biography of Richard Wagner, that placed him in the forefront of contemporary musicologists. When Walter Legge took fire from reading Newman's book on Wolf, it had not captured a wide readership, nor increased the appreciation of Wolf's music in England, which was at best minimal. Certainly nobody else had gone so far as to follow along the trail blazed by Newman in the way Walter now proposed to do.

Having obtained a copy of Wolf's *Mörike Lieder*, Walter began to work his way through each song, meticulously probing into the relationship between words and music that Newman had outlined in his book. Up to that time Walter's knowledge of German had been somewhat superficial – certainly scarcely adequate for the task he now set himself. He had a natural talent for languages, but hitherto, thanks to his enthusiasm for Verdi, it had been Italian which he had enthusiastically studied. Now, learning German properly became a labour of love, and he devoted more and more time to the study of a language for which he felt a strong affinity.

Newman had written that 'Wolf was the supreme master of form in music', and Walter was determined to give the music world an opportunity to experience at least some of his masterpieces. If he had suggested quite baldly that the company should make records of Lieder by a largely unknown Austrian composer, he would have been laughed out of the record department. Nevertheless, he would not, could not, get the obsession out

10

of his mind, and the seeds of an idea were germinating. In a quite Archimedean way, he awoke one morning with the plan fully ripened, and ready for assault on the HMV management. He knew at once that there was only one person to advise him.

Walter had first met Ernest Newman some years previously. One evening, during the interval of a concert at the Queen's Hall, Walter decided to introduce himself, a daring thing to do knowing Newman's dislike of meeting strangers. His misleadingly self-confident manner must have suggested to Newman that this was no ordinary young man, and possibly Walter's mention of Hugo Wolf's name persuaded him to take a closer look at this unknown. From that not-so-casual meeting there arose a friendship which lasted until Newman's death at the age of 90. Walter's admiration for the older man knew no bounds and it was therefore to him, as a son to a father, that he took his problems, both personal and musical.

So it was that one weekend in the summer of 1931 Walter telephoned to ask if he could call on Newman at his house in Surrey; he was one of the few guests who were always welcome there. When Walter laid before him his plan and discussed the way in which it might be brought to fruition, Newman soon became completely won over and offered to devote his next column in the *Sunday Times* to the project. This he did, and it made an immediate impact on his regular readers.

The scheme, seemingly so simple, was that The Gramophone Company should record a series of Wolf songs, to be published in one album containing six 12-inch records, if 500 members of the public would subscribe 30 shillings each to cover the cost of the whole operation. With Newman's backing assured, Walter's superiors at HMV accepted his idea for a Wolf 'Society' edition.

Once the project was announced in the autumn of 1931, there was an immediate and enthusiastic response. Several applications came from Japan, and that was before the airmailing of letters was possible. The Gramophone Company even made a profit. Walter had no difficulty in announcing who the artist for the first album would be: the German mezzo-soprano, Elena Gerhardt, who, with her usual accompanist, Conraad Bos, gave regular recitals at the Wigmore Hall in London, and was already well-known among the somewhat limited circle of Lieder *aficionados*.

The recordings, which were made in November and December 1931, were of course supervised by Fred Gaisberg, but as it was Walter's brainchild, Gaisberg generously allowed him to act as his assistant. This was the first time that Walter officially took part in a recording session, not merely as an onlooker but in his capacity as Editor of *The Voice*.

The success of the first Wolf song album encouraged HMV to promote further albums, and as is well-known, a total of seven volumes was made between 1931 and 1938, with singers of the calibre of Gerhard Hüsch, Herbert Janssen, Friedrich Schorr and Alexander Kipnis. Ernest

Newman, as he had promised when the recording plan was mooted, wrote all the accompanying analytical notes.

As a kind of back-up to the Wolf Society issues Walter decided independently to form the London Lieder Club. His aim was to promote the artists who had already recorded for the Society or were to do so shortly. The first venue of the Club was the Dorchester Hotel, where members in full evening attire attended each Sunday evening for two months (one Sunday excepted) in an atmosphere of quiet luxury to enjoy hearing the *crème de la crème* of contemporary Lieder singers. For the pleasure of attending these concerts members were asked to pay a subscription of three guineas. The list of patrons included the names of ten ambassadors; Walter did not believe in doing things by halves. Later, the Club held further Sunday evening soirées at the Hyde Park Hotel.

The success of the Wolf Society led to a stream of other Society issues, not all recordings produced by Walter, but originating in one way or another from his fertile brain.

When he was 28 years old, Walter first met Sir Thomas Beecham, and he soon became aware that Beecham would be willing to become involved in recordings for a proposed Delius Society. Beecham insisted that Walter should produce all his recordings, even though he was a Columbia artist, and they started work on a number of projects.

It seems almost unbelievable that while Walter was becoming more and more involved with record production, and spending more and more time in the recording studio, he was also, from 1932 onwards, a music critic for the *Manchester Guardian* (now the *Guardian*). He had quickly become known to several music critics in the close-knit music circles of London, and it was not long before he came into the orbit of another extraordinary character, Neville Cardus, who held the twin posts of music critic and cricket correspondent on the *Manchester Guardian*.

Cardus immediately recognised special qualities in Walter and arranged for him to be appointed assistant music critic on the *Manchester Guardian*, so that if Cardus were in Manchester attending a concert or a cricket match, Walter in London could attend a concert already agreed between them. After the concert Walter would go to the newspaper's London office in Fleet Street, write his copy and hand it in for transmission to Manchester for the next day's issue. He also wrote occasional reviews for the *Daily Telegraph*.

This double way of life continued for some years, until a conflict of duties and loyalties made it unavoidable but that Walter should resign from the *Manchester Guardian*. A most exciting project was now proposed, involving Sir Thomas Beecham. Walter had found it possible to persuade HMV to finance a complete recording of Mozart's *Die Zauberflöte* in Berlin. The Berlin Philharmonic Orchestra, a chorus which included the young Elisabeth Schwarzkopf, and a star-studded cast including Tiana Lemnitz, Helge Roswaenge, and Gerhard Hüsch, were to be conducted by Sir

Thomas, and sessions took place between November 1937 and March 1938.

The logistics of such an enterprise were quite staggering in those days. Walter had to assemble a cast of singers, which involved the difficulty of finding suitable alternatives if the first choices were not available. It was then necessary for Walter to go to Berlin ahead of Sir Thomas to coach the singers and at the same time ensure that the whole undertaking, including fares and living expenses, plus artists' fees, did not exceed the £3,000 that HMV had earmarked for the enterprise. It is astonishing, to say the least, bearing in mind the financial constraints, that the resultant recording should have been, in Walter's words some 40 years later, 'generally acknowledged as musically the best performance of Mozart's penultimate opera on record'.

Walter's career appears in retrospect to have followed a logical, almost inevitable course, but the facts now reveal that suddenly it took a quite unexpected turn. After the success of *Die Zauberflöte*, Beecham was obviously impressed with what Walter had carried out so effectively – even within the financial margin outlined by the HMV management. One day he invited Walter to lunch at his hotel, the Waldorf, and invited him to become his Assistant Artistic Director during the forthcoming International Opera Season at Covent Garden. With the confidence born of having been immersed in opera over the many years since his first visit to the Opera House, Walter felt quite ready to take on the responsibility.

The main obstacle lay with his employers. At the end of 1931 HMV, Columbia and Parlophone had combined to form one organisation, Electric and Musical Industries Ltd, and Walter felt sure that EMI would not readily agree to his non-appearance or irregular appearance in the office or the recording studios over a considerable number of weeks. What employer would? It was the powerful intervention of Sir Thomas Beecham who persuaded the then Chairman of EMI to grant Walter this very unusual leave of absence. Unusual, because Walter somehow managed to keep his hand on the controls of whatever recording plans were then under consideration. For several weeks he was either in his office; at Covent Garden; in his temporary flat in the vicinity of both HQs; dictating to one or other secretary; entertaining opera stars to lunch – or just in transit between them all. The strain on his constitution must have been outrageous, but Walter was happy, probably never happier, and thought he had the best of all possible worlds in his hands. The idea of a holiday would never have occurred to him.

This way of life lasted for two seasons at Covent Garden, 1938 and 1939. During the 1939 season it quickly became obvious that it would be useless to plan for a further season, with the threat of war becoming ever more likely. The atmosphere at the Opera House behind the scenes was tense and unhappy. A few weeks later war was declared, and life, in and out of the music world, was never the same again.

A few days before Neville Chamberlain's ominous announcement on 3

September 1939, Walter, who had a strong sense of what might befall, insisted that his widowed mother and sister should leave the capital, and accordingly drove them down to a charming rural area some 25 miles west of London, where he had been told by a colleague it would still be possible to find available property to buy or to rent. That Saturday, 2 September, they quickly found a delightful, recently built little house in Little Chalfont, Buckinghamshire, surrounded by a large, but as yet undeveloped garden. The owner was about to leave to stay with a married daughter, but kindly offered the three travellers accommodation until their furniture could be removed from London. Walter, however, felt like paying a dramatic farewell visit to 'England as we know it' and decided to embark on a quick tour around the countryside. The first night was spent in a roadside hotel at Burford aptly named 'The Gate to the Cotswolds'.

On the following day the trio embarked on a trip to the three cathedral cities of Gloucester, Hereford and Worcester. Each city is situated in delightful surroundings and Walter and his family felt a heightened sense of emotion at seeing these centuries-old cathedrals standing so securely in the face of possible impending disaster. On the road from Worcester, Walter found time to make a pilgrimage to Elgar's birthplace at Broadheath. For sure, the Legge family were the only visitors there on that particular day. When they reached a hotel which happened to be in the area known as Seven Springs, where the River Thames has its source, they found, while ordering their lunch, that the declaration of war had already been made.

Back in London on the Monday morning, Walter found that the situation in EMI was fluid. Several members of the staff were already due to join the forces, and a general transference of responsibility was being organised by the management. Following the semi-retirement of Fred Gaisberg earlier in the year, Walter had been given wider responsibilities, but now, in the changing situation, he had to modify his recording plans to supervise recordings of so-called 'light' or 'popular' music of the time. This was certainly not to his liking but was a result of the need to adapt to altered circumstances.

By 1940, the reorganisation was nearly complete, and Walter, who had been rejected for war service because of his weak eyesight, was put in charge of all EMI classical recordings. He was able to sandwich in between the lighter music fare some further sessions with Beecham, and also Felix Weingartner's last recordings. Sir Thomas embarked for Australia and the Americas in April 1940, and so the Beecham-Legge collaboration was suspended until Beecham's return in 1944.

Before his departure, however, Beecham recommended to Basil Dean, the Director General of ENSA (Entertainments National Services Association), that he should appoint Walter to head a separate music department within the organisation. This Dean did, and in addition to his work for EMI Walter was occupied for the rest of the war in organising concerts for the forces in Britain and overseas, wherever it was possible to arrange transport and accommodation, however primitive. Many of these entertainments were similar to concert parties, with small groups of singers and instrumentalists combining to produce a varied programme guaranteed to appeal to the tastes of all ranks in the forces. The concerts provided a distinct contrast to the famous comedy shows, which also brought much-needed enjoyment to the embattled forces.

A band of intrepid musical performers, known as the 'Good Music Group', travelled to Egypt, and from there on to Iran and Iraq, finally coming to the end of their eastward travels in Mesira on the Gulf of Oman. The Group consisted of a quartet of singers – Miriam Licette (soprano), Nancy Evans (mezzo-soprano), Walter Widdop (tenor), and Dennis Noble (baritone), plus the violinist Alfred Cave and the ebullient accompanist Ivor Newton, who struggled in vain to make the mini-piano which had to travel with them sound something like a proper concert grand.

In addition to the concert parties, Walter also organised events under the title, 'ENSA Orchestral Concerts for War Workers'. For this particular purpose he used the Liverpool Philharmonic, the City of Birmingham and Hallé orchestras, and when the venues were near London, some of the orchestras of the metropolis. Many notable performers of the day willingly undertook to perform wherever they might be sent. They included such pianists as Solomon, Louis Kentner, and even Moiseiwitsch, who, in spite of his involvement with the Lunchtime Concerts at the National Gallery, found time to take part in the opening concert of the Southern Command Symphony Orchestra. When the British Army invaded continental Europe the performing artists moved in after them in order to ensure that the troops could continue to be supplied with good music.

Working from the Theatre Royal, Drury Lane, a stone's throw from Covent Garden, Walter was fully stretched with this new undertaking, as he was still involved in a demanding recording schedule. Since the beginning of the war he had been living in Buckinghamshire, in the house he and his family had taken. It was convenient for London as no private car owners were allowed to buy petrol for the duration of hostilities, owing to supplies being restricted to essential use. The general public had to endure long delays when travelling by train, with military needs being given priority. Added to the difficulty of getting to and from his home and the erratic hours he was working, Walter also had to make frequent trips to recording sessions in Birmingham, Liverpool and Manchester, which were deemed to be safer than London. The effort had to be made so that the record-buying public, more numerous now than ever, could be provided with a supply of new recordings to help them while away long blackout hours.

During the Covent Garden opera season in 1939 Walter had become acquainted with a beautiful young singer named Nancy Evans, near the beginning of her career. He met her again later, when she was already working for ENSA, and their friendship developed rapidly. It was no surprise to their friends, therefore, when it was announced in 1941 that

Walter and Nancy were to be married. After no more than a two-day honeymoon, they endeavoured to settle down to married life. Their commitments hardly ever coincided, which made their chance of a successful marriage in wartime less and less likely. They tried to continue their relationship right up to the end of the war, but by then it was evident that their lives could not be adjusted to two such widely different careers. The one true joy of their marriage was the birth of their daughter, Helga Maria, in 1942, and towards the end of his life, Walter had the satisfaction of seeing his three grandchildren secure the continuation of the family line.

Walter left ENSA in 1945 and resumed full-time work with EMI. He made plans for an ambitious project, the formation of a completely new orchestra under his sole control. He believed that he could attract the best players in the country to the new body, if he could offer them regular employment and acceptable terms. Soon he had assembled a nucleus of those best players, and in 1945 the Philharmonia Orchestra was born.

2

The Reviewer

As Mrs Tobin reveals in Chapter 1, Walter Legge started to write reviews for the *Manchester Guardian* in the early 1930s. A selection is reprinted here. They remind us of the richness of London's musical life during this decade, when legendary artists such as Rachmaninov, Adolf Busch and Mengelberg were regular visitors to the capital city. Also apparent are the acute critical perceptions and musical knowledge of the youthful writer: all the reviews that follow date from a period when Legge was between 27 and 31.

Galli-Curci at the Royal Albert Hall   21 January 1934

The reappearance of the famous Italian coloratura soprano Amelita Galli-Curci at the Albert Hall this afternoon was an occasion of interest psychological rather than musical. Nearly 6,000 people had travelled across London through a fog that promised to develop into a 'pea souper' and paid high prices for the privilege of hearing her sing a programme that contained not more than half a dozen songs of musical worth, a faded operatic aria, and an odd assortment of café songs and ballads. By way of relief from the sound of the human voice the accompanist and a flautist played groups of solos. And yet there have been several occasions during this musical season when programmes of great music have been performed in splendid fashion to rows of empty seats.

It is true that this audience contained none of the usual set of concert-goers – the people whose faces are familiar to those who make a habit of attending the Queen's Hall and Covent Garden whenever there is good music to be heard. But why should 6,000 people elect to go to this rather than to any other concert? By its behaviour this audience proved that its interests were other than purely musical. It received a group of old Italian songs politely but frigidly; it coughed and rustled its programmes through some Debussy pianoforte pieces. But it clapped its hands in naive delight when the singer sat down at the piano to play her own accompaniment, and it held its breath at the acrobatics of the Shadow Song from *Dinorah*.

Nine years have passed since Galli-Curci first sang in London. Time has not changed her. Her voice has lost none of its suavity, it has still that oiled ease that delighted us when we first heard it through the medium of the gramophone. She can still fearlessly match herself with an able flautist and perform the vocal parallel of trapeze acts to which her uncertainty of intonation serves but to add a spice of excitement of the 'will-she-do-it' variety. With the exception of a lapse in Rossini's *Tarantella* (wherein she coyly transposed the final note down a tone without having previously warned her accompanist) her intonation was surer than of yore, but it still has that uncertainty that prevents the sensitive listener from enjoying to the full her lovely tone and otherwise accomplished vocalisation.

Kulenkampff at the Queen's Hall   10 February 1934

Even the announcement of Brahms's Violin Concerto to be played by a violinist new to London but of great Continental reputation failed to attract a large audience to last night's concert of the Royal Philharmonic Society. The 10,000 of London's so-called musical public that flocks to the Albert Hall to hear Gigli or Tauber is decimated by an orchestral programme containing a couple of unfamiliar works. Apparently it takes more than the experience-born knowledge that Beecham never gives a dull concert to induce 2,000 of London's seven millions to listen to Strauss's *Le bourgeois gentilhomme* Suite and a symphony by Balakirev. The Strauss suite is one of the most engaging works in the whole orchestral repertoire – that alone should have drawn a large audience, and surely there are enough musicians curious to hear, if only once, a symphony by Balakirev!

Whatever the reason for this mass capriciousness, the smallness of the audience that turned up at the Queen's Hall last evening seemed to have at the outset a depressing effect on the orchestra. In its usual form, the London Philharmonic Orchestra would have given a magnificent performance of Strauss's graceful, brilliant suite. Tonight the trumpet 'fluffed' a passage which must be played perfectly or not at all; the pianist lacked the rhythmic vitality on which so much of the success of the work depends; the intonation of cellos was often uncertain. And yet, for all its faults (the omission of three movements was not the least among them), the performance was a good one, for the work is fiendishly difficult. Beecham has found exactly the right tempo for the Minuet and the 'Dance of the Tailors'; both the woodwind and the trombone played superbly, and Paul Beard mastered the treacherous violin solo. With a few more rehearsals and bigger audiences, Beecham will make this work as popular as it deserves to be.

Herr Kulenkampff, who, together with Furtwängler and Backhaus, controls the musical destinies of Nazi Germany, is a violinist of the first class. His tone is full and round, and his technique makes even the difficulties of the Brahms Concerto seem mere child's play. But he lacks warmth, he plays as if he admires music but bears it no love. His playing belongs to the realm of science rather than of art.

The Balakirev Symphony is well worth its place in a programme, but it is hardly likely to become part of our staple musical diet. Its first movement, save for the second subject, that is a close relation of the Ivan theme of *Ivan the Terrible*, is more German than Russian in feeling, and the really Russian movements are rather long for their contents.

Sir Hamilton Harty: Philharmonic Society   23 November 1934
Presentation

Tonight, for the second time this month, Sir Hamilton Harty has conducted the London Philharmonic Orchestra at a concert of the Royal Philharmonic Society. Three weeks ago he took over a Beecham programme, a typically Beecham programme; tonight he has conducted his own Violin Concerto and three works obviously of his own choice – the Overture to Berlioz's *Beatrice and Benedict*, Mozart's Divertimento No. 17 and Brahms's Fourth Symphony.

One could feel tonight why he is so devoted to Berlioz, why he rates him above all other composers, why he conducts him with such sympathy, understanding, and expressiveness. His mind has much in common with Berlioz's. Berlioz loves the vivid, the exciting, and he wrote hyperbole. His criticisms, essays, and letters are vehement and eloquent; what a normally pulsed man would call large, Berlioz called colossal, stupendous, and pyramidal. He felt life like that. Harty gives the impression that he feels music in that way, so that one wonders why a comparatively low-pulsed composer like Brahms features so frequently in his programmes. Harty's fire, his eloquence, his persuasiveness, his charm are wasted on Brahms. It was Wolf who said that 'Brahms cannot exult'. Tonight Harty tried to make Brahms exult and in a way he succeeded, but much as one could admire the colour and passionate intensity of it all one missed the browns and greens and the reticence that most of us believe to be the real Brahms.

At the end of the first half of the programme Lord Londonderry presented Sir Hamilton Harty with the Royal Philharmonic Society's gold medal. In a short speech of thanks the conductor made witty and pointed reference to the fact that much of his conducting is done abroad and said that since the medal is a tribute from musicians – men of his own profession – it will go with him as a mascot and a reminder of the faith that his fellow musicians in Britain have in him. As if to pay its tribute to the conductor, the orchestra played better than it has ever done for any man but Beecham.

Paul Beard was the soloist in Harty's Violin Concerto; only three movements of the Mozart Divertimento were played.

William Walton's Symphony –   4 December 1934
first three movements performed in London

After various announcements and postponements of the first performance of William Walton's Symphony, three movements of that work were given for the first time by Sir Hamilton Harty and the London Symphony Orchestra at the Queen's Hall this evening. That this still unfinished work should be thus presented is unfortunate for the composer, particularly as we learn that the opening bars and the last three minutes of the missing movement are already completed. It is not fair either to the composer or to the audience to expect a final opinion based on these three movements, any more than it would be to estimate the worth of Sibelius's Fifth Symphony without having heard its superb finale.

On first hearing Walton's Symphony strikes one immediately and repeatedly as having been written under the influence of Sibelius. The hold that the great Finn has taken of our best composers is significant. The younger fashion-chasers among our musicians talk long and loud of the importance and all-powerful influence of Stravinsky and of Schoenberg, of how these two men are cutting the new paths that music must now and henceforward follow. But it is the influence of Sibelius that shows in the later works of Bax and in this new Walton work. It may be that the style we now regard as Sibelian is 'in the air' but it is difficult to credit that in this symphony Walton has not been consciously or subconsciously writing on Sibelian lines. Time and time again, particularly in the first movement, the character of the melodies as well as of the scoring suggests that Walton knows his *Tapiola* as well as the Fifth and Seventh Symphonies. The ascending string passages, the dramatic stabs of brass *sforzandi*, the melodic fragments with arresting rhythms in the woodwind are almost as evident in this symphony as in Sibelius's most characteristic works. There, however, the likeness ceases. Walton is too definite a musical personality to surrender himself to another mind, and the first two movements have, in spite of the modest orchestra, a brilliance and intensity of colour that we know from *Belshazzar's Feast* to be Walton's own. The first movement, like that fine choral work, is perhaps too vehement, too insistent. It forces its way along with terrific concentrated energy, but it is indubitably of the stuff of which great music is made.

The scherzo, marked 'Presto con malizia' is reminiscent of Holst in its rhythmic power and ingenuity, and one felt that the greater part of the audience was cowed by its forces. It is an angry, fierce movement and a superb piece of writing. In the slow movement there is more of the Walton we know from the Viola Concerto, the sensitive, fine-nerved composer who can and does write exquisite melodies. But while one delights in the beauty of this movement *per se*, it will not be until the whole four movements are given that we can judge it in relation to the whole. Enough here to say that this foretaste promises a complete symphony that will rank with the finest works of its epoch.

Kreisler at the Albert Hall   28 January 1935

The nine or ten thousand people who braved the northeaster, the snow and slush and slippery roads, to hear Kreisler at the Albert Hall this afternoon were rewarded with the best violin playing that has been heard in London since Kreisler last played the Elgar Concerto. To hear Kreisler play as he did this afternoon is the best medicine and a necessary medicine, for both the habitual concert-goer and the musical critic. To hear him is to realise the true meaning of the word 'great'. He readjusts one's standards, raises them again to heights from which they have lapsed through too frequent meetings with the competent or the very able, or the nearly great. His interpretation of the classics has never been disputed, and he goes to the heart of French and Spanish music as surely as he does to that of Elgar. The last item of today's programme, the dance from Falla's *La vida breve*, was a striking example of his penetration into Spanish music. He had been playing some of his own little pieces in the Viennese style, but as he began the dance in question his tone took on an entirely new colour – so different that it might have been a different instrument, another artist. He played as Supervia sings, with a passionate meridional warmth and a certain intense roughness (without sacrificing the essential beauty of tone) that was the perfect violinistic counterpart of Supervia's singing of Falla's songs.

The most important works in the programme were Bach's B minor Partita, which received an unforgettable performance, and the D major Concerto No. 4 of Mozart. In a lifetime of listening to music I have heard nothing finer than Kreisler's playing of this concerto. In style, in timing, in tone, in technique it beggared description and defied criticism. There is but one criticism. Why should we be made to listen to Kreisler playing a concerto with only a piano as substitute for an orchestra? The Mozart concerto demands only a small orchestra – six first violins, five seconds, four violas, four cellos, three basses, two oboes, two horns would have sufficed – 23 players in all, and a conductor. The cost of a first-class orchestra would have been in the neighbourhood of £60. Add £50 for a good conductor, and we could have had three such concertos perfectly performed.

Heifetz and Beecham   7 March 1935

When Heifetz came here seven or eight years ago he was a far better player than he was when he first appeared in London as a child prodigy, but those who had been then most prominent in pronouncing him faultless now deplored his frigidity, his aloofness, and his detachment. One suspects that that expressed view was not untinged by resentment at what was felt to have been too generous praise long since lavished. Last night at the Royal Philharmonic Society's concert what was probably over-praise of the child Heifetz and what was certainly under-praise of the young man Heifetz were things of the past, and Heifetz the man played Beethoven's Violin Concerto and proved that he is one of the really great violinists of our time. His technique is as flawless as anything of human agency can be (you should have heard the run up in sixths at the beginning of the cadenza) and his tone is ravishing and as rich in colours as the spectrum itself. And in his hands the violin might well be a keyboard instrument perfectly tempered; he plays with such faultless intonation that one is tempted to wonder if the violin as an instrument is capable of producing a tone that is out of tune. All this is done with such an appearance of simplicity that the listener might well imagine that he has only to pick up a violin and put a bow to it, and he will play the Beethoven Concerto as well as Heifetz.

Yes, Heifetz is unquestionably one of the supreme violinists of our time; he is certainly the least fallible. He lacks, it must be admitted, the warm, human, lovable tone that makes Kreisler the king of violinists, and he has not the highly strung, quivering sensibility of Szigeti, but his classic poise and lofty style, his sensitive musicianship and phrasing make him such an artist that one can listen with pleasure to his playing even of the silly cadenza that delays for several minutes the end of the first movement of the Beethoven Concerto. It does not matter whether Beethoven himself wrote this cadenza or whether it was perpetrated in 1882 by a committee consisting of Brahms, Joachim, Wolf, Richard Strauss, and Wagner; it is an excrescence.

Having devoted so much space to Heifetz there is but little room to accord just praise to Sir Thomas Beecham for his part in this magnificent performance of the concerto or for the exciting reading of Wagner's *Faust* Overture with which the concert began and his warm and lovely performance of Schumann's Third Symphony that concluded the programme.

'New' Schubert Symphony –   28 March 1935
First English Performance Last Night

Tonight Weingartner and the BBC Symphony Orchestra have played Schubert's Seventh Symphony – the real Seventh Symphony, the one in E major that Schubert left in sketch form. Too long has there been confusion and doubt as to the correct numbering of Schubert's later symphonies, and we can only regret that the BBC did not take the opportunity that tonight's performance presented of playing their part in the establishing of the truth of the numbering.

The Royal Philharmonic Society has recently led the way by correctly announcing the great C major as 'Symphony No. 9 in C major', and it would have avoided future confusion if the BBC had boldly marked this E major symphony as 'No. 7', as it undoubtedly is.

This work has a curious history. Schubert began writing it in August 1821, and completed the scoring in detail as far as the 110th bar of the first movement. Then, it seems, he grew impatient of the sheer physical labour of scoring, and henceforward he made mere memoranda of the course of the work, albeit memoranda so complete that there is no doubt as to his structural intentions. Every bar is drawn in, the tempi and the names of the instruments are written in at the beginning of each movement, all the nuances are marked, and he even wrote 'fine' at the conclusion of the fourth movement.

The themes are set out in full, and there is not a bar in the whole work in which he has not written clear indication in one part or another of what was to happen. No doubt he had the work finished in his mind, and intended to fill in the details when he had the leisure, but that leisure never came, the inexhaustible spring of his inspiration gushed too fast, and when he died the symphony was left in this sketch form.

The manuscript sketch passed from Schubert's brother to Mendelssohn, who contemplated completing it (but fortunately did not), and eventually by his brother to Sir George Grove, by whom it was given to the library of the Royal College of Music. A copy of the sketch reposes in the library of the Gesellschaft der Musikfreunde in Vienna, and it is from this copy that Weingartner has done what he calls the 'carrying out of Schubert's plan' that was played tonight.

He is not the first to have undertaken the task of completing the symphony. Over 40 years ago John Francis Barnett scored the work as he believed Schubert would have done, and his version was given at the Crystal Palace by Augustus Manns on 5 May, 1883. For those who are interested there is a pianoforte reduction of Barnett's score published by Breitkopf & Härtel which is well worthy of attention.

In the main Weingartner has done the job admirably, and in the first three movements there was nothing that might not have been written by Schubert himself. In the finale, however, there were several places where one felt, 'This is not how Schubert would have handled it.' And yet with Schubert one never knows. Had the great C major been left as incomplete as this E major Symphony, and been finished by another hand, as Schubert himself completed it, should we not have said of the magical horn passage in the second movement and of the trombones in the finale, 'This is not as Schubert would have handled it'? I think so.

In brief the E major Symphony in Weingartner's arrangement is a valuable addition to the concert repertory. It will not displace the B minor *Unfinished* nor the *Great* C major from their favoured places, but its charming, graceful melodiousness will secure for it a far more permanent position in the repertory of the future than Stravinsky's more recent effusions are likely to enjoy. It has, of course, all Schubert's characteristic repetitions, that make one feel that he was reluctant to leave a phrase or a melody until he had worked out the vein, and this may eventually count against it. But in the meantime let us be grateful for so engaging a work.

Koussevitzky in London   18 May 1935
Second of the BBC 'Festival' Concerts

Tonight Serge Koussevitzky has conducted the second of the series of concerts organised by the BBC and honoured with the imposing sounding title of 'The London Music Festival', and with two hours of magnificent music-making he has silenced nearly all the criticism that has been levelled at the BBC for the unenterprising nature of the programmes of this so-called festival and for the unsatisfactory performance of Bach's B minor Mass with which the series began.

The programme was orthodox enough in all conscience – Mozart's *Le nozze di Figaro* Overture and two great symphonies, the *Eroica* and Sibelius's Second; but our distinguished guest gave performances of such insight and sensitiveness and bewitched the BBC Symphony Orchestra into playing so far above its normal form that, whatever delights the subsequent concerts of the festival may hold in store, those of us who were fortunate enough to hear the two symphonies have already food for reflection to last us for many weeks to come.

The impression that Koussevitzky is an excitable, over-emotional conductor dies hard. It dates from the time when he introduced us to Scriabin, and his nervous orgiastic performances of the *Poem of Ecstasy* that swept so many of us off our feet 20 years ago have not yet been lived down; rather have they become a legend inseparably associated with Koussevitzky's name. If ever that legend is to die it will be at the hand of tonight's performance of the *Eroica*.

The performance of the *Figaro* Overture with which the concert began was of the 'That's *Figaro* – that was' order. One had hardly time to notice the perfect articulations of the strings at even that breakneck speed before Koussevitzky was back in the artists' room with the first item of the programme finished. After that one was prepared for anything except what came – a performance of the *Eroica* of such nobility, restraint, dignity, power, and emotional depth that one is tempted to say 'I will never hear that work again. Let me live on the memory of this performance.'

It was not by any means the 'biggest' *Eroica* we have heard. Its muscles were those of the perfectly trained athlete rather than of the professional strong man, but it was beautiful beyond words. There is no man living who merits a funeral march of such noble pathos as Koussevitzky gave us in the slow movement.

In the Sibelius symphony we missed some of the richness of string tone that we have enjoyed in recent performances of the work by the London Philharmonic Orchestra. There was volume in plenty, but not the intensity of tone that the London Philharmonic produces. Before another two years have passed this work will occupy the places in the affections of conductors that Tchaikovsky's Fifth and Sixth have enjoyed. There is no great work in the repertory better calculated to excite an audience. From conversations one overheard in the hall, it is clear that for many people the principal interest in this particular performance lay in deciding how Koussevitzky's reading compared with those of Kajanus and Beecham – a sort of contest to decide who is 'top conductor'. 'Which,' in the words of *1066 and All That,* 'is a bad thing.'

Il barbiere di Siviglia   25 May 1935

Wagner is credited with having said: 'Rossini, Rossini – how I love him: but do not tell my Wagnerians – they would never forgive me.' How surprised Wagner would be to see himself sharing a festival at Covent Garden with Rossini; how Rossini would laugh at the strange turn of the wheel of fate that has brought some of his forgotten works back into the repertoire.

Until tonight the Rossini boom has had a slightly false ring. The enthusiastic welcome accorded to *Cenerentola* last year has been perceptibly cooler at this year's performances. Sir Thomas Beecham, who has made this Rossini boom what it is, overlooked one factor when he set out to reinstate Rossini – the reaction of the British public to style in musical art. Sir Thomas has a more acute perception of and more highly developed feeling for style than any man in this country, and it is possibly the purity of Rossini's style in his particular *genre* that has won his affection. But English audiences have little sense of the style of Italian comic operas, and, deaf to Rossini's style, they are left with what no doubt seems to them a succession of rather ordinary flimsy tunes and some pleasant-mannered fooling. In *Barbiere* Rossini's style is at its best, but the tunes and the plot are vastly superior to those of *Cenerentola* and *L'Italiana in Algeri*. So that however innocent we may be of style, there is music and action that we can all appreciate.

The double attraction of Rossini's enduringly popular opera and the Covent Garden début of Lily Pons attracted a huge audience. Physically she is the Rosina of our dreams, a mere slip of a girl who is, and who looks and sounds, young. Vocally she is gifted with a voice of exceptionally lovely quality and remarkable size, and she sang all Rossini's ornaments, and some that were not his, without apparent effort. Although she was followed about the stage by a spotlight throughout the performance, the honours of the evening went to Pinza, whose Don Basilio was, after Janssen's Gunther and Kurwenal, easily the best individual performance of the season. Like Janssen, Pinza creates for each role a distinct character and personality. For the rest, Inghilleri, as Figaro, sang splendidly, but his acting was the very negation of the mercurial Figaro. Heddle Nash, in spite of a 'frog in his throat' that gave him a lot of trouble in the first act, sang better than any tenor we have heard at Covent Garden this year.

Prince Igor at Covent Garden   15 June 1935

Last night's performance of *Prince Igor*, making due allowance for the difficult conditions under which the opera had been staged, was a splendid achievement. The singing of the soloists was in many cases magnificent, and the orchestral playing (apart from a curious misunderstanding after the Polovtsian March in the first scene of the third act) had, thanks to Sir

Thomas Beecham, rare loveliness of texture, brilliance of colour, and vitality of rhythm.

It cannot be denied that in places Borodin's scoring is thin and that occasionally he wrote what has since become musical commonplace, but when all is said and done, *Igor* is one of the loveliest and most exciting works in the whole of the operatic repertoire. What it needs is production as perfect in its way as the singing that Jaroslavna's music had from Rethberg. She alone of the whole cast made the German language sound fit and proper for the music, and in every detail of phrasing and colouring and inflection and beauty of tone she proved herself the most accomplished woman singer we have heard in London in the last decade.

Of the men, Janssen in the title role took chief honours; the rest of the cast seemed strangers in a strange land. Schöffler, as Galitzky, suggested nothing of a villainous Russian Prince; Kullman, for all the fresh charm of his singing, seemed to have wandered, style and all, out of *La bohème*, and as the two comic drunkards Habich and Fleischer were but Alberich and Mime on a conducted tour of Russia. Even Kipnis, the one Russian in the cast, was, curiously enough, as Germanic as the rest of his Wagner-singing colleagues.

La bohème   30 September 1935

This evening's performance of *La bohème* attracted the first large audience of the London and Provincial Opera Society's London season to hear the best performance the society has given us and see a Mimi they will not quickly forget – Signorina Lisa Perli. She was beyond question the most natural and convincing Mimi I have ever seen. Nature or a dietician has given her the figure for the part, and she made hardly one conventional operatic gesture during the whole evening. She conveyed as no other artist within memory Mimi's shyness in the presence of her noisy Bohemian friends.

Never for one moment was she an opera singer acting Mimi or showed that she was aware of the existence of an audience. She played to her colleagues as if the proscenium opening had been a brick wall. So real and human was her performance that when at the end of each act she came before the curtain to make her curtsy with her all-too-obviously operatic colleagues one felt a shock of pained surprise that the Mimi whose love and suffering one had watched through the act should have the courage to walk before the curtains of an opera house.

Vocally she more than held her own with singers around her. She has power enough, an exquisite *mezza voce*, and an extraordinary instinct for expressive musical phrasing. For the beauty and pathos of her 'Addio senza rancor' one willingly condones a certain hardness and an occasional uncertainty of attack of high notes. Considerable interest naturally centred in the identity of this artist, whose voice has a curiously familiar ring but who surpassed the achievements of the person who in colour of voice and shape of face she so strikingly resembled. But although no statement has been made, I am prepared to wager that Signorina Lisa Perli bears the same relation to Dora Labbette that Tantris bore to Tristan.

The acting of the remainder of the cast naturally suffered by comparison with that of 'La Perli', but there was some excellent work from that subtle artist Octave Dua and some capable conventional work from Signori Bettoni, Baracchi and Ponzio and Mr Heddle Nash.

The conductor was Sir Thomas Beecham.

BBC Symphony Concert – First of the Season   25 October 1935

At the Queen's Hall last night Adrian Boult conducted the first BBC Symphony Concert of the season. The programme was given over to the 'three Bs' – that is to say, the three universally accepted Bs, Bach, Beethoven and Brahms, and to their august company was admitted – not, we hope, solely for the sake of alliteration – a contemporary B, Alban Berg.

The sight of the platform just before the concert began would have delighted the eyes and heart of Berlioz (yet another B). How he would have fired off the mighty adjectives to which he was so addicted at the sight of 20 first violins, 16 seconds, 14 violas, 11 cellos and ten double basses. Such a body of strings is admirable and enviable in music that calls for thickness and richness of tone if the rest of the orchestra is proportionately enlarged, but the Sinfonia to Bach's church cantata *Ich liebe den Höchsten von ganzem Gemüthe* does not call for such a mass of tone. We heard when the Busch ensemble played the Brandenburg Concertos last week how Bach's orchestral music can sound and should sound when the balance between strings and woodwind is properly held. Last night the few oboes and horns were almost inaudible through the ocean of string tone.

Berg was represented by his own arrangement for string orchestra of three movements from his *Lyric Suite*, a work which, in its original form for string quartet, dates from 1926. The content of the movements has remained virtually unaltered, and the arrangement consists mainly of alternations in the layout of the string parts to lighten the players' tasks. Berg's position in music is a curious one. As the most eminent pupil of Schoenberg he is an acclaimed and self-confessed atonalist. But although his heart and his thinking mind may dictate to Berg that he is a Schoenbergian, his unconscious mind and his natural tendencies lead him elsewhere – he is instinctively a post-Wagnerian. *Tristan* dogs his steps; he may start out determined to be as conscientiously atonal and mathematical as Schoenberg, but before he has gone far the Wagnerian influence overtakes him.

These three movements – Berg has taken the second, third and fourth of the *Lyric Suite* – are not yet, perhaps, everyday food for the everyday listener, neither are they ever likely to achieve such popularity, but there is no denying their fantastic, haunting, but elusive beauty – the

27

Tristanesque passion that creeps into the *Andante amoroso* and the *Adagio appassionato* and the tenuous gossamer of the *Allegro misterioso*.

The remainder of the concert was devoted to Beethoven's Violin Concerto, in which Carl Flesch was a sensitive and musicianly, if rather small-toned, soloist, and Brahms's First Symphony. With three seemingly interminable cadenzas and its last movement consisting of almost innumerable repetitions of one catchy tune the Beethoven concerto is, at the best of times, a thorny rose.

Beecham and Huberman   4 November 1935

There were both quality and quantity at this afternoon's Beecham Sunday Concert at the Queen's Hall; quality enough to still the critical impulse and rather too much quantity. The British public has never been at its most receptive on Sunday afternoons, and it is sheer waste of excellent performances, Sir Thomas's energy, and his players' time to give a programme that lasts from a quarter past three until half past five. No audience can concentrate for so long.

The concert began with a superb performance of Beethoven's Second Symphony, with the first 20 bars of which Sir Thomas knocked the post-prandial lethargy out of both his orchestra and his enormous audience. Sir Thomas's view of this work has changed. A few years ago he played it with rather more delicacy and refinement than many of us thought compatible with either the score or Beethoven's mind. Today's performance was altogether bigger-framed and stronger-muscled. There were delicacy and charm enough in the details, but there were intense nervous vitality and a freedom of stride that his earlier performances lacked.

Tchaikovsky's symphonic poem *Romeo and Juliet* is an undeservedly neglected masterpiece. The fact that it does not quite conform to the English idea of a musical representation of Shakespeare is no reason why some of the composer's best music should remain virtually unknown to us. In all his output there is nothing lovelier than the exquisite passage for muted strings that is held by some commentators to represent the garden beneath the balcony at night.

After an interval of some 20 minutes – too long for an ordinary concert interval, but in proportion to the excessive length of the concert – Huberman played Brahms's Violin Concerto. Of the handful of great violinists of our day Huberman has had the poorest deal from the British public, probably because he has made least concessions in the way of playing popular trifles. In Berlin and Vienna, where audiences demand no such concessions but rather resent them, he is the most popular of all the violin virtuosi. Huberman's approach to the Brahms Concerto is unlike any other. Heifetz stands aloof from it, observing all but seemingly remaining unmoved by it. Kreisler comes to it with love and reverence, and, without disturbing the unity of the work, shows us each of its wonders like a connoisseur lovingly proud of his treasures. Huberman sees with so many of us that Brahms lacks inner vitality, and, again without disturbing the shape of the work, infuses it with his own quick, intense vitality. It is impossible to imagine finer-nerved or more sensitive fiddling than Huberman gave us. The repose of the second movement was feline in its soft restfulness and feline in its readiness to spring to active life. And when it came to the finale Huberman showed the electrifying power that Reményi must have had to leave on Brahms the indelible affection for the abandoned Hungarian.

Sibelius and a New Schoenberg Work 9 November 1935

Locatelli, Sibelius, a new work by Schoenberg, Dvořák, and the presentation of the Royal Philharmonic Society's gold medal to the Finnish Minister, Mr Gripenberg, who received it on behalf of Jean Sibelius – there was something for everybody in the Philharmonic Society's concert that Sir Thomas Beecham conducted last night.

The lovers of old music no doubt felt that when the charming Concerto grosso by Locatelli was finished their innings was at an end. Little did they know what Schoenberg had in store for them: little, too, did the out-and-out modernists, the atonalists and the cacophonists, anticipate what the high priest of the twelve-tone scale was going to spring upon them. The new work was described in the preliminary announcements of the concert as 'concerto for violoncello and orchestra'. We were prepared to face an abstruse, complicated puzzle, a nut that would take some cracking. Not even his intimate friends suspected that this new work would be a mere pastiche, an arrangement of a 200-year-old concerto by a forgotten composer, unoriginal and unadventurous. As a work it has no interest whatever except that it has been written by the man who has created *Verklärte Nacht*, the *Gurrelieder*, *Pierrot Lunaire*, *Die glücklichen Hande*, and the *Variations for Orchestra*.

Knowing that Schoenberg has spent the last two years of his life in America we might surmise from the orchestration, muted quack-quack trumpet and trombone effects and the like, that he had found a new interest in the tricks of the American dance-band orchestrators. But this is not the case. This concerto is one of two works written in Berlin five years ago — this 'after the concerto for clavicembalo composed in 1748 by Gustav Matthias Monn', and the other for string quartet and orchestra after a concerto by Handel. Harmonically and rhythmically it is as normal and respectably dull as any student work. It is not even good or clever pastiche. Other contemporaries, Stravinsky in *Pulcinella* and Strauss in *Le bourgeois gentilhomme* and the *Couperin* suite, have displayed great taste and sense of style in pastiche. This new Schoenberg concerto is but a pointless joke with a cruelly difficult solo part.

Sibelius's Sixth Symphony received the best performance it has had in London. It is of all his symphonies the least likely to make its way with the general public; it is too quiet, reticent, and indefinite ever to become a popular favourite. It has no quick and no slow movements, no highlights, little variety of colour, and indefinite tonality; it reminds one in turn of all his works and yet is, in spirit, unlike anything else he has produced. For the student of Sibelius it provides a host of problems, and it gives him rare and subtle pleasure, for it stands in character midway between the full and generous First, Second, and Fifth Symphonies and the bare, concentrated Fourth and Seventh. Of all his works it is the best illustration of the truth of his statement to a publisher that 'whereas most contemporary composers are engaged in manufacturing cocktails of every hue and description, I offer the public pure cold water'.

After the interval there was a magnificent performance of Dvořák's Fourth [now known as Eighth] Symphony.

The soloist in the Schoenberg work was Emanuel Feuermann.

London Symphony Orchestra's Elgar Concert   19 November 1935

The attendance at tonight's concert of the London Symphony Orchestra was a disgrace to London and to London's so-called music public. Events have proved in recent weeks that 8,000 people will pay high prices to hear a tenor sing film-theme songs, and yet there were hardly 1,000 seats occupied to hear a programme consisting of three of Elgar's best works conducted by the only conductor in the world who can do justice to them. If the attendance at concerts in London were more than a mere fashion the Queen's Hall would have been sold out to hear Sir Landon Ronald conduct the Prelude to the *Dream of Gerontius, Falstaff* and the Second Symphony. The orchestral playing was as good as any English orchestra, not excluding the London Philharmonic, can give us, and Toscanini himself could not have penetrated so deeply into the mind and spirit of the composer as did Ronald. It was like having Elgar himself back in command of his favourite orchestra to hear the perfect timing and balance and to feel the intense inner fire of the *Gerontius* Prelude.

It is difficult to speak with restraint of the performance of *Falstaff*. Both musically and imaginatively it was an extraordinary feat of penetration of its creator's mind by that of the interpreter. In the whole realm of music there is no greater masterpiece of orchestration, and while giving every thread of that wondrous fabric its due, and holding the whole closely-knit work together, Sir Landon Ronald gave us all the humour and wit and splendour and pathos of Elgar's imagining. Falstaff and Prince Hal, as Elgar saw them, came to life with all their idiosyncrasies. In the opening bars one watched Falstaff 'in a green old age, mellow, frank, gay, easy, corpulent, loose, unprincipled, and luxurious'. One could almost hear the slightly wheezy ring of his laughter. And so it was throughout the work, until, in the final pages, his repudiation and death were a personal tragedy and grief to us. Of the symphony, too, the performance was flawless. If

30

Elgar's executors have the power they would do well to vest the exclusive right of performing his works in Sir Landon Ronald during that conductor's lifetime. In his hands Elgar's artistic reputation is safe and assured.

In the audience were the musical critics of several foreign newspapers who are on a visit here to savour a typical week of London's musical life. It will be interesting to read their views and learn their reactions to this all-Elgar concert. Will the Germans and Austrians find, as we do when we listen to Bruckner in Germany and Austria, that he is a great composer when listened to on his native soil? Whatever their impressions, they can rest assured of one thing – that whether or not they agree with us as to the greatness of Elgar's music, they could not have heard better performances.

Furtwängler   2 December 1935

Furtwängler and the Berlin Philharmonic Orchestra began their lightning tour of Britain with two concerts in London. At the first on Friday, the programme was virtually the same as for many concerts they have given here in the past – the Schubert C major Symphony, Stravinsky's *Firebird* Suite, and the *Tannhäuser* Overture. But tonight they broke entirely new ground, as far as our acquaintance with them goes, by playing Sibelius's Seventh Symphony. The remainder of the programme was conservative enough – Handel's Concerto Grosso in D major, Weber's *Euryanthe* Overture, and Brahms's First Symphony.

Two years have passed since this orchestra last played in London and it is still, as it was when Furtwängler first brought it to London, a magnificent, responsive, subtle instrument. The new leader, Hugo Kobiger, is not as good a player as his predecessor, Szymon Goldberg, and Hans Bottermund, the leader of the cellos, does not yet adequately replace Piatigorsky; but we cannot yet boast that our crack orchestras are better than those of Berlin. Comparison is made difficult because of the difference in outlook between Furtwängler and, let us say, Beecham. Furtwängler plays the Brahms C minor Symphony on the splendid instrument that he has built; Beecham and the London Philharmonic make music together. Beecham's discipline is not the less firm, but it is the discipline of cooperation; Furtwängler's is that of dictatorship.

With his superb Covent Garden performances of *Tristan* still fresh in the memory, we were prepared to revise all our previous estimates of him as a concert conductor. Our good resolution held throughout the lovely Handel concerto. The whole performance was broadly spaced, sensitively imagined, and perfectly moulded. Handel was left to speak for himself. Only the violins wavered in pitch at the end of the Largo and so marred an otherwise perfect performance.

The first note of the Sibelius symphony knocked good resolutions sky high. As the work went on they were scattered to the four corners of the earth. The symphony begins simply *piano* and *adagio*, with soft drum taps followed by an ascending scale. The whole point of this opening is the steady mysterious growth from nothing. The tympanist slogged at the drum as if he were at the beginning of the Scherzo of Beethoven's Ninth Symphony, and Furtwängler got away cleanly from this starting pistol, accelerated through the scale and was doing a nice *moderato* in no time. This unsatisfactory start was never recovered from. The rich polyphony of the wonderful passage for strings was obscured by too much attention to the 'top line', the exciting *vivacissimo* section did not move with the lightness, speed or spirit that Sibelius intended, the passage that Sibelians call the Scherzo, the stretch with the elfin, rather Italianate tune, was assessed as if it had been a tenor aria in a Puccini opera. If the Germans like Sibelius to be played like this, one cannot wonder that they do not consider him a great composer.

With the Weber overture the tide turned again. This is the music that Furtwängler does to perfection; the German romantic idiom is in his blood and in the blood of his orchestra. I doubt if Englishmen will ever play it so well, with just the right amount of sentimental warmth in the phrasing of the big tunes, the unconsciously right weight of tone, and the right degree of attack and dynamism.

Harty and the London Symphony Orchestra   3 December 1935

If there were any intellectual curiosity in London's so-called musical public the Queen's Hall would have been full this evening. Three virtually unknown symphonies by recognised masters were being given, one of them for the first time. But in London concert-going is now a matter of fashion, of vogue. One goes to the Philharmonic Concerts and to the Beecham Sunday concerts no matter what the programme may be. To attend the London Symphony Orchestra concerts is 'not done', no matter how interesting the musical fare. The blocks of empty seats at tonight's concert were a disgrace to the city. For intelligent and enquiring music-lovers the programme was the most interesting of the whole winter season – an early and rarely played symphony by Mozart, No. 30 in D major, the first performance in England of Bizet's only symphony, and Dvořák's seldom-heard Second [now numbered Seventh] Symphony in D minor. Yet there were not enough people even in the cheapest part of the house to line the first of the six rows of the upper circle.

For the Mozart symphony Sir Hamilton Harty wisely used a mere handful of strings. It is little more than a slender four-movement divertimento, charmingly laid out for two oboes, two horns, two trumpets and strings. This work by the 18-year-old Mozart did not compare at all favourably with Bizet's only symphony, written, it is believed by some writers, when he was but 16. It has a curious history, and for its rediscovery the world is indebted to Mr D.C. Parker, a Glasgow writer on music and the author of the best English biography of the composer. None of the books on Bizet, not even as far as I remember Mr Parker's, even mentions the existence of the work.

2. *The Reviewer*

Not since the early symphonies of Schubert has there been a gayer, fresher work in the form. It is in all things Southern. It is as if Nietzsche had said 'The symphony must be Mediterraneanised' and Bizet had obeyed. What does it matter that one or two of the themes savour of Offenbach's *opéras bouffes*? The whole work is in flawless taste, the craftsmanship is exquisite throughout, and the colouring unfailingly lovely. Not for many a day have we had a new symphony with so beautiful a slow movement tune as Bizet's – admirably played by the first oboist. Here is a work that the Hallé Committee must certainly present to Manchester next season.

After the interval came Dvořák's Second Symphony, a work with a strangely Brahmsian flavour. We know how deeply indebted Dvořák was to Brahms for help in his career, but we did not know until tonight that the Czech had acknowledged his indebtedness by very nearly quoting as the second subject of his first movement a tune that Brahms himself used twice, once as the cello solo in the Second Pianoforte Concerto and once for the beginning of *Immer leiser wird mein Schlummer*.

Belshazzar and Gerontius   30 March 1936

In ordinary circumstances one would be moved to protest against the excessive length, nearly three hours, of this afternoon's concert by the Royal Choral Society. But it so happened that the juxtaposition of two great works was so instructive that one would not willingly have missed the experience. The two works are *Belshazzar's Feast* by William Walton, and Elgar's *The Dream of Gerontius*, and the opportunity of hearing the two in one afternoon made strikingly clear certain essential differences in the minds of two of the most distinguished British composers of our time.

Belshazzar's Feast commands our admiration by reason of its terrific vitality, its fierce energy, its brilliance, power, and splendour. Had Strauss decided to introduce into *Aus Italien* a section depicting Vesuvius in a state of violent eruption he could not have written more exciting music than Walton has used for the Babylonian banquet. The greatest qualities of *The Dream of Gerontius* are its poignancy and its lofty spirituality. The question of whether or not one agrees with the dogmas that so concern Gerontius has nothing to do with our appreciation of Elgar's oratorio as a work of art. The core of its subject matter is problems of life, death, and the hereafter, and our imaginations and sensibilities are moved by the voracity with which Elgar, all matters of creed apart, handles the agony and terror of death, and the power of his imagination in creating the serenity of 'Not does one moment differ from the next' and the lustrous peace of the finale of the work.

Walton is magnificently successful as the Babylonian king's Master of the Musick, producing three heathen rites and barbaric festivities, but when Belshazzar is dead and the Children of Israel make a joyful noise to the God of Jacob, Mr Walton is not so ready to oblige. Strauss has already

33

been in that dilemma. Remember his letter to Hofmannsthal on the subject of Joseph's legend: 'The chaste Joseph is hardly in my line, and I find it difficult to write music for a character that bores me; a God-fearing Joseph like this I find infernally hard to tackle.'

Elgar's problem was the converse of Walton's and Strauss's. Gerontius's ecstasies and agonies, fears and hopes, and the Angel's solace were his home ground. It was the demons howling abuse at virtue and saints who eluded him. To them he could give only pantomime rage and pantomime abuse, making them mere nursery bogies who sing music comically like that he wrote for Germans in *The Spirit of England*. If only Walton had been old enough to write the demons' music for *The Dream of Gerontius* in exchange for Elgar's help with the chorus of the rejoicing God-fearing Israelites!

Both works were, on the whole, admirably performed. Malcolm Sargent achieved the almost superhuman feat of leading the vast forces of the Royal Choral Society through the rhythmic intricacies of Walton's work not only without mishaps, but with precision, and finely controlled dynamic contrast and considerable subtlety of phrasing. The honours in *The Dream of Gerontius* went to Astra Desmond and Heddle Nash. Miss Desmond has often sung the Angel's music well, but never in our experience with such beauty of tone and moving tenderness. It is doubtful if any singer will again bring to the part of Gerontius the sacramental quality that made Gervase Elwes's performance a never-to-be-forgotten experience. Elgar, however, often said that he wanted that part sung 'in the Italian manner'. This Nash did, and revealed unsuspected beauties in the 'Sanctus fortis'.

Der Rosenkavalier   2 June 1936

Tonight's performance of *Der Rosenkavalier* marked the beginning of a new chapter in the history of that opera in England. Each of the principals was singing the opera in England for the first time, new scenery and costumes had been provided, and it was Fritz Reiner's, the conductor's, first *Rosenkavalier* here.

The classic post-war cast for *Rosenkavalier*, Lotte Lehmann, Delia Reinhardt, Elisabeth Schumann and Richard Mayr, together with Bruno Walter, was imported as an already perfected ensemble from Vienna. When one considers the difficulties under which Covent Garden operates – the necessity of producing 15 or 16 operas within a space of seven weeks – it becomes clear that the principle of bringing over an ensemble of stars accustomed to working together is the only way in which first-class results may be obtained under present Covent Garden conditions.

None of the principals of tonight's performance had sung together in this opera before, and two of them, Elisabeth Rethberg (the Marschallin) and Stella Andreva (Sophie) were new to their parts, so it is not, perhaps, surprising that the entertainment savoured of a general rehearsal rather than of a finished performance. Musically it was fairly accurate and some of the parts were magnificently sung, but the attention of a producer was needed to fuse the material into a living artistic unity. The opera in itself is such good 'theatre' and so intensely human that it needs only reasonably good acting and expressive singing to enchant any audience, highbrow, lowbrow or no-brow; but not even Strauss's poignant music and Hofmannsthal's bitter-sweet text can make its effect when the Marschallin delivers half of the first act facing the audience as if she were singing Bach's B minor Mass.

This is the first performance of the opera we have seen in which the title role emerged as the leading role. In others, particularly when Lotte Lehmann was the Marschallin, her young lover has been only incidental. Tonight Tiana Lemnitz, as the Rosenkavalier, dominated the action. She is far and away the best of post-war interpreters of the part. Here, for the first time in our experience, was a Rosenkavalier who was so strikingly male in walk, in gesture and mental attitude that it seemed incongruous that this dashing, impetuous cavalier should sing with a woman's voice. There was not a false touch in the whole creation: even when dressed up as Mariandel she was essentially a young nobleman in his teens acting the servant girl. And she gave us magnificent singing; not since Rosa Ponselle sang at Covent Garden have we heard such ravishing *pianissimos* from a lyric soprano.

The Marschallin, it appeared, was indisposed, but Elisabeth Rethberg kindly consented to wear her clothes and sing her music. She sang it gloriously, every phrase, every note was a joy to the ear, but there was no suggestion of the pride, the passion, the sadness, the regretful withdrawal, the wit or the charm of the Marschallin. She showed so little interest in the Octavian that it was difficult to believe that there had ever been anything between them. Neither her movements nor her tone colour led one to believe that she was anything but a great vocalist singing the notes Strauss had written. The last 20 minutes of the first act which contains the most moving and expressive operatic music written since Wagner's death counted for nothing but ravishing singing. Stella Andreva sang Sophie's music with considerable charm, but introduced to the stage too strong a flavour of the musical comedy heroine. There was little in her performance to bring before our eyes Hofmannsthal's 15-year-old girl 'good, pretty and commonplace with a basic simplicity of manner'. Simplicity of manner is exactly what she lacked.

The Baron Ochs was Emanuel List. The part suits him better than any he has sung here, and his free employment of the Viennese dialect lent a fine porty flavour to the whole performance. But his reading of the part is more Ochs than Baron. Mayr was in many ways more gross and less jovial, but he did at least convey that Ochs was a nobleman. The right reading of the part would show us three different facets of the baron's character. In the first act he should behave with an outward show of manners in the presence of the Marschallin: she should be the focal point of his attention, and the incidents with Mariandel should be but by-play. In the second act, in the house of Faninal, his social inferior, he should be pompous and more obviously gross, but the full extent of his revolting lecherousness should be reserved until the Inn Scene. List sang the part with considerable skill – it does not call for much in the way of *legato* singing – but he robbed his part of much of its effectiveness by gagging incessantly. If Hofmannsthal and Strauss had wanted Ochs to chatter incessantly we may rest assured that they would have written the words they wanted and not left it to the caprice or ingenuity of their interpreters.

The orchestra, under the command of Fritz Reiner, played somewhat clumsily and with more volume than vitality, so that not only the exquisite quality of Strauss's scoring but much of the singing was obscured.

The Salzburg Festival August 1936

Within the space of three days Toscanini has conducted the two great comic operas of the nineteenth century, *Die Meistersinger* and *Falstaff*. He was working under conditions that gave him little assistance. The singing rarely rose above the adequate, and frequently sank to the deplorable: the Sachs was changed at the last moment, and in the disused riding-school that Salzburg seems to consider suitable for a Festival Opera House the orchestra is seated level with the audience, yet in spite of these handicaps he gave performances so revealing, so true, so beautiful, that those who heard them must inevitably judge future performances of these operas by the new standards which Toscanini set.

Klemperer's dictum of 'the inevitable rightness' of Toscanini's performances could not have been better illustrated than in *Die Meistersinger*. The great majority of conductors see the work from only one point of view. After Kapellmeister A has conducted it one is aware that he has regarded the whole opera through the impassioned and enraptured eyes of Walther and Eva. Dr B regards it from Sachs' standpoint, Herr C as a great manifestation of the Germanic spirit. Toscanini's approach is through the score without any preconceived notion or particular sympathies, and consequently he reveals as no other conductor has done Wagner's unerring dramatic instinct which made him see the drama from the point of view of each of the characters. Toscanini's *Meistersinger* cannot be generally described as youthful, or philosophic, or Germanic; it was just and true to each of the protagonists, intensely alive. The meeting of Eva and Walther in the second act was electrifying in its youthful passion, the Prelude to the Third Act was more tenderly resigned than we have ever heard it, Walther's Trial Song and Prize Song soared with rapt lyrical ardour, yet the whole conception was drawn in one noble span from the first bar of the Prelude to the last bar of the Third Act.

Toscanini's clarity of texture and the balance that he holds between the inner parts was as remarkable in the complexities of the riot scene at the end of the second act as in the quintet. This *Meistersinger* under his direction can be compared only to the experience of seeing in full score for the first time a work one has known intimately all one's life only from the pianoforte arrangement, or one's first sight of the Duomo and Campanile in Florence when one has had but a vague impression of them from photographs.

The best singing came from Hans Hermann Nissen (Sachs), who stepped into the role at the last minute owing to Schorr's indisposition, and Charles Kullman (Walther) who has everything that the part requires but power of voice and distinction of bearing. He sings musically and without a trace of the bleat that affects the majority of German tenors and their audiences, but he does not yet ride over the orchestra in climaxes. Lotte Lehmann's Eva was distinguished by a voluptuousness of tone that would have been admirable and apt had she been singing Venus, Thaïs or Kundry in the Second Act of *Parsifal*, but that made Walther seem the mere victim of a clever and experienced woman's wiles. It was only in Hermann Wiedemann's finely drawn and splendidly sung Beckmesser that the stage came near to matching the wonders that Toscanini was performing in the orchestra.

A special word of praise is due to Robert Kautsky (the stepson of Ilse Köchert, one of the three children for whom Wolf wrote *Epiphanias*) for his delightfully picturesque settings and his skilful suggestion of space on a small stage.

The performance of *Falstaff* was orchestrally speaking incomparably brilliant-spirited, witty and graceful. At tempi that seemed at times perilously fast the brass and woodwind played with machine-gun-like accuracy, reminiscent of Horowitz's octave playing, and yet had time to phrase expressively. The singing was immaculately accurate, and the intricate ensembles were as finely balanced as the best quartet playing, but little that came from the stage charmed the ear. Stabile's voice is not now a conspicuously beautiful musical instrument, but it is used with discretion, taste and restraint rare among Italians, and his variety and command of inflection are a delight to the sensitive listener.

The Mistress Ford was an American using the name Franca Somigli, whose accomplished singing was a welcome relief from the shrillness of her colleagues. Her obviously Anglo-Saxon bearing showed up their comic paper caricature make-up.

The gyration of the buxom chorus of elves and fairies flatly contradicted Verdi's nimble music in the Forest Scene, and the desiccated tone of the young lovers belied the orchestra's tender treatment of the love music, but Salzburg has not yet discovered singers who can seriously detract from the magic of Toscanini's performances.

2. The Reviewer

Wagner at Bayreuth 15 August 1936

In recent months it has become something of a fashion to pick holes in the performances of opera, and particularly of Wagnerian opera, given at Covent Garden. The impression seems to obtain in some quarters that only at Covent Garden do singers and conductors fail at times to see eye to eye in the matter of tempi, that the lighting is illogically employed, that a cyclorama ripples and bulges in a back-stage breeze.

Unfortunately there have been few English visitors to Bayreuth this year, or these fallacies would have died a quick death, for Bayreuth, which is generously financed by the German Government and has at its disposal the whole resources of German operatic talent, has been, in the first cycle of *The Ring*, quite as far as Covent Garden from the ideal.

The artistic direction of the festival is in the hands of Germany's most distinguished men in their various fields – Furtwängler, Tietjen and Preetorius as conductor, producer and scenic designer respectively – and the orchestra, chorus, stage staff and singers were rehearsed for five full weeks before the festival began. But only in *Lohengrin* and to a lesser degree *Parsifal* has the work on the stage suggested that the performances have profited by these weeks of preparation.

In neither *The Ring* nor in *Parsifal* was the general level of the singing of the principal roles as high as that to which Covent Garden has accustomed us, and the lack of cooperation between the stage and the conductor led to mishaps some of which had to be heard to be believed. There were two such major accidents in *Götterdämmerung*; one when Siegfried parted from both Brünnhilde and the orchestra, the other when the Rhine Maidens and Dr Furtwängler lost touch for several bars and both parties tried almost every expedient but that of a complete stoppage to get into stride again.

The most striking feature of *The Ring* performances was the quality of the orchestral playing. Judged by the highest standards it is a magnificent orchestra, an instrument of ravishing tone, marvellous precision, subtlety and sensibility, and almost inhuman in its infallibility.

Yet, for all the excellence of the playing the performance of *The Ring* was, as a whole, under-vitalised. Rarely was there a real *fortissimo*. *Pianissimi* there were in plenty, and several grades of tone further down the scale into the regions of the inaudible. And rhythmically as well as tonally the cycle was lifeless.

Only at rare moments, as in the scene between Siegmund and Brünnhilde in the second act of *Die Walküre* and the second act of *Götterdämmerung* was the music given its full stature. One felt that Dr Furtwängler was a tired man, able to muster the requisite tension of nervous vitality only under the stimulus of the heroic singing that Frida Leider occasionally gave him.

Most of the singers are familiar to London audiences. Frida Leider was at her heroic best throughout *Die Walküre* and in the first and second acts

38

of *Götterdämmerung*, but could not conceal the strain that the last acts of *Siegfried* and *Götterdämmerung* imposed upon her. Max Lorenz does not appear to be the solution of the Siegfried problem. In appearance he could hardly be better; he looks young and heroic, has a fine figure and moves easily about the stage, but his voice lacks the necessary weight and brilliance.

Rudolf Bockelmann as Wotan was in his best vein, but the other bass parts were less well filled than at Covent Garden. Jaro Prohaska's Gunther is not to be compared either vocally or dramatically with Janssen's familiar characterisation, and Robert Burg as Alberich indulged in the 'Bayreuth bark' of the old tradition.

The best singing of the cycle came from three singers who have made only occasional appearances in England, Margarete Klose (Fricka), Maria Müller (Sieglinde) and Franz Völker (Siegmund). A handsome young soprano, Liselotte Ammermann, made an excellent impression as Freia, but it was left to Fritz Wolff as Loge to give the most intelligent performance in the whole *Ring*.

The attenuated orchestral tone that Dr Furtwängler had maintained throughout *The Ring* was better suited to *Parsifal*, and after the disappointments of the four Nibelung days one was refreshed to hear a performance more worthy of the Bayreuth tradition. As Gurnemanz, Ivar Andrésen sang better than he has done for many years, but it was again a Covent Garden favourite, Herbert Janssen, who carried off the honours of the performance with his heart-rending and gloriously sung Amfortas.

The Kundry was Marta Fuchs, who will be heard in London as Ariadne and the Marschallin during the visit of the Dresden State Opera in November. She is a noble singer and a handsome woman, but she lacks some of the sensuous charm of phrasing essential for the seduction scene. Helge Roswaenge sang Parsifal. He too is a fine singer, but neither the timbre of his voice nor his temperament is suited to the part.

It was not until the performance of *Lohengrin* got under way that one could see the result of the five weeks of intensive rehearsal or reap the rich harvest of the cooperation of Tietjen, Preetorius and Furtwängler. There were some minor mis-castings and the singing was not uniformly admirable; there were moments when one could not endorse Dr Furtwängler's occasionally capricious tempi, but these details were dwarfed to insignificance by the magnificence of the whole creation. Preetorius and Tietjen have triumphed as no stage designer and producer have ever triumphed. In *Lohengrin* the action takes place almost at the natural tempo of life. Wagner's genius was great enough to let the drama unfold itself without theatrically piling incident upon incident, and without unduly holding back action for lyrical expansion; and aided by this naturalness of pace Tietjen has put *Lohengrin* on the stage so convincingly that one almost ceased to be aware of stage or theatre. The most lavish stage productions we have seen pale beside this superb Lohengrin.

Delight in the production was further intensified by Franz Völker who as Lohengrin proved himself to be the greatest German tenor of our time. To tone as mellifluous as that of the best Italian tenors he brought beauty of phrasing, intelligence, musicianship and such tenderness of feeling as have never before in recent times been heard from a tenor in Wagnerian opera.

Señor José Iturbi as Conductor-Pianist   13 October 1936

Señor José Iturbi, who has long enjoyed an enviable reputation as a pianist, made his English début as a conductor and in the dual role of conductor-pianist this evening at the first Courtauld-Sargent concert of the season. It is easy to appreciate Señor Iturbi's ambitions to become a conductor. The prizes are high and there are few formidable contestants for the places in the front rank – too few adequately to fill all those places. He has so easily won his prominent place in the harder fight for pianistic fame, in the face of keen competition and in an epoch rich in fine players of the piano, that it is but natural for him to look for fresh fields to conquer and that he should choose conducting. He is not alone in this. Horowitz will make his first appearance as a conductor in New York in a few weeks' time. True to his pianistic training, Iturbi conducted without score, and it is difficult to visualise how with his spacious beat he could have a score within reading distance. His is a beat that admits of no misunderstanding, but so wide is its sweep that if the players in front of him were to follow it to its extremes of latitude they would be turning their heads from side to side like court-side spectators at Wimbledon.

The performance of the *Leonora* No. 3 Overture was clear but rather under-vitalised. Then the real fun of the evening began. A battalion of men trooped on to the stage, removed a section of the wall of the platform, and proceeded to wheel out from its concealed hangar, much to the amusement and surprise of the audience, a pianoforte. Iturbi seated himself before the instrument and began to conduct Beethoven's C minor Pianoforte Concerto. There is nothing new in a pianist conducting a concerto from the keyboard, but Iturbi gave the feat a new interest by his over-scrupulous attention to the orchestra. He is not content, as Mozart and Beethoven were, to use his hands and, when necessary, his head for the guidance of the players. He performed feats of prestidigitation in picking up and dropping his baton which would have made Cinquevalli envious. He took nothing for granted and seemed positively to resent having occasionally to give his attention to the keyboard and leave the orchestra to look after itself. When either of his hands was playing a solo passage the other beat time and gave entries as if the London Philharmonic Orchestra were a collection of nervous amateurs. It was worth the price of a whole row of stalls to see the admonishing first finger of his left hand tell the orchestra to sit still until the cadenza was over and he could again give them the benefit of his guidance. It reminded one of a poem by Mrs Hermans learnt in early childhood:

'Now don't you go till I come', he said,
'And don't you make any noise';
And toddling off to his trundle bed
He dreamt of his pretty toys.

And the joke of it all was that the orchestra gave him their full attention only when they admiringly watched his facile playing of the cadenza.

After the interval we were given the first performance of an intermezzo from Eugene Goossens's new opera *Don Juan de Mañara*, which is to be produced at Covent Garden next June. This short excerpt whets our appetite for the opera. If all the music is up to the quality of this finely organised, harmonically subtle, and intensely vital fragment, and if the opera is really well written for the theatre, *Don Juan* will be the first great English opera since Purcell.

Paul Cinquevalli was a famous Polish juggler.

Vienna Symphony Orchestra   20 October 1936

The Vienna Symphony Orchestra, the official orchestra of the Vienna Broadcasting Station, made its English début last night at the Queen's Hall. The programme was not of the type which usually attracts English concert-goers, but it gave the visitors ample opportunity of displaying both their versatility and their virtuosity. The first half was given up to four short romantic works – Weber's *Oberon* Overture, Hugo Wolf's *Italian Serenade*, Liszt's *Mephisto Waltz*, and the rarely heard *Sakuntala* Overture of Goldmark. After the interval Beethoven's Fifth Symphony was played. Felix Weingartner conducted, and the presence of a director whose qualities are familiar enable one to form a fair impression of the orchestra's capabilities.

The first and most lasting impression is of the superb quality of the string players. Good as the front desks of our own orchestras are, it is rarely that we hear such unanimity, precision, and clarity as that of the whole string body of the Vienna Symphony Orchestra. Every man pulls his weight, the last desk as well and as earnestly as the leader. The tone produced is a sound fit for the ears of gods. It has rare vitality and variety. It sings with the vehemence and gusto of a North of England choir and the thrilling opulence of Flagstad, and it can fall as softly and sweetly on the ear as the sigh of an Aeolian harp. In the quickest passages every detail of figuration is as clear as in the printed score.

The English Channel behaved so inhospitably to our visitors that it would be unfair to criticise the rather uneven brass and woodwind playing in the Weber and Wolf pieces. The thought of blowing down a metal tube after a buffeting in the Channel is enough to turn the stomach of any man. After a bubbly start, the brass settled down to show us how much we miss by hearing German romantic music played on the narrow-bored instruments generally in use in this country. One looks eagerly forward to hearing at the next concert the great slow movement of Bruckner's Seventh Symphony and *Till Eulenspiegel* played by this open-throated brass choir.

Weingartner was at his best in the *Oberon* Overture and Liszt's amazing *Mephisto Waltz*. His handling of Wolf's exquisite and delicately poised *Italian Serenade* was rather heavy. But the fires of passionate, romantic youth blazed fiercely in the mad, whirling dance of Liszt's orgiastic *Mephisto Waltz*.

Bruckner's Seventh Symphony 23 October 1936

England is giving Bruckner a new deal. On Tuesday evening his Sixth Symphony was broadcast by Adrian Boult and the BBC Symphony Orchestra: last night at the Queen's Hall his Seventh Symphony was played by the Vienna Symphony Orchestra, conducted by Oswald Kabasta (by whom it will be played in Manchester on Saturday): next week the Philharmonic Society is giving the Fourth Symphony, and the E minor Mass is already scheduled for next year's Leeds Festival. Little did the sponsors of the Linz Festival of Art and Culture in Brucknerland think that their modest effort to make their city a centre of tourist traffic would have such far-reaching effects as the establishment of a Bruckner faction in English musical life. The kindly hospitality of a few businessmen has succeeded where great conductors have failed.

The Seventh Symphony is generally considered to be Bruckner's most easily appreciated work. It was the first to carry his fame beyond the confines of his little coterie of Viennese admirers, and the first to establish his name in Central Europe. The Seventh, as it was played tonight, is much edited by the Schalks and Loewe, but this is the form that has earned the love and devotion of Germany and Austria.

Two features peculiar to last night's performance tended to confirm the long-established English prejudices against Bruckner. The symphony was placed at the end of an already long programme, which inevitably stressed the size of the work, since London audiences are unaccustomed to be in the middle of a slow movement at half-past ten; and the episodic nature of Kabasta's treatment of all the works in the programme intensified often criticised defects of Bruckner's structure. Even so the symphony made a tremendous impression. Its thematic material is proportionate to the length of the movements. Sibelius, the master of concision, is satisfied with thematic fragments of a bar or so for his 24-minute symphonies: Bruckner builds his symphonic pyramids with vast themes.

The first subject of the work soars aloft for 21 bars, and Bruckner spends nearly 20 minutes in discussing it. The glorious slow movement, the elegy for the death of Wagner, is even longer, but when length is so filled with beauty and interest time ceases to matter.

In the first part of the programme the Viennese orchestra readjusted

London's standards of string playing, and in a delightfully genial performance of *Till Eulenspiegel* demonstrated the necessity of playing German
music with German brass instruments.

Dresden State Opera in London   4 November 1936

Judged by the standards of Covent Garden's summer seasons, the singing
of the Dresden State Opera Company in tonight's performance of *Tristan
und Isolde* was far from distinguished. With the exception of the Isolde,
none of the principals is vocally of the calibre of the eminent performers
who grace the same stage in May and June. But Wagner spent a great part
of his life in proving that opera can be and should be more than singing,
and tonight, as last night, the Dresden company came nearer to realising
the composer's intentions than do our summer constellations. Again the
conductor, the producer, the scenic artist, and the lighting technician gave
life to music drama instead of mounting opera. It was necessary for the
proper understanding of the Dresden company's qualities that they should
give a performance in which the singing was undistinguished. The listener's mind is left the freer to study the other points of their work – the
work of the conductor, the orchestra, and the producer.

Karl Böhm ranks with the best conductors of *Tristan* we have heard. He
works, not as the virtuoso conductors do by playing on the orchestra, but
as the guiding spirit in a vast artistic plan. He sings or recites to himself
every word of the text and holds the orchestral part in the finest, subtlest
relation to the stage word and action. His sense of tone gradation is
uncanny, and his restraint in the employment of the full intensity of
orchestral tone enables him to give the necessary climaxes almost unbearable effect. The power and life of sound at the crucial moments – Isolde's
curse, the entries of Tristan in the first and second acts, and just before
Tristan's death – had to be heard to be believed. The soft playing was no
less impressive. In Hans Strobach and Alexander Schum he has producers
who contrive the action on the stage in equally convincing manner.

Anny Konetzni was the Isolde. She has a magnificent voice, noble, rich,
and generous, but we should better be able to appreciate its beauty if she
would hold it still so that we could properly get it in focus. Her Isolde has
unusual dignity and majesty, so much, indeed, that one almost regretted
to see the raging queen of the first act transformed by philtre into a
passion-racked woman in the second. Julius Pöltzer was more of a William
Morris than a Wagnerian Tristan. His voice is thin and desiccated to such
an extent that it is hardly a musical instrument in the proper sense of the
words, yet, like every member of this fine team, he is clearly an artist who
has given thought and love to every detail of his part.

2. The Reviewer

Richard Strauss as Conductor   9 November 1936
Close of his London visit

London's Richard Strauss week came to an end this afternoon when the great composer conducted the Dresden State Opera Orchestra in a programme consisting of Mozart's G minor Symphony and his own *Don Quixote* and *Till Eulenspiegel*. Admiring Strauss the composer the world has of recent years somewhat overlooked Strauss the conductor. In the long run it is all to the good that Strauss should have given the greater part of his life to the activity that produces enduring results, and future generations will resent the time that he has given to conducting that might have been spent in writing music. If he had not been the creative artist he is his interpretative gifts would still have made him world famous. The performances he gave today will be talked of for years to come by those who were so fortunate as to hear them.

Strauss is the least demonstrative conductor we have ever seen. He seems to the uninitiated to be perfunctory, laconic. His right hand beats time with little visible arm movement, his left hand hangs limply at his side and is rarely used for any more important function than that of turning over the page in the score. It would be impossible to make less show or fuss than he does. His methods are the antithesis of those of such men as Toscanini, Beecham and Koussevitzky, all of whom in conducting become an integral part of the music in hand. These men seem to enact within their beings the performance they wish to conjure from the orchestra, they live and feel each work as they play it within themselves and communicate that playing to the orchestra. Strauss remains aloof, calmly, coldly watchful. He leaves it to the orchestra to play and to feel the music; he is at the conductor's desk to watch points, so to speak. His conducting is a perfect example of his own famous dictum about Tristan – 'The brain which conceived that score must have been as cold as ice.'

There have been more dramatic readings of Mozart's G minor Symphony than his – especially of the first movement – but none in which the beauty of the work was more evident. He made, incidentally, an unusual repeat in the third movement, by playing first the minuet and trio, both with repeats, then repeating both the minuet and the trio. In his own works the clarity of texture was a refutation of the charge which has so often been brought against him of over-filling his scores with detail. While those who heard this concert still live there will be testimony against any conductor who makes a Strauss work sound thick or fussy that, properly played, these works are as clear and transparent in texture as Mozart's.

Josef Lhévinne   5 January 1937

There were two exhibitions of virtuoso accomplishment in London's concert halls on Saturday. In the afternoon at the Wigmore Hall Mr Josef Lhévinne made a welcome reappearance after several years' absence; at the Queen's Hall the Glasgow Orpheus Choir gave its annual London concerts to its annual crowded audiences. It is only because Lhévinne plays so rarely here that his name is not a household word as are Horowitz's and Rachmaninov's: in this era which is so rich in pianists of immense dexterity and brilliance Lhévinne provides us with new and no less exciting experiences than those we have had from Horowitz, Rachmaninov, Hofmann, and Petri. He is less insinuatingly and indolently persuasive than Rachmaninov and more preoccupied with the keyboard than Hofmann; he does not attain Petri's superb intellectual mastery and breadth of style, nor equal Horowitz in his infallible accuracy; yet he plays some passages, and frequently for minutes on end, with dexterity and grace and power that seem to belong to the realm of necromancy rather than to human agency. After all the great pianoforte playing one has heard it still seems beyond credibility that only eight human fingers and two human thumbs could play the last two variations of the first book of the Brahms-Paganini variations as Lhévinne seemed to play them yesterday. A part of this skill is due to the enormous span of his hands – he seems to stretch and play at speed an octave and a fifth as easily as most great pianists play ninths.

BBC Symphony Concert   4 February 1937

The function of the conductor in a performance of Brahms's Double Concerto for violin, cello and orchestra is more that of referee than director. On one side there are the two soloists, on the other Brahms and the orchestra, and it is the conductor's task to see that the soloists are not swamped by Brahms's turgid scoring. Tonight at the Queen's Hall the contestants were Adolf Busch (violin) and his younger brother Hermann (cello) and the BBC Symphony Orchestra. Sir Adrian Boult was the conductor-referee. The normally heavy odds against the soloists were almost doubled by the fact that all the 72 string players of the BBC orchestra were pitted against them.

The first and last movements went almost entirely to the orchestra; only in the Andante, where they sweetened their usually rather dry tone, did the soloists make any real headway. Here their exquisitely modulated phrasing and perfectly timed playing of the triplets in the middle section of the movement temporarily dispelled the gloom of this harsh-sounding work which, more than any of Brahms's, justifies Wolf's accusation that 'Brahms cannot exult' and Nietzsche's dictum on 'The melancholy of impotence'.

After the interval the glorious sunshine of Schubert's C major Symphony revived our dampened spirits. Sir Adrian is invariably at his best in this symphony, one of the seven wonders of the world of music. His rhythm is steady, yet elastic. Its steadiness sets forth the noble proportions of the work and makes the maximum effect of the grandly forged climaxes; its elasticity encourages the wondrous blossoming of Schubert's divine melodies. That he was so admirably served by his strings and brass must have consoled him for the uncertainty of the woodwind.

Béla Bartók   11 February 1937

Béla Bartók has reached an age – he will be 56 next month – at which the world of music should be able to assess his true worth with a reasonable degree of accuracy. He is not an unknown quantity. He was one of the moderns, together with Sibelius and Delius, whose work Busoni sponsored in his much-discussed Berlin concerts nearly 30 years ago, and each of his new works is quickly given in most European centres of musical culture. Yet both amateur musicians and professional critics fight shy of committing themselves to a definite opinion on the very forthright works of this direct little man.

Judgement is still suspended principally because Bartók cannot be pigeon-holed or labelled. Like Sibelius, he defies classification and goes his independent way, seemingly uninfluenced by predecessors or contemporaries. Last night at the Cowdray Hall he gave the first performances of 27 pianoforte pieces from his *Mikrokosmos*, and joined Zoltán Székely in playing his First Sonata for Violin and Pianoforte and the Second *Rhapsody* for the same instruments. This concert brought us no nearer a solution of the Bartók problem. The first movement of the sonata, a work more than 14 years old, still sounds shapeless and chaotic in a wilful, perverse way. The second movement occasionally attains almost to the strange (Tristanesque) beauty of the First Quartet, and the finale, a savage and passionate movement, is a convincing subtilisation of the Hungarian folk-dance style.

The programme offered no elucidation of the significance of the title *Mikrokosmos* beyond the titles of the 27 pieces. Some, such as 'First Chromatic Invention', 'Fourths', 'March', 'Variations', and 'Ostinato', were self-explanatory, but one at least, the cryptically named 'From the Diary of a Fly', was, to say the least, inexplicit. These pieces make pleasant, stimulating, and often amusing listening, and they certainly provide amateur pianists with engaging and not too difficult novelties. They are all cleverly devised, forceful, and unaffected, and often witty in a manner reminiscent of Mussorgsky.

Yet on one hearing this collection of miniatures brings one no nearer to a fuller understanding of Bartók's style. His uncompromising directness and his subtle harmonic sense are evident here as in his other works. Perhaps a close study of these pieces would throw light on the mental processes which have gone to the making of the large and undeniably important works. If not, why the title *Mikrokosmos*?

Sibelius's Violin Concerto   5 March 1937

For some reason the violinists of sufficient eminence to be itinerant have avoided playing Sibelius's Violin Concerto in London. Most of them have avoided it altogether, preferring the beaten track of Beethoven, Mendelssohn, Brahms and Tchaikovsky and the grateful puerilities of Wieniawski and Vieuxtemps to the harder path of the Sibelius masterpiece. As far as the last 20 years are concerned we have no recollection of a public performance of this work in England by a great virtuoso – as distinct from an able violinist. The few performances that the work has had here have been the fruits of the devotion and labour of two or three fine craftsmen. But this concerto, with its enormous technical difficulties, was written with master players in mind, and tonight at the Queen's Hall Jascha Heifetz gave London its first post-war chance of hearing the work played with the authority the composer had in mind.

As a young man Sibelius's one ambition was to be a great violin virtuoso. He failed in his ambition, but he revenged himself on the whole breed of fiddlers by writing a concerto which only the greatest can play. Heifetz is the first violinist we have heard who can approach the work with the sublime confidence that he is master of all its difficulties. It holds no terrors for him. His bow arm and left hand are seemingly infallible, his tone rides easily over Sibelius's scoring. Previous performances have left one wondering whether the composer had perhaps been guilty of an occasional miscalculation in scoring. Heifetz proved that Sibelius knew his job when he wrote the concerto, that he put down nothing impossible. He was merely exacting.

The style, the technique, the dignity, and the command of Heifetz's performance have to be heard to be believed. Paganini at his best cannot have played harmonics at speed with the sureness and beauty of tone that Heifetz displayed tonight. It is cold comfort to hear this concerto played with a pianoforte as inadequate substitute for the finely-wrought orchestral part, but Manchester must hear Heifetz play this great work in that watered-down form at his recital on March 13 rather than be deprived of the experience of his performance of the solo part.

After the interval Nicolai Malko conducted Prokofiev's *Classical* Symphony. It is said that the composer intends this work to be taken seriously as what Mozart would have written had he lived in the twentieth century. As such it is merely a farce. Taken as a skit upon the eighteenth-century symphony the piece is an excellent joke, but it needs really brilliant and accomplished playing, particularly from the strings. The London Symphony Orchestra worked hard, but it lacks the superb technique and unanimity necessary to point the racy jest.

Walter Legge had produced Heifetz's HMV recording of Sibelius's Violin Concerto in December 1935.

Covent Garden Opera – Otello   20 April 1937

The Coronation Season of international opera at Covent Garden opened brilliantly tonight with a performance of Verdi's *Otello* under the direction of Sir Thomas Beecham. This is the first occasion since the post-war re-establishment of summer seasons of international opera at Covent Garden on which an Italian work has been given on the first night. The plan, which held for ten years, of devoting the first month of the season to the serious business of German opera, then trailing off to the lighter pleasures of Italian and French opera, had much to commend it. In the next few weeks we are to have Donizetti rubbing shoulders with Wagner and *The Flying Dutchman* sandwiched between *Tosca* and *Falstaff*.

Of all Italian works *Otello* is the most suitable for beginning a season, although with the Italian school of singing at its present low ebb it is virtually impossible to stage a performance comparable with those that Covent Garden gives of German opera. There are no young singers in Italy comparable with stars of pre-war years, and the directors of Covent Garden had no option but to entrust two of the principal roles in *Otello* to singers who were already famous 25 years ago.

The Otello was Giovanni Martinelli, who first sang here in 1912 and who has spent the best of his singing years in the United States. He is by nature and experience a lyrical tenor; it is only in the last year that he has turned his attention to this, the most exacting tenor part in the Italian repertoire. The part was written for Tamagno, a man with the physique of a bull and a voice like a trumpet. Martinelli has neither the compelling presence nor the vocal power to suggest the magnificent animalism of the Moor, but he surpasses all the Otellos we have heard since the war in the more lyrical music.

If the full extent of Otello's tragedy is to be brought home to an audience it is essential that in the opening scene one should be impressed by the power and glory of the triumphant general. The fate of the jealousy-racked victim of Iago's machinations loses half its poignancy unless one sees the man at the height of an awe-inspiring splendour. Shakespeare managed the contrast better than Verdi and Boïto. In the opera the hero has only two minutes of unshadowed command. If he fails on his entry announcing the annihilation of the Turks to impress us as the Lion of Venice, his subsequent misfortunes are but those of an ordinary, jealous man.

Martinelli's entrance was not impressive. He sang the music well enough, but failed, partly because of the comparatively light timbre of his voice and partly because of a lack of inner fire, to dominate the scene. The listener felt that he had only to wash this Moor's face and he would find a charming Rodolfo. But from that point onward the singer became more and more impressive. He is, without a doubt, the most musicianly and cultivated Italian tenor we have heard in London for more than a decade. A thread of pure gold runs through his voice and he shapes his phrases like a great cello player. He could not say, with Shakespeare's Othello:

Rude am I in my speech
And little bless'd with the soft phrases of peace.

The exquisite sensibility and polish of his singing showed to disadvantage the rough and ready methods of his colleagues. The Desdemona was a young soprano new to London, Fernanda Ciana, a handsome person with a good voice of which she has not yet learned to make the best use. Cesare Formichi sang Iago. His voice is still rich and warm in its lower registers, but the top is not of the fineness that the music demands. As an actor Formichi seemed to have a somewhat hazy notion of Iago's character. A general of Otello's prowess must necessarily be a shrewd judge of men, but not even the most gullible mercenary in the Venetian forces would have been taken in by the furtive, tip-toeing rogue that Formichi made tonight of honest Iago.

The best and most consistent performance of the evening was given by the London Philharmonic Orchestra. Not since Sir Thomas last conducted Italian opera in London have we heard a Verdi score played with such accuracy, fire and delicacy.

Covent Garden Opera – Ariane et Barbe-bleu   21 April 1937

An accident to Mme Germaine Lubin, the principal lyric soprano of the Paris Opéra, delayed by 50 minutes the start of the second performance of the Covent Garden season. A quarter of an hour after the curtain was due to rise Sir Thomas Beecham came before the curtain and gave the first news bulletin – that Mme Lubin had met with an accident in her hotel but that by an effort of will, and after receiving medical attention, she was now on her way to the theatre. It was particularly unfortunate that this artist should thus have been handicapped, for she was making her first appearance in London, and in one of the most exacting soprano parts ever written.

The opera was Paul Dukas's 30-year-old *Ariane et Barbe-bleu*, which was being given for the first time in this country. The performance was the first of the series which is being given at intervals during Covent Garden's Coronation Season by the joint forces of the two Paris opera houses, the Grand Opéra and the Opéra-Comique. The title of this work whets the appetite for a Strauss-Hofmannsthal or perhaps an Offenbach extravaganza in which the Ariadne of mythology finds herself involved with the Bluebeard of fairy tale. But Maurice Maeterlinck provided Dukas with the libretto, and instead of fantasy the audience beholds symbolism. 'Ariane,' explained Dukas, 'is youth and hope.' She is also the symbol of light. Nevertheless, most of what little action there is in the opera – it consists of the unlocking of doors and the symbolic breaking of a window – takes place in blue Maeterlinckian darkness.

Symbolism is all very well in its way, but it is not the stuff of which great opera is made – except by a composer of Wagner's stature and theatrical genius. Although Ariane is on the stage for nearly every minute of the opera and singing away with all her might and main, it is impossible to be really interested in her either as a dramatic personality or as a symbol. At no time in the opera does her fate or what she stands for become a matter of personal interest for any member of the audience.

It happened tonight that the part of Ariane was sung by an artist of exceptional charm, personality, and skill, and, although Mme Lubin was severely shaken by her accident, she made a profound impression. Her voice is a lyric soprano of no great range – it appears to lack substance in the lower registers and overtones at the top – but of exceptional warmth and colour. The other parts are of minor importance. Ariane apart, the principal interest is centred in the orchestra, for which Dukas wrote with consummate skill. The orchestral texture is of ravishing, luminous quality, so personal that it does much to disguise the Wagnerian and 'Massenettian' origins of a great deal of the material.

Before the opera began one deplored the smallness of the audience as indicative of a lack of intellectual curiosity among London's opera-goers. By the time the second act had finished one had come to the conclusion that *Ariane et Barbe-bleu* is already known here.

The conductor was Philippe Gaubert.

Tosca at Covent Garden – Lawrence Tibbett's first appearance in England

15 May 1937

Lawrence Tibbett, the American baritone of film and gramophone fame, gave his first performance in England this evening at the Covent Garden Opera House in an extraordinarily vital performance of *Tosca*. From the first arresting announcement of the Scarpia theme the level of the performance was conspicuously higher than that of any London presentation of Italian opera in recent years.

Given three good singers who can act, a few capable small part character-singers, a competent orchestra, and a vital conductor, *Tosca* is the most effective of all operatic melodramas. Apart from the brief lapse at the shepherd's little song and the unison passage for soprano and tenor in the third act, it sweeps along in a torrent of action from first bar to last. The lyrical episodes are short and to the point, and though they may at first hearing seem to hold up the onward urge of the drama – and this is particularly true of Tosca's aria 'Vissi d'arte' – in point of fact they serve to accelerate the otherwise swift sequence of events and intensify by suspension each succeeding horror.

This evening's performance stressed, as none other we have seen, the terrible sadism of the opera. This was in part due to John Barbirolli's steady and powerful handling of the orchestra, and in part to Tibbett's conception of Scarpia. Puccini's lyrical moments were made more than ever lulls before storms of brutality. The fact that the sometimes tender, sometimes jealous, interplay between the successful opera singer and her painter lover was so realistically sung and acted by Gina Cigna and Giovanni Martinelli threw into higher relief the ruthlessness of Tibbett's Scarpia. The conductor and these three singers, ably aided and abetted by the small-part people, made the nightmares of Strindberg seem pleasant dreams beside this terrible combination of Sardou and Puccini.

It is impossible to take full measure of Tibbett on his work in this one part, but he is evidently an artist of remarkable personality and command. His voice is a noble organ, unusually dark in colour and of exceptional power. Its freedom and richness remind one of Titta Ruffo, as does also his habit of singing up to G flat straight from the chest. He is certainly the most impressive Italian-singing baritone we have heard at Covent Garden in the last 15 years.

Die Zauberflöte at Glyndebourne   22 May 1937

The extent to which Mozart's operas are an expression of the spirit of his time is by no means generally recognised. His first successful opera, *Die Entführung*, was at once the first German opera and the first artistic manifestation of the independent German spirit. *Le nozze di Figaro*, based on Beaumarchais's *Le mariage de Figaro* – a play which has been described as 'the flambeau of the French Revolution' – was the outward and visible sign of the unrest and dissatisfaction under the abuses and tyrannies of the ruling classes. Figaro, the quick-witted servant outmanoeuvring his dissolute master, is symbolical.

Mozart's last opera, *Die Zauberflöte*, voices the hope and idealism of the Revolution. It is the 1791 belief in the friendship of man to man, and the universal brotherhood of men. The creed was young then, untried and unsullied. Forty years later Beethoven, who had matured in the post-revolutionary world, set out to express the same ideals in the finale of his Ninth Symphony. Comparing the community-singing-to-keep-up-the-courage bombast of the finale of the Ninth with the simple faith of *Zauberflöte* we see how far realisation falls short of ideals.

If the full significance of *Die Zauberflöte* is to be clear to an audience the simplicity of its humour and the solemnity of its rites must be kept free from any trace of theatricalism. The opera begins with a fairy-tale and grows into a rite, and so far as the singers in tonight's performance at Glyndebourne are concerned neither extreme was fully realised. The naive humours of Roy Henderson's musical and engaging Papageno were marred, in spite of the programme's specific statement that the opera was performed in the original German, by some childish gags in English. At the other extreme was David Franklin's Sarastro. When Bernard Shaw wrote of Sarastro's part that this was the only music which could be put without blasphemy into the mouth of God he did not mean Claudius the god and in truth Mr Franklin's Sarastro suggested a Roman emperor rather than the priest of Mozart's imagining. This music calls for the combined qualities of a Prospero and a Gurnemanz, a voice at once benign and noble, a voice remote from human passion but welling with human love. This singer has magnificent material, but neither his mind nor his voice is yet ready for the task tonight allotted to it. The new Queen of the Night, a Nicaraguan by the name of Sinaida Lissitschkina, proved to be one of the best singers of the part we have heard. She does not yet express all the rage that belongs to the music, but she sings every note with remarkable clarity and precision. A particular word of admiration must be said for Rautawaara's Pamina. She has nearly reached the ultimate stage of singing 'Ach, ich fühl's' so movingly that no member of the audience dare applaud. The other roles were filled by artists now familiar to Glyndebourne audiences, and Fritz Busch conducted with his customary precision and authority.

Verdi's Falstaff   2 June 1937

Verdi's *Falstaff* was given last night at Covent Garden by a company of Italian singers who placed Sir Thomas Beecham and the London Philharmonic Orchestra in the awkward and unsatisfactory position of giving a witty and brilliantly delivered running commentary on a pre-arranged series of events which did not come off according to plan.

Musically speaking, *Falstaff* is the only aristocratic and elegant opera written by an Italian since the death of Donizetti. It is, so to speak, a fine champagne grown in a country which for a century has habitually and otherwise exclusively produced fiery and full-blooded Chianti. It was the misfortune of this evening's performance that the singers were of an extremely Chianti order, while Sir Thomas and the orchestra remained faithful to the spirit of the champagne work.

Falstaff is a witty but in no wise a humorous opera. It has nerves, but no blood. While it is superficially the most faithful of all Shakespearean operas, it is intrinsically the least Shakespearean. It glitters, but is not the gold of humanity. There is no laughter in it, yet it is high-spirited. The heart does not laugh with or at it. Only the eyes sparkle and the lips pay curling service to its swift hard wit.

The instrumental part of this performance was admirable, transparent, exquisitely worked and modulated, darting, sparkling, and gracious. Sir Thomas's beat was a model of clarity and precision. But only one of the singers consistently phrased with him. The ensembles in the first and second acts were inelegant point-to-point races.

Of the several singers in the cast new to London Maria Caniglia made a pleasant impression of having an unusually good voice and a style free from most of the aggravating mannerisms of present-day Italian singing. She did some excellent work in the first act. So did the Nanetta (Licia Albanese). But as a work for the stage Falstaff stands or falls by the player to whom the title role is entrusted. It fell.

Caniglia took the part of Mistress Ford. Falstaff was played by Cesare Formichi.

Paray and the Colonne Orchestra 24 November 1937

When we left the Queen's Hall yesterday evening, nearly half an hour after the time at which orchestral concerts usually end, there were three substantial works yet to be played. We had already listened for more than two hours. The concert was the first of two which are being given by the Colonne Orchestra of Paris and its regular conductor, Paul Paray, and had been arranged by the Anglo-French Art and Travel Society as a counterpart to the visit of the London Philharmonic Orchestra and Sir Thomas Beecham to Paris last March.

The first 20 bars of Liszt's *Faust* Symphony, with which the programme began, made clear that this concert was no mere polite exchange of international compliments but an unusual opportunity to hear an orchestra different in character from our native teams. The tone, by comparison with that of English orchestras, is light and, at first hearing, rather thin-blooded. One misses in the first half-hour of listening the sonority and depth of string tone which is characteristic of the English and German orchestras of the front rank. This difference seems to come from the school and tradition of French string playing, and as one becomes accustomed to the sound one appreciates that the whole string section of the Colonne orchestra is a branch of the tree which produced as its finest fruit Ysaÿe and Thibaud. The style is in the best French tradition – light, elegant, and graceful.

The woodwind section of this orchestra is the best we have heard for years; in the enthusiasm of the moment we would even say the best we have ever heard. We have one good oboe player in England but no flutes, cor anglais, or clarinets to match these superb French players. For English ears the German bassoon, with its fuller, lower register, is preferable to the reedier French instrument; but in their way these Colonne bassoonists are remarkable players.

The light, transparent, and exquisitely musical tone of this orchestra would not, of course, suit all music, as we quickly became aware when it was applied to the Prelude to *The Dream of Gerontius*, but the experience of hearing such alert and finely poised playing is one which should have been shared by a larger audience than that which was in the Queen's Hall. The programme was partly to blame for the sparse attendance. The British public has never shown much inclination to listen to Liszt's *Faust* Symphony, which, with all its repetitions and in spite of the vulgar tune in the first movement, is his masterpiece. To the lightness of this orchestra's tone we may attribute the fact that the Faust section seemed to speak of the sorrows of Werther rather than of Faust's constant doubtings, but the Gretchen movement has not been more beautifully played in London, and the irony of the Mephistopheles movement was the keener for the swift, direct playing it received.

After the interval a compliment was paid to English music in the shape of a performance of the *Gerontius* Prelude, which with the best intentions was made to sound related to both Auber and D'Indy.

It is said that in his Pianoforte Concerto Ravel intended to follow the tradition of Mozart and Saint-Saëns, the two composers who, in his view, had furnished the best examples of this type of composition. Ravel is so devout a disciple that he keeps a more than respectful distance, and in doing so gets into all sorts of bad musical company – Massenet, Stravinsky, and even Gershwin. We can only regret that the inclusion of this tiresome piece so delayed the proceedings that we were deprived of hearing Fauré's *Pelléas et Mélisande*.

The soloist in Ravel's Piano Concerto was Yvonne Lefébure.

Moeran's Symphony   15 January 1938

The Royal Philharmonic Society perseveres with its old irking policy of relegating a new work to the end of the programme. This evening at the Queen's Hall E.J. Moeran's first symphony was played for the first time, but the performance began only a few minutes before ten o'clock, by which time the audience had had the fine edge worn from its sensibilities by 80 minutes' music and the noisy, nudging disturbance of a 20-minute interval.

The right place for the 'novelty' in a programme of orchestral music is immediately before the interval; the orchestra is fresher, the audience more alert to gather and enjoy new impressions, and those whose pleasure and duty it is publicly to express their opinions on the new work are given more time in which to organise and consider their views.

More than 12 years ago Moeran was invited to compose a symphony for the Hallé, but the work which he began then was abandoned because he felt that he was not in a sufficiently advanced state of development properly to write his first symphony. The work which was played tonight was begun in 1934 and completed last summer. It contains only a few ideas from the sketch made in 1925, and the same dedication to Hamilton Harty.

This symphony is above all things intensely and passionately musical. The politicians of music who so rail at the mechanisation of the art by gramophone and wireless have failed to see that the form of mechanisation really dangerous to the art is that of idea and form. Music for Moeran is beauty of sound. He writes and, it seems, means to write tunes. Some of them are too locally Irish in accent to let the work speak an international tongue, but the symphony as a whole is refreshingly free from the parochialism that is the bane of British music.

In recent years we as a nation have flattered ourselves that British music has taken an eminent place in the world's music. There is no evidence to be found abroad that this is so.

The rhapsodical nature of Moeran's structure will count against this new symphony; but the fault is a good one in a composer who is clearly destined to develop slowly. To check a spate is easier than to eke out poverty so that it looks like abundance.

Like most really musical British composers, Moeran is much influenced by Sibelius. There is a passage in the finale of this symphony strikingly like the famous string climax in *Tapiola*. The effect of the influence does not end there. The rushing string figures pivoted around a central note, the nature and crack of many entries of the brass, the spacing of the woodwind writing all doff respectful caps to Sibelius. But in company with this undisguised assimilation of the greatest musical genius of our time, there is in Moeran's symphony freshness and a musical spirit rare in an epoch which is more notable for its mathematical skill in the handling of musical symbols than the outpouring of beauty.

Leslie Heward conducted the London Philharmonic Orchestra.

Mengelberg and the BBC Symphony Orchestra   20 January 1938

Dr Willem Mengelberg conducted the BBC Symphony Concert this evening at the Queen's Hall, and again showed his extraordinary command over an orchestra. London has good reason to remember this aspect of his skill. Seven or eight years ago, when the London Symphony Orchestra had fallen into half-hearted and haphazard habits of playing, Mengelberg took charge of it for a season and galvanised it into new life. The BBC orchestra is no subject for such rejuvenation, but the obedience with which it followed Dr Mengelberg's unusual tempi and variations of tempi in Brahms's Third Symphony testified in another way to his mastery. Only a man of remarkable persuasiveness and determination could induce an orchestra to give a performance so unlike the traditional way of playing this work.

There were not 20 bars in any of the first three movements which went their accustomed ways without some surprising check or onward spurring of the natural impulse of the music. Generally speaking the conductor's attitude to these movements was to take the imposing beard from Brahms's face and show the mild eyes and soft mouth and chin of the portraits taken in the composer's twenties. The glory of the first movement is its striding athleticism, but in his care for polishing details the conductor made it watch its step along by-paths instead of stretching its limbs across fields. The two middle movements minced where they should have ambled. It was only in the finale that Brahms emerged in his full stature, and there the listeners' pleasure was marred by faulty intonation in the woodwind.

Hindemith's *Philharmonic Concerto* passed without leaving any impression but wonder that the piece should have been played for a second time in London.

In Strauss's *Also sprach Zarathustra* we were best able to appreciate the advantages of Mengelberg's virtuosity, and hear how a man of his command can make every point in so complicated a score tell with the fullest effect. Not a detail, not an inner part was missed; such a performance justifies the composer's orchestral demands, even though it cannot disguise the vulgarity and inherent weakness of the work. This tone poem is the most penetrating criticism of Strauss that has yet been written. Nothing that his most calculating detractor could say in words would cast a crueller light on his deficiencies than the super-cinema sentimentality of the section headed 'Of the inhabitants of the unseen worlds'. Strauss's devout music is no better than that of Barnby, or the most modest contributor to *Hymns Ancient and Modern*. Unlike Luther, he believes in letting the Devil have all the best tunes.

Furtwängler's Concert at Queen's Hall   22 January 1938

Furtwängler confined adventurousness to the performances in his concert this evening at the Queen's Hall. The programme was a model of conservatism, consisting of the *Leonore* No. 2 Overture, the Fifth *Brandenburg Concerto*, and Brahms's D major Symphony.

Furtwängler's repertory seemed to be restricted, but it could never be said of him that he repeats his performances. His attitude is rather that of the student who finds in his pet subject unending food for thought and speculation. No two performances of any one work are identical; each one is, for him at least, a new experience in search of beauty. For him there is no final and objective truth about any music, no performance of which it can be said that 'this is what the composer had in mind when he set these notes on paper'. His first concern is beauty of sound, beauty of texture, and he pursues that end often at the expense of cohesion of design. The slow movement of the *Brandenburg Concerto* was teased out to timelessness because he was lost in the enchantment of the sweetness he was wooing from the pianoforte. The preoccupation with beauty stamps all his work, and it leads to a form of auto-intoxication which induces certain excesses. He reacts instantaneously to the effect he is producing. If that sound is soft he seeks to make it even more dulcet; if the orchestra is playing *forte*, he craves intensification in that direction. Only thus can one account for the extremes of dynamics in which he delights.

His preoccupation with sweetness of sound romanticised the Beethoven overture until it became almost Schumannesque, and the Bach concerto into the perfumed languor of Chopin. His mood found its natural counterpart, however, in the Brahms symphony, the warm lyricism of which he keyed up to passionate fervour which compensated in some measure for the flaccidity of the Beethoven and the Bach.

It was good again to hear the exquisite string playing of the Berlin Philharmonic Orchestra, particularly the violas and cellos, which far surpass their counterparts in any British orchestra.

London Symphony Orchestra   23 January 1938

Too much time was spent during the concert given by the London Symphony Orchestra last evening at the Queen's Hall in operations which have no vital bearing on the proceedings proper to a symphony concert, so that neither the audience nor the orchestra properly settled down to the serious business of enjoying music. After 12 minutes nearly half the orchestra disappeared, since it had been decided to play a Mozart concerto with a small orchestra, and the full forces of the orchestra did not reassemble for Elgar's First Symphony until a few minutes before ten o'clock.

Mr Anthony Collins, who was for several years the principal viola player of the London Symphony Orchestra, was making his first appearance as the conductor of a full-dress symphony concert in the Queen's Hall. He began well by giving an unaffected and musicianly performance of Brahms's *Tragic* Overture. His second task, that of conducting Mozart's *Coronation* Concerto, with Wanda Landowska playing the solo part, would have tested the skill of most conductors of longer experience than his. Mme Landowska played this work in an unusual and charming manner, but the freedom and subtlety of the rubato she allows herself demand either untold hours of rehearsal or the simpler expedient of conducting from the pianoforte. The refinements of rubato are as personal and individual as fingerprints; they also vary with the occasion, and it is not to be expected of any conductor that he shall perfectly match the playing of an orchestra to the fanciful caprices of a soloist who plays as freely as an inspired improviser.

The slow introduction of the Elgar symphony was magnificently done. Elgar would have chortled with delight to hear his broad-shouldered tune so grandly played. It was good to see a conductor carve the air in the practical way that Elgar himself employed for this section. But when the more nervous first subject came along one missed the surging lyrical impulse that the composer used to give to the music. His beat used so often to look clumsy, but there is no master of all the subtleties of stick technique who can bring his works to the intense life they had when he conducted them.

New Works by Prokofiev   28 January 1938

Serge Prokofiev was the guest of honour at tonight's BBC Symphony concert. Having the first part of the programme to himself, he conducted performances of his now familiar *Classical Symphony* and two works new to concert halls – the Symphonic Suite No. 2 from *Romeo and Juliet* and his Second Violin Concerto.

His *Classical Symphony* makes an excellent first piece on a programme. It is as short as most classical overtures of the nineteenth century. No time is wasted, no tune outstays its welcome. The Haydn-Mozart style is parodied in a manner which is obvious to the most unsophisticated man in the audience yet fine-pointed enough to delight the connoisseur. Prokofiev played the work at slower tempi than those to which we are accustomed – perhaps out of consideration for the violins of the BBC orchestra, which, even with these allowances, made some unmusical sounds in the jumps over two octaves in the second subject of the first movement.

Twenty-one years separate this diverting *jeu d'esprit* from the two new works played at this concert, but neither the *Romeo and Juliet* Suite nor the Violin Concerto leads one to believe that the composer has changed or developed during that time. He is still a clever, exuberant child up to all sorts of amusing tricks, but they are intrinsically the same tricks, the only difference being that he plays them rather self-consciously now.

The build of his melodies has not altered one whit since the *Classical Symphony*. They are nearly all based on a simple run up or down the scale or on the notes of the common chord, and the dash of spice in the form of over-running the scale by a note or sharpening one of the notes of the chord only concentrates the attention on the essential sameness. Even more exasperating is his unfailing and perky good humour, his irrepressible exuberance. No shiny-faced office boy ever whistled 'The music goes round and around' with more unfeeling persistence than that with which Prokofiev keeps the wheels of his facile musical garrulousness going round and round. His mind is so restless that even when, as in the middle movement of the Violin Concerto, he produces a beautiful lyrical idea, he runs off to some quite irrelevant bauble like a child excited by the varied novelty of a new toy-box.

The programme note was discreetly non-committal about the ballet *Romeo and Juliet* and its relation to another famous entertainment of that title. There must be some connection because there are Montagues and Capulets in both. There is not, however, as far as we remember, a dance of West Indian slave girls in the old work. This does not matter as much as the reader might think; there was little difference to be discerned between this dance and a piece described as 'The parting of Romeo and Juliet'. The tedium of the 35 minutes devoted to this ballet suite was relieved by some exquisite and original orchestration.

BBC Symphony Concert   4 February 1938

Miss Myra Hess played Mozart's Pianoforte Concerto in C Minor last night at the Queen's Hall, accompanied by the BBC Symphony Orchestra, in a variety of keys in that vicinity. Intonation is the most essential part of music-making, and although one is willing to make reasonable allowances for the difficulty of keeping woodwind instruments exactly in tune in a concert hall, the temperature of which rises from the moment the audience is assembled, one cannot condone the persistent 'out of tuneness' which has made some of the recent concerts of this orchestra a trial to sensitive ears.

2. The Reviewer

Nearly all the performance of this work sounded like a rehearsal, rather than the result of rehearsal. It had neither the elegance, firmness, and precision to which Beecham has accustomed us in the playing of Mozart, nor the unity of style which should hallmark any properly prepared performance. The soloist rightly and consistently took a romantic view of the music, but the orchestra dallied in a manner which paid more attention to decoration than to the powerful build of the structure. They rarely met on the common ground of seeing the work with one mind.

Unlike the orchestra, Miss Hess did not produce an unlovely sound, but we do not believe that her beautiful luxuriously soft tone is right for this music. The instruments of Mozart's time were incapable of producing so dulcet a tone, the upholstered comfort of which was foreign to the late eighteenth-century mind. Mozart left no cadenza for this concerto, but Miss Hess played one written by Bruce Simonds, pianist and professor of music at Yale University, for all it was worth.

After the interval Sir Adrian Boult conducted Elgar's Second Symphony. The intonation of the orchestra in regard to pitch of notes was now more satisfactory than in the concerto, but the spirit of the performance was not yet in tune with the composer's. It differed from his in most characteristics and many essentials. The worst that can befall Elgar's music happened when its composer died.

It implies a criticism of the intrinsic worth of that music, perhaps to protest that only its creator could show its full quality in performance. The fact remains, with one exception. Last night's performance was accurate after a somewhat shaky start, but like to the original only in the way in which a son of different personality is strikingly like his father. The features were tantalisingly reminiscent, but the character was changed. Sir Adrian has not yet caught the intense alertness of Elgar's spirit, its eloquent compelling rhetoric, or its rapt tenderness. Elgar's rhythm was firmer and more resilient. He tightened the reins after a *rallentendo* more sharply than does this conductor, who is too much inclined to let this music sprawl. Elgar's music calls for more whip-lashes and gentler coaxing than it received last night.

Weingartner in London   5 February 1938

Felix Weingartner conducted the London Symphony Orchestra last evening at the Queen's Hall in a programme which was hardly distinguishable from 20 or 30 others he has given in London – Schubert's *Rosamunde* Overture and the *Unfinished* Symphony, a short Beethoven work, and Brahms's Fourth Symphony. It is easy to criticise a conductor for his conservative habits in programme-making, but it is difficult to see how a musician of Weingartner's intelligence can happily and freshly play the same works year after year for 50 years.

Any man who has watched Furtwängler and compared his performances of one work can see why he can restrict himself to a small repertoire.

With him, as with many virtuoso conductors, each performance is an experience, an attempt at the realisation of the self. Many conductors delude themselves that they are seeking the essential qualities of each composer and each work when they are in fact only searching for the realisation and consummation of their own personalities. They are, so to say, only Cynara conductors – 'I have been faithful to thee after my fashion.'

Weingartner has long passed this Cynara stage – if ever he experienced it. He is faithful to the composer, and therefore supremely faithful to himself and to the conductor's highest aim. His performances do not differ a hair's breadth from each other. He has decided what each composer wanted and meant in every phrase, and he reproduces that and nothing more.

If Weingartner had more of the tense vitality of Toscanini or the intoxicating persuasiveness of Beecham in him he would play Schubert and Brahms differently. For the interpreter is always a channel which imparts the contours of his own personality to every work which passes through him. But in his quiet, impersonal, yet dictatorial way Weingartner comes as near to abiding and personal truth as can any mortal who cannot at once be an affinity of more than one creative artist.

Between the two Schubert works Beethoven's concert aria *Ah! perfido* was sung by Miss Vera de Villiers. The programme note diplomatically stated that this aria is 'something of a test for the singer'. By this test Miss de Villiers finds it more difficult to sing softly than loudly.

Mahler's Eighth Symphony   11 February 1938

Mahler's Eighth Symphony, which was given at the Queen's Hall last night, is as long as a concert and it needs an orchestra and choruses the size of a large audience. Not for nothing do the Germans call it 'The Symphony of a Thousand'. The participants in last night's performance filled the platform, the organ loft, nooks and crannies around the organ, and overflowed into the auditorium, meeting the audience, so to say, half-way.

To call it a symphony is taking the term to its limits. How is one to describe a work which keeps eight soloists, two choruses, a boys' chorus, a mammoth orchestra with quadruple woodwind, eight horns, nine percussion instruments, celesta, piano, two harps, harmonium, organ and mandolins fully occupied for nearly two hours? Not even Berlioz dared to ask so much. The word 'megalomania' persists in the listener's and observer's mind. Was it really necessary to Mahler's ideas thus to solve the problem of unemployment among musicians? It seems to have been. The symphony is the logical culmination of the search for greater splendour and sonority of tone which obsessed nearly all the post-Wagnerian, Teutonic composers, and Mahler was tackling the subject dearest to the heart and mind of every thinking Teuton, the end of the second part of *Faust*.

2. The Reviewer

It is easy to dismiss Mahler – England has been doing it for nearly 40 years – but it is nonsense to dismiss a man who was a genius and who sacrificed himself and his life on the altar of truth in art. Whatever its faults, this symphony is the fruit of the passionate conviction of a great man and a great musician. One differs from Mahler's conception unless one shares his medieval view of a heaven full of singing angels, trumpets, and harps. The difficulty that the ordinary sensitive man has with Mahler, and particularly with this work, is one of outlook. It is already a period piece in that its melody, harmony, and scoring are stamped circa 1905, but its outlook is peculiarly that of a convert to Catholicism who, like Bruckner, was 'half-God, half-child'. That is where Mahler and Goethe part company. Goethe's words are eternal manifestations of ideas which have obsessed humanity for thousands of years. Mahler has localised them to the Vienna of a particular decade and expressed his own view of them. His heaven is a sweeter and grander form of the sugar-plum house of *Hänsel and Gretel*. His Pater Ecstaticus sings of 'rapture of endless fire blazing in ecstasy', as Tauber sings of 'Vienna, city of my dreams', and in like accents, not because of any weakness in his musical equipment but because he felt simply and affectionately and like a child about the heavenly host. It is modern mankind's misfortune that it quickly sympathises with the Mahler of the *Kindertotenlieder* and the long-drawn pessimism of *Das Lied von der Erde* and understands the transience of happiness and the sorrow of parting.

The performance, which Sir Henry Wood conducted with the patient energy he always brings to unfamiliar works, was weakened by a team of soloists who lacked in most cases the range and power needed to master music to which only a team of Flagstads and Melchiors could do justice.

Schumann's Posthumous Violin Concerto   17 February 1938

Circumstances have provided a better background for the first performance of Schumann's posthumous Violin Concerto than any which a publicity agent could devise for stimulating interest in a new operetta by Noël Coward or a million-dollar 'spectacle' from Hollywood. The tangle of spiritualist seances attended by a famous diplomat at which Schumann 'spoke' to an eminent violinist, contradictions, protests, interference by a government, postponements, controversies and disclaimers savours more of a Phillips Oppenheim romance than the peaceful art of music.

The excitement which culminated in the first English performance of the work this evening at the Queen's Hall began last summer, when it was stated that Miss Jelly d'Aranyi had discovered an unknown violin concerto by Schumann as the result of a message received from Schumann at a seance. The account of this discovery is given in *Horizons of Immortality* written by Baron Erik Palmstierna. There would have been a greater stir among musicians than this pronouncement caused if the existence of this concerto had not been known for nearly 30 years.

2. The Reviewer

It was written in the autumn of 1853 and was Schumann's last completed work. He was already a sick man; the signs of the mental disease which were to lead to his confinement in an asylum were evident. His conduct was often eccentric. He suffered from delusions in which he fancied he heard one particular note or certain harmonics, or that the spirits of Schubert and Mendelssohn brought him musical themes; but between these attacks he was normal and self-controlled. The concerto was written for Joachim, who read it through once at a rehearsal with the Gewandhaus Orchestra. Clara Schumann was present and decided then that it would be unfair to her husband's memory to allow the publication of the work.

When Breitkopf & Härtel were preparing their complete edition of Schumann's works the question of publication was again raised. On this occasion Frau Schumann consulted with Brahms and Joachim and it was again agreed to withhold the score. When Joachim died his heirs deposited the manuscript at the Prussian State Library in Berlin on the condition that it should not be published until a century after Schumann's death. This stipulation has now been disregarded, 19 years early. The concerto was first performed in Berlin last November by Kulenkampff, in the United States in December by Menuhin, and in England tonight by Jelly d'Aranyi.

Now that Schumann's reputation is firmly established and his worth safely estimated, the publication and performance of this concerto can do him no harm provided that the state of his mental health at the time of its composition is borne in mind. In general it is no weaker than many of the late pianoforte pieces which are already published, and there are long stretches of remarkable freshness and originality which justify Menuhin's statement that it is 'the historically missing link of the violin literature'. There are so many phrases in the first and second movements which anticipate Brahms's Violin Concerto that one cannot escape the conclusion that Brahms was familiar with this manuscript. If the authorship were unknown one would more readily attribute it to Brahms than to Schumann. The opening tutti is full of good music, but the entry of the soloist sets the composer wandering aimlessly along in ineffective passage work. The second subject would be more charming if it did not so outstay its welcome. The second movement, in which Joachim felt 'an unhealthy tendency to brood and ponder', seems to us a consummate achievement, fresh and tenderly romantic yet adventurous and finely organised. The finale bears all too evident signs of its creator's enfeebled mind. The lifeless and ungainly subject-matter never strides naturally in its polonaise rhythm, the figuration for the soloist is weak and ineffective. The movement wanders on, repeating itself mechanically and pathetically. The brain which created it had ceased to imagine, the fancy which had given *Carnaval* and great songs to the world was functioning only as an engine works when the force which drives it has stopped – a few more dying turns in the accustomed direction and then all is still.

Sir Adrian Boult conducted the BBC Symphony Orchestra.

2. The Reviewer

Courtauld-Sargent Concert   22 February 1938

George Szell conducted a Courtauld-Sargent concert this evening at the Queen's Hall in a twilight more suitable for receiving spirit messages from dead composers than for the intelligent appreciation of music. Concerts of this type should be given in a hall sufficiently well lighted for every member of the audience to follow the performances with a miniature score if he feels so inclined. This evening it was impossible to read even the programme notes. Such sentimental gloaming, in association with the super-cinema luxury of the Queen's Hall seating arrangements, produces a state of ease and mental relaxation in which music is heard but not listened to.

Szell is not the conductor to shake an audience out of such luxurious restfulness. He is a conductor to be watched with keen mind, ears and eyes if one is to get the most out of his careful, watchful work. He takes no risks with the orchestra and no liberties with the composer. Every tempo he adopts seems to be decided upon after consideration for the comfort and peace of mind of the orchestral players. Nothing is allowed to hurry or flurry them into the danger of a mistake. Every lead is given so clearly that no player could miss an entry. Painstaking solicitude of this order does not make for exciting performances, but it secures accuracy, clarity, and beauty of tone. Unfortunately it also imparts a sameness of character to composers intrinsically as different as chalk and cheese. Mozart's E flat Symphony sounded strangely academic, not to say schoolmasterish, under this treatment. One became unusually aware of the structure but less conscious of the spirit of the work than usual. Dvořák's Violin Concerto fared better because Szell gave the impression, as often before, of being temperamentally in sympathy with this composer. Much of the slow movement soared out of the lecture-room into the realm of poetry, and carried the soloist, Adolf Busch, with it into a rapt detachment he too rarely wins.

The orchestra was the London Philharmonic Orchestra.

Yehudi Menuhin – From Adolescence to Manhood   7 March 1938

The proceedings at which Yehudi Menuhin made his reappearance before the London public today were more in the nature of an exhibition than a concert. Nearly 10,000 people had come to the Albert Hall to see and hear how the young artist had developed in the critical period between adolescence and manhood, and the programme consisted simply of three concertos for violin and orchestra – those by Schumann, Mendelssohn, and Brahms.

It stands to reason that there are interesting differences between what the preface to the programme described as the prodigy of yesterday and the genius of today. Menuhin's most remarkable characteristics as a child and adolescent were his cool-headed musical sagacity and his clear-eyed freshness and athleticism of style.

Nearly everything that was heard today suggests that the latter quality has been supplanted by a vibrant and exquisitely sensitive sensuousness. He was always a passionate player, but the nature of the passion has changed; the seeker of light has become a seeker of delight. His treatment of quick movements is more rhapsodical than before, and he lingers more lovingly in slow movements. This last feature of his playing was particularly noticeable in the slow movement of the Mendelssohn Concerto, where each note fell like the heavy drops of sweet moisture from an exotic flower. There were moments in the slow movement of Brahms's Concerto when this honeyed tenderness weakened the span of the melodic line, and these were made the more evident by Léon Goossens's flawless playing of the oboe solo.

This change is a natural one, and it has been made without the sacrifice of any of the old technical sureness, the vitality of rhythm, and the insistence on firm tempi that hallmarked Menuhin as a child; but it is not without corroborative significance that the prodigy who so frequently played Bach, Mozart, and Beethoven chooses for his reappearance three out-and-out romantic concertos.

Even though the acoustics of the building put a muddy complexion on the orchestral part of Schumann's 'newly discovered' concerto, the work made a better effect than on the occasion of its first London performance, partly because no attempt had been made to improve upon the composer's figuration of the solo part and partly owing to the adoption of a brisker tempo for the finale.

Sir Henry Wood conducted the London Philharmonic Orchestra.

Herbert Janssen   8 March 1938

Herbert Janssen sang Hugo Wolf's three *Harfenspieler* Lieder with the composer's own orchestrations this evening at the second Serenade Concert. It is almost superfluous to say that such singing and such a voice as his have never been heard in Sadler's Wells, but there is pleasure in recording that the applause bore evidence of the audience's appreciation of the fact.

Neither the songs themselves nor Janssen's performances of them are likely ever to appeal to a large public. Those three studies in melancholia are the songs sung by the old harper in Goethe's *Wilhelm Meister* – 'Wer sich der Einsamkeit ergibt', 'An die Türen will ich schleichen', and 'Wer nie sein Brot'. There is nothing in all music, not even the last act of *Tristan* nor in *Parsifal*, that so searches out the depths of human suffering as these songs. They live in a world of pondering upon spiritual torment, a world of solitude and gnawing grief lit only by the glimmer of the hope for pity.

The miracle of Wolf's settings of the poems is that they penetrate not only the general and particular sorrows of the words but the personal, morbid anguish of Goethe's half-crazed harper. And it is the wonder of Janssen's art that he lives in Wolf's songs as completely and self-effacingly as the composer absorbed himself in the poet's imaginings. The naturally elegiac timbre of his voice is an advantage, but he seems to have been born with a peculiar sympathy for and understanding of Wolf's mind that enables him to cut to the very core of the musical as well as the emotional texture of the songs.

Mr Menges does not seem yet to have developed that understanding. He gave the impression of one who follows willingly but yet hesitates to probe into the mysteries around him. His willing following caused us an uneasy moment in the second song, where he appeared to fear for a moment that the syncopated orchestral part was lagging too far behind the singer.

Herr Janssen also gave a magnificent account of the Count's aria from the third act of *Figaro*, and Mr Menges conducted performances which included the *Midsummer Night's Dream* Overture and a capitally arranged suite from Monteverdi's *Orfeo*.

The orchestra was the London Philharmonic Orchestra.

Rachmaninov 14 March 1938

Rachmaninov was not invariably in his best form for his concert at the Queen's Hall yesterday afternoon. He gave the impression of being at times preoccupied and at others as weary of the whole business of concert-giving. It is not unlikely that the mystification of his audience at the end of the first piece on the programme unsettled him. According to the printed programme and the analytical notes he was to have played Liszt's variations on a theme of Bach, *Weinen, Klagen, Sorgen, Zagen*. This work is well known to concert audiences and it lasts about 12 minutes. Rachmaninov played for about five minutes and then stopped at what appeared to be the end of a variation. The embarrassed silence was relieved by some tentative applause from various parts of the hall. What had happened was that Rachmaninov had played an earlier form of the variations, unaware of the fact that the programme had made no mention of the fact. In works by Chopin and in short pieces by Liszt he was his incomparable matchless self, swift and sure of finger and wrist, the supreme pianistic poet of our time. Only Debussy's *Suite bergamasque* seemed strangely to elude him. The execution was flawless, but the music was made to sound as un-Gallic as a performance of *Boris* sung in German sounds un-Russian.

Kreisler in the Brahms Concerto 28 March 1938

Fritz Kreisler has played Brahms's Violin Concerto often enough in London for the public to know that his performance of this work is an experience which should not be missed. The most vital service which musical criticism can perform in relation to his playing of this masterpiece at the Albert Hall this afternoon must therefore be directed at the public, which did not entirely fill the hall.

The fact that other famous violinists have recently played the same concerto in London has no real bearing on the matter. Kreisler is mortal; he cannot go on for ever and no life is full which has not included in its experience Kreisler playing the Brahms Concerto. His art begins where that of other fiddlers ceases. There are three or four other players who can produce the notes as surely as he, but not another who can live as he does in the soul of this music. His performance is not to be measured in terms of tempo, rhythm, phrasing and intonation. It is in its way a feat of imaginative re-creation which raises his part to a function comparable with the composer's.

Our elders tell us that those who did not hear Jean de Reszke sing Tristan or Richter conduct *Die Meistersinger* have no idea of how those works can sound. If by some tragic mischance Kreisler should never play again, those who were at the Albert Hall this afternoon have experienced a performance which neither sentiment nor the flattering illusions of memory can enhance. Dr Malcolm Sargent conducted.

The orchestra was the London Philharmonic Orchestra.

Rachmaninov and Beecham 4 April 1938

Rachmaninov remembers that in the 1790s Beethoven was a popular virtuoso. He does not confuse the lionised composer-pianist of the close of the eighteenth century with the brooding lion of the late pianoforte sonatas and the posthumous quartets; neither is he of the school which seeks to read Schopenhauer into Chopin. So he played Beethoven's First Pianoforte Concerto this afternoon at the Queen's Hall with the sympathetic understanding of a fellow composer-pianist. Anatole France said that it is the critic's duty 'to think himself into the state of the creator's mind in which each work of art was conceived'.

This is equally the interpreter's duty, and Rachmaninov fulfilled it admirably in his performance. He played with the virtuoso's delight in beauty and variety of tone, in accuracy and grace of execution, in giving pleasure to his audience, and he was rivalled, aided, and abetted in the friendliest way by Sir Thomas Beecham and the London Philharmonic Orchestra. Only careful and understanding rehearsal can produce a frame and background of the confident unanimity within and before which the participants are free and safe genially to compete in exquisite nuancing of phrasing and accent. The collaboration was no less happy in Rachmaninov's own *Rhapsody on a Theme of Paganini*. There is subtle and unfortunately rare pleasure in observing two fine minds exercised in the performance of concertos.

Beecham and his orchestra also played Haydn's B flat Symphony (No. 102) and Sibelius's *Tapiola*, each with a peculiar understanding of the antithetical styles. The colour and character of the orchestral tone in the two works was as different as eighteenth-century Vienna from twentieth-century Finland.

Ireland and Bliss   9 April 1938

The announcement of two modern British compositions had its usual effect on the size of the audience last evening at the Queen's Hall and resulted in hundreds of people missing a magnificent performance of Richard Strauss's *Ein Heldenleben*.

There was nothing to fear in these native works – John Ireland's Pianoforte Concerto and the concert suite from the ballet *Checkmate* by Arthur Bliss – they are neither folkish nor freakish, as is the way with so many contemporary native products. The Ireland concerto is a likeable work, individual, concise, and at times sensitively lyrical. The composer knows what he wants to say and he knows how to say it. The only drawback to this music is that it says things of such essentially Anglo-Saxon interest that one cannot imagine any but a British or an American audience understanding it or listening to it. One takes the liberty to doubt if even the composer's compatriots who are not also his contemporaries will respond to its esoteric appeal.

Arthur Bliss conducted his own loud and vehement piece which was written for a ballet and which, divorced from its natural twin, the stage action, is as tedious as the orchestral part of an early Verdi opera. This music is as hard, ruthless, and busy as everyday business life, unsentimental as a high-powered locomotive. It sets the listener no problems, but it gives him no rest from insistent clamour. Perhaps Mr Bliss is the true modern musician, faithfully reflecting the spirit of his times.

The sentiment of *Ein Heldenleben* has dated. It belongs as recognisably to the turn of the century as *Le mariage de Figaro* belongs to the dawn of the French Revolution, but it has faith and a sense of beauty which Bliss's music lacks. The passing of 40 years has not drained this work of its soaring nervous vitality or its power to excite. Strauss's music is under a cloud at the moment, but it needs only half a dozen performances like last night's to bring it back into favour. Beecham and his orchestra played like men possessed. From first bar to last this was a brilliant, exuberant, and beautiful performance.

The soloist in Ireland's Piano Concerto was Clifford Curzon.

3

Pre-war Associations

I. JEAN SIBELIUS

Early in 1934 Walter Legge met Sir Thomas Beecham and from then until 1945 produced all his recordings for Columbia and HMV (see Chapter 1). Legge had already corresponded with Sibelius, but now, working with one of the greatest exponents of the Finnish master's music, he was able to strengthen an important acquaintance with the composer. The first two Sibelius Society sets were conducted by Sibelius's friend and disciple Robert Kajanus, with the addition of a live performance of the Third Symphony in which Serge Koussevitzky conducted the BBC Symphony Orchestra. In 1933 Kajanus died, and Beecham was his obvious successor as conductor in future Sibelius Society projects.

[translated from German] 13 June 1933.
Järvenpää.

Dear Mr Walter Legge,
Thank you very much for the records. They are excellent and I am completely enchanted by Dr Koussevitzky's conducting. Wishing you all the best, I sign, with all good wishes.

Yours,
Jean Sibelius

19 January 1934.

Dear Professor Sibelius,
We have just started work on the Third Volume of the Sibelius Society which will contain the String Quartet and some of your orchestral works, probably *Lemminkäinen zieht Heimwärts* and *Nachtritt und Sonnenaufgang*. The conductor will be Sir Thomas Beecham who, more than any conductor in England, has popularised your music and who has, during the past winter, given magnificent performances of your First, Second, Third and Fourth Symphonies, the Violin Concerto and *Tapiola*. Have you any other short works which you suggest we might record instead of these two, in addition to them?

When we are recording these works we are anxious to do another large one. Is there any hope of our having the score and parts of the Eighth Symphony by May or July? Naturally, we should not arrange a public

68

performance of that work unless you wish, but we are extremely anxious to record the Symphony as soon as possible.

You will, I know, be pleased to hear that your music is now the sensation of London, and that your Symphonies are being frequently performed in all the important Provincial Cities. During the past three months all the Symphonies, except the Sixth, have been played here and both the First and Second have been repeated by popular request. The Swedish soprano, Göta Ljungberg, gave a recital of your songs and had a very great success. She and I propose to come and see you at Helsingfors in July.

Please accept the very best wishes of Mr Ernest Newman and myself and of the hundreds of your admirers who formed the Sibelius Society.

Yours very sincerely,
[Walter Legge]

Plans for the third Society volume were in fact changed, and Beecham's participation in the series was postponed. The String Quartet, *Voces intimae*, played by the Budapest Quartet, formed the third volume in company with the Sixth Symphony, recorded in London during June 1934 by the Finnish National Radio Orchestra under another compatriot of Sibelius's, Georg Schnéevoigt. Live recordings of Schnéevoigt and the orchestra in the Fourth Symphony and *Luonnotar* (with the soprano soloist Helmi Liukkonen) were also made during a London concert on 4 June, but these remained unpublished until 1976.

[translated from German]

3 February 1934.

Dear Mr Legge,

Please accept my apologies for having to write to you in German. It will give me great pleasure to see you and Miss Ljungberg here in the summer.

I admire Sir Thomas Beecham as an eminent artist and am happy that Sir Thomas is performing my works.

I will write to you soon in more detail about my new symphony, which is as yet unfinished, and about some shorter work which I would like to suggest to you. In the meantime I want to thank you, my dear sir, for the great interest you are showing in my music and send my very best wishes to you, to Mr Ernest Newman, to Sir Thomas Beecham and to my friends in the Sibelius Society.

Yours sincerely,
[Jean Sibelius]

My old friend Professor Schnéevoigt is coming to London in May with his orchestra and wants to play my Symphony No. 6 and the *Oceanides*. How do you feel about this? He plays these works very well.   JS

69

3. Pre-war Associations

14 June 1934.

Dear Professor Sibelius,

First of all let me congratulate you on the success of the concerts of the Finnish Orchestra: they were a triumph for the orchestra, but a far greater triumph for you. London regarded the concerts as a Sibelius Festival, the audiences were enormous and the English musical world is more than ever 'Sibelius mad'.

As you suggested, we have made records of the orchestra playing your Fourth and Sixth Symphonies and *Luonnotar*. Copies of the records are being sent to you today and I wait anxiously to hear from you that they please you. I am sure they will, particularly those of the Sixth Symphony.

Do please write to me as soon as you have heard them for I am anxious to publish them together with your Quartet played by the Budapest Quartet for the Third Volume of the Sibelius Society; and your recommendation of the records as delighting you and having your entire approval will be the greatest help in spreading the knowledge of your music throughout Europe and America as well as in Britain and of these two works in particular which are, as yet, very rarely performed here.

Ernest Newman, Cecil Gray, Arnold Bax and Harriet Cohen ask me to send their warmest greetings to you.

I hope you are keeping well and that the Eighth Symphony is nearly finished.

By the way, I hear you have written a Cello Concerto. Is it true? Is the work published?

Please accept my kindest regards and best wishes.

Yours very sincerely,
[Walter Legge]

Legge's first visit to Sibelius duly took place, and following this he made arrangements for EMI to present the composer with a new gramophone. In October 1934 he made some live recordings of Beecham and the London Philharmonic Orchestra at the Leeds Festival. These included excerpts from Sibelius's incidental music to *The Tempest*. In due course he sent copies of the test recordings to the composer, but they remained unpublished.

[translated from German]

11 November 1934.

My dear friend Mr Legge,

The pleasant hours we spent together made me very happy. I am and feel myself constantly enriched when dealing with 'the youngsters in the production team'. Concerning a gramophone I have 220 volts and alternating current.

I am very curious about the records. Up to now I have not received them. I find the photos excellent.

I really appreciate your friendship and send you and all my friends my best wishes.

Your devoted
Jean Sibelius

[translated from German]

25 November 1934.

My dear friend Mr Legge,
    Re: *The Tempest*
In the prelude the woodwind and brass must be louder and the strings muted.
TT 1805 Canon. The canon in the middle cannot be heard. Must be played more softly – a bit.
TT 1807 The 'Chorus of the Winds' does not fit here. It must be left out.
TT 1808 'Dance of the Nymphs' much slower: minim = 132.
TT 1809 'The Naiads' slower: *Andantino p. con moto*: minim = circa 80.
    Much is fine, for example Miranda where Sir Thomas's firm hand is clearly evident. I would like to write about much of the rest but my hand is troubling me.
    Sincerest best wishes to you and to all my friends.

Your devoted
Jean Sibelius

PS. In a few days' time I will write to you in more detail. Many of the pieces are quite suitable for recording. Others (eg 'The Oak Tree') are not. Everything is done in such an unclear way and the players must get the feel of the music more.

[translated from German]

18 December 1934.

My dear friend Mr Legge,
    You can well imagine or rather not imagine what joy I felt about your right royal gift. I am totally astonished by the perfection of this equipment which is a veritable miracle.
    The Tempest music sounded completely different. The prelude under the direction of the eminent Sir Thomas Beecham certainly sounds excellent in the reproduction. The same is true of the 'Oak Tree'. Other than that I can only repeat what I have already written to you.
    I send my best regards to you and all my friends.

Your humble and grateful
Jean Sibelius

The records have to be improved here and there. I find the 'Chorus of the Winds' is now just right.

Late in the year Legge set down some impressions of his visit to Sibelius in an article for the *Daily Telegraph*.

A Visit to Sibelius   15 December 1934
The Table-Talk of a Great Composer

For four or five years the musical world has been waiting for the news of the completion of Sibelius's Eighth Symphony. Nearly two years have passed since the first performance in London was announced, and still there is no sign of the long-awaited work.

I had hopes that, coming face to face with Sibelius himself, I might find him willing at least to say whether or not the new symphony might be expected to materialise in 1935. Early this year he had written to me promising soon to write more fully of his 'new and fast-growing symphony', but, although privileged to spend a great deal of time in his company, I discovered only one thing about the symphony – that to attempt to discuss it is unwise.

On any subject except his own music Sibelius is a brilliant, illuminating and amusing talker. When he does somewhat reluctantly mention his own music he is no less illuminating, even though he maintains that, 'liable as musicians are to be wrong in discussing music, the composer is most liable to be wrong when talking of his own'. But Sibelius is the last man in the world from whom we can expect an intimate autobiography; his way of personal revelation is through his music, not words. It is when he talks of other men and other music that he reveals most of himself.

In his recollections of the great composers he met in his young days in Vienna, one sees reflected his own fastidiousness in dress. 'I remember Brahms well – an unsavoury-looking fellow, untidily dressed in a shabby suit that bore evidence of many a previous meal and grey with cigar ash.' He saw Wolf too. 'A curious, nervous-looking little man with extraordinary bright, intense eyes.' And Bruckner. 'Another untidy man with a broad back and a squeaky, high-pitched voice – we used to call him the hippopotamus with the nightingale voice.'

At one time Sibelius and Mahler had a long discussion as to the form of the symphony. 'Mahler maintained that the symphony should be like the world – embracing all types, the great and the small. His own did – that is their greatest fault. His great gifts, apart from conducting and his extraordinary capacity for organising music, were lyrical. The songs are the best of Mahler.'

Sibelius's essentially classical attitude to the symphony was defined thus: 'Since Beethoven's time all the so-called symphonies, except Brahms's have been symphonic poems. In many cases the composers have told us or, at least, indicated the programmes they had in mind; in others it is plain that there has been some story or landscape or set of images that the composer has set himself to depict or illustrate.

'That is not my idea of a symphony. My symphonies are music conceived and worked out in terms of music and with no literary basis. I am not a literary musician: for me music begins where words cease. A scene can be expressed in painting, a drama in words; a symphony should be first and last music. Of course, it has happened that, quite unbidden, some mental image has established itself in my mind in connection with a movement I have been writing, but the germ and the fertilisation of my symphonies has been solely musical. When I set out to write symphonic poems it is another matter. *Tapiola, Pohjola's Daughter, Lemminkäinen, The Swan of Tuonela*, are suggested to me by our national poetry, but I do not pretend that they are symphonies.'

This non-literary view of music colours Sibelius's taste in other men's music. Part of his lack of sympathy with Wagner may be traced to this source; he dislikes Hugo Wolf for the same reason. 'His fine taste in poetry', Sibelius said to me, 'is proved by his choice of poems, his appreciation of their subtleties, by the perfection of his declamation, of his word-setting. But why urge the music on at one point and check it at the next in obedience to a poetic impulse? Why obey the dictates of poetry?'

Reminded that he had written over a hundred songs himself, he replied, 'I was young. Every young man writes songs.'

Sibelius had several hard things to say of conductors. 'I have found it a rule, with so few exceptions as to be almost a law of nature, that as a conductor grows older he becomes more sentimental, more inclined to drag out slow movements, to distort them, lingering with senile sensuality over the phrases which he seeks to make "more expressive". Some composers may like this "expressiveness", it may suit some music; but it is foreign to mine and I do not like it. My slow movements are to be played just as they are written, without any of the tender caressing and *rallentandos* to which they are often subjected.

'This wilful overloading of sentimentality has led to the popular misconception that my first two symphonies are Tchaikovskian. My musical mind and my methods are the very antithesis of Tchaikovsky's. I cannot think, I have never been able to think, the Tchaikovskian way, and it is the conductors who are to blame if the public thinks it sees in my early works a Tchaikovskian influence. That I admire Tchaikovsky is true, but I have never written in his style. All I ask of the conductors who play my music is that they should obey my markings implicitly, neither hurrying nor dragging, and to remember that my scoring and my dynamic indications are intentional.'

He talked of conductors who have performed his music. 'I owe a great deal to the men who played my works in my young days. Busoni was a great worker and a great friend. Toscanini I have never met, but 30 years ago he was playing my music, and I have heard glowing accounts from friends who understand my intentions. Both Sir Henry Wood and Bantock have been splendid to me. It was Wood who first performed many of my works in England, and he has worked magnificently to make my music known. To Bantock I owe more than I can say; as a young man he did more than a dozen men could do to get a hearing for my works, and best of all he induced orchestras to let me conduct them.

'The best conductor my music has ever had, as far as my own experience goes, was Kajanus. When we were young men he was a passionate Wagnerian, and although he never entirely deserted his first love, he worked and studied and sought unceasingly to play my works exactly as I wanted them to sound.

'It often happened, particularly with my Fourth, Sixth and Seventh Symphonies, that at first he could not see what I was driving at. He would come back from rehearsals and say, "I've played exactly what you've written – but you can't mean that." And when I had carefully assured him that I did mean precisely what I had written he would go back and work again until he had thought himself completely into every detail of the work. His patience was as remarkable as his self-effacement in conducting. His sole idea was to serve the composer and to prevent his own personality from intruding upon that of the composer. And even though, in the last years of his life, he became passionately devoted to Tchaikovsky, he kept that apart from his performances of other works. Tchaikovsky is the composer for the very young and the very old musician.

'Of the men who play my music today, and whose performances I have heard, I prefer Beecham and Koussevitzky. Of Koussevitzky I have heard only the Seventh Symphony records published by the Sibelius Society, but with those I am entirely delighted. Beecham's performances have come to me by wireless, and they are superb. He is a remarkable man. It gives me the deepest pleasure and satisfaction to see how great an interest he takes in my music and to know that it is he who is playing so much of my music to the British public.

'During my lifetime the musical centre of the world has shifted three times. When I was a youngster, Vienna was the musical Mecca. Then, until the war, it was Berlin; after the war and until the slump America enjoyed it; now it has shifted to London, where you have more and better music than one could hear in any city in the world. Your tastes are more catholic than anywhere in the world, you give new composers a fair hearing, and you are freer than any country from nationalistic prejudice.'

[translated from German; the quoted section was in English]

11 January 1935.

Dear and esteemed friend,

Many thanks for your letter. I am very pleased that the equipment sounds so good and that you now find that the records of *The Tempest* are worthy of merit.

At the end of January Sir Thomas Beecham will conduct your Fourth Symphony. He has already held three rehearsals and has worked like a horse with the Schnéevoigt records, but there are many things in these records which do not correspond to the score. Sir Thomas has therefore asked me to obtain an answer from you to several questions. Here are the questions:

I have listened to the Finnish Orchestra's gramophone records of the Fourth Symphony of Sibelius; comparing them with the printed score I find many differences in respect of tempi and dynamics. It is with the tempi that I am most concerned, and I should like Professor Sibelius's ruling on the following points:-

First Movt.
The opening marked is *Tempo molto moderato quasi adagio*. The time adopted by the Finnish Orchestra is M.M. quaver = 48-50. As this is easily the slowest speed of any known piece yet written it should be marked *Adagio molto*. All the more so because the so-called *Adagio* at Letter B is M.M. quaver = 76-80, a much quicker time. The execution of the 3/2 bar after Letter B is clearly indicated, but the four bars which follow it are, I presume, to be played about M.M. quaver = 76-80. The sixth bar of Letter C is played by the Finnish Orchestra as *Adagio*, although it is not so marked. After this we come to *Tempo primo*; obviously we should return to the first tempo (quaver = 48-50), but the record reveals a tempo of quaver = 80, and therefore it is misleading to everyone that the passage should be so marked. At Letter F the record reveals an *accelerando poco a poco* during five or six bars, when we arrive at a tempo crotchet = 60. This sounds right. The bar at Letter I is marked *Adagio* but it is not played very *adagio* on the record. I propose to take it about crotchet = 48.

Second Movt. Letter I, page 24; the whole of the viola passage fails to sound either on the record or in rehearsal. Does Professor Sibelius agree that the second violin part be marked *pp* with only the very slightest crescendo?

Third Movt. Letter A; In the printed parts the Horns are marked *con sordini*; in the record they are *senza sordini*. Which is right? Letter C; in the record the tempo is here quicker – quaver = 66 – as compared with the previous quaver = 56. Is this right? There is a further quickening of time beginning five bars after letter D, and this tempo – quaver = 80 – continues to the end of the movement. Should this be?

Fourth Movt. The record begins with minim = 144, which I find too quick. The playing as shown by the record is very loose and hurried. Apparently the conductor also found this to be the case because after Letter F he slackens the time to minim = 132 and does not return to the original minim = 144. I find minim = 132 to be about right for the whole movement. At the close of this movement, from Letter W to the end, the conductor of the record makes a *rallentando poco a poco*. Indeed he begins it somewhat earlier than Letter W. He firstly slackens to minim = 120, then (8 bars after W) to minim = 96-100, and finally (in the last six bars) to minim = 80. He also makes a marked *diminuendo* during these last six bars, ending *pp*. This seems good and natural, but it is not marked in the score! What does Professor Sibelius want here?

The best thing to do would be to send me the metronome marks for the whole symphony, if that is possible. Please be kind enough to send me an answer immediately by airmail. The next rehearsal is on 18th January.

With kindest regards,
Yours,
[Walter Legge]

16 January 1935.

WALTER LEGGE JABBERMENT TELEX LDN

SATISFIED WITH SIR THOMAS JUSTIFIED CRITICISM LETTER FOLLOWS

GREETINGS SIBELIUS

[translated from German]

17 January 1935.

My dear friend,

Many thanks! I am very pleased with Sir Thomas Beecham's observations. Here are the answers to the questions. I hope you can decipher them. In haste!

Best wishes,
Your devoted
Jean Sibelius

Symphony No 4, Jean Sibelius

First Movement

Tempo primo	crochet = 52-60
Letter B to Tempo primo (page 5)	crochet = 40 (-45)
Tempo primo (page 5)	crochet = 60
(i) Adagio (page 11)	crochet = 40
Tempo primo (page 12)	crochet = 60

Second Movement

Second violin. Letter I *pp* with only the very slightest crescendo

I. Jean Sibelius

Third Movement
Letter A. Horns – if played firmly: *con sordini* (sound as with the Finnish Orchestra. *senza sord*)

Fourth Movement
Tempo minim = 132. From letter S on, gradually becoming softer and softer until minim = 100 at letter W. From letter W until the end minim = 100. The last 6 bars: *mf*. As solemnly as possible and without *ritardando* (tragic, without tears, resolutely).

The letter which follows implies that Beecham's performance of the Fourth Symphony was recorded, either live or in the studio, though no documentation or other evidence of a recording has seemingly survived (Beecham did make a recording of the work in December 1937 which was published).

[translated from German]

1 February 1935.

My dear friend,
    I think this is excellent. Perfect. While listening to it I noted the following:

Second Movement:. page 19 and 20. *Tranquillo*, if this were a bit softer it would have a greater effect I think.

Third Movement: page 36.

Strings

even more *largamente*.

Fourth Movement: page 65. The passage between R and S could in fact be more powerful. But?

I must now express my deep admiration for Sir Thomas Beecham's masterly conducting. For me it was something unique and remarkable.

Best wishes,
Your devoted,
Jean Sibelius

3. Pre-war Associations

10 April 1935.

Dear and honoured Friend,

Sir Thomas Beecham and I are working out the plans for a grand Sibelius Festival to be held in November in London in honour of your seventieth birthday and we are anxious to include in the programmes of the concerts (there will be five or six of them) as many unfamiliar works as possible. We are particularly anxious about *Kullervo, Lemminkäinen und das Mädchen* and *Lemminkäinen in Tuonela* since they have never been heard here. I know that the manuscripts do exist and Sir Thomas asks me to ask you if you could possibly arrange that we should borrow those manuscripts to have them copied. Would this be possible?

Another question. This one is entirely Sir Thomas's, and knowing how you hate to discuss the matter I hate to raise it – but he insists. Is there any hope of your Eighth Symphony for performance in November?

How are you? Well I hope. You will, I know, be pleased to know that the Fourth Symphony was played in Birmingham last night by Sir Thomas Beecham and had a great success.

Kindest regards from Sir Thomas, Ernest Newman and, of course, your very sincere friend

[Walter Legge]

[translated from German]

20 April 1935.

My dear friend,

Many thanks! I feel really blessed. The manuscript scores of *Lemminkäinen and the Maidens* and *Lemminkäinen in Tuonela* do not belong to me. They were lost for 40 years. I will send them to you as soon as possible. However I would advise you against doing *Kullervo*. I will send you a choral work with, unfortunately, only the rough texts.

I cannot say anything about Symphony No. 8.

My best regards to Sir Thomas Beecham, Ernest Newman and yourself.

Your grateful friend,
Jean Sibelius

Apparent ambiguities in the above text are due to Sibelius's idiosyncratic use of German.

A potentially difficult situation now arose with Schnéevoigt, and Fred Gaisberg, Legge's chief, wrote to him for advice.

MR. WALTER LEGGE   17 May 1935.

I see that Schnéevoigt has gathered from the manuscript, some early works of Sibelius, dated about 1893. I quote you from his letter:

At the great Finnish Kalevala festivals, which were held at the beginning of March last, I produced two works by Sibelius, composed 42 years ago, and which have hitherto only once been presented, 42 years ago. These two works are *Lemminkäinen in Tuonela* and *Lemminkäinen and the Maidens of Saari*. They were a sensational success at the festival, these two works being regarded as the *clou* of the whole.

The work of setting the two scores in order was extremely laborious, but the result was the most brilliant possible. After the festivities I secured from the composer the first production rights for London. Now I beg to propose that you, by inviting me to London, should avail yourself of the opportunity of making records of these two works.

I possess the whole orchestral material, or rather, this belongs to the Helsingfors Town Orchestra, whose head I am, as is known, and [they] have the material at hand. Each work occupies about 15 minutes. These works are among Sibelius's most inspired creations and it would certainly be a grateful task for you to be able to offer the world these two works in records on the Master's seventieth birthday. I am at liberty during the summer and could come across at any time.

At the same time I beg to inform you that I possess the score and orchestral parts for the original arrangement of Sibelius *En Saga* and that I should greatly like to have this work of genius included in your collection of Sibelius records. As is well known, the score of this work was lost, but, as I had had the same copied more than 40 years ago, it has thus been saved for posterity. This original composition differs greatly from the later adaptation, and is undoubtedly of greater power and wilder contents than the latter.

As this music is still in manuscript and in Schnéevoigt's hands, it means having him do it or not doing it at all.

I have simply answered the letter saying I shall look into the matter. Please telephone me about it.

F.W. GAISBERG
INTERNATIONAL ARTISTES' DEPARTMENT.

20 May 1935.

Verehrter Meister!

I was so happy to receive your letter and the promise of the loan of the scores of *Lemminkäinen und das Mädchen*, *Lemminkäinen in Tuonela* and *Kullervo*. Sir Thomas and I wait anxiously for their arrival. I have had a letter from Schnéevoigt in which he says that he has discovered these works, that he has recently played them with great success in Helsinki, and that you have given him the sole right of performing these works in England. If that is indeed so it is not for me to dispute your wishes, but I am sure you will understand that Sir Thomas Beecham will be greatly disappointed if Schnéevoigt, who is regarded here as a third-class conductor, is given preference over him. Moreover, I cannot believe that Schnéevoigt would give performances comparable with those of Sir Thomas.

The plans for the Festival are going well and we anxiously await the arrival of the scores.

My best wishes to you. I hope to be in Helsinki again in December.

> Yours very sincerely,
> [Walter Legge]

[translated from German]

28 May 1935.

My dear friend, Mr Legge,

I will send you the manuscripts for copying.

Unfortunately they do not belong to me. I would be only too happy if Sir Beecham [sic] were prepared to perform the pieces.

> With best wishes,
> Jean Sibelius

PS. There is something wrong with my hand.

27 June 1935.

Dear Professor Sibelius,

I know you will be glad to hear that I have at last succeeded in inducing the publishers of your First and Fourth Symphonies, *Tapiola*, *Der Schwan von Tuonela* to publish miniature scores of those works.

I learn that my friend Koussevitzky is conducting some concerts in the Festival that is being held in your honour in Helsinki in September. I shall make the journey to Finland for these concerts so that we shall meet again soon.

May I ask a favour? You know how enthusiastically Sir Thomas Beecham has worked in the last three years in the presentation of your music – and you have yourself heard by Radio how he understands it. It would create a great impression in this country if you would use your influence to arrange that Sir Thomas should be invited to Helsinki – in September if possible – to conduct at least one concert of your music. I have not, or course, mentioned this to him, but I am confident that he would accept and that nothing would give him keener pleasure than to be invited to your country to conduct a concert in your honour.

I look forward with delight to the prospect of seeing you again in September.

With warmest greetings and kindest regards,

> Yours sincerely,
> [Walter Legge]

I. Jean Sibelius

[translated from German]

1 July 1935.

My dear friend,

I am sending you today *Lemminkäinen and the Maidens*. At last! Soon I'll send you *L. in Tuonela*!

With best regards,
Jean Sibelius

4 July 1935.

Dear Mr Legge,

Thanking you for your kind letter of June 27th I congratulate you for the results obtained with the miniature scores. I felt very happy about them.

Regarding the planned visit of Mr Koussevitzky in September I understand he is coming to conduct some of my compositions. This, I believe, has no connection with my birthday, which is on December 8th. There have been some plans for celebrating my birthday but until now the matter has not been discussed with me. I personally am very much against any kind of celebration and if it will be possible it is my intention not to participate in any festivals. This will explain to you why I do not take any part in the contemplated arrangements, beside I never tried to influence the musical life of Helsinki.

It will be a great pleasure for me to meet you again in September.

I beg you kindly to convey my most respectful personal regards to Sir Thomas Beecham, and to explain to him my admiration and profound gratitude for the marvellous way he works for my art.

Yours sincerely,
Jean Sibelius

Volume Four of the Sibelius Society was now being prepared, and on 23 January 1936 Adrian Boult and the BBC Symphony Orchestra recorded *The Oceanides*, *Night-ride and Sunrise* and *The Bard*. Presumably technical problems prevented publication of the last-named work, since the composer evidently approved the performance. Jascha Heifetz and Beecham had recorded the Violin Concerto on 26 November and 14 December 1935.

[translated from German]

4 March 1936.

My dear friend,

I have sent you today new records of your *Bard*, *Oceanides* and *Night-ride and Sunrise*. Records of the Violin Concerto played by Jascha Heifetz and Sir Thomas Beecham will also follow in a few days' time. Please be kind enough to write me a few lines on what you think of the records.

I hope you are well.

With my best wishes I remain,

81

Your admirer and friend,
Walter Legge

[translated from German]

2 April 1936.

My dear friend,
   The records are marvellous. I was really delighted with them. Please convey my gratitude and my regards to Sir Thomas, Mr Heifetz (his playing is masterly) and Mr Bouldt [*sic*].
   The best title in English would be: *Night Cavalcade and Sunrise*, and in Finnish *Oinen ratsastus – retki ja aurigon nousu*.

Best regards,
Your devoted
Jean Sibelius

Beecham made a second and successful recording of the Fourth Symphony on 10 December 1937 for Volume Five of the Sibelius Society, but before entering the studio he sought to consult the composer once more.

19 November 1937.

PROFESSOR SIBELIUS JARVENPAA HELSINGFORS FINLAND

PLEASE SEND AT ONCE METRONOME MARKINGS FOR ALL MOVEMENTS OF YOUR FOURTH SYMPHONY GREETINGS

WALTER LEGGE LDN

20 November 1937.

METRONOME MARKINGS IN ALL FOUR MOVEMENTS ARE ABOUT AS FOLLOWS ONE QUARTER NOTE 54 THREE QUARTERS 96 ONE QUARTER 50 ONE HALF NOTE 108 IMPOSSIBLE TO GIVE THEM EXACTLY

GREETINGS SIBELIUS

[translated from German]

28 November 1937.

My dear friend,
   I have just received the records. As this symphony is hardly suitable for the gramophone one needs to perform much of it with a different balance than indicated in the full score. The solo passages sometimes cannot be heard at all. Unfortunately I cannot really comment on the overall sound as the equipment which you sent me is now completely ruined after being repaired locally. I must therefore travel to Helsingfors, albeit reluctantly, to listen to the records again and I will write to you about this in more detail.

The tempi were fine although I would suggest playing more softly in the last movement from letter S.

> With best greetings,
> Sincerely yours,
> Jean Sibelius

WALTER LEGGE LDN   30 November 1937.

DISCS BY SIR THOMAS ARE EXCELLENT CANCEL LETTER 28/11

GREETINGS SIBELIUS
SIBELIUS JARVENPAA HELSINGFORS FINLAND

21 December 1937.

I READ THAT YOUR EIGHTH SYMPHONY IS FINISHED MAY SIR THOMAS HAVE FIRST PERFORMANCE FOR LONDON NEXT YEAR WE BOTH SEND GREETINGS FOR CHRISTMAS AND NEW YEAR

WALTER LEGGE

WALTER LEGGE JABBERMENT TELEX LDN   24 December 1937.

NEWS CONCERNING SYMPHONY PREMATURE STOP GREETINGS SIBELIUS

11 May 1938.

My dear Friend,

Sir Thomas Beecham wants to give a Festival of your works in London this autumn. There will be six concerts – five with large orchestra, and one with small orchestra, quartet and singers. Sir Thomas himself will conduct all the concerts. We propose to do all the Symphonies, as well as the following works:-

Finlandia: Pohjola's Daughter: Luonnotar: Scènes historiques: Night Ride and Sunrise: March of the Athenians: Storm and Incidental Music to the Tempest: Origin of Fire: Valse triste: Violin Concerto: The Bard: Two Romances for violin and orchestra: Karelia – Intermezzo; Alla Marcia: Tapiola: En Saga: In Memorium: Lemminkäinen Suite.

We hope to get Heifetz to play the Violin Concerto and the Two Romances for violin and orchestra, and in short, no effort will be spared to make this Festival really worthy of you and your works.

Only one thing is wanting. That you yourself should come over to attend it, so that you may be properly honoured in the country where your works are so popular.

The Festival will take place during the last week of October and the first fortnight of November.

May I ask you on Sir Thomas's behalf, and as a personal favour to your tens of thousands of English admirers, and to me, to agree to come to London for this great occasion. Everything will be done to ensure your comfort and peace, and to make your stay as happy as you would wish it to be.

> With my kindest regards,
> Your Friend,
> [Walter Legge]

[translated from German]

17 May 1938.

My dear friend,
    Your letter has brought me great pleasure.
    It is a splendid idea and of the greatest importance to my music. Sadly I cannot promise to come to England this autumn. I will write to you later about this.

> With cordial greetings,
> Your Friend
> Jean Sibelius

At this point correspondence between Sibelius and Walter Legge seems to have come to a halt: they resumed contact after the Second World War (see Chapter 7).

II. GERHARD HÜSCH AND HERBERT JANSSEN

In the early 1930s Walter Legge started to produce Lieder recordings and he also founded the London Lieder Club (see Chapter 1). The baritone Gerhard Hüsch and his accompanist Hans Udo Müller visited London in April 1933. Under Legge's supervision they recorded Schubert's *Winterreise* song cycle at EMI's Abbey Road Studios on the 8th, 10th and 11th days of that month, and they also gave several recitals. The London recording sessions yielded satisfactory results in only 11 of the 24 *Winterreise* songs, and the remainder were successfully re-recorded at the Beethovensaal, Berlin on 1 August.

2 March 1933.

Dear Mr Legge,
    I received today from the Gramophone Co. the travelling permit from the Minister of Labour for Herr Udo Müller and myself. The permit seems to be only endorsed to recording, as it says 'employment: recorder W6'. May I ask you therefore to have the permit for Mr Müller and for myself extended for your concerts if this is necessary. The permit for recording is valuable for two weeks. Will you excuse me if I have not so far told you that Herr Udo Müller will also accompany my five recitals at the Lieder-club in London. This was simply a mistake on my part.
    Herr Müller is looking forward to his week in London and would agree – even with a heavy heart – to a fee of £8 per evening.

I have the first night of the opera: *Cobert Chabert* [*sic*], on March 4th and on the following day I shall be in Cologne for the performance as I am in *The Tsar and the Carpenter*.

In consequence I cannot tell you definitely of the programme concerning the Wolf songs for the recital of the Lieder-Abend.

Naturally I shall take your suggestions as much as possible into consideration. Also I should be delighted to record for the Wolf Society in London.

I thank you very much for the trouble you took concerning a *pension*. May I ask you to let me know your suggestions as soon as possible and also the charges. My second Lieder-Abend in Berlin takes place on March 28. I enclose the programme. I gave the same recital with the exception of Schoeck on Feb 22nd in Bremen. I enclose also the critics.

> Best regards,
> G. Hüsch

[translated from German]

17 March 1933.

Dear Herr Hüsch,

I am in the process of arranging for your work permit. Please be so kind and send me your Wolf programme as soon as possible. I would be glad if you could take my programme into consideration as much as possible. As I previously mentioned one of our most renowned critics, an admirer of Wolf, has drawn up the programme.

As regards accommodation may I recommend the Anglo-German Club. They would be only too happy to make you an honorary member and you will get a comfortable room there for 8/- a day. That is a little more than five Reichsmarks. The cost of meals is very reasonable – 2/6d for breakfast, etc.

If you wish to make use of a piano there is also a good one there.

> With all best wishes,
> [Walter Legge]

[undated – mid-March 1933.]

Dear Mr Legge,

Many thanks for your letters and for the trouble you took over our arrangements.

You can imagine how unpleasant a refusal concerning the concerts would have been for me. I am therefore overjoyed that everything has turned out satisfactorily.

Herr Udo Müller and myself will leave here on Saturday evening 10 pm and we shall arrive at Croydon after the English time 16.05 pm.

We should be very obliged to you, if you could give us the exact address of the Anglo-German Club, and let them know that we shall be staying there until Monday morning. Would you also arrange for our stay from April 7-12.

We would of course like to have a piano at our *entire disposal*.

We must leave on April 3 by air via Amsterdam-Hannover for Berlin. On the 7th of April we return to London by the same route. We shall make our first recordings on the 8th, on the 9th is the Hugo Wolf-Abend, on the 10th and 11th are again recordings and we shall leave on April 12. Herr Udo Müller for Berlin so I shall go to Bremen for the *Matthäus-Passion* (13.00 14/4).

I am much obliged for your suggestions concerning the Wolf-pro-session [*sic*] and shall consider it as much as possible. Unfortunately I shall not be able to send you a programme until Sunday.

I am highly delighted that everything turned out all right.

> With best wishes,
> Yours,
> G. Hüsch

[translated from German]　　　　　　　　　　　　10 September 1933.
　　　　　　　　　　　　　　　　　Berlin-Zehlendorf-West
　　　　　　　　　　　　　　　　　Adalbertstrasse 57
　　　　　　　　　　　　　Fernruf H4 Zehlendorf 0690.

Dear Mr Legge,

I am enclosing a copy of the letter which I have just sent off to the Electrola Company to put you in the picture about my selection of the *Winterreise* songs. Everything is now looking so rosy that I rightly feel rather proud about the happy outcome of your great undertaking. Let us hope the first title succeeds in the coming week, as we all wish, then all who took part can feel satisfied. Let's also hope that it turns out well commercially. May I ask you now when the complete cycle will be published? Which company is responsible and when is it likely to appear in Germany? I could indeed well make use of it for my own publicity purposes here. It will be broadcast repeatedly by all the German radio stations as I have now been generally led to believe. For the time being let's keep our fingers crossed that the title 'Gute Nacht' turns out as well as we hope next week.

Best wishes to you yourself, your sister and Mr Gaisberg.

> Hans Udo Müller and Gerhard Hüsch

Another baritone who made Lieder recordings with Walter Legge and sang at the London Lieder Club was Herbert Janssen.

[translated from German]　　　　　　　　　　　　13 April 1933.
　　　　　　　　　　　　　　　　　189 Kaiseralle
　　　　　　　　　　　　　Wilmersdorf, Berlin.

Dear Mr Legge,

In your last letter you informed me that you wanted to try to reschedule the concert of the 30th of April to the 6th of May. Since then I have not heard from you. I have been ill with 'flu these last three weeks and as a consequence have had to cancel every one of my concerts and all my arrangements have now changed. I am going to Baden-Baden in the next few days to recuperate until the end of April and will therefore not be in a position to draw up the programme you wish.

As I have to sing on my London visit between the 8th and the 18th of May three times at the opera and once on the radio, I would find a whole evening singing Lieder just too much.

Could you possibly re-arrange the concert programme so that others could participate leaving me with only a few songs to sing? I would of course agree a correspondingly reduced fee with Mr Richardson.

If this proves possible Sunday the 14th would suit me best. Don't be angry with me for making things more difficult for you but everything has been thrown into confusion by my illness.

It would give me great pleasure to see you soon.

> With best wishes, I remain
> Yours,
> Herbert Janssen

[translated from German]   14 January 1936.
                                                                      11 Nymphenburgerstrasse
                                                                      Schöneberg, Berlin.

Dear Walter,

A thousand thanks for your nice letter which I was very happy to receive. I too feel in fine fettle. I'm enormously pleased that the records have turned out well. I would of course be only too happy to make some new Lieder records but I regard it as much more important at the moment to make orchestral recordings (Amfortas or suchlike) which would indeed sell fabulously well in London during the season and equally in Bayreuth.

I will be in Brussels from the 31st of January until the 2nd of February – staying at the Hotel Atlanta – and I would of course be delighted to be able to see you there. Otherwise there is nothing new to tell you. I have contracted for 11 evenings at Covent Garden where I'll sing Kurwenal, Gunther, Amfortas and Kothner.

Looking forward to seeing you at the earliest opportunity.

> With best wishes,
> Your old friend
> Herbert

                                                                      6 July 1936.

My dear Herbert,

I want you to make the Wolf records we discussed as soon as possible – the end of September would be ideal.

Here are the titles:-

Lied eines Verliebten	)	Mörike.		
Zur Warnung	)	"	1 side	

Fussreise	)	"		
Auftrag	)	"	1	"

Alle gingen, Herz zur Ruh') Spanisches Liederbuch.
Dereinst, dereinst   )   "   "   1 side

Im Frühling (1 Ton tiefer) Mörike   1 side

Wo wird einst. Lieder nach
verschiedenen Dichtern   1 side

Selig ihr Blinden (in D flat)) Italienisches Liederbuch
Tief im Herzen trag'ich Pein) Spanisches Liederbuch   1 side

Will you get these songs ready in your spare time.
I wait anxiously for your answer to my last letter.

Always your friend,
[Walter Legge]

As always, plans changed, and there were problems and disappointments in the recording process. Janssen undertook no more Wolf sessions until February 1937. Four of the songs listed above he did not record, and only his May 1937 recordings of *Alle gingen* and *Tief im Herzen* were issued on 78s. A 1937 recording of *Wo wird einst*, and 1938 recordings of *Lied eines Verliebten* and *Fussreise* were eventually issued on LP over 40 years later.

[translated from German]

17 October 1936.

Dear Walter,

My sincerest thanks for your nice letter. Naturally I will gladly sing Jokanaan (John the Baptist) and Orestes and take a holiday at the same time, but I must know well beforehand.

I will begin studying the Lieder as soon as I have got through my two 'first night' performances (*Don Carlos* and *Halka*).

For now, in haste, all my best to you and your sister.

Your old friend,
Herbert Janssen

[translated from German]

14 November 1936.

Dear Walter,

We made the Schubert and Schumann records on the 10th November and I think they turned out very well. But I would ask you from the bottom of my heart to release them only if they really are first class, otherwise I would prefer to record them again.

88

I hope you are well and that you are not as busy as I am at present. For now, all the best to your sister and yourself.

> Your friend,
> Herbert Janssen

PS. The Wolff [*sic*] Lieder will follow in December.

[translated from German]

6 December 1936.

Dear Walter,

I'm writing to you today about an urgent matter which I beg you to sort out for me and reply by return post.

As you know Sir Thomas has offered me through Dr Geissmar in Bayreuth the parts of Amfortas, Kurwenal, Dutchman, Gunther and Donner in the coming London Season of 1937 and I have accepted them. Up to now I have still not heard another word from London although in previous years all contracts were already settled by about this time.

Please make enquiries as to why I have heard nothing from Covent Garden, preferably via Dr Geissmar or Miss O'Donell, and let me know the answer by return.

How did the Schubert-Schumann recording go? Why are you such a bad correspondent that you don't write and tell me about it? On the 4th of January I'm singing the Wolf Lieder and let us hope they turn out fine. I have already agreed 13 Bayreuth evenings for next summer.

So Walter, please get moving and reply without delay.

> Your old friend,
> Herbert Janssen

The recordings turned out to be satisfactory, in fact, and were issued. Janssen undertook no more Wolf recordings until 10 February 1937.

[translated from German]

15 December 1936.

Dear Walter,

A thousand thanks for your nice letter. I'm sorry to hear that you have not been well. Take care and look after yourself. In the meantime I have received the invitation from Dr Geissmar to do the Dutchman, Amfortas, Kurwenal and Gunther for this season. I am glad the Lieder turned out well, but please arrange for a record to be sent to me soon.

For the moment best wishes to you and your sister and get well soon.

> Your old friend,
> Herbert Janssen

Shortly after this time Janssen fell foul of the Nazis and was warned that he should leave Germany. He came to England, where he was met by Walter Legge's sister at Victoria Station and taken to temporary lodgings. He then settled in Vienna, from where he fled to Paris when the Nazis invaded Austria.

[translated from German]   19 December 1937.
                                                                 14 Himmelpfortgasse, Vienna.

My dear Walter,

I was delighted to hear your voice recently on the telephone. Unfortunately the conversation was too short to tell you everything. Please send me straightaway the precise dates for the March concerts in England, by cable would be best, as at that time I have been asked to do three well-paid *Figaro* performances in Paris. Please do not forget.

Everything is marvellous here. The audience idolises me and the newspapers are full of the highest praise. Nevertheless, I do not want to stay here permanently. I would, of course, be very pleased to conclude a contract for festivals every year, but America beckons even more. I have received from Mertens an offer for Chicago, San Francisco and Los Angeles, and in addition as many concerts as I want if you add the Metropolitan and South America (Engel is already negotiating with Mertens on my account). I will have so much that I do not know whether I will manage it all. Yesterday evening I sang Scarpia here with tremendous success, and after that have 12 evenings with the Opera here up to 12th May. You see, everything is going just as I would like it – touch wood – my voice is in excellent form and I am now already looking forward to London. I would ask you to let Norman know once again, that Toscanini wants to have me for Wolfram, Kurwenal and Kothner in Salzburg. I am not going back to Germany in the near future under any circumstances. What are you doing for Christmas? I would be delighted to see you here. Erna is staying here over Christmas and is going to Berlin on 26th December to clear out my flat completely, and will only come back to me at the beginning of January. She sends you her best wishes. If, as we hope, you are to come for Christmas, please bring me my little yellow writing case which you have in your office.

For now I send you my very best wishes – do not forget the March dates.

> Your old friend
> Herbert

Very best wishes to your sister and Erika.

The soprano Erika Storm was a friend of Walter Legge. Erna was Janssen's future wife. Mertens was an agent.

[translated from German]

                                                                            16 January 1938.

Dear Walter,

Thanks for your letter. I told Beecham initially and repeated it to you in September that I will not sing Sachs. You will certainly have also heard from Tietjen that it is not a part suitable for me and I would only harm myself by doing it. I cannot learn *Rigoletto* in such a short time as I still have new roles to study here including the *Mass of Life* and the *Alto Rhapsody* as well. So it is completely out of the question. You really should have told me earlier as I had time enough to learn it in London. Why didn't you bring it up then? I accept the concert of the 7th of March and the *Mass* concert also.

You can see from the enclosed letter from Ibbs and Tillett what sort of difficulties these people create for me. Where am I to obtain the orchestral parts? It is taken for granted that at such large concerts the orchestral parts are provided by the organisers. I am relying on this being the case as I have none anyhow.

I'm not feeling well and my nerves are in shreds. If I don't start to feel better I'm going off to the mountains for three weeks. In such an eventuality I will then telegraph you requesting you to send me £60 by the fastest means possible, but I will communicate further on this later.

There is one thing I would like you to bear in mind at all times and never to forget and that is that my nerves are not made of steel and now less so than ever. We all have an overriding interest in keeping ourselves fit enough to work as long as possible ...

[text incomplete]

[translated from German]

25 January 1938.

My dear Walter,

What is actually going on? What is happening with the Delius Mass? Am I to learn it and when will it be performed? I really must know this now since time is running out. Why are you changing the concert programme of the 7th of March? I do not know any Bach arias and I must at the very least know what you have in mind otherwise I'll sing the five Wolf Lieder which you suggested.

My dear Walter – it is no easy task to produce programmes without my knowing what you intend especially if it includes works with which I am unfamiliar.

So please be kind to your old friend Herbert and let me hear from you as soon as possible.

Have you already instructed Erika to find some accommodation?

Most sincerely,
Herbert

[translated from German]

15 March 1939.
Saint Briac (France)
Ille et Vilaine
Villa les Korrigans.

Dear Walter,

This is to confirm again that I have listened to my records which were made in November and found them to be fine and I ask you to put them on

91

the market as soon as possible. Likewise the *Sonne der Schlummerlosen* which I unfortunately did not hear and which you said was the most beautiful recording. I also did not hear *Der Lindenbaum*. What has happened to it then?

I will still be here till the 19th of August and I do ask you to send me all my records which I made in your country (including all the most recent), every one – so that I may have them all.

> With kindest regards,
> your
> Herbert

Sonne der Schlummerlosen was published: there is no documentation to suggest that *Der Lindenbaum* was recorded.

[translated from German]

> 13 May 1939.

My dear Walter,

Further to our recent telephone conversation, I have to tell you once again that, after mature reflection and for many pertinent reasons, I am sticking to the decision I have already given you to sing a Wanderer or Wotan this season – come what may. I would ask you not to torment me with this any more as it would be pointless. I have also written in this vein to Sir Thomas.

> Your old friend,
> Herbert

III. ARNOLD BAX

After Sir Arnold Bax's death in 1953 his close friend Harriet Cohen sent some scores to Walter Legge.

> (undated)
> London W1.

Dear Walter,

When I saw the name 'Philharmonia' on these two old scores of Arnold – I thought – 'Walter should have those'. I think you were once very fond of him.

I was with him in love. We had a very happy time ... that is comforting. He was here mostly all the summer. And he did dote on this little cottage, so I am staying here *Deo volente*!

> Yours,
> "Tania"

III. Arnold Bax

17 December 1953.

Dear Tania,

I am deeply touched by your thoughtfulness in sending me these two scores from dear Arnold's library, but I am not in any way surprised, as I know from long and grateful experience the essential goodness and kindness of your own nature.

You cannot know what a deep affection I had for Arnold. The four or five years immediately before the war I had the privilege of spending a good deal of time with him; we had ridiculous schoolboy outings together, particularly on Summer Sundays, driving down Thames, lunching and wining at *The Compleat Angler* or the *The Wedge and Beetle* or one of the other Thames-side Inns he knew so well; then rowing through the afternoon and dining and wining at another hostelry and driving back to Fellows Road, with Arnold drawing from his extraordinary memory the gems of great poetry and verses. In those sun-drenched days I had before me a rare glimpse of a great spirit, of a fine mind, rich and suffused with the love and understanding of beauty.

In those days, our friends thought it the best joke in the world that grown men should love Strauss and Wagner and, since I was then at an age when many famous contemporaries were barking round the Stravinsky tree, it was an invaluable reinforcement of my spirit to know that Arnold shared my enthusiasm.

Having had the privilege of knowing him thus, I can understand, in some measure, what you have lost and I hope that your work and your friends will, to some extent, speed the healing of the wound that only time would otherwise do.

My best wishes for Christmas and the New Year,

Yours always,
[Walter Legge]

4

Wartime Activities

I. SIR THOMAS BEECHAM

Walter Legge's close association with Sir Thomas Beecham spanned a total of nearly seven years before and into the Second World War. In 1940 Sir Thomas left Britain, but the two men remained in occasional contact during the next few years. After Sir Thomas's return to the UK in 1944 he and Legge resumed their work in the recording studios, but for a period of little more than a year. The story of how Beecham became discontented after returning to a London Philharmonic Orchestra which was now self-governing; and how after conducting the first public concert of Legge's new Philharmonia Orchestra in October 1945 he had a disagreement with him, and formed yet another new orchestral body, the Royal Philharmonic Orchestra, in 1946, is well-known but germane to the correspondence which follows.

> 7 January 1941.
> Palace Hotel, San Francisco.

My dear Walter:

I hope that all is well with you, and that the old firm is flourishing. I have had no news about musical affairs in England since last August, when I was in Australia, a very odd country, by the way. The orchestras there, although weak, and uneven on the technical sides, are remarkably musical and everywhere gave me some admirable performances, more intrinsic than many I have had with older, and better trained organisations. Indeed, the musical community (public as well as performer) is the best thing in that continent which in nearly every other respect is culturally like its general appearance – a desert. I think it is unlikely that I shall return there for some years to come, as I, in common with most Englishmen, find the attitude of the majority not only unsympathetic, but frequently hostile. Anyway, owing to its removed position, and ossified mental condition, it will be generations before there is any real development of the country on a big, and modern scale.

I expect to return to England about the beginning of April, and will remain there for something like six weeks, after which I shall go back to Canada. During my stay, I may give a few public performances, concerts of course, but what I should like particularly to do is a complete recording of *A Village Romeo and Juliet*. In this town, as in many others, there are several Delius enthusiasts, who have all the hitherto published albums of the Society, and there is a unanimous demand for this piece. Unlike *A Mass of Life*, it is not difficult to execute as the chorus plays a very limited part in it, and can be of moderate size. The principal singers, there are really only three, should be easily procurable. The tenor is the only part about which there might be any difficulty, but there must be someone, somewhere capable of singing it in the right way. Perhaps Lisa might have some ideas about this; at any rate it would be worthwhile to talk it over with her.

Since my arrival here from Australia two months ago I have given concerts in Vancouver, Toronto, Montreal, St Louis, and San Francisco, as well as a number of lectures in other places, and have yet to appear in Detroit, Cincinnati, Los Angeles, Philadelphia and New York, the last named date being just prior to my departure. In addition to this I have another score of lectures to deliver, mainly in University centres, and mostly in the middle west states.

I should like you to consider well, and explore all the possibilities of recording the Delius opera, as undoubtedly the public here will welcome a new album. You might also, if you have time, think of some useful task I could accomplish in the concert room with the orchestra: you are in touch with present conditions over there, and are better able to gauge the taste of the moment than I am.

> With kindest regards, always yours most
> Sincerely,
> Thomas Beecham

Lisa was the soprano Lisa Perli, a friend of Beecham who began her career in her real name of Dora Labbette.

[mid-January 1941.]

My dear Sir Thomas,

Your letter and the news that you are returning in April are the lightest tidings I have had for months. I have delayed a few days in answering you so that I might discuss with Lisa the matters you raise, and others.

Since you have had no musical news from England since August I will at the risk of wearying you with length give you an account of the gloomy state of music in this country.

Your own orchestra is financially speaking, doing quite well for itself. Jack Hylton's venture of which you have certainly read kept them going through the Autumn and they have left again today for two weeks to play twice nightly in music halls in Newcastle and Liverpool. They have just finished a provincial tour which they ran on sharing terms in the Midlands. Holt keeps them going on Sundays with the so-called Beecham Sunday Concerts which, in spite of despicable performances, are always well filled and frequently sold out. That the standard of playing has fallen far from its old level is due to a succession of talentless conductors under whom they have to perform. For their music-hall concerts they are quite appropriately in [the] charge of Flash Harry. On their own provincial tour the conducting was divided between Cameron and Keith Douglas under whose direction they are also giving a series of Beethoven Concerts in the Queen's Hall on Saturday afternoons. It is undoubtedly the appearances of Myra Hess and Moiseiwitsch as soloists at these concerts which is drawing the public. Charles Hambourg has charge of most of the Beecham Sunday Concerts!

The LSO is not better, or better off, than of yore. Cameron and Douglas have also taken this band on tour. The BBC Orchestra is now confined to broadcasting and to a few lunchtime concerts in the Colston Hall. The studio concerts are divided between Dame Adrian, Clarence Raybould and Gideon Fagan, and the slovenliness of the playing has to be heard to be believed. The only occasions on which this band plays with passable intonation, accuracy and style are when they are in [the] charge of Leslie Heward who is working extremely well. His own band in Birmingham has been sadly depleted by the predatory moves of the BBC who have taken nearly all his woodwind players either for their Manchester Orchestra or their Variety Orchestra.

To complete the catalogue of London's orchestras I must inform you that Sidney Beer has formed the Sidney Beer Orchestra. The personnel is worthy of better handling for the string sections are led by the Blech and Grinke Quartets and the wind section is enlisted from the best of the LSO. This incidentally is a small band – only 42, and Beer has the enterprise to give programmes which would be attractive if they were more faithfully realised.

Beer is alone in avoiding the beaten track.

[text incomplete]

19 July 1943.
31 East 79th Street
New York City.

My dear Walter:

You will be receiving a letter from Charles O'Connell of the Victor Company on the subject of the Phillips-Miller records I made at Covent Garden in 1939. In view of the recording impasse here, O'Connell sees great possibilities in transcribing or commuting these records into ordinary disc form.

So much time has gone by that I scarcely remember what operas we did record, although I have some recollection that *The Bartered Bride, Don Giovanni,* and *Aida* all came out pretty well. There were seven or eight others, I think. I have written to Phillip Emanuel that when you and O'Connell find yourselves in a position to begin the recording, he is to put you in possession of the films.

Kindly keep in touch with me frequently over this matter, otherwise there will be a series of unnecessary delays. I should very much appreciate from you an impartial account of the musical situation in London, more especially as it concerns the orchestras. I have a particular reason for making this request as you are the only person I know qualified to give me an answer.

> I am, with kindest regards,
> Yours very sincerely,
> Thomas Beecham

Phillip Emanuel was Beecham's legal representative.

The London Philharmonic Orchestra
Founder and Principal Conductor: Sir Thomas Beecham Bart
> 23 October 1944.
> 53 Welbeck Street, W1.

My dear Walter,

I have received the telegram from Mr Alfred Clark to which you referred in our very agreeable conversation at Nottingham.

This message which is pleasant enough so far as it goes contains no indication that The Gramophone Company is prepared to carry out your undertaking to me that my contract on behalf of the London Philharmonic Orchestra with the Victor Company will be honoured to the full. It also increases rather than diminishes the mystery to which I alluded, for undoubtedly I have the clearest evidence that someone in your organisation was perfectly aware of the terms of this contract and had taken upon himself (or herself) to protest vigorously to Victor. The evidence is in this office and consists of two cables, one from the Victor Company itself, and two letters from my representative in New York.

In order that the matter may be placed upon a basis where no ambiguity can arise I think that I should receive a formal letter from your organisation indicating its intention to accept the conditions of the Victor contract and to cooperate with me in fulfilling them satisfactorily.

I am out of town for the next few days, but have a little free time over the coming weekend. I should be greatly obliged if you will secure the official confirmation of the assurance that you gave me at Nottingham.

> I am, with best wishes,
> Sincerely yours,
> Thomas Beecham

> 30 January 1945.
> 113 West 57th Street
> New York City.

Dear Walter,

I have given much thought during the past four months to the unfortunate position of music in England, and I have come to the following definite conclusions.

97

4. Wartime Activities

1. Without a complete reformation or transformation of the policies and practices of the London Philharmonic management within the next three months, I cannot see my way to continuing any association with this body. There are many reasons for this decision, but the only one material to future possibilities is that I doubt the capacity of the orchestra's management to provide me with the instrument I require for the adequate performance of great music. In connection with the above-stated opinion I do not seriously think for a moment that this desirable metamorphosis will take place; but for the sake of appearances as well as for that of old association I am giving the institution I founded a full measure of time in which to put its house in order.

2. I have no intention in the event of my finding it necessary to bring about or cooperate in the formation of a new orchestra of beginning in any other than a grand way. You may recall how in October 1932 I produced the new LPO to the startled eyes and ears of the London public like a conjuror extracting the familiar rabbit from the hat. Therefore if we are to have a new orchestra which will be associated with me for some years to come it will make its first appearance at full strength next autumn and under the most auspicious conditions of glamour and *éclat*.

3. I will not anticipate the effect I have in mind to produce by wasting five minutes of my time on preliminary effort this summer with a reduced combination. In other words I deprecate entirely the plan of giving a Mozart festival.

4. The new orchestra will bear the name of the 'Beecham Symphony Orchestra'. This is the only title that will be accepted by all parties in the United States as well as in South America where I intend to take it next year. Through its numerous recordings the LPO has a name tolerably familiar to the public here and means something. The name Philharmonia or any similar title has been flatly rejected, as signifying nothing, capable of causing much confusion, as well as sounding slightly preposterous.

5. To preserve the high standard of excellence vitally necessary in the new body all points and questions touching artistic policy and control shall be exclusively in my hands. For instance no other conductor whatsoever shall be engaged as guest or otherwise without my consent or approval. I have no intention of once more viewing the melancholy spectacle of my labours being vitiated continually by the butchering hand of oaf or clown.

6. Provided all the above conditions are realised to my satisfaction, I should be prepared to find a sum of not less than £10,000 per annum (pounds) for a definite period of years, on my own account toward the upkeep of the orchestra as from Jan 1st 1947.

I cannot help thinking that in view of the potentialities of this scheme you should make an effort to come over here at the earliest possible moment. A matter of this sort cannot be initiated or prepared by correspondence. Furthermore there is a strike on here which means that cabling is next to impossible. Lastly, I should like you to realise that if I enter this project it will be carried through in a big manner and must have the effect of eliminating from all possible idea of competition every other institution in the country within 12 months.

> Best wishes
> Yours very sincerely,
> [Thomas Beecham]

PS. I have received copies of letters passing between you and the advisory committee of the Delius Trust. The new orchestra would of course play in the proposed concerts sponsored by the Trust. I believe that the RPS [Royal Philharmonic Society] has some intention of inviting me to take up again my old position of musical director. If this be so one of my conditions of acceptance would be that the new orchestra be engaged for *all* the concerts of this society. It is time that the hen-witted policy of engaging a variety of orchestras under indifferent conductors should be abandoned by this ancient, respectable and distinguished institution.

'Firstly and finally', as Dogberry would have said, you will kindly bear in mind that not a whisper of anything that I am writing about shall get abroad for at least three months, dating from the receipt by you of this letter.

II. SIR HENRY WOOD

Walter Legge had little artistic contact with Sir Henry Wood, but as the letters below indicate, the doyen of British conductors was responsive to the younger man's approaches and to his initiatives, though with the passage of time it is now unclear as to what the ideas actually were.

> 11 February 1940.
> Old Ship Hotel, Brighton.

Dear Mr Walter Legge,

I know I was not sufficiently alive yesterday afternoon after my concert to evince the very great interest I feel with regard to your suggestion for putting an orchestra, or orchestras, on a permanant basis by means of your penny a week system, but to tell you the truth, I am always much too involved in the music performed, to bring myself completely to another angle of it immediately after a performance.

I want very much to discuss your ideas fully at the earliest possible moment, but I fear a weekend here is out of the question until after Easter – and that is I think leaving things 'till possibly too late to be of service, as obviously the recent correspondence in the D.T. [Daily Telegraph] is bearing fruit in one way or another!!

Of one point, I particularly want you to enlighten me, and that is, do you propose financing one orchestra, or more, in equal proportions?

In this scheme, one must not lose sight of the fact that the G.P. is an unknown quantity, and extremely unreliable, whereas, a Government

Subsidy would be a *security of tenure* as it were, and one, I think much to be desired, providing a scheme could be devised whereby an independent organisation could work the subsidy, for of course, anything in the way of a MINISTRY OF ARTS (such as I have seen advocated) would be to place music in the hands of a civil service régime as stultifying as is that of the big house!

Look at my diary, from which you will see, that unless we meet in town, or merely a day during a week here, it seems utterly impossible to have this chat.

What do you say to Friday March 1st, after a morning rehearsal at Queen's Hall? We could lunch somewhere of your choice, since I know you must find the stolid old Langham just as dull – though very useful – as we do, and we could return to the latter for a quiet chat, or go up to your office at Abbey Road. On the other hand, if you cared to come here for the day of Friday 23rd, and share the rather dull Old Ship fare, we have that day completely free, and should be so pleased if you would spare the time to come, and spend the night, although we should leave you to your own resources on the 24th as we have to be off early for a rehearsal with the Philharmonic Orchestra, at Tunbridge Wells.

> With all good wishes,
> Sincerely yours,
> Henry J. Wood

> 29 June 1940.
> Four Grand Avenue
> Hove, Sussex.

My dear Mr Walter Legge,

Of course Derek McCulloch is the man, and if I find any possible chance of getting *Peter and the Wolf* into one of my programmes – I doubt it is possible during the Promenade Concert season, as the Prospectus is out – I shall do so, and thank you for bringing it so much to my notice.

I never suggest that the BBC should follow my advice in anything, but again should I find a suitable opportunity I will bear in mind your splendid programme for the *Children's Hour* or for a Children's Concert.

The situation is indeed very anxious making, and although I am sure we are in for a trying time, we shall pull through I am sure – in time.

So glad you raided the young people, and hope you will take the law in your own hands and repeat the attack – it's good for them, as I am sure they get shut within their own shell too much these days, and as we find much of the kindred spirit about you which pleases us and gives us so much pleasure in our meetings with you, we like to know you will visit them.

With kindest regards from us both.

> Sincerely yours,
> Henry J. Wood

15 November 1940.
Shandon
Winton Road
Bowdon, Cheshire.

Dear Mr Legge,

Delighted to hear from you, we have so often thought of you and spoken of you.

Your letter is splendid and certainly ought to do the trick – call upon me for any assistance.

I have been here for four weeks, directing the Hallé Orchestra at Sunday afternoon concerts in Manchester – on other days I have been touring with them and visiting such lovely places as Bolton, Blackpool and a lot more Bs during the other days in the week, just off to Morecambe and Blackpool again for return visits.

Sold out at every concert, so all goes well, and here in Bowdon we sleep the sleep of the just – it's the quietest place I have ever struck and I expect that is why Richter and Brodsky and even Hallé lived here. Sorry for delay in replying to your note of the 13th but only received it one hour ago. My wife joins me in kindest regards and best wishes.

Yours always,
Henry J. Wood

13 March 1941.
Cromwell Hotel
Stevenage, Herts.

My dear Mr Walter Legge,

It is interesting to learn that this scheme owes its existence to yourself, and I am all the more pleased to become a member of the Advisory Music Council of ENSA and only hope I shall be of some real service, once I know just what it is all about, and for what it is actually designed.

I hope to attend a meeting on March 21st as near 10.45 am as my train up from here will allow; the delays these days make rail travel a positive nightmare.

Thank you yes, we are better and making every endeavour to carry out our engagements, but there is no doubt this 'flu does take its toll!!

With kindest regards from us both,

Sincerely yours,
Henry Wood

III. LEOPOLD STOKOWSKI

What survives of an exchange of letters between Walter Legge and another great conducting figure of his time speaks for itself, and reveals that Legge's achievement in founding the Philharmonia Orchestra was not his first attempt to establish a new and great British ensemble.

4. Wartime Activities

16 April 1942.

Dear Mr Stokowski,

First of all let me thank you for your friendly and enthusiastic interest in my project. Under your guidance we will teach the British Public what an orchestra *should* sound like!

In the last year there has been a great increase in orchestral concerts throughout the country. Unfortunately, however, there is not now a conductor here of first class talent, let alone of genius. Consequently the standard of orchestral playing has deteriorated steadily – particularly since Beecham's departure. What passes here for good playing is a mere travesty by American and Central European standards. Britain's most urgent artistic need is for a great conductor who can weld the good players here into a first class orchestra. You are the only man who can do this and stimulate audiences here from the acceptance of the humdrum into the demand for great performances.

It fortunately happens that my views are shared by Mr David Webster, the Chairman of the Liverpool Philharmonic Society. He and his Committee are willing to collect the finest players in the country and contract them for a new orchestra if you will come here to conduct them for a season of seven or eight months, beginning in September next.

Subject to your acceptance we plan to engage a permanent orchestra of the following constitution:

Triple Woodwind, Four Horns, Three Trumpets,
Three Trombones, Tuba, Harp, Two Percussion,
Strings – Twelve, Ten, Eight, Six and Five.

The orchestra would be engaged for 32 hours playing time per week. This time will be allotted to six concerts and 20 hours rehearsal. Not more than two different programmes will be given each week. You will have three weeks' preliminary rehearsal in which to prepare the orchestra for its first concert. You would not, unless you wished, be asked to do all six concerts in any week: an assistant – the best of the native conductors – would be engaged to direct those concerts which we mutually agree you should not do.

The headquarters of the orchestra will be in Liverpool where the Philharmonic Society has a new and magnificently appointed concert hall. There will be two concerts a week in that hall with series of concerts in the principal cities throughout the country. The short distances between important towns makes this a simple matter. You will naturally agree to conduct only the Liverpool Philharmonic Orchestra during your stay here – and while we do not wish to hamper your other arrangements we naturally would like to have the option of inviting you to take charge of the orchestra for three subsequent seasons.

As far as the financial arrangements are concerned, it would be best for you to cable your suggestions as soon as you receive this letter. Under the present laws it is not permitted either for citizens or visitors to take from this country any money earned here. But knowing your high ideals and your indifference to commercial considerations if they interfere with your artistic convictions, I am sure that this will not affect your decision. The really vital matter for all concerned is the establishment here of an orchestra of unprecedented quality and the giving of great performances under your direction.

One other point, we naturally would like you to include your own transcriptions and important American works in your programmes. It would be necessary for you to arrange for the scores and parts to be sent here.

In conclusion let me say how keenly I look forward to you coming here and assure you of my personal readiness to stop at nothing to make your visit the happiest period of your artistic life.

Please cable your reactions to this letter.

Yours very sincerely,
[Walter Legge]

PS: In case you do not remember me I am and have been for five years recording and artists manager of HMV, and for the two years before the war was assistant artistic director of the Royal Opera, Covent Garden.

7 May 1942.
Hotel Sulgrave
67th & Park Avenue
New York City

Dear Mr Legge,

As I cabled you today, to Recordabox, Maida, London, England, greatly to my regret, it is impossible for me to accept your invitation to conduct the Liverpool Orchestra, because since I first received your cable many new developments have happened here, and all my time is now taken for the next season in various parts of the United States.

Please thank the directors of the orchestra, and tell them that I hope some time in the future still to be able to conduct for them.

With friendly greetings to you personally,

Leopold Stokowski

IV. CONSTANT LAMBERT

Legge and the composer and conductor Constant Lambert had been friends since the early 1930s, and they worked together quite frequently until Lambert's early death in 1951 at the age of 46. For many years Lambert was musical director of the Sadler's Wells Ballet. Wartime restrictions meant that he frequently had to dispense with an orchestra and give performances with two pianos, one of which he played himself. A great deal of touring was also involved.

103

4. Wartime Activities

4 October 1939.

Working 10 hours a day. No time to write properly. Ballet not doing too badly. Profits small but increasing each week.

You have no conception how hideous *Checkmate* sounds on two pianos. Could you send *Orpheus – Joyeuse marche* to

> Miss Laureen Goodare
> 25 Conway Street W1.

Thanks so much.

> Yours,
> Constant

Next week Leeds.

[undated, probably late January/early February 1940].
Wednesday.
Royal Station Hotel, Hull.

Dear Walter,

Sorry to miss you before I left and sorry you had to miss the *Dante Sonata* which was a howling success. It is definitely the best ballet of its kind ever done and everyone for once is agreed. I hope to get it going as a concert piece, I think it would go well with another short concerto. Kentner was very pleased with it and though I say it as shouldn't it really makes a splendid shindy. Do you think there is any chance of recording it? The length is just right – 16 mins and I am sure it would have a big sale with ballet fans quite apart from the general public.

It was a thousand pities we had to go back on tour just when we had had such a big success. I shall be back in London March 18th and hope to rectify matters at that eleventh hour. Heard from Paddy who enclosed a programme and notice of his Caius Concert. The old dirge seems to have gone down quite well.

We go to Blackpool (The Grand) next week and then I shall be back in London for a few days.

The BBC I am glad to say seem inclined to give me more work next year, which is encouraging. How is the recording situation? I ask because I have a lust for the baton again.

I look forward to sharing a tolerable meal and bottle of house red with you on my return to London. Excuse this disjointed letter, but am dead tired. This town however, is by no means bad, with a really beautiful theatre of the best nineteeth-century vintage.

> Yours ever,
> Constant

IV. Constant Lambert

8 February 1940.

Dear Constant,

I got back yesterday afternoon, after some adventures that were more exciting than comfortable.

I read, some days after the event, several criticisms of the *Dante*, all of which made me feel that I was missing something exceptionally good.

Before I give a definite 'Yes' to your suggestion for recording, I should like to hear and see the Ballet for myself, so if your tour should bring you anywhere within reasonable reach of London, let me know when the *Dante* is to be done and I will come up to see it.

Kindest regards,
Yours always,
[Walter Legge]

25 February 1940.
Stork Hotel, Liverpool 1.

Dear Walter,

Dante Sonata lasts approx 16 minutes and divides up well into four sides. Naturally the strings will have to be increased. I had calculated 8, 6, 4, 4, 2 as minimum, but naturally what you suggest will be better. When you decide finally could you get in touch with Shadwick at the Wells and ask him to get the necessary duplicating done by G[oodwin] & Tabbs. This is *important* and should be put in hand as soon as possible.

As regards the Ireland I have always thought it the best modern English pf. concerto and would be very pleased to do it. Have not performed it in public but know the score well and have rehearsed it several times at College. Much as I would like some additions to Irelandiana I will only record it on condition that the old sod is kept firmly in the Channel Islands if necessary by FORCE! Otherwise the sessions might drag on as long as the war. Not having done *Malédiction* on the wireless I have no timing of it, alas. The only time I heard Petri do it, I was slightly disappointed. But apparently he and Timber [Wood] had only had a week or so to study it. Both waited for the other and eventually the work got so slow that it nearly stopped. But naturally I don't doubt that Petri could do it superbly. Kentner could obviously do it well and I know that Franz Osborn (who I did it with at Lady W's) is altogether excellent in it. I can't understand why he isn't better known.

The moment I get my matinée days at Brighton I will let you know. Friday that week is bound to be free but I'm not quite sure if the first matinée is Tuesday or Wednesday.

Yours ever,
Constant

Dante Sonata was Lambert's arrangement of Liszt's solo piano work *Après une lecture de Dante* as a ballet score for piano and orchestra. It was recorded by HMV on 20 March 1940, with Louis Kentner as soloist and Lambert conducting the Sadler's Wells orchestra. A recording of Ireland's Piano Concerto was not made until 14 January 1942, and was in fact conducted on Columbia by Leslie Heward, with the Hallé Orchestra and Eileen Joyce as soloist.

> 2 January [1941].
> Dartington Hall
> Totnes, S. Devon.

My dear Walter,

Many thanks for the card which I enjoyed. There are two superb cats here, one a small, neat frisky tabby called Giles Farnaby and the other a magnificent eunuch slightly broader and heavier than myself called Don Thomas Tomkins. A kindly old abbot with a friendly word for all his parishioners.

The *Wanderer* is going splendidly and we have already started the finale.

If (unlike Schubert) he can keep the inspiration up to the end it should be the best ballet for years (though I doubt if it will be Newman's cup of tea). Life here is pleasant in a pseudo-monastic way and when I find the atmosphere too intense I slide down the hill to Totnes (a pleasant little town) and have a pint of bitter in bourgeois surroundings.

Can you help me over two things?

(a) *Sleeping Beauty*. Please keep the pf. score for me. It is now worth its weight in gold.

(b) Pianos for our season. Ninette de Valois is going to act for me about this and I told her that if there was any trouble with Steinways to ring you up and find out the gangster who really controls things there. I couldn't remember if he was called Hungerdunger or Shenectady.

The London raids sound pretty grim. I hope the town doesn't look as sad as Bristol which depressed me very much the other day. I have quite a pleasant lunch hour concert there in February made up of four of my favourite composers, viz, Borodin, Handel, Lambert and Chabrier.

Is there anything palpable on the carpet regarding my Sunday concert at the Phil? The Sibelius symphonies have I'm afraid been apportioned to some of the older boys (including the Owl of the Remove).

Looking forward to London though I'm afraid that a series of matinées cuts out our genial lunches.

> Love to Nancy,
> Yours,
> Constant

The Wanderer was a ballet with music by Schubert. Frederick Ashton was the choreographer (presumably it is he who is referred to in the above letter), and the first performance took place on 27 January 1941.

IV. Constant Lambert

On 24 February 1941 Lambert recorded Tchaikovsky's Fantasy-Overture *Romeo and Juliet* with the City of Birmingham Orchestra for HMV. For some reason the name of the orchestra was not indicated on the record labels.

> 1 March [1941].
> Cross Keys Hotel, Burnley.
> Royal Hall, Harrogate next week.

Dear Walter,

Just a line to thank you for the good time I had in Birmingham and also for sustaining me during that very trying piece of recording. I like to think we had one good master of each side in the end.

I have finished the ballet arrangement of *Orpheus*. Only two voices will be needed (one doubling Eurydice and Amor) but they must be good ones. Any suggestions?

We don't open at Bournemouth until the Tuesday, so could we lunch together on Monday week? Also could you possibly fix up a meeting that afternoon with the old boy who runs Aschenberg's? Waldteufel is again on the carpet.

Sorry to treat you as a dragoman like this, but it is so difficult to arrange things on tour.

I have had bad news about Kit [Lambert's son] who seems to be developing trouble on the other side of his neck, poor child. It is all very worrying and upsetting.

> Yours ever,
> Constant

> 23 November [probably 1942.]
> Royal Hotel, Bristol.

Dear Walter,

I gather that one of your nefarious nixies using my mother as an innocent dupe has managed to purloin for you my copy of Borodin No. 2. Such deeds do not go forgotten. Until it is returned you will not ever hear of Sibelius *Tempest* again.

Back on Sunday night.

Any chance of lunch at Pag's [Pagani's] on Monday? If so drop a card or leave a message at Peel Street.

> Yours,
> Constant

> [undated, but probably autumn 1943.]
> Thursday.
> 42 Peel Street, W8.

My dear Walter,

You have seen it on the screen, you have read it in the daily press, you may even have heard it on the wireless machines – I have what the doctors describe as – the 'FLU'. Fortunately very slightly and hope to start getting up tomorrow. Back to work I hope on Monday.

In the meanwhile cannot telephone anybody so could you get your secretary to get the publishers

(A) to send me the following:
Goodwins Borodin 2 (preferably a copy I have used before)
España (In the reduced Gabriel-Marie edition I suppose)
Check up on the parts of this
Suggest getting original trpt and cort parts as we have three trpts. also original tuba.

(B) OUP [Oxford University Press]. Walton's Welltempered Spitfire

(C) B & H [Boosey & Hawkes]. See that they have got all the material of *Merchant Seamen* shipshape.

Rehearsals:
a) What time and where?
b) Shall not need solo pianist till Monday
c) Will need *orchestral* pianist on Friday

Sorry to land you with all this but have no telephone extension and daren't risk standing about in a cold hall in a negligée. Every now and then my eyes well up with tears as I gaze at the grapefruit squash and cough linctus beside me and think of the sardines and entrecôte of what seems now yesteryear.

> Yours ever,
> Constant

P.S. Preparing formidable list of lesser-known Russians.

Merchant Seamen was a 1940 film score by Lambert. In 1943 he arranged some of the music into a suite for concert performance.

> 25 November 1943.
> as from 42 Peel Street
> London W8.

My dear Walter,

As I have just been writing to B and H confirming that you must have the material of the old Commercial Spunk by Dec. 8th it suddenly occurred to me that in my usual unbusinesslike way I never gave you the account for the Albert Hall perf.

As I never write letters in London I thought I'd write out a bill now (not that I know how to write one but I know you will be able to see to it).

I don't want to seem grasping but I paid out a lot for the copying and am at present £15 down on three perfs! You will of course point out that this is purely a hire account and that my own services were of course given free.

> Yours ever,
> Constant

IV. Constant Lambert

[undated, probably late 1944/early 1945.]
ENSA/HQ
BLA Paris.

My dear Walter,

Please excuse no letter so far but life has not been easy. One week in Brussels I had six rehearsals, seven shows and two talks in French on the wireless! I have to do all the organisation and rehearsing and my assistant (who leaves us tomorrow) has been very little if any help. Also not wanting to present *Rake's Progress* in Paris with a reduced orchestra, I have had to do all the brass parts myself. Hence the pyramids. (If you see Gavin tell him it now sounds terrific.) Brussels I found bourgeois but most friendly and unexpectedly gay. Concerts a great success. The national orchestra are charming, first-rate readers and without ever touching the Caruso-like heights of Rome Radio are every bit as good as a pre-war London orchestra at its best. Old pros every one. The Sibelius arrived too late for perf. (incidentally you sent the wrong one) so did a ham perf. of *Enigma* instead.

We really must get together and see that each capital town and/or headquarters has a minimum permanent library of at least six English classics.

Horoscope went down very well indeed and I took the liberty of adding *Aubade héroïque* to my second programme.

Willie's [Walton's] fiddle concerto (done twice) made an enormous impression and should have been heard by the civilians. Owing to otherwise routine programme I was able to give it a lot of rehearsal. Grumiaux is all that you said and more. A second Heifetz no doubt. The string players in my orch. were knocked sideways. He must do it in England.

Being in Paris is a mingled pleasure for someone who has known it backwards for 20 years. Too many ghosts for my liking though there are compensatory highlights. Have been too busy to properly contact my friends though I had a very pleasant dinner with Poulenc who took me to a concert conducted (and damned well) by Desormière – slight but pleasant works by Milhaud and Ibert and the new dance suite of Stravinsky (*Baiser de la fée*-cum-*Jeu de cartes*) which is his best work in that style if you like that kind of style which I don't.

General impression in art galleries is of good taste but *déjà-vu*. Have seen nothing so far as interesting as Sutherland or Ayrton. Being freer this week hope to get more in touch with things.

The Champs-Elysées is a barn of a place but has a good orch. pit.

The extras from the Conservatoire are first-rate and most genial. Off to do *Hamlet* tonight. Hope it is as successful as *Gorbals* which made great impression. Do try and get me some concerts in Paris later on. As quondam Parisian would like to join in the Anglo-French party not unnaturally. Conducting at the Marigny prevented me from hearing Alan's perf. concerto but I hear on all sides it went v. well.

As regards English concerts can settle nothing until I get back.

Our South American tour is off and I am faced with the prospect of a

London season minus second conductor unless Corbett gets out. The whole thing is most complicated and cannot be settled by signals.

I know you will understand.

Best wishes,
Constant

(Shortage of time and paper imposes Mr Jingle style)

The Rake's Progress is a ballet score by Gavin Gordon; *Horoscope* is Lambert's own ballet score, and *Aubade héroïque* is a short orchestral piece, also by Lambert. The new Stravinsky work was presumably *Scènes de ballet*, and *Miracle in the Gorbals* is a ballet score by Bliss. 'Alan' was Alan Rawsthorne.

V. LESLIE HEWARD

Another conductor who died prematurely at the age of 46 was Leslie Heward. Shortly after his death Legge wrote a tribute to a valued friend and colleague in *The Gramophone*.

Leslie Heward   June 1943.

The fact that Leslie Heward had been a sick man for several years and that he had been gravely ill four times since the beginning of the war did not in any way lessen the shock of his death. Those of us who knew him well had seen him recover so quickly from bouts of illness that would have killed most men that in spite of the grave reports that came from Birmingham in the last two months, we hoped and expected he would soon be back at the work he loved so well.

He will be mourned more deeply by professional musicians than by the concert-going public as a whole. He was too fine-fingered and modest an artist and too little of a showman to impress himself quickly on the general mass of concert-goers. Even some of our professional concert-givers were reluctant to engage him because they felt he lacked the platform manner of a great conductor. What he needed was a manager who could induce him to change his customary light cloth cap for a black hat, but he was not amenable to that sort of discipline. He was not really interested in the public as such; he was a musician who loved music with all his heart.

He was born near Bradford in 1897. The family was poor: his father had married on 15 shillings a week. When he was only five he started to learn the organ from his father, who had been made organist of the little Moravian Church in Lower Wyke. Within three years he had progressed far enough to accompany the whole of *Messiah*. At this time he began to make a reputation for himself at competition festivals where he almost invariably won first prizes for playing and singing at sight, solo singing, solo violin, theory and ear test. This sequence of successes ended only when Sydney Nicholson, then organist and choirmaster of Manchester

Cathedral, gave young Heward a scholarship to the Choir School. He was only 11 at the time, but almost at once he achieved professional status as a singer and teacher, and a few years later as organist and choirmaster of a Manchester church. He liked to walk round those scenes of his youthful successes after recording sessions with the Hallé Orchestra and recall the games as well as the music he had played. In those years he was a good athlete, and he captained his school at cricket and football.

At 16 he was an associate of the Royal College of Organists and a little later he won a composition scholarship to the Royal College of Music. While he was still a student he became music master first at Eton, then at Westminster. His first engagement as a conductor was at the Gaiety Theatre, where he took over, at a couple of hours' notice, the orchestra for the opening of Maeterlinck's *The Betrothal*, and he stayed for the run. His next engagement was as an organist at a Brighton cinema, but he soon got clear of that and joined the musical staff of the British National Opera Company.

It was on Basil Cameron's recommendation that Heward was invited to become Musical Director of the Cape Town Municipal Orchestra and the newly formed South African Broadcasting Service. It was uphill work. In his first year he had to give four or five public concerts a week and split up his orchestral resources to provide the light orchestras, dance bands and chamber music combinations that broadcasting needed. He was conductor, part time announcer (in Afrikaans – learned parrot-wise – as well as English), actor, producer, Children's Hour Uncle and utility pianist – jazz as well as musical. After a year he brought his Cape Town Orchestra to England for a tour of England and some performances at the Wembley Exhibition, and took back with him a wife he had married in Westminster Abbey.

He returned to England in 1927, bringing with him the seeds of the tuberculosis which eventually killed him. He rejoined the British National Opera Company, now as conductor sharing the repertoire with Eugene Goossens and John Barbirolli. In those days he specialised in Wagner. The singers who worked with him in those days remember well his fantastic musical memory. On more than one occasion he rehearsed the whole of *Meistersinger* at the piano without a note of music. Three years later he succeeded Adrian Boult as Conductor of the City of Birmingham Orchestra, and he remained there to finish what he intended to be his last season there. Early this year he resigned from Birmingham expecting to take over the Hallé Orchestra; but in March he collapsed after a rehearsal with the CBO under what proved to be the final assault of the disease which he had fought with all his will for 15 years.

Only those who worked with him knew the depth and scope of his talents. It is the orchestral players and the soloists who played with him who knew how vastly superior he was to the majority of those who profitably pursue the occupation in which he was a master. Music was his nature.

He was an excellent pianist and as such made some records for Decca. He could play at sight from a complicated full score better than most musicians from a pianoforte reduction. In rehearsal his ear for intonation and wrong notes was not less remarkable than Toscanini's. Directing an orchestra came so naturally to him that he was unaware of baton technique as such. He did not even need or want a baton. For rehearsals and recording he was perfectly happy with a pencil and even preferred it to a stick.

The outstanding qualities of all his work were its untarnished musicianship, its touching sensitiveness of line, and its clarity and beauty of texture. He did not want to impose his own personality on music and he did not try to make it effective. I have never known a man more sensitive to beauty. He loved it in music, in poetry, in prose, in painting, in women and in flowers and it brought him often to the verge of tears. Many a time during recording sessions I have seen his kind, light eyes moist and over-bright from some expressive piece of phrasing from Pat Ryan, the first clarinet of the Hallé or some other exquisitely musical player. And he would turn his back on the orchestra, brush his eyes with his sleeve like a child and say, 'Damn this music! I wish it didn't get me like this!' He loved words, unusual, apposite words, and would delight in the discovery of one that pleased him. 'Nub' was a pet of his. He would delight in planning to get a word like 'kempt' as opposed to 'unkempt' into a broadcast talk. Between recording sessions, and often far into the night, he would sit in a bedroom of the Midland Hotel, Manchester, talking about English poetry, of which he had a wide knowledge, or reading and translating Heine and Goethe's early lyrics. They were pleasant days, lit by his intense love of life, his quick sympathy and charming talk roaming from Nicholas Bentley to Goya, Mozart to James Joyce, Richard Wagner (Dick Carter as Leslie translated it) to John Haig.

He had, musically speaking, a large heart. It included Mozart and Sullivan, Wagner and Sibelius, Grieg and Edward German, Wesley and Walton, in its wide embrace. Like Beecham, he was prone to over-estimate Dvořák, and unlike Beecham to over-estimate Brahms, and he shared Beecham's and Harty's understanding of Berlioz. But he maintained a rather resentful dislike of Puccini, whose work he regarded as insincere and bogus.

Heward's first records were made for Decca. His connection with the EMI group began about seven years ago. He had conducted a BBC Symphony Concert in the Queen's Hall doing, among other things, a superb performance of the Sibelius Fifth Symphony and a concerto with Egon Petri as soloist. Petri and I were so delighted with his work on that occasion that we arranged for him to conduct two major works with Petri, the Liszt A major Concerto and the *Fantasia on Beethoven's Ruins of Athens*. It was in the last three years of his life that he did his best work for the gramophone, first with his own City of Birmingham Orchestra, and later with the Hallé. He has left behind him an impressive record of his work, a selection as eclectic as his own taste and at the same time indicative of it. At the head of it all stands the Moeran Symphony. He gave the first performance of that symphony and he loved and knew it as if it were his own: although he was tired, limping and in pain at the time of the recording he summoned up enormous strength and vitality to give that superb performance. The Haydn *Drum Roll* Symphony shows the clear-sighted and unaffected rightness of his work in the classics. Of his personal favourites he recorded Sibelius's *Rakastava* Suite with the lovely 'Elegy' from the incidental music to *King Christian*; the Overture to *Prince Igor*, Dvořák's *Notturno*, *Eine kleine Nachtmusik*, and the *Fledermaus* Overture, over which we spent more than three hours. His deep and kindly love of his fellow creatures and his understanding of them made him the ideal conductor of concertos and for singers. He seemed to anticipate their phrasing as if he read their thoughts. Some of his best work as a recording artist is to be found in the concertos he did with Moiseiwitsch and Eileen Joyce, the arias with Isobel Baillie and Joan Hammond and in the magical records with Maggie Teyte of songs by Berlioz and Duparc.

In all of them there is the sense of easy and tender beauty that made Heward, musically speaking, the most satisfying conductor this country has had since Beecham.

VI. BRITISH COMPOSERS

In his work for ENSA and as EMI's recording manager during the war Legge came into contact with several British composers. Letters from three of them have survived.

18 May 1942.

Dear Legge,

In regard to your enquiry about the orchestral March I have done for the BBC, this is to be tried over at Bedford on Friday 29th May, with Boult, at 7pm. If you could be present you would receive a more definite idea than from my playing it on the piano.

However, as I am coming up on Wednesday, I could call on you at Abbey Road about 11 or 11.30 on Thursday morning. I will ring up to find out if this suits you. Boosey & Hawkes have the full score, so I am not sure if it will be available.

I am assuming that your enquiry was not purely facetious.

Yours sincerely,
[John Ireland]

The work in question was the *Epic March*, which received its first performance at a 1942 Promenade Concert under Sir Henry Wood.

4. Wartime Activities

10 December 1942.
Little Sampford
Saffron Walden, Essex.

Dear Legge,

I hear that the recording of my Cello Sonata, made by Antoni Sala and myself, is to be or has been withdrawn from the Columbia catalogue. It is true the recording is not up to the present standard, nevertheless this sonata receives more performances, at any rate in this country, than any other British work in this medium, in fact, I am told, more than any modern cello sonata, and it seems a pity no recording should be available. Perhaps you might consider a fresh recording, with myself at the piano.

The original record had a very good sale when it was issued – about five times the sales of my Piano Concerto, if I am to trust figures and amounts received in both cases.

Yours sincerely,
[John Ireland]

A recording of Ireland's Piano Concerto with Eileen Joyce as soloist and Leslie Heward conducting the Hallé Orchestra had been made for Columbia under Legge's supervision in January 1942. Dr Ireland was not given the opportunity to re-make his 1928 Columbia recording of the Cello Sonata, and in fact he only recorded on two more occasions, once for Decca (the Second Violin Sonata with Frederick Grinke in 1945) and once for HMV (the piano piece *April*, for the second time, in 1950).

10 December 1943.
The White House, Storrington

My Dear Walter,

I have finished the piece you asked me to write for ENSA. This is an overture lasting about nine minutes, I suppose, 48 pages, all moving fast. It is called *Work in Progress* and scored for a comparatively small orchestra: 2 fl 2 ob 2 clar 2 fag 4 horns, 2 trumpets, 3 trombones and tuba (no harp) percussion and strings.

It would be well if the strings had half an hour's rehearsal by themselves, as most of the intended brilliance relies upon them.

What about Manchester? Is the recording definitely fixed for the last days of the year?

Yours,
Arnold [Bax]

Arnold Bax's Third Symphony was recorded under the auspices of the British Council for HMV by John Barbirolli and the Hallé Orchestra at the Houldsworth Hall, Manchester, on 31 December 1943 and 12 January 1944. Walter Legge was the producer.

VII. Gerald Moore

15 September 1944.
Gravel Hill, Kington, Hertfordshire.

Dear Walter,

I went to Manchester last week and heard my piano and orchestra *Rhapsody* properly for the first time. Iris Loveridge is an excellent intelligent pianist with a first-rate technique. She gave the work an exuberance, vitality and brilliance which were painfully lacking before and I have now come to the conclusion that this F sharp *Rhapsody* is a really good effort on my part.

I am hoping soon to learn from you about our proposed trip to hear the ENSA overture.

As they say, I am all agog to hear the sound of it.

I take it that there is a photographed copy of the score. I have the original here; I wrote to Boosey & Hawkes to send it to me when the flying bombs were blasting at London as I did not want it to be destroyed.

Have you any Bruckner symphonies for sale at HMV? I can't find them in the catalogues; but I know they exist for last week I was spending an evening at a house in Manchester where two of them (Nos. 4 & 7) were produced.

I have just finished my new work, a small symphony or more strictly speaking, sinfonietta, in the key of C, three movements and small orchestra.

Please let me know soon if you have been able to arrange a performance of the overture as I want then to get on with the engraving and must hear it first.

Yours,
Jack Moeran

E.J. Moeran's *Overture to a Masque* was the ENSA commission.

VII. GERALD MOORE

Walter Legge had made many Lieder recordings with Gerald Moore at the piano by the time he came to write an appreciation of his colleague's art in *The Gramophone*. Before submitting the article he sent a copy of it to Moore for his approval.

20 July 1942. My birthday!
235 Sussex Gardens,
London, W2.

My dear Walter,

I must write to say how grateful I am to you for the article you are in the process of writing about me. It would be churlish if I did not admit that I am delighted with it – I shall like it still more when it is in print. Naturally your praise of my work gives me special pleasure since I feel you would not write anything above your signature, where music was concerned, that you did not mean.

The picture of the remarkable English boy pianist in an Eton jacket and drinking rye whisky on the side is too rich to be omitted – that's a real W.L. touch. Could you tone down a little the paragraph about my mother? She was not – is not – a virago. She was not 'annoyed' about the rival pianist. Perhaps you could find another term. Also 'that woman' is still alive but her poor daughter died in tragic circumstances – I tell you this as that sentence might cause pain. Perhaps you could perform an operation and turn the girl into a boy. Your account of my being taken on to the platform by my mother by the scruff of the neck is absolutely true.

And now the Pole. I think the Polish passage should be hermetically disinfected, plugged and sealed. I cannot deny that it made my hair stand on end; and the allusion to the 'night-ride' still tickles me. But you and I are the only people who know what you are talking about. To anyone else this paragraph is quite irrelevant and boring.

Since you have expressed yourself so generously about me, my dear Walter, allow me in my turn to say that our years of association in the recording studio have been memorable ones for me. You have been an inspiring critic, counsellor and friend – and I can do my best work when you are around. Long may it continue! Nobody could write about our recordings as you are able, with the intimate knowledge and authority of a true artist.

> Yours always,
> [Gerald Moore]

Gerald Moore   September 1942.

The contract which Gerald Moore has recently signed by which he records exclusively for the EMI group, is a significant tribute to a remarkable artist. It acknowledges his pre-eminence in his art and shows that his share in making good records is larger than the formula 'pianoforte accompaniment by Gerald Moore' suggests.

He was born at Watford in 1899. As a child he showed no liking for music, and he was forced to the pianoforte only because his mother resented that a neighbour's child of Gerald's age had excited local interest by playing at a school concert. His first appearance, an end-of-term concert at the Watford School of Music, was a triumph only of maternal authority. Gerald was taken by the collar and pushed on to the platform where he sobbed his way through a Gurlitt Sonatina. In spite of this inauspicious start he made good progress. His parents took him to Canada in 1913, where he at once won a scholarship to the Toronto School of Music. His teacher was Michael Hambourg, Mark Hambourg's father. Two years later he began his professional career, touring the length and breadth of Canada billed as 'The Remarkable English Boy Pianist'. On the platform he wore an Eton jacket, and in the artists' room he learned to drink rye whisky neat. Through Campbell McInnes he met the American baritone David Bispham, who perceived his talent for accompanying and advised him to specialise in that art rather than enter into the fierce competition of solo pianists. But young Moore had set his heart on returning to England to complete his studies as a soloist. By working sometimes as a pianist, sometimes as a church or cinema organist, he had saved enough by 1921 to make the journey and pay for his tuition.

In London he had a few lessons from Mark Hambourg who took him to Landon Ronald and to the concert agent E.A. Michell. Ronald, whose help to young artists has not yet been sufficiently acknowledged, quickly weaned him from his solo ambitions, and Michell gave him his first engagement here – a Max Mossel tour in which he played for Pauline Donalda and Mischa Leon. His second Mossel tour brought him into contact with Renée Chemet. It was she who introduced him to HMV, and he made his first records with her at Hayes in 1922. Through Peter Dawson, with whom he next recorded, he met John Coates.

This meeting was a turning point in Gerald Moore's career. In weeks of rehearsal to prepare one concert programme Coates exacted from him the scrupulous attention to detail, and put him on the track of the niceties of phrasing and balance, the crispness and subtlety of rhythm which have eventually made him the most remarkable accompanist of the present day.

The importance and the practice of the accompanist's art is little understood by the larger part of the musical public. For them the accompanist means about as much as 'Wigs by Clarkson' does to the playgoer. First-class accompanists are rarer than first-class pianists – partly because brains are rarer than brawn. Several solo pianists have made world-wide reputations and handsome fortunes on no more musical capital than the ability to play half a dozen concertos, a like number of sonatas, and a few groups of shorter pieces effectively and from memory. Some of the most popular of them are quite unmusical, unable to read at sight, and abysmally and happily ignorant of all music except their own little repertoires. When a famous pianist of this order was asked to write 'something short' in an autograph album, Moriz Rosenthal, who was standing at his elbow, prompted him quickly: 'Write out your repertoire.' This is a favourite story among musicians and it is justifiably told of nearly a dozen famous players. The very nature of the accompanist's work presupposes skilled reading at sight, and the practice of it makes him familiar with a wide range of music. The tricky transpositions at sight which I have seen Gerald Moore do in recording studios and on concert platforms would baffle all but a select few soloists. The real art of accompanying is on a higher plane than the technical accomplishments of dexterity, tone, reading and transposition. Like all the higher forms of musical achievement, it is a blend of musicianship, imagination and sensibility. Its nature is most nearly that of operatic conducting. A great accompanist can and does contribute as much to a performance of a solo singer or instrumentalist as a Toscanini or a Serafin does to an operatic performance. When I was writing for the *Manchester Guardian* it was my duty to attend many of those depressing first recitals given by young singers at the smaller London concert halls. More often than not the young women were hopelessly incompetent to tackle the programmes they had chosen, but there was usually the compensating pleasure of hearing Gerald Moore's playing. I suggested at the time that the only way to make these concerts attractive to musicians was to announce them as 'Accompaniment Recital by Gerald Moore' – and at the foot of the bill in the small type habitually used for accompanists' names 'at the voice Miss ...'

When I first knew him Moore excelled in accompanying string players. It was not until he acquired a working knowledge of German that he developed into a great player of Lieder. Even ten years ago some eminent singers were reluctant to accept him. One famous bass resented being pulled up by this Englishman who drew his attention to the disparity between his performance and the composer's markings. It was even more difficult in the recording studio. This singer had different ideas from Gerald and me on the proper balance between voice and piano, particularly on records. His views were intensified when he saw Gerald Moore's name printed in the same type as his own on some record labels. Nothing that Moore could do was right for him. He insisted on having his own accompanist brought over from Germany; a player so self-effacing that he made a Steinway Concert Grand sound like a distant harpsichord. Nearly all the results of this collaboration were rejected. Eventually, after months of coercion and dispute the singer capitulated and he became an enthusiastic admirer of Gerald's work.

The first great Lieder singer to acknowledge Gerald Moore's superiority to the German accompanists was Herbert Janssen. With him, Gerald and I have spent some of our happiest working hours. Time did not matter. Day after day, at Abbey Road or in Gerald's charming studio, we worked at Wolf and Schubert songs, phrase by phrase, bar by bar, nuance by nuance. Then, after an evening's recording at Abbey Road, there was the excitement of hearing the first pressings and, in the light of that experience, more rehearsal before recording again. In some cases the production of what we considered a satisfactory record of a song was spread over years. And when we were satisfied there was the pleasure of taking the records down to Ernest Newman for his approval.

In spite of our mutual conviction that our trio was essential for the best artistic results, conditions made it necessary that Janssen should make one record with a German accompanist. It is his worst record. Compare the pedestrian *Serenade* (HMV DB3024) with the magical version (DB5797) which we made together in Berlin in 1938 and you will know why we were happy in our work and hear what a difference Gerald Moore's cooperation makes to even 'the prince of German singers'.

That trip to Berlin in 1938 was a triumph for Gerald. We had decided to record Schubert's *Schwanengesang* – that superb series of songs which he wrote at the end of his short life – and the second volume of the Brahms

Song Society, to complete the sixth volume of the Hugo Wolf Society and, if possible, to make substantial progress with the seventh volume. Not all the German artists concerned took kindly to the idea of the importation of an accompanist from England to record German songs with German singers, but the intimation that we were more willing to alter our choice of singers than accompanist had the desired effect. We all met in Berlin – Moore, Marta Fuchs, Janssen, Roswaenge, Karl Erb, Hüsch and I – and started rehearsals in earnest, usually eight or nine hours a day. I have rarely seen a musician happier than Erb in those days. He was already 60 and terribly crippled by a fall in which he had broken both legs and both arms, and badly twisted his back. The physical effort of supporting himself with his crutches before the microphone must have been torture to him, but his pleasure in finding English collaborators who loved and knew Schubert and Wolf as intimately as he did, and his delight in Moore's exquisitely sensitive playing, were such that he insisted on recording for six hours with only half an hour's break.

The Sunday morning on which we made the Hugo Wolf Society's record of *Feuerreiter* and *Gesellenlied* was unforgettable. Roswaenge had already made some tests of *Der Feuerreiter* with his own accompanist. They were accurate, but dull and taken at about half the proper pace. We knew it would be hard work to galvanise that reserved and unemotional Norwegian into the frenzied pyromania of Wolf's vivid masterpiece, but in the course of a dozen tests and playbacks we had hypnotised the singer into giving a performance which so frightened his ten-year-old child that it had to be taken home. At a quarter to one Roswaenge apologised that he must leave in three-quarters of an hour: he had some friends lunching with him to celebrate his birthday. That apology was a gift from Heaven. I sent out for a bottle of champagne. The effect of two glasses on that reluctant and almost teetotal singer was magical. His inhibitions and Nordic restraint dropped from him: he sang like a man possessed. When Roswaenge heard that record a fortnight later he did not and could not believe he had ever sung like that. I doubt if he believes it even now.

The reader may well wonder what has happened to the fruits of these Berlin sessions. The war prevented both the completion of the Brahms volumes, and us from remaking two unsatisfactory sides of the *Schwanengesang*. This had been planned for September 1939! As evidence of the quality of those splendidly productive days and the treasures that HMV have in store for the time when German is no longer an enemy language, there have been published three Brahms songs: *Wie bist du meine Königin*, *Minnelied*, and *Nicht mehr zu dir zu gehen* (DB3941), which were made for the second volume of the Brahms Songs Society, and the previously mentioned *Ständchen* and its coupling, the deeply tragic *Doppelgänger* (DB5797), which are fair samples of the quality of the complete *Schwanengesang* recording of which they are a part.

The war has naturally restricted Gerald Moore's activities, but he has found compensating stimulation in working with Maggie Teyte, who works and understands work as no other singer in this country. The magical records of French songs Maggie Teyte and Gerald Moore have made together were not improvisations. Such matching of magical sensibility and subtlety comes only when two artists of rare quality rehearse together unselfishly as they do. What British singers lack is not voice, but the will, the intensity, and the unquenchable desire for perfection that have brought Maggie Teyte as near to perfection in her own sphere as any mortal may hope. He is a man who practises hard, and thinks about his art.

The war has made a successful broadcaster and lecturer of him. His first broadcast of a record programme was clearly the work of a man with a natural microphone voice. His easy, friendly manner, which is so helpful in the recording studios, loses nothing in the broadcasting studio. His fine intellectual grasp of his job has enabled him to talk informatively and interestingly about accompanying, both over the air and at the National Gallery.

The best British accompanists of the previous generation, Hamilton Harty and Landon Ronald, became eminent conductors. It is not likely that Gerald Moore will follow their example even though he is better qualified for that career than many of those who are profitably practising it on us today. His heart is in what is called accompanying. It is because he realises that the pianoforte part of a great song by Wolf or Schubert is often half, sometimes more than half the song, that he is peerless. For this reason he may one day become a great chamber-music player. He is not really an accompanist, he is a collaborator. And as John McCormack said of him this very day: 'He's such a hell of a good artist than whom there is none better.'

5

The Philharmonia Orchestra

The story of how Walter Legge formed the Philharmonia Orchestra has been told by more than one commentator, and also by Walter Legge himself: his own account of the orchestra's origins and early years can be found in Chapter 3 of *On and Off the Record*.

I. Dennis Brain

A founder member of the Philharmonia was the great horn player Dennis Brain.

19 April 1956.
Hampstead, NW3.

Dear Walter,

    Thank you so much for your suggestion that I should record the Haydn Concerti.

    Nothing would give me greater pleasure, except perhaps that Elisabeth and you would find a way to come to my concert on April 27th – to lend invaluable encouragement.

    You have been so helpful so far, in helping me to avoid clashes, that I think it only fair that you should hear something of the result, and I personally would value very much your opinion.

    I find the first Haydn much better than the second, which is apparently doubtful, and have a photostat score of it, which is quite interesting. It has in the second movement writing which is much more adventurous than Mozart, and a finale which is not in 6/8!

    I was sorry to hear of Mr Ackerman's indisposition, and hope he will soon be well.

With kind regards,
Dennis

Dennis Brain did not live to record the Haydn concertos, since sessions for these works were not planned to take place until the winter of 1957/58. Stephen Pettitt's *Dennis Brain – A biography* (Robert Hale, London: 1976) chronicles Brain's association with Legge's orchestra which lasted until 1 September 1957, when he was killed in a car accident on the way home from playing with the orchestra at the Edinburgh Festival. He was 36 years old. Walter Legge's tribute to an admired friend and colleague was published in *The Gramophone*.

Dennis Brain   November 1957.
17 May 1921 – 1 September 1957

Music has suffered irreparable loss by the tragic death of Dennis Brain. He was, in the exact sense of the word, unique. Even among experts opinions differ on the respective and comparative merits of half a dozen conductors, singers, violinists and pianists, but since the days when he first became internationally known there was no voice to dispute that Dennis Brain had achieved unequalled pre-eminence in his art. In his warm and serene person all the essential qualities of the great interpretative artist were blended in perfect harmony.

He was innately musical in a way which defies description or analysis. He shaped phrases with an instinctive rightness that seemed inevitable. Technical problems did not exist for him. He had tamed the most notoriously intractable of all instruments to be his obedient servant and raised it again to sing the song the sirens sang. Over his instrument's whole range he had a mastery of intonation, of *legato*, of *staccato*, of dynamic range and, above all, of expressiveness that no other horn player has matched. But neither the listing of his qualities nor their sum explains the essential quality of his magic. That all these attributes should be embodied in one young man was miracle enough. But there was a still greater magic – the personality of his tone.

An unmistakable, immediately recognisable personal tone is an attribute shared by the few great instrumentalists and singers of every generation. In Dennis Brain's case its sunny radiance was the outward manifestation of a warm and serene nature. His sound was balm to the ears, to the mind and to the spirit. Its essential character did not change in all the 20 years I knew him. Neither his growth to supreme mastery, the deepening of his perceptions, nor even the change from an old French horn (held together in later years with adhesive plaster) to a modern German instrument altered the basic character of his tone. It was the audible radiation of his basic goodness.

Dennis was only 16 when he first blew himself into my awareness. From a studio which I believed to be empty there came the most impudent imaginable utterance of the *Till Eulenspiegel* theme. In the studio I found a cherub-faced schoolboy standing alone with a horn in his hands. Unable to believe the evidence of ear and eye I asked him, 'Was that you playing?' He blushed and said, 'Yes. Aubrey Brain is my Dad.' He was there to record the Mozart D major Divertimento with his father and the Léner Quartet.

When his time for call-up came, Dennis went into the RAF Central Band at Uxbridge. All honour to Wing-Commander O'Donnell for the service he did to our post-war musical life. In wartime Germany and Italy music was a reserved occupation. It was otherwise here. But O'Donnell laid his net so that every exceptionally able young instrumentalist knew that a place would be found for him in the RAF Band. Dennis landed there, and acquired a nickname that stuck to him for ten years – 'Dubbie', to

Walter Legge's mentor, the critic Ernest
Newman, pictured in his Surrey home.

Herbert Janssen (above). Gerhard Hüsch
(left), pictured with his accompanist Hans
Udo Müller on the right. Janssen and
Hüsch both made many pre-war
recordings with Walter Legge.

Jean Sibelius, in a photograph which he presented to Walter Legge.

Wieland Wagner (second left), Herbert von Karajan (centre) and Walter Legge (right) with some younger members of the Wagner family.

Signed photograph of the conductor Wilhelm Furtwängler, referred to in Walter Legge's letter of 5 July 1954 (see p. 163).

Sir Thomas Beecham conducting Mozart's *Die Zauberflöte* at the Berlin State Opera in 1937.

Walter Legge consults balance engineer Harold Davidson at a recording session.

Walter Legge discusses a point in the score with Herbert von Karajan.

A pause for thought at a recording session conducted by Sir William Walton (right).

The conductor Antonino Votto (left), Walter Legge, and the soprano Maria Callas listen to a recording session playback while musical assistant Antonino Tonini looks on.

Two principal clarinettists in the Philharmonia Orchestra - Frederick Thurston (left) and Bernard Walton.

The Maharaja of Mysore

Walter Legge in paternalistic pose with (left to right) Manoug Parikian (leader of the Philharmonia Orchestra), Gareth Morris (principal flautist), Jane Withers (Managing Director of the orchestra) and Dennis Brain (principal horn). Lucerne, 1954.

Otto Klemperer listens to a band concert at the Hotel Kurhaus, St Moritz, in August 1959, while recuperating from an illness. Walter Legge stands behind him, while Jane Withers (left) protects herself from the sun.

The conductor André Cluytens (left), soloist David Oistrakh and producer Walter Legge at the recording in Paris of Beethoven's Violin Concerto in October 1958.

Elisabeth Schwarzkopf listens to a playback of Mozart's 'Ch'io mi scordi di te? … Non temer' with Alfred Brendel (centre, obbligato pianist) and Walter Legge (producer) in March 1968.

Walter Legge at a recording session with conductor George Szell.

distinguish him from Denis (one 'n') Matthews. The goodwill tour of the
RAF Band in America laid the foundation of Dennis's American reputation
and brought him an offer from Stokowski to go as his first horn to
Philadelphia 'when the war is over'.

During the war Dennis made several records, all of which have disappeared from the catalogues, through the advent of tape recording and
long-playing records. For Columbia he made the Fourth Mozart Horn
Concerto with the Hallé Orchestra, and the Beethoven Horn Sonata with
Denis Matthews. Decca recorded Britten's *Serenade*, written for Dennis,
Peter Pears and the Boyd Neel Orchestra and Brahms's Op. 17, Four
Songs for female voices, two horns and harp. In most of Sidney Beer's
wartime records with his National Symphony Orchestra, Dennis was the
first horn.

He was still officially an airman when I realised my long-laid plan of
forming the Philharmonia Orchestra – the name retained from the Quartet I had formed in the early days of the war. Naturally, Dennis was first
horn. The first time the orchestra met was to record the Tchaikovsky
Concerto with Moiseiwitsch, Weldon conducting, in the Friends Meeting
House. In the interval Dennis came to me and said, 'This is going to be
good. I didn't think we should ever have an orchestra like this here.' Many
battles were to be fought and some years to pass before the orchestra
began to sound as I had dreamed. But that is another story. In the late
1940s Dennis was first horn of the Philharmonia, soloist with orchestras,
the most sought-after horn player for chamber music and, when Sir
Thomas Beecham first formed the Royal Philharmonic Orchestra, first
horn there. Dennis formed his own Wind Quintet and toured it here and
abroad. He seemed tireless, but always relaxed. The story is told that on
one occasion he played two concertos, Mozart and Strauss, with a provincial orchestra, the two appearances separated by a classical symphony and
the interval. During the interval Dennis was missing from the Artists'
Room. The conductor said jokingly, 'He's probably giving a half-hour recital
at the BBC.' Dennis was!

Neither the great fame he achieved nor the admiration and affection of
the most eminent conductors altered Dennis's nature. He remained, until
the day of his death, the laughing, cherubic-faced schoolboy I had first met
nearly 20 years previously, always arriving punctually at the last minute
for a concert or a session, always racing out first to the canteen.

His only interests in life, apart from music, were his family and motor-
cars. I do not believe he ever played a rehearsal or recording session or
even a concert session without having the latest copy of *The Autocar* or *The
Motor* open on his music stand. The day of the Philharmonia's first concert
in Zürich my wife bought a second-hand Hudson saloon, a huge vehicle
that was afterwards nicknamed the Atlantic Liner. We invited Dennis to
drive with us down to the next concerts in Turin and Milan. I drove. We
planned to drive back to Zürich through the night after the second Milan
concert. As we were about to leave Toscanini summoned my wife and me

to his home to tell us that he would come to London to conduct the Philharmonia. By the time we got back to the hotel it was well into the night and I was much too happy and excited to trust myself at the wheel, so I asked Dennis to drive. At dawn we were at the foot of the Gotthard Pass. Although the road was not officially open to traffic, Dennis insisted that we should drive over it rather than wait for the first train to take us through the tunnel. The whole road was hard, polished ice, with snow piled up nine or ten feet high on one side, and often sheer drops of several hundred feet on the other. Dennis handled that unmanageable brute of a car on a Serpentine skating-rink surface with a cool mastery that I have never seen equalled. To this day I blush to think of having driven in the presence of such a master. Curiously enough, it was only when he was driving that Dennis shed his endearing, irresponsible boyishness. It is terrible that his only relaxation should have cost him his life.

Their passion for cars forged an extra-musical link between Dennis and von Karajan. They both knew by heart the specifications, advertised and actual performances, structural details, advantages and disadvantages of every fast car, and never tired of discussing them. When Karajan told Dennis that he was giving up cars in favour of flying Dennis looked at him in hurt astonishment, then smiled and said, 'Yes, but you'll need a car to get to and from the aerodrome.' One of his happiest hours was when Karajan let him drive his Mercedes 300SL in Lucerne.

For an artist of his greatness Dennis has left a slender legacy of records. The fault lies in the repertoire rather than with the recording companies. As a soloist we have on Columbia the four Mozart concertos with the Philharmonia conducted by von Karajan and now, posthumously published, the two Strauss horn concertos with the Philharmonia conducted by Sawallisch. Decca has the Britten *Serenade*, a work which did much to make Dennis famous. Still unpublished is Hindemith's Horn Concerto conducted by the composer, recorded early this year by Columbia, who had planned for him to record all the Haydn concertos and the Brahms Trio this winter. But in the short history of the long-playing record his unmistakable voice is to be heard in nearly every major work in the orchestral repertoire and, in an impressive way, of opera. There is still much to come. The four Brahms symphonies conducted by Klemperer, Mozart's B flat Divertimento with Karajan which, when he played it in America, prompted a critic to describe Dennis as 'the only man who has the right to blow his own horn'. And *Der Rosenkavalier* the horn-player's opera par excellence! I doubt if anyone told Dennis that Strauss was depicting an orgasm at three bars before Figure 5 in the Prelude, but Dennis played it.

There is no knowing how Dennis would have developed. One of his unfulfilled ambitions was to play *The Ring* with a great conductor. His other ambition was to conduct, an activity he had already begun.

Deeply though I grieve his death, as a friend, as an artist, and as a matchless jewel in the Philharmonia Orchestra's crown, I cannot recall his art without smiling. Smiling at the impudent confidence of his mastery of his instrument, with anticipatory pleasure at the unconcerned and seraphic ease with which we knew beforehand he would play the notorious deathtraps in the whole symphonic literature, smiling in admiration and in gratitude for the joy of hearing such playing.

It was my privilege to have Dennis Brain as first horn of the Philharmonia Orchestra from the first day the Orchestra was assembled for our first rehearsal to the last day of his life. He is irreplaceable, but his art and his influence have left their permanent mark upon horn playing. His father, Aubrey Brain, had already effectively demonstrated that the bubbles and cracks which were the rule rather than the exception in horn playing 30 years ago were the faults of the players: there was nothing wrong with the instruments. Dennis has done still more. He restored to the repertoire Mozart's four horn concertos and established Strauss's two concertos. He inspired contemporary composers (among them Hindemith and Britten) to write works for the horn. And he has proved and established as a tradition that the horn at the lips of a devoted artist is one of the noblest and most expressive of instruments. We shall never hear his like again, but the standard of horn playing throughout the world has been inestimably improved by his example.

II. TWO CLARINET PLAYERS: FREDERICK THURSTON AND BERNARD WALTON

Frederick Thurston was the Philharmonia Orchestra's principal clarinet from 1949 until November 1953, when illness ended his career. He died a month later at the age of 52 and was succeeded by his deputy, Bernard Walton. Walton was the orchestra's principal clarinet until 1966, and also became the first chairman of the self-governing New Philharmonia Orchestra after Legge's departure in 1964. He died at the age of 54 in 1972.

Frederick 'Jack' Thurston – A Tribute   [January 1954]

In the interval of his first rehearsal with the Philharmonia Orchestra, Toscanini said to me, 'The man who cannot make music with this orchestra has no right to stand before an orchestra. The first clarinet – that is a great artist! He plays with the accents of a human voice.' The first clarinet was 'Jack' Thurston, and Toscanini's remark was the sincere appreciation of one great artist by another.

Thurston's playing had two incomparable characteristics: his noble tone, and his exquisitely musical, sensitive phrasing. His was an art at times near to tears and his playing, particularly of slow melodies was elegiac poetry suffused with wounding pathos.

Before he joined the Philharmonia Orchestra, Thurston had already enjoyed a career of musical distinction. He was principal clarinet of the BBC Symphony Orchestra from its inception until he resigned shortly after the war. As soloist in the Mozart Clarinet Concerto and as a chamber music player he had no rival, and as a teacher he had the priceless gift of infecting his pupils with his own selfless devotion to music.

To have experienced his solos in the great classic symphonies and in the repertoire from Tchaikovsky and Richard Strauss to Bartók is a lifelong enrichment of musical experience. There is not a colleague who has not been stimulated to better playing by the affecting but never affected expressiveness of his *cantilena*. And there is not a conductor who has made music with him who does not cherish the recollection of the magic that Jack Thurston poured 'from his full heart in profuse strains of unpremeditated art'.

Bernard Walton [1972]

The early death of Bernard Walton has robbed the world of one of its few great clarinettists who was also one of the finest orchestral players of the post-war period. I knew him from the early days of the London Philharmonic Orchestra. At that time he already produced a beautiful sound and phrased musically but an inborn reticence of manner prevented him from playing solo passages with the power, expressiveness and flair necessary for the woodwind soloists of a great orchestra and which he developed only much later.

When I formed the Philharmonia Orchestra in 1945 I engaged Reginald Kell, a brilliant and naturally extrovert artist, as first clarinet. When Kell decided to settle in America, I told Walton that he was not yet ripe for the responsibility of being the Philharmonia's first clarinet and that I was engaging Jack Thurston as Kell's successor, but that if Walton would give me first option on his services he should have every opportunity of doubling first clarinet or playing third or fourth when required so that he might learn from Thurston's expansive style and highly sensitive phrasing. At that time Walton could have had the first chair in any other orchestra but he gladly accepted my offer. Soon Thurston began to show signs of the illness which eventually killed him. At the Philharmonia's first concerts at the Edinburgh Festival Walton sat next to Thurston (to double the first clarinet in the tutti) and – this was so typical of Walton's gentle and modest nature – played all the exposed first clarinet passages so superbly that neither Herbert von Karajan nor I noticed the ruse. Only later did Thurston tell me how Walton had helped him.

When Thurston resigned I immediately appointed Bernard Walton first clarinet, a position he retained until I suspended the Philharmonia Orchestra. As evidence of the esteem in which Walton was held by great conductors it is not inopportune to recount that when Karajan was appointed Musical Director of the Berlin Philharmonic Orchestra he said to me, 'If we were not old friends I would immediately engage Walton for my Berlin orchestra.'

As first clarinet of the Philharmonia Walton at once blossomed into a unique artist and in company with Gareth Morris, Jock Sutcliffe and later

Gwydion Brooke those leaders of my woodwind section became known in the profession as 'Legge's Royal Flush'.

He was the most cooperative of men and had an extraordinary sense of fairness which made him the ideal link between the management and the members of the orchestra whose whole-hearted and unanimous respect and affection he had. When, with heavy heart, I decided that conditions had made it impossible to maintain the standards of playing I had established and maintained, Walton used, unsuccessfully, all his powers of gentle, firm persuasion to induce me to keep the orchestra going.

He was the principal architect in the establishment of the New Philharmonia Orchestra as a self-governing body but on the few occasions we met after I left London he frequently assured me that an orchestra is happiest when decisions are in the hands of a benevolent dictator because individual members can always blame 'the management' for any displeasures they may have.

Walton was by instinct an intensely and superbly musical player with an uncanny flair for matching his big but enchanting tone and adjusting his intonation to that of his colleagues. His tone was marvellously matched throughout its whole range in a manner which was as equable as his disposition.

III. RUNNING AN ORCHESTRA

Walter Legge attracted many of the day's outstanding artists to the Philharmonia, but a rare failure was the great Spanish cellist Pablo (or Pau) Casals, who resolutely refused to visit countries which recognised the Franco régime.

13 April 1954.

My dear Friend,

Since we last met, I have created an Orchestra which our mutual friend Walter Schulthess will assure you is the best in Europe. It has been my privilege that in the nine years of the Orchestra's life nearly all the greatest artists of our time have played with it.

Toscanini himself heard this Orchestra in Milan and chose to make his only two appearances in London within the last 15 years as its conductor.

Comparatively speaking, we give few concerts but I shall not feel I have done my work well unless the Orchestra, which has many of your pupils in its cello section, has the privilege either of playing under your direction or with you as its soloist. I leave the choice as to which role you wish to play entirely to you.

If you conduct, I have the Royal Festival Hall and the Orchestra engaged for the 5th December 1954 or January 28th, 1955. As a soloist, either of these dates, with a conductor of your own choice. For a recital I can offer you the dates of January 23rd, February 13th, March 13th or March 20th.

5. *The Philharmonia Orchestra*

As a conductor or soloist in an orchestra concert, I would offer you a fee of £250 0s. 0d. For a recital, a fee of £400 0s. 0d.

I know how deeply you feel about your own Festival and its future, but I am firmly convinced that if only the London public might have the privilege of hearing you again, the Casals Festivals in Prades would gain enormously.

Yours,
[Walter Legge]

Walter Schulthess was a well-known Swiss artists' manager.

[translated from French]   21 April 1954.
                                                                                    Prades.

Dear Friend,

I had great pleasure in receiving your letter. I am happy to learn that, thanks to your efforts and abilities, you have succeeded in giving your country an orchestral ensemble of the first order, and I share your happiness most sincerely.

As for your kind invitation, I am most unhappy not to be able to reply in the affirmative, but I still live in the hope of being able to pay a visit once more to England and the other countries which for a long time have been most dear to me.

Please accept my sincere good wishes,

Pablo Casals

In his role as a self-styled 'benevolent dictator' Walter Legge sometimes encountered problems of discipline in the Philharmonia. He always acted promptly and decisively when the need to do so arose.

                                                                        23 September 1953.

To: all Philharmonia Orchestra Committee Members

F. Thurston, Esq.

Dear Mr Thurston,

No doubt you have been reading the *Daily Telegraph* in the last week or two, and I know that you will have been experiencing with me, the same concern on the misguidedness of private communications with the press by members of the Philharmonia Orchestra.

I feel sure that you will feel, as I do, that the well-being of the whole Orchestra and the individual prestige of every one of its members can be, and indeed has been, put in danger by a not unnatural desire, on the part of certain of your colleagues, to express their individual opinions. This must never be repeated, and I would like your advice on the best way in which we can together establish it as a ruling that no artist playing with the Philharmonia Orchestra should express his or her personal opinion, either in a letter or personal statement to the press, without first placing the text of these views before the management of the Orchestra, so that we may avoid giving to anybody, either inside or outside of the Orchestra, the opportunity of reflecting unfavourably upon the qualities of your colleagues.

Yours sincerely,
[Walter Legge]

On a slightly later occasion he required Jane Withers to take action on his behalf. Miss Withers was appointed Secretary of the Philharmonia Concert Society in 1951. A year later she was made Managing Director, and ran the orchestra for Legge until 1964.

12 October 1953.

Dear Jane,

I am leaving it entirely to your judgement whether it is in the Philharmonia Orchestra's best interest that you discuss with the Committee or the Orchestra as a whole, certain matters which have – for some time past – but particularly in the last days, been causing me the gravest concern.

I know that you are aware to some extent of the situation, but I am sure you do not know how serious it has become. Otherwise you would not have let it happen.

The matter is quite simply the lack of manners and inattention of the Philharmonia Orchestra.

In the last two years only Toscanini and a very few other conductors – and also soloists – have not commented privately to me about the Orchestra's lack of attention and its noisiness during rehearsals and recording sessions. It goes further than this – The Gramophone Company's staff also complains because the Philharmonia are late to start; late back after the interval; they ignore signals; they are best known as the noisiest Orchestra. All this is a waste of The Gramophone Company's money.

Quite frankly, I forsee that unless there is an immediate and permanent improvement in their attitude towards conductors and in their sense of responsibility to the people who provide them with their income, that those incomes must inevitably suffer.

Both conductors and soloists have told me that they have regretted not walking out on occasions at rehearsals. For an orchestra of the Philharmonia's quality it is only natural to expect – and insist – that the behaviour should be comparable to the musical performance.

I have received complaints about the deplorable manners of the Orchestra at the concert for which the Philharmonia was engaged at the Royal Albert Hall on October 11th, and I am sorry to say there were specific references to some of the musicians whose playing and position in the Orchestra make them the ones whom I would most expect to regard it as their professional duty to correct any sign of slackness.

It is your personal responsibility to see that every person who employs

129

the Philharmonia Orchestra gets the best value for his money and you must ensure that there is no further cause for complaint.

I am not prepared to be forced to apologise for the heedlessness of a group of artists – for whose music making I have the greatest personal regard – when they behave to conductors and soloists in a manner which they themselves would be the first to resent if they were either the conductor or soloist. Neither am I going to have the reputation of the Philharmonia Orchestra, or the Orchestra itself, destroyed by all, or any one of its members. Either you see that the Orchestra behaves itself as well as it plays or we part company.

It is up to you to see that their manners are as good as their finest performance.

Yours sincerely,
Walter Legge

In March 1964 Walter Legge attempted to disband the Philharmonia Orchestra, but the players resolved to carry on as a self-governing body under the name of New Philharmonia. One of the players on the board of management was the principal flautist, Gareth Morris. He attempted to make a bridge between the new orchestra and its previous chief. He wrote to say that he had had 15 happy years in the Philharmonia, and he asked Legge to wish the orchestra luck in its new venture.

28 September 1964.

Dear Gareth

Luck is not an element for good or ill in music.

I am proud that you had 15 happy years working with me and I most sincerely hope that you and your colleagues will constantly remember that there is no adequate substitute for a great artist and that the standard we achieved together was due to unremitting hard work. While it was still possible for me to maintain those standards they were happy years for me too.

With all good wishes,
[Walter Legge]

6

Wilhelm Furtwängler

Walter Legge maintained professional contacts with Wilhelm Furtwängler over a span of eight years; between 1946, when Legge made his first attempts to arrange recording sessions for the great conductor, until Furtwängler's death in 1954. It was not always an easy relationship, and remained very formal. Furtwängler was wary of Legge's friendship with his great rival Herbert von Karajan, and he was less willing than other artists to accept the Englishman's ideas for recording and concert projects.

The two men had a sharp disagreement before the recording sessions for Wagner's *Tristan und Isolde* in the summer of 1952. As is now well known, Furtwängler at one point refused to go ahead with the recording if Legge was the producer, but the Isolde, Kirsten Flagstad, insisted that Legge should produce the opera, which he did. After the sessions Furtwängler was extravagant in his praise for Legge's work during the recording sessions, yet never again did Legge produce a recording by Furtwängler. Even so, that was not the end of the relationship. Legge was anxious that Furtwängler should maintain his association with the Philharmonia on the concert platform, and he continued to cajole the older man into accepting engagements with his orchestra.

*

In 1947 Furtwängler's career was still very much overshadowed by allegations regarding his activities during the Nazi régime in Germany, even though he had been cleared by de-Nazification courts in April of that year. The charity concert referred to below was one of several conducted by Furtwängler in England during February and March 1948. Furtwängler's first recording sessions with Legge were to take place during the Lucerne Festival in late August 1947. It is noteworthy that Furtwängler sought Legge's advice on a matter connected not with his orchestra but with the London Philharmonic, whose Chairman and Managing Director was Thomas Russell, assisted by Berta Geissmar. Dr Geissmar had worked for Furtwängler in Germany before fleeing to England when the Nazis came to power.

[translated from German]   3 July 1947.
                                                  Villa l'Empereur, Clarens.
Dear Mr Legge,

I am sending you enclosed *in the strictest confidence* a copy of part of a letter from Mr Russell regarding the planned Charity Concert. It is not really possible for me at this distance to make a realistic judgement. There is no doubt that the concert in December would have to be preceded by a publicity campaign in the press. The only thing that I personally am afraid of is that my willingness to conduct for the Jewish Charity, which corresponds completely with my whole personal attitude, will simply be branded as sheer opportunism, taking advantage of the occasion. That must be avoided at all costs. I do not want to link any specific political attitude with it, but rather to show that art is above politics. I will always be prepared to offer my artistic skills – for humanitarian reasons – either for the Winter Aid Concert in Germany at present or for the Jewish Charity Concert in London.

Please let me have your opinion without delay. Perhaps it would also be possible to arrange the concert a little later, e.g. January or February?

I am of course to some extent dependent on Mr Russell releasing me from the promise I gave him, but I do not want to give up the fight prematurely of my own accord. If you should wish to telephone me, just wire the Clinic. I shall be there at the appointed time.

> With best wishes as always,
> Yours sincerely,
> Wilhelm Furtwängler

PS. What worries me most about the concert is the prospect of having to make music in the enormous Albert Hall, where, in my opinion, artistic success (such as can be achieved, for example, in the Berlin Titania Palast) would scarcely be possible, because in spite of really intensive efforts on the part of the orchestra everything would sound too pale and insignificant (especially in the Beethoven).

[translated from German]

8 July 1947.

Dear Mr Legge,

So we shall just have to wait and see what the decision is next week regarding entry. I would like to ask you one more thing: which Jewish Charity is involved? Miss [sic] Geissmar informed me that there was no such thing in London. You will understand that I can only withdraw the promise I gave to Mr Russell on these grounds. I am committed to make my first appearance in London with Russell/Geissmar (otherwise I am not committed to anything, something I would like to make very clear). Only if there were some important outside and generally comprehensible reason, would I be able to disregard this commitment. The invitation of this Jewish Charitable Society would seem to me to represent such a reason. I would be grateful if you could give me some further information which I could use *vis-à-vis* Russell/Geissmar. If the latter maintain that this is opportunism, as I have already written, this might be interpreted as an affront from my point of view and in particular would give completely the wrong impression to the English public who are particularly sensitive in such matters. I must confess that I find the accusation that I would do something like that out of opportunism anything but pleasant, simply because it is not true. I am therefore writing this to you because you yourself recommended this way out at the time in your telegram with the proviso – 'if public response as good as expected'. You yourself were therefore not completely certain at the time about the effect. In which way have you been able to clarify your views in the meantime? Or in which way would it be possible to assess such a reaction before the matter is announced, when it would perhaps be too late?

Please forgive these belated misgivings. My desire to do this concert remains unchanged, but you will understand that these misgivings are understandable, especially as you yourself have expressed them.

If it would not be advisable at present, I would ask whether some other, somewhat later, date could be arranged which would not be so provocative. The concerts agreed with Russell/Geissmar are not until March. If they could begin, for example, in February with the J.Ch.Soc., no one would be able to say anything against it. Perhaps you could think this over once again.

I am writing this to you to ask you to contact Ingpen & Williams at your end. I do not know Mrs Ingpen personally and would not therefore like to repeat all these misgivings to her. If you would do that, however, I would be grateful. It is, however, an awkward situation.

I intend to leave here for Salzburg on about 9th August. The rehearsals are to take place from the morning of the 11th, the concert on the 13th. I would therefore have either to leave for Lucerne straight away on the same evening by train or on the following morning by car. How about you? Will you be able to take us from Switzerland to Salzburg or from Salzburg to Switzerland? In any case, the journey here from Salzburg is wonderful as I know from experience. We would then have to leave early on the morning of the 14th.

The rehearsals in Vienna always take place on the Thursday and Friday before the concert, i.e. on 6th/7th, 13th/14th and 27th/28th November.

> With best wishes,
> Yours sincerely,
> Wilhelm Furtwängler

In December 1949 plans were being made for a production of Mozart's *Don Giovanni* at the 1950 Salzburg Festival. Dr Egon Hilbert was the Intendant of the Vienna State Opera: given his good working relationship with Elisabeth Schwarzkopf it seems unlikely in fact that he applied his dictum to her. Furtwängler often referred to his arch-rival Karajan as 'K'.

[translated from German]

2 December 1949.

Dear Mr Legge,

I hear that Schwarzkopf has not yet promised to do the *Don Giovanni*. Dr Hilbert is of the opinion that the common method (also familiar to K

6. Wilhelm Furtwängler

and others) is to delay in answering and then perhaps to refuse at the last moment. I would therefore recommend that she makes up her mind straight away, in a positive sense. It is not, of course, possible to change the repertoire in Salzburg, but every opportunity will be seized to include such a performer. I am thoroughly in favour of Pamina, but only with Seefried's approval. I would ask you finally to reply to my letter regarding the record programme. I do not want this matter only to be resolved in Vienna under duress and would be grateful for a clear opinion from you. I am going to Germany for a few days on the 11th of this month, and hope to hear from you before then.

I hope that in the meantime you have made a complete recovery as regards your health and send you my best wishes.

Yours sincerely,
Wilhelm Furtwängler

Although Furtwängler conducted the Philharmonia in a March 1948 recording session (the 'Immolation Scene' from Wagner's *Götterdämmerung*, with Kirsten Flagstad) he did not conduct them live until 22 May 1950, in the concert when Flagstad gave the first performance of Strauss's *Vier letzte Lieder*. It was a constant battle on Legge's part to persuade the German conductor to come to England. Furtwängler did in fact conduct the Philharmonia on two dates later in the year, 13 November and 1 December, since his visit to Egypt did not take place. The 19 February engagement in fact became part of a recording session when Edwin Fischer and Furtwängler recorded Beethoven's *Emperor* Concerto.

[translated from German]   17th August 1950.
Waldburg, Salzburg-Aigen.

Dear Mr Legge,

Unfortunately my last discussion with you was somewhat rushed because of the pressure of all the work I have here. Now, only a few days later, it is clear that it will not be possible to keep the December date which I gave you.

A visit to Egypt had originally been planned in this period for the Berlin Philharmonic, which had fallen through in the meantime. Now the Minister Taher Pasha is here and has approached me again regarding this visit which was agreed in principle at the time. I cannot refuse *vis-à-vis* the Berlin Philharmonic for whom this visit represents a considerable income.

Only two concerts have actually been fixed so far, i.e. in November, 13th, and in February, 19th.

Will I see you next week in Luzern?

I have serious misgivings about the exchange of singers between Bayreuth and Salzburg. I will tell you more about this when I see you in person.

With best wishes for the present,
Yours sincerely,
Wilhelm Furtwängler

134

To come back to financial matters once again: I have heard that Karajan received a total sum of £300 – under various headings. I would ask you to let me know once again, what the position is in this respect. Quite apart from the fact that I cannot continue to conduct in England for my continental fee, it is really regrettable from everyone's point of view that one is obliged, whether one wants to or not, to take into account this pressure exerted by Karajan as regards fees, especially in comparison with the actual fees offered to me on an international basis.

[translated from German]   16 November 1950.
Clarens.

Dear Mr Legge,

Unfortunately the telephone connection this morning was not successful. I would propose the following for the programme of the next London concert:

> a) Mendelssohn: *Hebrides* Overture
> b) Schubert: Entr'acte from *Rosamunde*
> c) Bartók: *Concerto for Orchestra*
> ———
> d) Tchaikovsky: Fifth Symphony

or:

> a) Overture and Entr'acte from *Rosamunde*
> b) Bartók Concerto
> ———
> c) Tchaikovsky Fifth.

You also mentioned a Sibelius piece. We could also do the following:

> a) Bartók
> b) Sibelius: *En Saga*
> ———
> c) Tchaikovsky

The Sibelius would, however, be rather tiring after the Bartók which is not short. It is an entertaining piece, but rather long drawn out, so that I think that one of the other versions would be better for the audience.

> With best wishes,
> Yours sincerely,
> Wilhelm Furtwängler.

The programme for 11 December was that listed in the first alternative above, plus the 'Ballet Music No. 2' from *Rosamunde*. Furtwängler conducted the Philharmonia in two concerts in February and March 1951.

6. Wilhelm Furtwängler

[translated from German]

5 June 1951.

Dear Mr Legge,
    I have been asked to organise a visit for the Vienna Philharmonic to London and Paris. Some concerts would take place in London at the end of January. Will this affect our concerts with the Philharmonia Orchestra? (Please remember that I have commitments *vis-à-vis* the Vienna Philharmonic.)

> With best wishes,
> Yours sincerely,
> Wilhelm Furtwängler

With many thanks for your and your orchestra's kind messages during my illness. I am feeling much better.

[translated from German]

7 June 1951.

Dear Mr Legge,
    What do you think about a concert on 25th October and 24th April? I shall, however, only be able to make a definite commitment in two weeks' time. You were going to write to me regarding possible suggestions for the programmes.
    Shall we discuss this in writing *or verbally*? I shall be staying here until the middle of the month as I still do not feel completely well, but then I must go to Berlin for a few days, if at all possible. From 22nd June I can be reached at the Dolder Hotel in Zürich.

> With best wishes,
> Yours sincerely,
> Wilhelm Furtwängler

11.6.1951.
DR WILHELM FURTWANGLER VILLA L'EMPEREUR, MONTREUX, SWITZERLAND.

AM CONSULTING PHILHARMONIA COMMITTEE ON YOUR LETTER STOP UNTIL I HAVE DECISION CANNOT ANSWER STOP WOULD YOU DO THREE PHILHARMONIA CONCERTS BEFORE XMAS OR TWO MARCH AND APRIL SINCE HAVING CONSULTED SOME MEMBERS FIND DIVISION OPINION WHETHER YOUR CONCERTS FOR SOCIETY SHOULD BE BEFORE OR AFTER VIENNA VISIT STOP FOR YOUR PRIVATE INFORMATION DOUBT WISDOM OF VISIT OF FOREIGN ORCHESTRA THIS WINTER AS PUBLIC SPENDING ALL MONEY ON FESTIVAL CONCERTS NOW STOP OUR PLAN TO GIVE YOU NEXT SEASON GREAT SOLOISTS EACH CONCERT CALCULATED TO COUNTERACT SITUATION STOP FROM PRELIMINARY

DISCUSSION WITH COMMITTEE BELIEVE STRONGEST OBJEC-TIONS WOULD BE RAISED IF YOUR VIENNA PHILHARMONIC CON-CERTS HAD EMINENT SOLOISTS STOP DELIGHTED YOU ARE WELL AGAIN.

GREETINGS W.L.

[translated from German]

11 June 1951.

Dear Mr Legge,

Many thanks for your telegram. I will be writing to you in a few days, as to what, if anything, is going to happen as regards the Viennese*. If you are coming to Zürich (Dolder Hotel) between 22nd and 28th June, we will not need to correspond regarding suggestions for the programme, otherwise please keep me informed.

> With best wishes,
> Yours sincerely,
> Wilhelm Furtwängler

* also in connection with this, about the dates suggested by you.

The projected London and Paris concerts with the Vienna Philharmonic and Furtwängler did not in fact take place.

3 July 1951.

Dear Dr Furtwängler,

We had a full committee meeting last Friday morning and discussed at length the programmes for next season at which I placed before my Committee the best of the suggestions that I had been too tired to discuss with you before we met in Zürich.

For the first programme on October 25th we should particularly like the following:

Hugo Wolf – *Penthesilea* (first concert performance in England of the *Urfassung*).
Beethoven – Piano Concerto No. 3 in C minor – (Soloist Myra Hess)

INTERVAL

Brahms – Symphony No. 1

For the second programme on April 24th with Kirsten Flagstad we would like the following:

Haydn – Symphony in G – *Paukenschlag*
    or Symphony in D major – *Londener*
Handel – Arias – (Flagstad)
Smetana – 'Moldau'

INTERVAL

Beethoven – Symphony No. 8
Wagner – 'Schluβszene' *Götterdämmerung* – (Flagstad)

As you know I am an old and incurable Wolf enthusiast and his only *Tondichtung* has never been played in the London concert halls in its original form, and it is a piece which I am sure you would do better than anyone.

About the rest of the first programme I am sure you will have no complaints.

If, in the second programme, you would prefer to do the 'Rheinfahrt' and 'Trauermarsch' or the *Siegfried Idyll* in place of the Beethoven Symphony we should be equally happy.

Do please let me know as quickly as possible as we must announce these concerts before the middle of July.

> With kindest regards,
> Yours always,
> [Walter Legge]

[translated from German]

4 July 1951.

Dear Mr Legge,
I promised to write to you from here about the London concerts. It is, however, still difficult for me to do so as two dates, i.e. the date of my engagement in La Scala and that of a visit with the Viennese in October to Switzerland and Germany have not yet been finalised and so I do not know whether your dates will be affected by this. Furthermore, what you said about programmes has not greatly encouraged me. It would indeed be possible to do an accompanying concert with Flagstad, if some new Strauss Lieder were available, but a second time, without even performing a large substantial symphony, does not really attract me, however much I like Flagstad personally, and a Brahms concerto with an English pianist whom I do not know and who possibly would give the usual routine, painstaking version of these concertos, also does not attract me. I would prefer to have a concert without soloists, which you, however, probably do not want because you think that a concert with soloists is not any dearer, as I would receive only half of the fee. What I would like to do is to perform for once a choral work such as the Brahms Requiem or the Ninth Symphony with your orchestra. There are so many choirs in England which would do those well and that would have some purpose.

> Awaiting your reply,
> With best wishes,
> Yours sincerely,
> Wilhelm Furtwängler

PS. As soon as I have confirmation of my dates, I will write to you again. You also have to make arrangements your end after all.

9 July 1951.

Dear Dr Furtwängler,

I think our letters about programmes must have crossed; I thought my suggestions rather good! – *Penthesilea* – Beethoven with Myra Hess, whom you have already had as a soloist with the Berliner Philharmoniker, and Brahms 1. And the other programme ought to give us both the pleasure of that sight so rare in the Albert Hall – a full house!!

The Brahms Requiem is a notorious house emptier in London – and neither Schwarzkopf nor Seefried is available at that time.

If, for the first Concert in October, you would prefer a purely orchestral programme we would have no rooted objection but we have unfortunately learned from expensive experience that one cannot rely on good receipts for a purely orchestral concert, whereas a programme including a Beethoven concerto, particularly when you conduct, makes a great difference to the size of the audience.

Starting with your results with Yehudi [Menuhin], here the public has learned that a Beethoven concerto is a great orchestral work with soloist and not merely a concerto with orchestral background.

> With all good wishes,
> Yours sincerely,
> [Walter Legge]

PS: Since you told me, after Hess's concert with you that you were happy with her, and we had already agreed to have a soloist (Edwin [Fischer] is not available at the time required), the office here has engaged her for the October date and I should not like to cancel her, particularly because she is looking forward with great pleasure to playing with you. My motive here was her great influence in America; to play with her can only help you in the USA!

[translated from German]

6 July 1951.

Dear Mr Legge,

I can see that making up for records which are not completely successful is very complicated. We can talk about this again in Bayreuth. By the way: the Ninth in Bayreuth should not be recorded under any circumstances. If it is to be done, then not in this ambience which is certainly not very favourable from an acoustics point of view.

As regards your programmes, they seem to me to be somewhat depressing. I do not have the feeling that there is any point in my conducting concerts in England in this way. Myra Hess is, of course, a worthy and charming artist and to create a complete Beethoven or Brahms evening with her help would perhaps have some purpose. Apart from the opening section, Wolf's *Penthesilea* is an extremely weak piece and although I value Wolf highly as a composer of Lieder, I would find it difficult to warm to this piece, just to make something of its rarity. I am too old and too critical for that.

As regards the second concert, you know how highly I regard Flagstad, but an accompanying concert with her would only be possible if I either had something really new like the Strauss Lieder at the time, or could do a full-blown symphony such as Bruckner or something similar as well. As it is, it is neither one thing nor the other and would not give me any pleasure. I would like to suggest in fact that you find another conductor for the two concerts; as you are principally concerned, as I suspect, with financial factors, you will be able to find someone.

> With best wishes,
> Yours sincerely,
> Wilhelm Furtwängler

The performance of Beethoven's Ninth Symphony to celebrate the opening of the first post-war Bayreuth Festival was in fact recorded, and issued after Furtwängler's death in the absence of the studio recording which had been planned.

11 July 1951.

Dear Dr Furtwängler,

Thank you for your letter of July 6th. I have already answered you about the first paragraph of your letter; as far as the rest of it is concerned your observations are rather a shock, however, that is beside the point.

I have reserved the Hall and the Philharmonia Orchestra for you on the October and April dates, to say nothing of Flagstad for the latter, and I do not want – particularly in view of your own letter some weeks ago, in which you said how much you valued the continuity of the thing we had begun together – to let that be disturbed through a mere difference of opinion on programmes. The fact that my Committee will protest violently is my headache – not yours.

Now let us take the first programme. As I explained to you in my letter sent yesterday Myra Hess has been engaged, so will you consider as quickly as possible and let me have your reactions to the following suggestions:

(1) — following your own lead on a Beethoven programme:

Egmont
The C minor or G major Concerto with Hess

Interval

Eroica Symphony

(2) Bruckner Fourth Symphony (It is the only one we can risk in England apart from the Seventh which you have already done).

Interval

Beethoven C minor Concerto with Hess
Three pieces from the *Damnation of Faust* ...
... or
Meistersinger Overture

Since the second half of this suggested programme is short we could, if you like, begin with a Weber Overture.

I would suggest an all Brahms programme if I were not convinced that no woman can play either of the Brahms Concertos to your satisfaction, or, for that matter, mine.

If you want to do a first performance in England we could begin the Concert with the Berger *Rondo Burleska* which is short and effective, or for that matter with *Moldau*.

Now about the Flagstad programme .... Nothing you ever conduct is a *Begleitkonzert*. Flagstad has never sung Handel in public, and that is why I had set my heart on Handel arias and it is rather a waste to have her for the closing scene of *Götterdämmerung* only. I still think, if only you would ponder on it, that you will agree my last suggestion for the programme with Flagstad as soloist has a great deal to be said for it. If you don't like the idea of the Haydn Symphony, there is a wonderful one with a slow movement, really after your own heart – No. 88 in G major; perhaps you would like to look at it and let me know what you think, or, if you want to change the programme completely how do you like the following?

Gluck – Alkestis ...
... or Gluck/Wagner *Iphigenia* Overture
Handel – Arias (Flagstad)
Beethoven – Eighth Symphony (which you have done so little in London)

Interval

Schumann Fourth Symphony
Wagner – Closing scene *Götterdämmerung*

or would you rather consider doing, in the first part, one of the Mahler song recitals with Flagstad; not, I think, the *Kindertotenlieder*. I don't think Flagstad would be happy with that sort of pathos, or, we could have another Wagner concert.

Let me have some suggestions from you.

> With kindest regards,
> Yours always,
> [Walter Legge]

At length the programmes agreed and played were as follows:

6. Wilhelm Furtwängler

25 October: Beethoven: *Grosse Fuge*; Piano Concerto No. 4 (Hess). Brahms: Symphony No. 1

24 April: Schumann: *Manfred* Overture; Symphony No. 4. Ravel: *Rapsodie espagnole*. Wagner *Wesendonk Lieder* (Flagstad); *Götterdämmerung* 'Immolation Scene' (Flagstad).

Information from Switzerland and difficulties with the French branch of HMV now caused Legge to send a memorandum to his departmental head at EMI, Brenchley Mittell.

Mr Mittell   18 December 1951.

Jecklin telephoned me today to say that Furtwängler, having read of the split between Columbia England and Columbia America, had expressed his desire and intention of going to Philips because he wanted to be on Columbia America, so I telephoned Furtwängler. He tells me that the contract with Mr Bicknell is almost in order. There are still details outstanding (I am inclined to believe Jecklin rather than the dear Doctor). He told me, however, in the course of the conversation that by agreement with Mr Bicknell he had recorded not only his own Symphony for Deutsche Grammophon but the Schubert C Major. I presume that it was agreed but I regret the oversight which neglected to inform me of this. I am sure that you will see that such oversights do not occur again.

Now the question of the closing scene from *Götterdämmerung* with Flagstad. I made it clear to everybody after I played the test of the LP to him that this record was not to be published as it stood. I told de Jongh this myself. In spite of this, France published this same side with a coupling not by Furtwängler but by Böhm. Furtwängler was naturally furious. First of all, that we had published the record that he had forbidden and, secondly, we had published the Flagstad coupling with him as conductor on one side and Böhm on the other. How in heaven's name can we keep artists happy if this sort of nonsense is going on? Mr Hughes managed to get the sales stopped but by then the damage was done. Here again is concrete evidence that the only way we can pull the business together is to centralise the authority in this country.

Walter Legge

Paul Jecklin was EMI's agent in Switzerland: his family owned a large musical instrument business in Zürich.

Mr Walter Legge   21st April 1952.

As you know Dr Furtwängler has just concluded a new contract with the Company. He feels that in view of your close association with Herr von Karajan, it would be preferable for all his, Dr Furtwängler's, recordings under the new contract to be handled by a separate artists manager. I have, therefore, asked Mr Bicknell to take over the supervision of all recordings with Dr Furtwängler starting with *Tristan and Isolde*.

This change of managership must not alter your former enthusiasm for Dr Furtwängler and his art, of which I know you have always been so great an admirer. Please be particularly careful not to allow it to cause you to utter any criticisms nor make any comments which might be construed as unfavourable to Dr Furtwängler. I stress this, because there are only too many people ready to put a wrong interpretation upon any words which are not entirely favourable to an artist.

B. Mittell.

Inter-departmental MEMORANDUM   Date: 25 June 1952.
To: Mr Mittell

Dear Mr Mittell,

The complete recording of *Tristan und Isolde* is finished in five sessions less than the time we had allotted for it. 132 kilometers (82 miles of tape)! As a bonus I have a Closing Scene *Götterdämmerung* (Flagstad/ Furtwängler), Mahler's *Lieder eines fahrenden Gesellen* (Fischer-Dieskau/ Furtwängler) and I hope to get, to fill up the time, at least one LP side for MGM with Susskind!

The results are magnificent and I shall welcome the efforts of any team in or out of the Company to equal the work Larter and I have done. Apart from the one row of which Bicknell has certainly told you things went peacefully to the end. Furtwängler cannot cease praising the Philharmonia ('Why do you want to record the Vienna Philharmonic in that hall when you have this wonderful orchestra and this splendid hall here?') and went so far as to congratulate and thank me for my valuable contribution to the artistic success of the performance and recording.

The Doktor asked me to have a private chat with him over our past and future relations which I stalled as long as possible. Last night there was no escaping it. I told him you had asked me not to enter into any discussions with him apart from the actual work on *Tristan*. We had an hour together after last night's session: the usual stuff, I had libelled him by comparing Karajan to Toscanini. For the hour he poured out venom against Toscanini, Karajan and every living conductor, and against Ernest Newman because he had criticised him adversely.

I told him that when he had wished, and you had agreed, that in future his relations with the Company should be maintained by other persons and that Collingwood should supervise his recordings I had accepted the situation regretfully, but as a *fait accompli*: I saw no reason to change the situation. Also that much as I admire him as an artist and enjoy working with him when he is in a good mood, neither my health nor my nerves will stand up to his 'explosions' and that I need a rest from them.

I have got Collingwood to do the sessions with Fischer-Dieskau and the Doktor, who nevertheless insists on having a chat with Elisabeth and me;

we have invited him to lunch tomorrow! I am, you'll be interested to hear, lacking in character, morals and a serious interest in the art of music because I do not actively protest against Karajan's activities as a producer and conductor of opera! In spite of all this he has the 'greatest sympathy and liking for me and admiration for my abilities'!!!

What really matters is that Victor have every reason to be pleased with *Tristan*.

Once I get back to the office for a day I will write in more detail. The next headache is called *Boris*.

> All good wishes,
> Yours sincerely,
> Walter Legge

PS. The lunch with Furtwängler went off in peace, even with gaiety, and we returned to the studios to hear the third act of *Tristan*. The old man is really delighted with the results. Now we have to make satisfactory LPs of them!

It looks as if we shall have to record *Tristan* again in Bayreuth. I talked with Karajan by telephone and he asked pointedly if we were trying to get out of our promise to him to record *Tristan* in Bayreuth because we have just done it with Furtwängler. To give him this handle at the moment would be fatal to our chances of getting another contract with him.

To my surprise the Wagners have not refused to let us record as they swore they would do if Elisabeth refused to sing there this year: they have asked me to go over at once to discuss the *Tristan* and future recording. I'll discuss this with [Leonard] Smith and Miss Mathias [of EMI's International Classical Artists' Department] and act on the outcome of our deliberations.

The recording of Mussorgsky's *Boris Godunov* took place in Paris in July 1952.

3.9.52

DR FURTWANGLER, VILLA L'EMPEREUR CLARENS VAUD

AFTER OUR CONVERSATION ON MONDAY FEEL IT ESSENTIAL IN YOUR INTERESTS SINCE YOU ARE NOT CONDUCTING VIENNA PHILHARMONIC'S VISIT TO LONDON THAT YOU STILL APPEAR DURING THIS SEASON SO HAVE MANAGED TO GET APRIL 20 AND 27 FESTIVAL HALL IN HOPE YOU WILL ACCEPT BOTH DATES AS NEAREST AVAILABLE PERIOD TO CORONATION STOP SUGGEST FIRST PROGRAMMES TRISTAN VORSPIEL EINE KLEINE NACHT-MUSIK SCHUBERT UNVOLLENDETE INTERVAL BEETHOVEN EIGHT TANNHAUSER OVERTURE WITH OR WITHOUT VENUS-BURG SECOND PROGRAMME BEETHOVEN SEVEN INTERVAL BEETHOVEN SIX LEONORA THREE STOP PLEASE TELEGRAPH

6. Wilhelm Furtwängler

REPLY KINDEST REGARDS WALTER LEGGE ORGANOL WESDO
LONDON

[translated from German]

22 November 1952.

Dear Mr Legge,

Herr von Westerman told me on the telephone with horror that Ibbs &
Tillett, and/or you had said that the Berliners will only get the date of 27th
April in the Festival Hall if I do the concert on the 20th with the Philharmonia. You know how much I enjoy doing a concert with the Philharmonia,
and I have reconsidered it in the meantime, but it really is not possible on
the 20th as I have a concert which has been scheduled for some considerable time in Berlin – at the beginning of the tour. If, however, you could
give me any other date which is possible, I should be pleased to do a concert
just in order not to let the season go by without making music with your
splendid orchestra, even if I had planned on doing other things with my
time.

Please write to me to Vienna I, (2 Schaufflergasse), where I shall be
until 3rd December or to Berlin-Dahlem (1a Meisenstrasse) from 4th to
10th December, with what other date you can suggest.

> With best wishes,
> Yours sincerely,
> Wilhelm Furtwängler

[translated from German]

6 December 1952.
1a Meisenstrasse
Berlin-Dahlem.

Dear Mr Legge,

I arrived here yesterday from Vienna; as you have probably heard, I
recorded several symphonies there, including the Fourth and the *Eroica*
once again. In the case of the *Eroica* I was particularly pleased to do it as
that was the first record we made, which I was not very happy with even
at the time. I hope that these records will be reasonably successful.

I really regret that I am not able to accept the Philharmonia Orchestra's
invitation for 22/4. I wrote you at the time that, if you still had dates free
which coincide with mine, I would be pleased to agree to do a concert with
the Orchestra in London for this season.

Nothing definite has yet been heard in Salzburg about the collaboration
with Frau Schwarzkopf in Salzburg – which I am really counting on. These
people must finally make up their minds and so I am quite confident that
I shall receive their agreement in the next few days. I am thinking of
producing *Figaro* in German this time.

Please let me know (preferably at Clarens where I should be back from
the 20th) whether and from when the *Tristan* record will go on sale and
what the recording was like. There are several points, as I have seen with

145

hindsight, which I am not absolutely satisfied with. Have you considered whether we could record some other Wagner excerpts?

With best wishes as always, also to Frau Schwarzkopf,

Yours sincerely,
Wilhelm Furtwängler

[translated from German]   11 December 1952.
                                    Hessischer Hof, Frankfurt.

Dear Mr Legge,

The dates indicated by you of 6th or 8th May are unfortunately impossible because at that time I shall be in the middle of my tour with the Berliners, which takes us from London to Brussels, Paris, Switzerland and Germany. I would possibly have certain dates free at the beginning of February, middle of March, beginning of April, for a concert with the Philharmonia Orchestra, but not the dates you indicated.

I am very pleased about Frau Schwarzkopf's agreeing to come to Salzburg. That you felt obliged to mull over the composition of the programme for London with Elisabeth, would make me regret it all the more if the concert were not to take place. But write to me here (until 16/12) in any case whether one of the other dates would still be possible. (From 17-19/12 I shall be in the Albergo Principe di Piemonte, Turin.)

With all best wishes, also to Frau Schwarzkopf,

Yours sincerely,
Wilhelm Furtwängler

The date of 27 March was eventually agreed for the London concert with the Philharmonia. On that occasion Furtwängler conducted a Beethoven programme. (The London concert with the Berlin Philharmonic also duly took place on 22 April.) Furtwängler was due to conduct a German language version of Mozart's *Le nozze di Figaro* at the Salzburg Festival, and also three concerts in Edinburgh with the Vienna Philharmonic. A very special project was a Lieder recital at the Salzburg Festival in which Furtwängler had agreed to accompany Elisabeth Schwarzkopf in a programme of songs by Wolf.

[translated from German]   14 January 1953.
                                    Atlantic Hotel, Hamburg.

Dear Mr Legge,

I have just heard via Böhm that Elisabeth is an incomparable Susanna. Please ask her whether this time she would sing the Susanna part in the German *Figaro*. I would then have Grümmer, who will also sing Donna Anna in *Don Giovanni*, to sing the part of the Countess, and would then have a completely new exciting *Figaro*. Perhaps Elisabeth would also find it exciting; Susanna is more different from the Elvira part than the Countess, otherwise I would try to get Berger for the Susanna part. Please let me have an answer as soon as possible to this vitally important question.

As regards the Lieder programme, I must check this on the basis of the individual Lieder. At first glance, it would seem to be a full, but very beautiful programme.

I must ask you to advise me once again regarding the programmes in Edinburgh. I do not know the other programmes being played there, but would ask you to consider what I could or should possibly suggest and how these concerts should best be grouped for the Edinburgh situation. I am not completely happy about the Edinburgh engagement as I feel rather like a spare wheel on the cart and the preparation with the orchestra will have to be very rushed. It will also be very tiring directly after Salzburg. If there were to be any difficulties regarding my proposals, I would prefer not to do the concerts. Please write me a few lines about this, however, and in particular about the Susanna.

> With best wishes,
> Yours in haste,
> Wilhelm Furtwängler

[translated from German]   2 May 1953.
At present in Baden-Baden.

Dear Mr Legge,

As regards your invitation to conduct a Beethoven Cycle with the Philharmonia Orchestra in the Albert Hall in London, there are two sides to this. On the one hand, it is very advantageous for you as an impresario; the Albert Hall is big and as we saw the last time, enough people will come to provide excellent financing for such concerts. From my point of view I see the matter differently, of course. This time in fact I have had the opportunity to get to know both the Albert Hall and the Festival Hall and compare them with each other. And although initially I was not much taken with the Festival Hall, I must say that it makes it possible for us artists to have contact with the audience far more than the Albert Hall. If I did the concerts in the Albert Hall, I would indeed be meeting your interests as an impresario, but at the expense of my own interests as an artist. You will certainly understand that I do not want to do that. Conducting in London is for me more a matter of artistic prestige in view of the tax situation etc. For this very reason I am reluctant to sacrifice this prestige to any material advantages. I would therefore make the following suggestion:

I will conduct several concerts in the Festival Hall so that each individual programme can be played twice. I assume that just as many people would be able to attend the concerts as in the Albert Hall and for my part I would ask for the same fee as if it were only one evening. What do you think about that? The decisive fact is whether dates can still be found which are suitable.

> With best wishes, also to your wife,
> Yours sincerely,
> Wilhelm Furtwängler

PS. I would like to remind you that your wife wanted to suggest other pieces instead of the *Zigeunerin*. I realise, by the way, that you have not taken up my willingness to conduct your orchestra on an international tour. I assume, probably correctly, that you have made other arrangements in this respect. It was a pity that you did not attend my Paris concert, when you would have had a good opportunity to experience the qualities of the Berlin orchestra.

Best Wishes!

6 May 1953.

Dear Dr Furtwängler,

Your letter has just arrived and I have spent two hours with Miss Withers working out the simple arithmetic of your proposals and these are the conclusions we reach. In the first place, I understand quite clearly your attitude to the Royal Albert Hall and I should not myself have invited you to give your last Concert with my Orchestra in the Royal Festival Hall if I had not felt that you would be happier there.

I am sure that you too understand that any suggestions I make with regard to playing in the Royal Albert Hall in preference to the Royal Festival Hall are only because I am desirous of giving you the best possibilities for working in London, and that the only reason I have to think many times about Concerts in the Royal Festival Hall is because I, personally, cannot afford to lose money on Concerts.

If I had the money, I am sorry to say my artistic wishes would not let me hesitate, but I have not got it; I can see that ten years hence a host of artists will be living in luxurious retirement on the money I have paid them (I don't mean you), while I shall be selling matches outside the Royal Festival Hall. The trouble would be that with my smoking habits I should expend my own stock and capital as a match seller!

I am deeply touched by your noble offer to conduct a series of concerts in the Royal Festival Hall, accepting for two concerts of the same programme the same fee which we have hitherto paid you for a single concert, and I accept it here and now.

The difficulty, of course, which I have not yet had time to investigate, is getting dates from the Festival Hall – which is very heavily booked – and then fitting those dates in with your available time.

In the last two hours I have worked out three possible arrangements for a series of Beethoven programmes:

Scheme I, six double concerts with Edwino [Edwin Fischer] playing the Third, Fourth and Fifth Piano Concertos, and – I hope you will accept my suggestion because I know it would endear you to the Philharmonia Orchestra even more – Parikian [Manoug Parikian, leader of the Orchestra] playing the Violin Concerto.

148

6. *Wilhelm Furtwängler*

Programme 1 *Coriolan*, First Symphony, Fifth Symphony.
" 2 *Egmont*, Fourth Symphony, *Emperor* Concerto.
" 3 Sixth Symphony, Third Piano Concerto, Seventh Symphony.
" 4 Second Symphony, Violin Concerto, *Leonora* No. 3.
" 5 Eighth Symphony, Fourth Piano Concerto, *Eroica*.
" 6 Ninth Symphony.

Scheme II, a series of five double concerts.

Programme 1 *Egmont*, Sixth Symphony, Fifth Symphony
" 2 Fourth Symphony, First Symphony, *Leonora* No. 3.
" 3 *Coriolan*, Second Symphony, Third Symphony.
" 4 Eighth Symphony, *Grosse Fuge*, Seventh Symphony.
" 5 Ninth Symphony.

Scheme III, a series of four double concerts.

Programme 1 *Egmont*, Sixth Symphony, Fifth Symphony.
" 2 *Coriolan*, Second Symphony, Third Symphony.
" 3 Eighth Symphony, Fourth Symphony, Seventh Symphony.
" 4 First Symphony, Ninth Symphony.

There has been no time to even investigate the possibility of dates at the Royal Festival Hall, but as soon as I can get a fairly firm list I will telegraph you.

If we cannot achieve this series in the season ending April 1954 can you NOW give me dates for us to put it on in the Autumn of 1954 in whichever of the three schemes appeals best to you. Personally, I would prefer that we should do the larger scheme because I find both schemes II and III too compressed to allow you and the music to take full expansion and for the public to fully appreciate the glories you will display to them.

There remains, of course, always the possibility of doing any one of these three schemes in the Albert Hall but I would prefer to wait until we have heard about the availability of the Festival Hall before we discuss this in detail. If we *cannot* get the Festival Hall in a way which will enable us to do any one of these schemes I feel fairly confident that we could get it for a series of three double concerts in which case I would suggest that you do for us in this coming season three double concerts of miscellaneous programmes:

Programme 1 *Meistersinger* Overture, *Eine kleine Nachtmusik*, *Don Juan*, INTERVAL, Brahms First Symphony or Tchaikovsky Fourth, Fifth or Sixth Symphony.
Programme 2 Brandenburg No. 3, B minor Suite, *Tristan* Vorspiel, *Till Eulenspiegel*, INTERVAL, Beethoven Fifth Symphony or Brahms First Symphony.
Programme 3 *Fliegende Holländer* Overture, *Siegfried Idyll*, *Tannhäuser* Overture, INTERVAL, Beethoven Seventh Symphony.

6. Wilhelm Furtwängler

If we have to postpone the Beethoven series until the Autumn of 1954 it will be a good thing to excite the public's anticipation by giving them a foretaste of your Beethoven performances in this season.

Now about the tour of my Orchestra that you suggested you would be prepared to conduct. Believe me that, if when you came here in the 1920s I had dared to hope that at some future moment in my life Furtwängler himself would have expressed his willingness to conduct an Orchestra of my creation on an international tour, or even an English Orchestra, I should have had myself quietly put away into a lunatic asylum. You cannot know how grateful I am.

You are wrong in thinking that the Philharmonia Orchestra has any other definite commitments of any sort; it has, however, several invitations.

My wife and I were prepared to lose money on the first tour because we felt – on the one hand the necessity for making the Orchestra known abroad, and on the other hand the Conductor accepted no fee. I gambled on the quality of the Orchestra inducing Toscanini to come to conduct the Orchestra in London and my gamble justified my own faith in the quality of the Philharmonia Orchestra. We cannot do a second tour on such a basis.

There is a third element in the gamble of the Orchestra's tour; the Philharmonia Orchestra's only source of income is records made without soloists, and recordings once made enable us to save on preliminary rehearsals for a tour.

For a tour of the sort you have in mind – and I and the Philharmonia Orchestra would dearly like to make under your direction – you and I and the Orchestra need, first of all, a repertoire which needs no preliminary rehearsals and gives the management of the Philharmonia Orchestra an implied guarantee that the result of the tour will increase the sales of the records made with the Conductor of the tour to repay the inevitable loss.

To make such a tour the success which would reward both you and the Orchestra therefore, needs that you and the Orchestra together, shall have made a series of records – at least three complete programmes – every piece in which will attract capacity audiences which are necessary.

When we last met you stressed so strongly your obligations to both the Berlin Philharmonic and the Vienna Philharmonic Orchestras that I saw no reasonable possibility of your having recorded with the Philharmonia Orchestra sufficient works to make such a tour possible for either party.

As far as the Wolf song is concerned, my wife is at the moment in Milan and I cannot find the programme anywhere so I am disposed to say simply leave out *Zigeunerin* – there is a good deal to be said for a quiet ending.

With kindest personal regards,
Yours very sincerely,
[Walter Legge]

6. Wilhelm Furtwängler

[translated from German]   15 May 1953.
                                                        1a Meisenstrasse
                                                        Berlin-Dahlem.

Dear Mr Legge,

Many thanks for your detailed letter with the programme suggestions.
I am therefore waiting to have details of any dates which are still free
in the Festival Hall; as I shall not be conducting much at all next year
(because of my own work), I can probably adapt better to your dates than
you to mine. As regards how the proposal for the trip affects me, I was
assuming that the receipts from such trips, especially in Germany, would
be considerably greater under my baton than under the baton of any other
conductor so that the resulting 'records' which you mention are not important. It would certainly not be bad for the orchestra. I hear, by the way,
that the fee offered by the orchestra for the weeks of the festival with
Karajan are getting 'cheaper and cheaper'. Naturally I do not want to
interfere with your arrangements in that connection.

> With best wishes,
> Yours sincerely,
> Wilhelm Furtwängler

                                                          3 June 1953.

Dear Dr Furtwängler,

While I am delighted that you are conducting a concert for us on March
5th, 1954 I am extremely depressed to know from Miss Speiser [Furt-
wängler's secretary] that you can only manage one concert in the whole
season – that is really too little. I have now managed to get May 7th – will
you conduct a Concert on this date as well as March 5th? Also, would you
please reconsider the January dates – 12th and 22nd. The Orchestra will
never forgive me if I only succeed in getting you to conduct one concert in
the season.

Now I have another favour to ask of you. I gather that your Recital with
Elisabeth in Salzburg was one of the first concerts to be sold out. While you
are here for the Orchestral concert on March 5th, will you not stay and give
a recital with her on March 7th at the Royal Festival Hall? There is nothing
she and I would like so much and I am sure it would be a great success.

Since you last conducted the Orchestra I have made a few changes. I
have a wonderful new First Trombone whose presence has enormously
improved the quality of the whole section; I have two new magnificent
viola players who make up a new second desk, and four new violins, all of
whom have substantially contributed to the weight and sound of the string
section. You see I have not failed to learn the lesson you taught in your
Concert with the Berlin Philharmonic.

> With kindest personal regards,
> Yours always,
> [Walter Legge]

151

6. Wilhelm Furtwängler

[translated from German]

6 August 1953.
Pension Waldburg
Salzburg-Aigen.

Dear Mr Legge,

I have just received your telegram and would like to make the following comments: in itself, of course, I find *Götterdämmerung* beautiful, but it would only really be relevant if Flagstad could be considered for it. Whether she is still able and willing to do it, is a matter which I cannot judge at present. If Flagstad could not be considered for it, then I would definitely be in favour of first tackling *Walküre*, which is easier to cast and would be even more rewarding for the record in particular.

I must tell you, however, that unfortunately the date suggested by you is not possible as I have a concert in Zürich on 23rd March (rehearsals from 20/3), which I cannot cancel under any circumstances. Another date would have to be found.

Best wishes,
Yours sincerely,
Wilhelm Furtwängler

16 October 1953.

Dear Dr Furtwängler,

Mr Legge, who is away, has asked me to write and tell you how delighted he is that you have agreed to do the recital with Madame Schwarzkopf and Mr Dietrich Fischer-Dieskau on May 7th at the Royal Festival Hall, and the orchestral concert on 12th March with the Philharmonia Orchestra at the Royal Festival Hall.

The programmes you will remember – which you have already accepted and which we have now printed, are:-

March 5th

Beethoven	–	Overture: *Coriolan*.
Beethoven	–	Symphony No. 8 in F.
Beethoven	–	Overture: *Leonora* No. 3.
Beethoven	–	Symphony No. 5 in C minor.

March 12th

Wagner	–	*Die Meistersinger* – Overture.
Wagner	–	*Siegfried Idyll*.
Strauss	–	*Till Eulenspiegel*.
Brahms	–	Symphony No. 2.

We will write to you again about these concerts in a week or two.

With best wishes,
Yours sincerely,
PHILHARMONIA LTD.

JANE WITHERS, Managing Director

6. Wilhelm Furtwängler

[translated from German]

25 October 1953.
Pensione Astoria
8 Via Varese, Rome.

Dear Mr Legge,

It is not correct that I accepted the programme of which you informed me via Miss Withers in a letter dated 16/10; this must be due to an error on your part. I find a programmme in which the *Leonora* No. 3 and Beethoven's Fifth Symphony are performed to be lacking in taste. You cannot present two such thrillers in succession, apart from the fact that I do not think it is necessary. If you want to do a Beethoven Evening, the programme could be something like the following:

First Programme:

> Eighth Symphony or Fourth Symphony
> *Leonora* No. 2
> ———
> Fifth Symphony

or:

> *Coriolanus* Overture
> Fourth Symphony
> ———
> Fifth Symphony.

How about the following programme:

> Haydn: Symphony in D Major
> Schubert's *Unfinished*
> ———
> Beethoven: Fifth Symphony

or:

> Handel: Concerto grosso
> Beethoven: Eighth Symphony
> ———
> Beethoven: Fifth Symphony

The second programme is also extremely loud. Would it not be better to have the following?

> Overture (eg. *Coriolanus* or Gluck)
> Brahms: Second Symphony
> ———
> Prelude to *Tristan und Isolde*
> Prelude to *Meistersinger*

As regards the programme for the Lieder Recital, I would ask you to send me precise suggestions, as to how you and the two singers see it and whether it would not be better to engage a different 'genuine' pianist.

I shall be in Rome until 27th November.

153

With best wishes,
Yours sincerely,
Wilhelm Furtwängler

9 November 1953.

Dear Dr Furtwängler,

Many thanks for your kind letter which I have just got because I have only been back in London for an hour.

As we agreed when I last saw you in Clarens, you must really do an all Beethoven concert, since you do so little in London.

I am inclined to agree with you about piling Beethoven Five on *Leonora* No. 3, for March 5th; how would it be with Beethoven Eight, *Leonora* No. 3 and Beethoven Seven? As far as I can remember, you have never done Beethoven Eight in London and you have certainly done the Seventh Symphony less than the Fifth Symphony.

About the second programme for March 12th, I still think the one we agreed to in Clarens is preferable to your last suggestion which contains three overtures:– *Coriolan* or Gluck, *Tristan* and *Meistersinger*. Besides, you did *Tristan* when you were last here with the Berliner.

If you feel you must change the programme, then let us put in something instead of *Eulenspiegels*, for example, the Schubert *Unvollendete*; the only disadvantage I see in this is that the basic tempo of the whole programme is rather slow.

As an alternative, how would you like:-

Meistersinger Overture.
Bartók *Concerto for Orchestra.*
Brahms Second Symphony.

or it might be better this way round:-

Meistersinger Overture.
Brahms Second Symphony.
Siegfried Idyll.
Bartók *Concerto for Orchestra.*

As far as the Lieder programme is concerned, I am waiting for Fischer-Dieskau's final suggestions, but I should not think of having any other pianist.

I think I had better announce it in this way.

Liederabend.

Dr WILHELM FURTWÄNGLER

Stimmbänder: Elisabeth Schwarzkopf
Dietrich Fischer-Dieskau.

STEINWAY FLÜGEL

Yours very sincerely,
[Walter Legge]

[translated from German]   29 November 1953.
                                                                      Clarens.

Dear Mr Legge,

I gather that the *Lieder eines fahrenden Gesellen* with Fischer-Dieskau, which we recorded, have still not been released. As I am doing *Kindertoten-lieder* with Fischer-Dieskau in Berlin in the next few days, it would seem to be a good idea to record this as well – instead of the *Amfortasmonolog* – if there is time. What to you think?

From: 2-10/12 I shall be at: 1a Meisenstrasse, Berlin-Dahlem, from 11-16: at 2 Schaufflergasse, Vienna 1, after which I shall be in Clarens.

With best wishes,
Yours sincerely,
Wilhelm Furtwängler

3 December 1953.

Dear Dr Furtwängler,

Many thanks for your two letters. I had already wired Fischer-Dieskau, suggesting that he should do the Second Mahler Cycle with you instead of the *Amfortasmonolog*, before I received your second letter.

Both my wife and I realise, fully appreciate and sympathise with your point of view about Salzburg. We were both deeply touched that you wanted her to sing *Freischütz* with you. You will remember that, for the last four years, I have been suggesting to you that you should do this opera at La Scala with her.

You know that neither she nor I have ever put the money question before the artistic question. We have, as you know, spent every penny we have earned in the last six years in the effort to make one first class orchestra in Britain, and Elisabeth has frequently accepted an engagement which she would rather not do to enable us to put on an orchestral concert where we were bound to lose money.

The problem in Salzburg is entirely one of prestige. Salzburg, as we are reliably informed, has paid certain Italian artists $500 a performance. It has rested in the hands of the Direction of the Salzburg Festival whose first duty, it would seem to me, to be to make you, as their Principal Conductor, happy; that they should secure for you the artists you want. If they do not consider Schwarzkopf sufficiently important to pay her the same fees as they do Italian artists, drawn into the ensemble, the reflection is not upon my wife or her artistic integrity, but upon the method of thinking of the Salzburgers.

There is another point of view which you no doubt find it difficult to understand – but each singer has to bear in mind; the greatest Conductors – you and others – are at the climax of their earning capacity in their

155

sixties, or later. The earning period of a singer is not only pathetically short, but is dependent upon the amount of rest taken in one year. The gentlemen in Salzburg have allowed three weeks to pass without making a counter proposition and, since Elisabeth could only deduce from this that they are not willing to meet your artistic wishes or her really modest request, she has, with a heavy heart, been compelled to take one or two other engagements for recitals at other Festivals.

We shall both always be grateful to you for the wonderful performance that she gave in Salzburg last year, under your direction, and for your generosity in making music with her in your joint recital, and it is our mutual hope that you will long make music together. She knows what she learns from you and the stimulus she has from working with you, so I beg you not to allow the question of Salzburg to interfere with the quite independent harmony of the London recital which is announced and already arousing the greatest interest.

I saw Fischer-Dieskau in Berlin, and we are now proposing the following programme:

Dichterliebe.
Frauenliebe und Leben.

Interval.

Fifteen duets (all very small).
About 17 minutes music, and all by Schumann.

With kindest personal regards,
Yours always,
[Walter Legge]

PS. It is getting more and more difficult to secure dates at the Royal Festival Hall and so I shall be grateful if you will let me know what period you may be free in the season 1954/1955 for four or five concerts with the Philharmonia Orchestra.

[translated from German] 12 January 1954.
Ebersteinburg Sanatorium
Baden-Baden.

Dear Mr Legge,

I have been in the Ebersteinburg Sanatorium in Baden-Baden for some days. I have to undergo a course of treatment which became necessary as a consequence of American antibiotics which were given to me – during my last bout of influenza in particular – and which cannot be got rid of in any other way. Consequently I had to cancel a tour with the Berlin Philharmonic and a series of other concerts (including one with my own Symphony) and am also unable to undertake the trip to Portugal with the Vienna Philharmonic which was scheduled for the second half of February.

In addition, the doctor here is putting a big question mark over the first concert in London which takes place immediately afterwards, and as I am a conscientious creature, I would ask you to allow me to conduct only the second concert taking place on 12th March, but to cancel the first concert and the proposed Lieder recital. It is all rather uncertain at present and I would not like either to have to make difficulties for you at the last moment, nor on the other hand to act against the advice of the doctor into whose care I have entrusted myself. I would therefore ask you to regard it as a case of *force majeure* and not take it amiss if I conduct only the one concert on 12th March instead of two, or rather three.

In that event I would, of course, like to change the programme: either to do the scheduled Beethoven evening or a mixed programme with great classical works. Perhaps you would write to me here and tell me what you think about it.

> I remain with very best wishes,
> Yours sincerely,
> Wilhelm Furtwängler

14.1.54

FURTWANGLER VILLA L'EMPEREUR CLARENS MONTREUX SWITZERLAND

TICKET OFFICES AND PUBLIC DEMANDING IMMEDIATE PUBLICATION YOUR PROGRAMMES FOR MARCH STOP PLEASE CABLE ACCEPTANCE TO FOLLOWING MARCH FIVE BEETHOVEN EIGHTH OR FOURTH LEONORA THREE BEETHOVEN SEVENTH MARCH TWELVE MEISTERSINGER VORSPIEL SIEGFRIED IDYLL UNVOLLENDETE PAUSE BRAHMS SECOND STOP LIEDER RECITAL ALL SCHUMANN DICHTERLIEBE FRAUENLIEBE UND LEBEN SELECTION FROM SIE UND ER

GREETINGS WALTER LEGGE

18 January 1954.

Dear Dr Furtwängler,

I am deeply sorry to hear from your letter, which has just arrived, of your unfortunate state of health and particularly that you will have to be so long in the Sanatorium.

For a man of your enormous physical and intellectual energy it must be an intolerable bore to be imprisoned in Baden-Baden, the home of the Zukunftsmusiker of your friend Strobel!

I regret your illness too because it will deprive my Orchestra of the stimulation of playing two Concerts with you; Elisabeth and Fischer-Dieskau, in what would have been an unforgettable Concert; and the London public of three Furtwängler Concerts – now reduced to only one.

Nevertheless, I accept your Doctor's decision and declare myself grateful for the small mercy of one Concert.

As far as the programme is concerned:-

Beethoven	–	Symphony No. 4 in B flat.
Beethoven	–	*Leonora* Overture No. 2.

Interval

Beethoven	–	Symphony No. 5 in C minor.

I am delighted with your proposal and we are announcing it immediately.
With all good wishes for a speedy recovery,

> As always,
> Yours,
> [Walter Legge]

Strobel was a well-known local figure who championed *avant-garde* music.

[translated from German]

2 February 1954.

6613 EBERSTEINBURG UEB BADENBADEN
LEGGE ORGANOL HESDO LONDON

SUGGEST ON DOCTOR'S ORDERS ONLY CONDUCTING 2ND
CONCERT. LETTER ON WAY PROGRAMME SUGGESTIONS
BEETHOVEN 4TH SYMPHONY 2ND LEONORA OVERTURE 5TH
SYMPHONY

GREETINGS FURTWANGLER

[translated from German]

7 February 1954.

Dear Mr Legge,

As my doctor has told me just recently that he can discharge me as early as 1st March, I have arranged with the Vienna Philharmonic to do some recording during that period – which I am writing to tell you about now to avoid any misunderstanding. If the doctor had given me his opinion earlier, I would not, of course, have cancelled the concerts in London; but after cancelling it would probably be unwise to revert to them now. I also assume that you made other arrangements some time ago.

I should be grateful if you would confirm the rehearsals for the concert on 12th March. One on the morning of the concert, the two others on the two preceding days?

> With best wishes, also to Elisabeth
> Yours sincerely,
> Wilhelm Furtwängler

PS. Incidentally, many thanks to you both for your kind birthday greetings.

6. Wilhelm Furtwängler

They are constantly telling jokes about you here, about your tremendous repertoire; I hope to have new ones when I see you next.

17.2.54

FURTWANGLER BADEN-BADEN SANATORIUM EBERSTEINBURG

TO GIVE YOU TWO REHEARSALS FESTIVAL HALL HAVE SIGNED CONTRACTS FOR REHEARSALS MARCH 11 9.30 HMV STUDIO AND 2.30 FESTIVAL HALL STOP GENERALPROBE MORNING OF CONCERT FESTIVAL HALL STOP UNFORTUNATELY ORCHESTRA IN CAMBRIDGE 8.9.10. STOP PLEASE WIRE ACCEPTANCE

GRUSSE WALTER LEGGE

[translated from German]

19 February 1954.

Dear Mr Legge,

I agree with the arrangements you have made for the rehearsals and will be in London in good time. Would it be possible, however, to change the second rehearsal on 11th March from 2.30 to 3.00.

With best wishes,
Yours sincerely,
Wilhelm Furtwängler

23 February 1954.

Dear Dr Furtwängler,

Your letter addressed to Mr Legge, dated February 19th, has arrived whilst he is abroad. However, I know he will wish me to thank you for your cooperation in agreeing to the two extra rehearsals being held on the 11th March which, as Mr Legge explained, was planned in order to give you two rehearsals at the Royal Festival Hall.

I am very sorry to have to tell you that it is not possible to change the time of the second rehearsal because the Festival Hall have to re-arrange their platform and prepare for another engagement to commence very early in the evening.

The Orchestra is looking forward immensely to the Concert with you, as we all are.

I do sincerely hope that you are now feeling very much better and that you will very soon be restored completely to full health.

Yours sincerely,
PHILHARMONIA CONCERT SOCIETY
Jane Withers

The concert on 12 March duly took place. This was to be Furtwängler's last appearance in London.

6. Wilhelm Furtwängler

[translated from German]
5 April 1954.
1a Meisenstrasse
Berlin-Dahlem.

Dear Mrs [sic] Withers,

Unfortunately I am unable to come to London on 5th December, as I am not conducting at all until the end of this year (October, November, December).

The concert on 28th January 1955 would appear to be difficult for me as I am to play with the Berlin Philharmonic in London on 18th and 20th January. Will the Philharmonia Orchestra still be interested in me if I have already appeared twice shortly beforehand? Perhaps another date could be found for this?

> With best wishes,
> Yours sincerely,
> Wilhelm Furtwängler

13 April 1954.

Dear Dr Furtwängler,

Miss Withers has shown me your letter of the 5th April.

I had hoped that, after your last London concert, the recollection of the public's warmth and the Orchestra's playing would have tempted you away from your voluntary retirement in the three last months of the year.

I am sure that you are right, both in your own and our interests, not to wish to conduct on the 28th January – so quickly after two concerts with the Berlin Orchestra. I think it is also kinder to the Berlin Philharmonic that you should not do a concert with the Philharmonia Orchestra so close to theirs because, if I know my Orchestra, they would burst themselves to show you and the public how good they are.

Of course we are interested in finding other dates, and I have asked Miss Withers, as soon as she has heard from you about your available periods, to try and change the December 5th date for the one which suits you, which you will, by now, know because of my telegram.

> With kindest regards,
> Yours sincerely,
> [Walter Legge]

P.S. I have two new stories for you.

13 April 1954.

FURTWANGLER VILLA L'EMPEREUR CLARENS MONTREUX SWITZERLAND

MUST SIGN CONTRACT FESTIVAL HALL SO PLEASE CABLE

160

6. *Wilhelm Furtwängler*

ALTERNATIVE DATES TO DECEMBER 5 AND JANUARY 28 AND I
WILL ENDEAVOUR TO GET HALL ON DATE WHICH SUITS YOU

WALTER LEGGE

[translated from German]

21 April 1954.

Dear Miss Withers,

You asked me about a possible tour with the Philharmonia Orchestra. I must confess that I would be delighted to appear with this excellent orchestra in some of the capitals of Europe, eg. Paris, Brussels, Frankfurt, Zürich and Milan. I do not know whether or when the orchestra would be able to undertake such a tour. As far as I am concerned it would have to be in the period after the middle of April 1955 as only then do I arrive back from America.

I will let you know in the next few days about the dates which I would like to suggest for London.

> I remain, with best wishes,
> Yours sincerely,
> Wilhelm Furtwängler

PS. I would suggest Walter Schulthess, who lives in Switzerland and is very reliable, as organiser for such a tour.

9 June 1954.

Dear Dr Furtwängler,

Thank you for your charming letter. I am delighted that you will do the Concert on the 18th April and, since you have been so kind in accepting the date so quickly, I will gladly wait 14 days before we finalise the programme.

I rather like the idea of an all Brahms programme and, if you decide to do that, I would only suggest that it should be:-

> *Haydn* Variations.
> Second Symphony.
>   Interval
> First Symphony.

or, as an alternative, you might remember that you have not done a Tchaikovsky Symphony in London for a very long time, so how does the idea of —

> Weber   *Freischütz* Overture.
> Schumann   First Symphony.
>   Interval
> Tchaikovsky   Sixth Symphony.

appeal to you? Or, to make the Orchestra love you even more than they

161

already do (if that is possible!), instead of the Schumann Symphony, a Mozart concerto with Parikian as soloist. Anyway, I look forward to hearing from you in the next two or three weeks.

Unfortunately there is no hope of me coming to Clarens because I shall be stuck in Milan from the 12th to the 30th of this month, recording Leoncavallo and Verdi. I can think of many more agreeable ways of spending the month of June than grilling in the heat and dust of Milan.

Incidentally, if you are doing any Wagner Operas or Broadcasts this winter I do beg of you and advise you to engage Hotter; he has just been here for ten days' recording and, in all the 17 or 18 years I have known him, he has never been in such wonderful form. The voice is fresher than ever and even more beautiful.

London is in the middle of a Ring Cycle. As [Fritz] Stiedry is conducting, I have spared myself the experience but, to all accounts, the singers they have engaged are almost uniformly disappointing, particularly Beirer and Frantz.

Since I try to keep my letters free of indecent jokes, I have only one mild story – but this is a true one – it has been announced in the English and French papers that Markevitch is conducting *The Ring* at Bayreuth in place of Clemens Krauss.

> With kindest regards,
> Yours always,
> [Walter Legge]

> 20 June 1954.
> Clarens.

Dear Mr Legge,

In order to have a Brahms-Evening without soloists, only one programme is possible, and that is the following:

Haydn Variations
Third Symphony

————

First or Second Symphony

You probably did not put on the Third because it is less effective outwardly; the Second and the Third on one evening seems to me to be too much. The following appears to me to be a possibility:

Weber Overture *Der Freischütz*
Schumann Fourth Symphony

————

Tchaikovsky or Brahms.

I will write to you shortly about the two London concerts with the Berlin Philharmonic Orchestra.

> Yours sincerely,
> Dr Wilhelm Furtwängler

6. Wilhelm Furtwängler

5 July 1954.

Dear Dr Furtwängler,

I want to tell you how grateful I am for your kindness in at long last sending me an autographed photograph. I assure you it will have an honoured place in my Office and be the envy of all my colleagues and visitors.

As far as the programmes are concerned, the reason I avoided the Third Symphony is because I dislike it personally. This is no criticism of Brahms – merely a criticism of my own blind spot on this particular matter and, since I shall certainly be at the Concert, I would prefer to hear you conduct something I love rather than something I do not love. However, if it would make you happy to do it, by all means keep it in.

The second programme I like a lot, apart from the Schumann Fourth Symphony, which has been done rather too often in London recently, and it seems an awful waste of your genius to do a Tchaikovsky Symphony. Since you give so few concerts with my Orchestra I would prefer that you do the music which lies closest to your heart.

How do you feel about:-

Weber *Der Freischütz* Overture.
Wagner *Siegfried Idyll.*
Brahms *Haydn* Variations.
Interval
Beethoven Symphony No. 7.

Will you please let me know about this as soon as you can, so that we can go to print.

With kindest regards,
Yours always,
[Walter Legge]

P.S. What is your latest information about Krips's departure from the LSO?

27 September 1954.

Dear Dr Furtwängler,

I am still waiting to hear from you about the programme for the concert with my Orchestra on April 18th.

Since we last talked I have had another idea in which I would dearly like to interest you – it is this; that you should give four Brahms concerts in two pairs on successive days, the programmes to be:-

First pair of concerts.

Brahms *Haydn* Variations.
Symphony No. 2.
Interval

Symphony No. 1.

and on the next day:-

Brahms: *Haydn* Variations.
Piano Concerto in D Minor (with Edwin Fischer or Géza Anda).
Interval
Symphony No. 1.

Second pair of concerts.

Brahms: *Academic Festival Overture.*
Symphony No. 3.
Interval
Symphony No. 4.

and on the next day:-

Brahms: *Academic Festival Overture.*
B flat Concerto (with Edwin Fischer or Géza Anda).
Interval
Symphony No. 4.

For each pair of concerts you would have three rehearsals for the first concert and a rehearsal for the concerto on the morning of the second concert.

Would you let me know when in the season 1955/56 – preferably after 10th February, 1956 – you would give us a week or, alternatively, two periods of three days; in the latter case not too far apart because I want the impact of your performance of the major orchestral works of Brahms to be concentrated into the shortest convenient period.

That being so, I would like to leave the Brahms out of the programme for April 18th and for this date I would suggest:-

Weber – *Freischütz* Overture.
Wagner – *Siegfried Idyll.*
Strauss – *Don Juan.*
Interval
Beethoven – *Eroica.*

I am particularly keen to do the *Eroica* because you have never done it with the Philharmonia Orchestra.

We are waiting to go to press with our prospectus and so I shall be very grateful if you will let me have your agreement on this programme by return.

> With best wishes,
> Yours sincerely,
> [Walter Legge]

6. Wilhelm Furtwängler

[translated from German]

4 November 1954.

Dear Mr Legge,

Your programme with the *Eroica* is quite nice, but I am not very happy always to be doing Wagner and Strauss. How would it be if I were to do the *Manfred* Overture and the Schumann Fourth Symphony as well as the *Eroica*? That would certainly be more original and something not everyone can do. The four Brahms programmes are fine.

I shall be in Switzerland now until the end of the year. Will you be coming this way some time?

> With best wishes,
> Yours sincerely,
> Wilhelm Furtwängler

P.S. As a specialist in singers have you any ideas as to whom I could have as a leading lady in *Magic Flute* in Salzburg?

Wilhelm Furtwängler [undated]
Born Berlin 25 January 1886 –
died Baden-Baden 30 November 1954

The death of Wilhelm Furtwängler has robbed the world of the last great romantic conductor. The dynasty of which he was the last heir began with Wagner and the great line, in its span of more than a century, was sustained by Hans von Bülow, Felix Mottl, Arthur Nikisch and finally Wilhelm Furtwängler, all names which will be honoured as long as nineteenth-century German music holds its place in the repertoire and in musical history.

The direct links with this tradition were Mottl who first engaged the young Furtwängler on the musical staff of the Munich Opera, and Nikisch from whom Furtwängler inherited the directorship of the Berlin Philharmonic Orchestra at the unusually early age of 36.

There are only two real schools of conducting. The one is the daily grind of the man-of-all-work in the opera house who has to drum the notes, the expression and the requisite style into the heads of singers, conduct the chorus and orchestra behind the scenes, hold the stage together from the prompter's box and bring the curtain up and down on cues: the other is the less exciting but still hard school of playing in an orchestra. Furtwängler went through the harder school. The man we were proud to honour and from whom all our generation has learned went through the operatic mill in Munich and Zürich – where one of his first public appearances was conducting *The Merry Widow* without rehearsal. To the end of his career the operatic training remained fresh in him: he called his singers to his dressing room between the acts of even a repeat operatic performance and sat at the piano to rehearse details of balance, rhythm, or nuance.

An orchestra, chorus, instrumentalist or singer meeting a conductor for

165

the first time, gives, according to his reputation: then the factor of the conductor's will starts to function. It was one of Furtwängler's most impressive characteristics that standing before an orchestra for the first time, his personality and will instantaneously hypnotised them into producing from the first beat the character of sound – the rich, sonorous bass, the intense glowing warmth that were the hallmarks of his unforgettable personal sound. In the eight years I worked with him there were opportunities enough to observe this power, but it was never more evident than at his first meeting with the Philharmonia Orchestra on Good Friday, 1948. We were together to record the closing scene from *Götterdämmerung* with Kirsten Flagstad. Few of that young orchestra had seen let alone had to play that unconventional quivering beat, but from the first moment there came from the consort of young British musicians the unmistakable Furtwängler sound. Such was his power of communication.

To the inexperienced eye it was a miracle that his beat, which seemed indecision made manifest, should have had the coordinating power essential to the conductor's job. On the one hand its very indecision commanded the greatest attention and concentration from the musicians before him and produced in the opening chords of a Beethoven or Brahms symphony an extraordinary spontaneous combustion of pent-up will from the orchestra. On the other, its lack of definition in lyrical passages avoided the hard drawn line which is the antithesis of the flexible, sensuous contours which were for him part of the essence of music.

Unconsciously he played a vital part in forming the present standards of orchestral playing in London. His visits to London around 1930 with the Vienna Philharmonic and Berlin Philharmonic Orchestras prepared the way for the foundation of the BBC Symphony Orchestra and later the London Philharmonic Orchestra. In the last six years of his life he made music with the Philharmonia Orchestra in London and in 1954 at the Lucerne Festival. These concerts endeared him to every member of the orchestra and they are already part of the texture of the Philharmonia tradition. The recordings he made with the Philharmonia, particularly the complete *Tristan und Isolde* are incomparable testimony to his greatness.

There are and will be other great conductors but there is none and will be no one with those magical qualities which will ever remind us of Wilhelm Furtwängler.

7

Post-War EMI Affiliations

I. HERBERT VON KARAJAN

Immediately after the war Walter Legge made visits to several European centres in order to find new artists for EMI and to renew contacts with established performers. In Vienna he sought out Herbert von Karajan, who had found accommodation in the city but was forbidden to conduct in public. It was Legge who re-established the conductor's career by arranging for him to conduct recordings with the Vienna Philharmonic, and this led to a close artistic partnership between the two men which lasted until 1960.

*

Although the following letter has no date, there are several references which suggest the approximate period. Karajan's reference to 'the whole mess' is probably an allusion to the fact that after having been prematurely de-Nazified by the Americans in 1945 and officially cleared by the Austrian authorities in March 1946, the matter was held up and then still further delayed by French intervention in March 1947, so it was not until August 1947 that Karajan was finally cleared. Furtwängler had evaded the process by accepting conducting engagements in Italy, which was beyond the four-power jurisdiction, but as his letter indicates, Karajan was not keen to follow suit. Nevertheless, Karajan had made his first recordings in Vienna during October 1946 (including Beethoven's Eighth Symphony), and he was due to record Beethoven's Ninth Symphony in the following November and December. Walter Schulthess was a highly-regarded Swiss musical agent. Turicaphon was the EMI-affiliated Swiss company which Legge had to use in order to secure a record contract for Karajan. Karajan's letters are reproduced here in their original somewhat eccentric English.

[undated – probably mid-1947]

Dear Walter,

Your letter was exactly what I expected it to be the right word in the right moment and the understanding help of my best friend – thank you!

And I promise you to pull myself together and try to forget about the whole mess. –

In any case I shall see you in Vienna. If you happen to pass by car or train through St Anton I would come with you. If not let me know the exact date of your arrival.

I was thinking very much of our forthcoming work in autumn and

167

specially of the Ninth Beethoven. We have to talk very much about it. I spent the last three weeks on this work and what I find now is the great difficulty of bringing the enormous conception of the work into the close and condense[d] form in which it is written. It was a great experience with the Eighth under your control to get the whole content into its really classical form. But what with the Ninth. For instance did you notice that in comparison with the Eighth nearly all metronomes are too fast in the first and third movement and too slow in the last to get out the enormous *Steigerung* which reaches to the stars. And all the slight tempo modifications which are essential, in short to get the fullest richdom of fantasy just in the purest form. That needs an utmost degree of *Selbstzucht*. In any case it is *very* important for me that you make it possible to bring with you the best two existing recordings that we get afterwards a close conception of what we want and I can work quietly in the summer on it.

A long and serious task it is and I feel that I must bring *mein inneres Beethovensbild* up to the present form in which I am feeling and thinking of music and the Ninth is probably the key to the other sinfonies after the experience on the Eighth. And *I need all your help* for it.

Speaking of more practical things of course, it would be delightful to go to Italy but I fear at the moment I would not get the visa and on the other hand it is dangerous to come at the present moment in contact with this country where everything is so easy and smooth it might induce oneself of staying there and work and I feel it would not be the right place to restart a career. I am certain I will conduct here in autumn but then I must start in the right place possibly London. Do you still have in mind a Beethoven cycle which would be just the right thing?

This all we can discuss in Vienna also the matter of the agent did you speak to Schulthess about it now that I see the end coming somebody must plan and arrange things for me.

Please let me know as soon as possible your definite plans to St Anton. If you come to Vienna please bring with you some of the Turicaphon test records I need them badly for working.

My dear don't overwork yourself we need our nerves on important things.

Look after yourself and thank you once more.

> Always yours,
> Herbert

> 1 September 1947.

My dear Walter,

Thinking of Sibelius recording I was telling you I would like to do the Seventh because the work is the one which comes nearest to me. But on the other hand we should decide whether from the point of recording the Fifth is not the better one, the instrumentation being more clear whereas the Seventh is rather thick and to compare to Brahms which generally does not so well record itself. I think it would be good to hear both works on records and then decide.

About my London concerts, please talk to Mr [*sic*: in fact Mrs] Ingpen about a possible soloist in the first concert, if there is a good one available.

About Salzburg plans please be very cautious not letting people know too much about the structure of the management.

If you see Hilbert don't forget to point out to him the risk he takes if the *Falstaff* does not materialise.

It was very nice of you both to have come to Anton in spite of the difficulties and I was very glad to have seen that the work with Schulthess will be very good, I was very impressed by his clear way of seeing things.

The most difficult thing to settle will be to get Strauss's permission for the *Danae* and to avoid my interference from the other side, he must be convinced that next year the work must come off in the planned way.

If you talk to him make it clear to him will you, but possibly after the *Salome* conductor has left.

I am very much looking forward to the recordings.

I shall be a week or so sooner in Vienna to prepare the choir. If you come we have to decide what number of singers we shall use.

Will you let me know the places where one can reach you in case something important happens.

Anita sends you her love and hopes that the journey back to Switzerland was not too tiring for you.

You would do me a great favour if you could get me in London an *abonnement* on the *British Motor*, if it can't be sent to a civilian in Austria please let it be on the name of Peter Schnabel.

Thanks for everything and let me have the news of the opera's performance in London.

> Love,
> Yours,
> Herbert

It was to be some four years before Karajan recorded his first Sibelius symphony, the Fifth. Karajan made his concert début with the Philharmonia in April 1948, and the soloist was Dinu Lipatti, who played the Schumann Concerto (they also made their famous recording of the work at this time). Ingpen & Williams were London concert agents. The *Salome* conductor referred to was Clemens Krauss: he directed the first performance of Strauss's *Die Liebe der Danae* at the 1952 Salzburg Festival.

*

In October 1947 Karajan recorded Brahms's *Ein deutsches Requiem* in Vienna. Before the sessions he and Legge had to agree the most appropriate breaks in the music for the 20-sided 78rpm set.

20 September 1947.

My dear Walter,

After three more days carefully timing I come to the conclusion that the *only* possible *artistic* way of dividing the Requiem is in linking the numbers 1, 2, 3 and 5, 6, 7 together. I give you now the full details. 1. part[itur] till C, 2. part to F, 3. part to C of number II, 4. part to G, 5. part to eighth bar after 6, 6. part to 16 bars after B, inf III. 7. part to 6 bars before F, 8. part to end of III.

The reasons are: one could with some hurrying come in the first part to one bar before D and with the second reach the end, but: you lose the tranquillity which is so important to establish right in the beginning and still more important you must hurry the last big expansion in the end of I and most dangerous you get the final chord right at the inner end of disc. As for number II my suggestion gives the 'so seid nun geduldig' the opening of the disc whereas if you have to divide number II 'selbständig' you have to cut this wonderful intermezzo in two pieces. Furthermore you would have to cut right at the beginning of the fugue which would be very bad because the anticipation of the theme in 'Aber des Herrn Wort' must lead through in the fugue without stopping which happens in my scheme. And more I have plenty of time in the *tranquillo* of the fugue which is so vital to bring this part to an end in peace. There too I avoid the final chord on the end of disc. In number III I can reach quite comfortably the part 'Nun Herr' and get the whole following complex 'eigner geistigen Einheit' in one piece whereas with normal cut you have to divide before 'Ich Hoffe' which is terrible.

Now for the second half: 9. part is number IV, 10 part to O of number V, 11. part to A of number VI, 12. part to E, 13. part to L, 14. part to 6 bars before B of VII, 15. part to 2 bars before Doppelstrich and 16. part to end.

In a normal cutting the number V must be divided in two rather shortish parts number VI would again cut right at the beginning of the fugue which would have to be played at an incredible speed and the whole majesty of the piece would have gone. Number VII *can't* be played in two parts so you have to cut in three and if you would cut it so that the wonderful middle part 'Ja der Geist' comes for itself as it does my scheme, the first part would be ridiculously short. Further you will notice that in my propositions no great *fortissimo* comes at the end of a disc with the exception of end of III but this is so timed that it comes only to about four inches so there is enough margin.

And chief thing of all, every idea is either carried to the end or in case it is part of a greater complex this is introduced and established before the cut comes. Also in normal cutting you come to 17 part instead of 16. And I know quite a lot of conductors who would vouch for the first because this gives them extra income without work.

But seriously think it over and you will agree with me that it is worth breaking with a tradition in this case for the benefit of a highly artistic thing, because its timing is so that in the important parts I never need to be nervous whether I can reach my time because there is in every record a margin of about 10-15 seconds. And if this work sounds hurried everything is spoiled.

Now think about it quietly and we talk in Vienna. The first choir rehearsal will be on 16. I am deadly frightened what will come out of this ensemble. Perhaps you can arrange to be there, already.

Be sure to have petrol because the current frequency will be according to the shortage of water terribly low.

Love your
Herbert

In February 1953 Karajan conducted four performances of Orff's *Trionfi* at La Scala, Milan.

[translated from German] 12 April 1952.
St Anton.
Dear Walter,

Many thanks for both your telegrams. I would be happy to meet Ashton and Margot Fonteyn at your place. I do not know if it would not be better if we first discuss the matter in principle without Orff. Possibly I will still meet him now in Munich and will in that case ask him to meet Ashton in Milan on the day of our concert, provided the question of the stage design has been cleared up etc.

I do not know what grumbles Horowitz still has regarding the programme: we have already altered it once. I am very grateful to Elisabeth for her suggestion, but I do not regard this combination favourably because the programme becomes much too long if this is done. You know I have a particular aversion to programmes which consist of three numbers before the interval, since inevitably one of the programme items is affected as a result.

A soloist of Elisabeth's calibre would have to appear with a much longer contribution after the first introductory piece and before the break and the *Don Juan* would then of necessity have to be dropped, and that is not really practicable, when the main purpose of the concert is to present the orchestra. I therefore think we would do better to leave everything as it now is.

Another point which is very irritating is that I have discovered through a detailed study of the D major Divertimento that in the outer movements it comes off significantly worse by comparison with the B major Divertimento which we once tried to record. The material of both these movements is noticeably weak compared with the latter, above all in melodic invention and what is more the two movements in the B major Divertimento, especially with the very charming violin solo at the end also affords the orchestra much greater potential. Since we are only talking about changing one number which in the event of the programme having

171

already been printed could be said to be due to a printing error, I would
suggest that we alter both the recording and the concert performance of
this latter work.

Perhaps I will be in Munich in the next few days as I must speak to
Preetorius and Reinking. I would in that case wire you my telephone
number. Vedder cables me that RIAS is possibly ready to pay the air fare.
I have already submitted the programme. If all this comes off it would be
a great relief for us.

Happy Easter, all my affection.

Yours,
Herbert v. Karajan

The pianist Vladimir Horowitz was favourably disposed to Karajan, but the
mooted concert did not materialise. Emil Preetorius was a renowned stage designer at Bayreuth in the inter-war period, and he had just worked with Karajan
on a production of Beethoven's *Fidelio* at La Scala. Wilhelm Reinking was also a
stage designer who had worked at Salzburg and Vienna. Rudolf Vedder was
Karajan's agent between 1938 and 1942, and still undertook some work for him in
the post-war period.

*

Celebrations to mark the bicentenary of Mozart's birth took place in 1956.

7 January 1954.

My dear Herbert,

I have been thinking over the best way in which you and the Philharmonia can profit from the Mozart Year.

I am afraid that the plan for an operatic tour is, on the one hand difficult
to realise because of the expense that would be involved in initial costs to
cover fees to artists of the quality you want, and because such a tour would
be a thing that happened only once without the possible chance of repeti-
tion. We are both at an age when we must do only those things which can
be profitably repeated or which will give us – over a long period – returns
for our initial expense, thought, energy and work.

I have an alternative suggestion which I believe will help us both and
give us the best dividends. You will remember that in Rome I suggested
that it would be economically wise for you to record all the Mozart
symphonies with the Philharmonia. Without a word from me Soria has
written a particular request that in view of the Mozart year for the Angel
mark 'it is essential Karajan should record all the Mozart symphonies and
that they should be ready by the early Autumn of 1955'.

In two or three concentrated periods I suggest we record all the symphonies and any other major works we need for a series of Concerts.

I would suggest that in January or February of 1956 we give the first of
12 Mozart Concerts in London including concertos and all major works –

these we could quickly agree upon together – the whole idea of the plan on the following lines taking as a basis for discussion the first week in February as the starting point.

Monday/Tuesday two sessions each day, and Wednesday one session – recording with large orchestra necessary repertoire. Not Mozart.
Wednesday one rehearsal. Thursday rehearsal and Concert.
Friday – rest.
Saturday rehearsal. Sunday rehearsal and Concert.
This plan to be repeated the following week.
Then on the last Sunday evening depart for two weeks tour, Belgium, Holland and North Germany – 6 concerts each week.
(That takes us through four weeks).
The fifth and sixth weeks as the first and second – (London).
The seventh and eighth weeks tour Scandinavia.
The ninth and tenth weeks back in London as first and second weeks.
The eleventh and twelfth weeks tour France and Italy.

With this plan we shall be able to get you and the Philharmonia into a number of cities which would not otherwise afford us and thus pave the way for future tours with you and the Philharmonia and the whole undertaking will advertise the records we shall have made together at the right time.

What are your views on these ideas?

> My love to you,
> Yours always,
> [Walter Legge]

Dario and his wife Dorle Soria ran EMI's Angel label in the USA. On 25 January Karajan apparently replied to the above letter and declined Legge's proposals, saying that they would take up too much time.

23 April 1954.

My dear Herbert,

You will have had my telegram about the American tour. I am firmly confident that this will materialise, either on the Efrem Kurtz/Gorlinsky plan or, if you are persuasive enough when we meet McLeod, with the Company paying the travel costs – which is what he himself suggested as a possibility.

If we do go to America in the Autumn of 1955, it will mean that the Orchestra is immobilised for recording for two full months next year and it is absolutely essential that, in addition to *Der Fledermaus* and *Rosenkavalier* – which the Sorias have already announced in America – that we should complete the Beethoven Symphonies (the Ninth is now number one priority). We have also to record Mozart from No. 29 to the *Jupiter*. We must do the *Missa solemnis* in view of the success of the B minor Mass, which, to my utter astonishment, is amongst the best selling records in England at the moment.

It therefore means deciding now on the exact periods for your recording in London for 1955.

We have already booked the Hall and the Orchestra in July for recording with you. In January and February you will be at La Scala.

Now, we have the following periods clear:-

March 7th – 12th
14th – 19th
21st – 26th
April 11th – 16th
18th – 22nd

(These are immediately before your first Concert on April 24th and *Der Fledermaus*).

We also have the periods June 20th to 25th and June 27th to July 2nd. All August is clear. I expect we shall go to Edinburgh again in September.

I have to fix recordings with other conductors but naturally want you to have first preference. Will you let me know which of these periods you can accept.

We have also to do a complete *Don Giovanni*, so I think it will mean your giving us a total of five weeks plus the *Don Giovanni* time and in addition to July.

We ought to complete the Brahms Symphonies and now, after the fantastic press for Sibelius 4, we must do Sibelius 2. We must also do some popular money makers; the best-selling orchestral recording in England is the Tchaikovsky Ballets, so we had better follow up that line of country with a series of similar money-making records.

I can hardly wait for your return from Japan, and you can count on me being at Rome Airport to welcome you.

> My love to you,
> Yours always,
> [Walter Legge]

The allusions in this letter are not all clear: Efrem Kurtz was a conductor and S.A. Gorlinsky a concert agent. John McLeod was Managing Director of Pathé-Marconi in Paris from 1948 to the mid-1950s. Sessions for *Fledermaus* took place in April 1955, but *Rosenkavalier* was not recorded until December the following year. Karajan did not record *Don Giovanni* for EMI, and only three Mozart symphonies with the Philharmonia were ever released. Karajan did not record the Brahms Third Symphony with Legge, and Sibelius's Second Symphony had to wait until 1960, although a coupling of the Sixth and Seventh was made in 1955.

II. 'THOSE WHOM THE GODS LOVE ...'

If the destruction and deprivations of war had not been enough, the health of post-war musical life was soon afflicted by the deaths of several young artists at a time when they were at the height of their powers. As we have seen in previous chapters, Walter Legge was deeply affected by these personal tragedies, and he was always willing to write tributes to lost colleagues. Some of his most eloquent and vividly expressed prose is to be found in his obituary essays. The three following articles first appeared in *The Gramophone*.

Maria Cebotari   July 1949.
10 February 1910 – 9 June 1949

Maria Cebotari's untimely death has robbed the European operatic stage of one of its most able, versatile and conscientious artists. Although she was only 38 when she died, she had been singing principal roles in the leading European opera houses for nearly 20 years. Born in Bessarabia, Rumanian and Russian were her native languages, and as little more than a child she joined the Moscow Art Theatre Company. Through a leading actor of the company, whom she later married, she was brought to the notice of Issay Dobrowen, at that time conducting at the Dresden Opera. Dobrowen secured her a scholarship to study singing with Daniel in Berlin, and within six months Cebotari was a useful member of the Dresden Opera Company.

Her rise to popularity was swift. She was not yet 20 when I first saw her *Butterfly* in Berlin. Ears accustomed to Aida and Tosca-type voices in the part were disappointed in the size of her voice, but eyes which had learned to accept the tradition of 14 stone Butterflies were delighted by a credible and slender child. I did not realise at the time how quickly her fame had spread. Only a few weeks ago did I find in the guest-book of the Gesellschaft der Musikfreunde in Vienna that the 20-year old Cebotari had been invited there to sing the Verdi Requiem.

Between the wars she sang in almost every important opera house in Europe. Conductors liked her; she was as reliable as the rock of Gibraltar, vocally and musically. Her physical toughness was unique in a profession that makes exceptional demands. She hardly ever cancelled a performance. Her skill and resourcefulness were such that she knew how to sing through a cold, and she had nerves of steel. Vocal chords too, of some equally durable material. She was physically and vocally tireless. When she was under contract both to Berlin and Dresden she sometimes sang six or seven times a week, flying backwards and forwards.

The first news I had of her after the second world war was in Switzerland in 1946. After the first performance of his Oboe Concerto Richard Strauss told me that Cebotari was the best all-round artist on the European stage. I met her a couple of days later in Zürich, after a performance of *Arabella*, and began discussions which led, a year later in Paris, to her signing an exclusive contract with His Master's Voice.

At the 1946 Salzburg Festival I had first-hand evidence of her toughness. She was seven months gone with her second child, but the most punctual and untiring person at every rehearsal; no producer could weary her, nor conductor catch her out on an untidy demi-semiquaver. In a ridiculously short time after her confinement she was back at the Vienna Opera rehearsing and singing. If anyone was ill or cancelled a performance at the last moment it was always 'Phone Cebotari'; she was always ready to sing.

The range of her repertoire was extraordinary; there was hardly a part feasibly within the range of her voice that she was not prepared to sing at a couple of hours' notice. Take Mozart. She sang all three women's parts in *Don Giovanni*; Constanze, Fiordiligi; the Countess and Susanna. Her other roles included Gilda and Salome, Turandot and Sophie, Butterfly and Mimi – the latter hundreds of times each – Amor and Eurydice, Carmen and Micaela, Margarethe and Frau Fluth, *Fledermaus, Zigeunerbaron, Bettelstudent*. Her boundless ambition recognised no vocal or human limitations. Last December after she had made a splendid record of Ariadne's aria, which showed a remarkable development in her lower register, I suggested to her that in a year she ought to be ready to sing the Marschallin. A month later she said that she was ready with the part! And she had set her heart on singing Isolde. I believe that if she had seen a chance of singing in a performance of Elektra, she would have learned Elektra, Chrysothemis and Clystemnestra – just in case.

I doubt if her own family could say how and when she worked. It was her pride that her family never noticed that she was a professional singer. As long as I knew her she ran her home with the same invisible and swift efficiency, brought up two children and was always ready at a moment's notice to jump in to help any opera director. If, during the last three years, I had been asked to take an opera house, the first person I should have engaged would have been Cebotari.

Already in the autumn she began to suffer the pains of the disease which finally devoured her. Armed with a little bottle of drops which deadened the pain, she sang her three, four and five performances a week, and recorded for three hours at a stretch without letting us guess of the battle she was fighting. She sang her last performance on 1 April, a new production of *Bettelstudent*. A few days later the doctors tried to operate. As late as ten days before her death she was talking of getting well quickly to be in her best form for Salzburg.

Her artistry was instinctive. Her singing, like her acting, was always the fruit of intuition not the product of consideration. By a sixth sense she was aware what was artistically necessary, and by some subconscious process she found the technical means to realise it convincingly. The Vienna Opera will already have discovered that Cebotari, like all other exceptional people, has made nonsense of the theory that 'no one is indispensable'.

Ginette Neveu   December 1949.
11 August 1919 – 28 October 1949

Ginette Neveu was the first of the remarkable batch of young artists I found for my companies in my post-war visits to the Continent. Within a few days of the liberation of Paris I looked up Jacques Thibaud, to find out who had come to the forefront in the war years. He mentioned three string players – Ginette Neveu, Pierre Fournier and Gyula Bustabo. I had known of Neveu before the war, first as Carl Flesch's best pupil in the middle 1930s, then as a young recitalist in Berlin – I think it was in 1938. Her first records, the Strauss Sonata and a posthumous Chopin *Nocturne*, were the fruits of that Berlin success.

Thibaud spoke glowingly of her extraordinary vitality and superhuman concentration, but it was with Francis Poulenc and Pierre Bernac that I first met her. Her first concert in London at the Wigmore Hall in 1945 was given under the patronage, if I remember rightly, of the French Cultural Attaché. It was what every concert should be – an experience that added to the sum of the life of everyone present.

It was at once evident that Ginette Neveu was technically a violinist of the front rank; but technically accomplished violinists are not all that rare. Her unique quality was the intense and passionate beauty of her playing, an incandescent and fiercely primitive passion that seemed always on the verge of breaking all restraint, yet just held in leash by powerful will and intellect. Her face was extraordinary; not conventionally beautiful in repose, and she had the slightly prominent eyes and throat that are often associated with over-active thyroid glands. But in the moment that her hand touched the strings her face was transfigured into a wild, ecstatic beauty. As she played she crouched over her fiddle like a tense pantheress about to spring, and the sound she produced pulsed with unspeakable intensities.

A couple of days after her concert she signed the recording contract, which was about to be renewed when she met her tragic death.

The first records we made together were the Sibelius Violin Concerto. It was in November 1945, and London was enveloped in a fog so thick that we could not see from the recording room to the stage in the big Abbey Road Studio. It was the only free day she had in the middle of a busy tour. I had not hoped to complete the work in two sessions. The orchestra – the Philharmonia – was doing its first major recording; Walter Susskind was doing his first international recording, and it was our first experience of Neveu in the studios. The gods and her fantastic concentration were on our side. Between two and five we had recorded the whole of the first movement. In the hour and a half interval between the sessions any other player would have rested; not Neveu. Striding up and down the Studio she practised the whole time through. By eight o'clock the neck abrasion, which is the violinist's trade mark, was an angry scarlet wound and the left side of her chin was near to bleeding. It made no difference to her.

Smoking incessantly she worked through until shortly before half-past nine, and asked that the orchestra should do half an hour's overtime to finish the work. Before ten o'clock the concerto was completed. All of us were exhausted – except Ginette Neveu. She came up to my room, and played through the Walton Concerto, which she was learning. When, a few minutes before midnight, I got her back to the Piccadilly Hotel, her only complaint was that there was no restaurant where we could sit and start to talk.

Later in Paris I learned to know her better. At that time she cycled round Paris in heavy shoes with short socks and bare legs, a tweed skirt, and a sweater, with her precious fiddle strapped across the handlebars. She had a mind. Lunch lasted sometimes four hours, and she talked in her heavy, hoarse deep voice with the same intensity with which she played of music, politics, life and art. One of these days I hope to write of her theory and practice of musical preparation – for those who have the energy, will and single mindedness; it is at once the most rigorous and improving régime I know.

I was in Vienna for her début there. It was a tribute to the quick understanding of that strange public which, as Karl Böhm said, is exceptional in that while most audiences can tell the good from the bad, the Viennese public can at once tell the exceptional from the good. Neveu gave what the Viennese call a double concert – the same programme Saturday afternoon and Sunday morning. The Saturday afternoon concert was more than half empty. The Viennese talk – and the word of Neveu's genius really spread overnight, so that on the Sunday morning the house was full.

She was granted but little time to enjoy the success she so well deserved. England, America and all the European countries fêted her as she deserved – except her own country. But she remained unchanged; simple, direct, outspoken and illuminated from within by a radiant intensity.

She made far fewer records than she, or we, would have liked. We had planned to do the Beethoven and Tchaikovsky concertos on her return from America, and all the Brahms sonatas with Edwin Fischer, whose glowing musicianship had been an inspiration to her from childhood. She made no record that does not convey her unique qualities, but as one who was privileged to know her, I feel that the suggestive power of her personality comes most strongly from the Ravel *Tzigane* and the Sibelius Concerto.

It is to be hoped that her executors will sanction the publication of the Chausson *Poème* and the Debussy Sonata, which she had yet to approve.

The Chausson and Debussy recordings were issued on LP in due course, and in common with all the other Neveu recordings they have been reissued on CD.

Dinu Lipatti   February 1951.
19 March 1917 – 2 December 1950

Dinu Lipatti had the qualities of a saint. The spiritual goodness of his nature, his modesty, his gentleness, his will's firm purpose, his nobility and loftiness of thought and action communicated themselves to all who met him, and to the remotest listeners in the halls where he played. His goodness and generosity evoked faith, hope and charity in those around him. We not only hoped – we had faith. Even his doctors believed that the incurable disease he had suffered for six years would miraculously yield to some hitherto untried treatment, or that some new cure would be discovered before it was too late. Last June and July we had reason to believe that this miracle had happened. Injections of Cortison, the American preparation which has had spectacular successes in the treatment of rheumatoid arthritis, arrested his malady's progress and gave him a brief summer of well-being, high spirits and energy. This treatment was expensive – the injections cost £18 a day – but as soon as the facts became known musicians like Charles Munch and Yehudi Menuhin, as well as private persons, many of them anonymous Swiss admirers, guaranteed him several months' supply. He was the cause of goodness in others. But Cortison was only a dam, not a remedy. When the injections ceased the disease resumed its inexorable course. Although he managed with Cortison's aid to give two more concerts, the inevitable end came on the afternoon of December 2nd. He was 33.

Lipatti was born in Bucharest and cradled in music. His father was a wealthy amateur who had studied with Sarasate and Carl Flesch, his mother was a good pianist; George Enescu was his godfather. Music was his preoccupation from infancy. His mother has told me that he could play the piano before he had learned to smile. At four he gave concerts for charity and began composing pieces describing the characters of his family and their friends. It was never in question that he should devote his life to music, but only later did circumstances dictate that he should become a professional pianist. He never attended school; professors from the University of Bucharest tutored him at home, building his general education around his music. His pianoforte teacher was a woman, Floria Musicescu. In winters in Bucharest and in summers on the family estate at Fonda she stood over the boy relentlessly building that incomparable technique and magical touch. Admitted early by special dispensation he entered the Conservatoire before he was old enough officially to take the entrance examination. In 1934 he entered for the International Competition in Vienna. At the stormy final session Constantin (his baptismal name, Dinu is a diminutive) Lipatti was awarded second prize, and Alfred Cortot resigned from the jury as a protest that Lipatti had not been given the first prize. Before he left Vienna Cortot invited Lipatti to Paris to study with him.

In Paris he worked at pianoforte with Cortot and studied conducting with Charles Munch. On the evidence of some compositions submitted to the Conservatoire Paul Dukas had accepted him as a pupil with the comment, 'We have nothing to teach him; all we can do is encourage him to compose and guide his development.' Dukas died shortly afterwards and Lipatti was put under the care of Nadia Boulanger, who at once became, in Ansermet's words, 'his spiritual mother'. That noble and energetic woman, who has been the artistic conscience and guide to three decades of musical life in Paris, remained a close friend to the end of his life and a powerful influence on him. It was Nadia Boulanger who first brought him to recording. In 1937 he recorded with her and four singers Brahms's *Liebeslieder Waltzes* and a selection – Nos. 1, 2, 5, 6, 10, 14 and 15 – of Brahms's *Waltzes*. By an engaging oversight in French HMV this latter record was announced as being played by Mesdames Nadia Boulanger and Dina Lipatti.

In 1936 Lipatti began to make his name as a pianist with concerts in Berlin and various Italian cities. At the outbreak of war he returned to Rumania, where he stayed until 1943 when, together with his fiancée, Madeleine Cantacuzene, he escaped from Bucharest, and by devious ruses and routes they arrived, via Stockholm, in Geneva with a joint capital of five Swiss francs. The fates and the Genevese were kind. His reputation as an artist and teacher spread rapidly. In Paris, in 1944, Francis Poulenc told me of 'this artist of divine spirituality', a judgement I was fully to endorse a few months later at a rehearsal of Chopin's F minor Concerto. From January 1946 Lipatti had an exclusive contract with Columbia.

He was already an ill man. Frail from childhood, the illness which was eventually to destroy him had taken its hold. From 1948 onwards his fame was such that he could command his own terms to play wherever he chose. Tours in North and South America, and of Australia, which would have provided him with the money he so badly needed, were arranged and at the last minute cancelled on doctors' orders, but his only complaint was for the inconvenience and expense that he had caused others.

Our first recordings were ill-starred. In July 1946 he made a series of records in Zürich which, owing to an unforeseen fault in the material, were not good enough for publication. After that unfortunate start all his recordings, except the last incredible achievements of July 1950, were made in the Abbey Road studios. Only his illness is to blame for the comparatively small number of records he made. Karajan's recording of Bartók's *Music for strings, percussion and celeste* was a last minute substitution for the recordings Lipatti was to have made for The Maharaja of Mysore's Musical Foundation of Busoni's *Indian Fantasia* and Bartók's Third Pianoforte Concerto. As recently as October Galliera recorded Respighi's *Brazilian Impressions* a year earlier than we had planned, owing to Lipatti's non-arrival to record Chopin's F minor Concerto.

Lipatti visited England four times; in October and November 1946, when he recorded one of Liszt's *Sonetti del Petrarca*, *La leggierezza* and the Chopin *Waltz* which is coupled with it, and made his English début at

Walthamstow Town Hall, where he played a Mozart concerto with the Philharmonia Orchestra and Karl Rankl. On his second visit in February and March, 1947, were recorded two Scarlatti sonatas, Chopin's D flat *Nocturne*, Chopin's B minor Sonata, and we began the long series of attempts to produce his ideal performance of Myra Hess's transcription of 'Jesu, Joy of man's desiring'. In September that year he recorded the Grieg Concerto with Alceo Galliera and the Philharmonia Orchestra, and repeated the Chopin *Waltz, Sonetta del Petrarca* and a Scarlatti sonata. All these became the definitive versions. 'Jesu, Joy' was also repeated several times, and although he was not completely happy with the results he yielded to the appeals of admirers in Switzerland and France by allowing the best of these recordings to be published – but only in those countries. For the final version we had to wait until July 1950. It is impossible to explain to those who have not experienced the wonder of his playing of this piece, its rapt beauty and fascination. It was always the first encore he played, and for him it was a prayer and utterance of thanksgiving to God. The sound was not of this world, it hovered in space like some celestial blessing. On his last visit in April 1948 he recorded the Schumann Concerto with Herbert von Karajan, the incredible performance of Ravel's *Alborada del gracioso* with its fantastic graduated *glissando* that I still cannot believe was played by human hand, and Chopin's *Barcarolle*. He was not completely satisfied with the latter. After that we made nothing but plans for visits to London, which were frustrated by his illness. Last Easter I went to see him in Geneva and promised that if he would get well enough I would find ways and means of recording him wherever or whenever it might be.

In the last days of May I had a private letter from a Dr Dubois-Ferrière in Geneva urging me at once to organise an expedition to Geneva to record Dinu Lipatti. As his doctor he had administered injections of Cortison and the improvement was remarkable. Unfortunately, he explained, the treatment could not be continued for more than two months, and since this was the first time it had been tried for Lipatti's complaint he could give no promise of its permanence or continued efficacy, but he begged me as a friend of Lipatti's to stop at nothing to make recordings in Geneva possible while the improvement lasted.

Dr Dubois-Ferrière had already collected subscriptions from friends and admirers of Lipatti to present him with a new Steinway pianoforte from the Hamburg factory – a luxury Dinu had long wished to enjoy. But it was not a concert grand, and I have a rooted objection to the lack of warm bass that seems inevitable in recordings made with short grands.

Those colleagues and friends who made those last Lipatti recordings possible have earned the gratitude of musicians and music lovers for decades, perhaps generations to come. W.S. Barrell, Director of EMI Studios, interrupted his holiday to find a suitable studio in Geneva. Radio Geneva rearranged their programmes so that the studios should be available to us day and night. Paul Jecklin, Columbia's agent in Switzerland, bought from Steinway in Hamburg and had sent to Geneva the first of those fabulously beautiful post-war concert grands to enter Switzerland, the instrument Lipatti had always wanted to use for recording. Our French company sent their superbly equipped new recording van directly from the Casals recordings in Prades.

I found Dinu in better health and spirit than I had ever known him to enjoy. Friends had placed at his disposal a house standing in its own small park, outside Geneva and a few minutes' walk from the French frontier. We christened it 'Haus Triebschenli', because it looked like a diminutive copy of Wagner's house on Lake Lucerne. Dinu loved the sun and the trees, and the weather smiled on us. For two radiant and blessed weeks the sun shone out of a clear blue sky and the thermometer settled itself comfortably in the nineties. Cortison had given him a ravenous appetite and restored his natural gaiety. Dinu laughed and made music. He had just heard the story of a great conductor, known among musicians for his nervous and seemingly undecided down-beat who, at the beginning of his first rehearsal with a famous Italian orchestra had been encouraged by a shout from the first contra-bass player 'Coraggio! Maestro, coraggio!' Whenever an arpeggio in the Chopin waltzes failed to come off with the desired clarity, accuracy and grace, Dinu stopped and called out either in apology or impatience 'Arpeggio Maestro! arpeggio'. It became a catch phrase which he cherished to the end. And when a *legato* passage was less smooth or chords less brilliant than he wanted it was always 'Doigts de Maccaroni' – maccaroni fingers – the contemptuous epithet which he used on himself and his pupils for a lack of controlled strength in the fingers.

The recording van stood day and night beside the Radio Geneva studios among lawns and well kept rose beds in rural peace. Both new Steinways were in the studio, Jecklin's noble concert grand and Dinu's exquisitely sensitive short grand, his 'virgin, whom no other hands have caressed'. We spent the first day satisfying ourselves by innumerable test recordings which piano to use, where it sounded best, which microphone to use and where to place it.

Let me here and now correct the current belief that the Chopin *Waltzes*, Bach's B flat Partita and Mozart's A minor Sonata were recorded all in one day. I can well believe that my illegible writing misled some friend, to whom and to all others I now apologise. The recording of the Chopin *Waltzes* took nearly all of nine days, from three to seven hours a day. We worked as a rule from nine until lunch time and from half-past six or seven until ten or after. The first seven sessions were devoted to the *Waltzes*. Apart from all the other problems Lipatti was particularly concerned with the fact that unlike the Studies, which were composed in two batches, and the 24 *Preludes*, Chopin's *Waltzes*, although sometimes played as if they were written at one period of his life, belong together only by virtue of title and rhythm. To differentiate between these works of different periods, to avoid applying a personal range of nuances or mannerisms of *rubato*, was his constant preoccupation while studying and recording them. We

182

decided, after seven sessions of waltzes, that it would be refreshing to make a change from waltz rhythm and Chopin's texture, and to record some Bach. That evening he recorded Kempff's arrangement of a *Siciliana* and returned, not for the last time, to the old problem of 'Jesu, Joy of man's desiring'. After six days eight of the waltzes had been completed to the satisfaction of the most critical trio who ever sat in judgement on performances – Dinu, his wife, and I. At supper late that night we decided to devote the Sabbath, the next day, to Bach.

Sunday 9 July was the hottest and most memorable of all the days in that spell of incredible happiness. At nine in the morning we began Bach's B flat *Partita* and it was finished before lunch. Fearing that the effort of recording those four perfect sides – most of them were done some four or five times – would be too much for him I counselled cancelling the evening session, but Dinu would not hear of it: his sun was shining and he was going to make hay. At seven he started on the Mozart sonata. If ever a player was inspired it was Dinu that evening. Mozart and Bach were the composers nearest and dearest to his heart, and this was his first Mozart recording. The music came to an intensity of life rare, if not unique, in my experience. Phrases took on human form and character, living their exciting lives before the mind's eye as in a perfect performance of some unwritten operas. In no other way could he have demonstrated so convincingly his belief that even in his instrumental works Mozart was at heart a dramatic, an operatic composer. By ten o'clock the sonata was finished and now there was no stopping him; we must try to get the outstanding waltzes while he was in the mood. He recorded five, not all finally, and when shortly before midnight the exhausted engineers were trudging wearily in search of a meal, Dinu, the freshest of us all, played 'Stormy Weather'.

In the next three days we again repeated the waltzes still outstanding, recorded the *Mazurka,* which is on the final side of that set – ('Let us see if we can whet the public's appetite so that you will ask me to do all the *Mazurkas* next year') – some Bach-Busoni transcriptions and – 'Jesu, Joy'. I have lost count of how many times that was repeated, but the last version made on 11 July at last pleased him. On 12 July he again repeated the fourteenth waltz and with it completed the recorded part of his artistic testament. It is comparatively small in content but of the purest gold.

He loved recording. Times without number he said to me, 'I do not want to give any more concerts – except perhaps as rehearsals for recording. Let us give our lives to making records together'. As an incurable perfectionist it delighted him to work in a medium wherein he could repeat until he was satisfied that he could do no better, where the slightest blemish, what he called his *bêtises* and *cochonneries* could be obliterated and a fresh start made. Such faults were rare: he had such a complete physical mastery that he was by nature the 'cleanest' player I have ever worked with. The innumerable repeats were made in pursuit of an ideal sensibility and beauty. His wife was his invaluable and incomparable collaborator. A pupil of the same teacher and herself a magnificent pianist and teacher – I doubt if she has her equal in the latter field – she hears and senses overtones and subtleties of nuance with ears that matched, and might have been, his. Her art, as well as her love and selflessness, are also in Dinu Lipatti's records.

This is not the place to write about Dinu Lipatti as a composer, neither have I yet had the opportunity of examining more than a small part of his output. There exists a recording he made with Hans von Benda and the Berlin Philharmonic Orchestra for the Rumanian Radio before the war of his *Concertino* for pianoforte and orchestra, a charming essay in the modernised classical vein reminiscent of Prokofiev's *Classical Symphony*. In the last months of his life he made some wonderful Bach transcriptions, a *Pastorale* in four movements, of which the manuscript is complete, and two which he played to me, which may or may not have been written down – the aria 'Schafe können sicher weiden' (Cantata No. 208) and the dance epilogue of the aria 'Mein gläubiges Herze'. Those works apart, those of Lipatti's compositions which I have seen have one astonishing characteristic. His Balkan blood, of which there was no trace in his playing of Western music, suddenly dominates him. The *Rumanian Dances* originally written for orchestra and played by Ansermet and later rewritten for pianoforte duet, as well as the *Sonatina for Left Hand* might have been written by Bartók.

I do not believe that there has been, or will be, a pianist like Dinu Lipatti. It is not a matter of comparisons of quality, it is a matter of difference in kind. Hard as he worked and thought on purely technical problems of touch, sonority and pedalling, he was not a 'virtuoso' in the word's modern and debased sense – but certainly in its seventeenth century application 'a connoisseur'. For himself he had no use for display or brilliance of execution as ends in themselves, though he was almost over-generous in his praise and admiration for his many contemporaries who have. He was a musician, a musician who used the pianoforte as a means of communication and expression. Only in terms of his qualities as a musician and a man can one hope to explain, to understand or describe him.

He was a good man in the highest sense, and a particularly sensitive one. He was in all things an aristocrat of the finest fibre, temperamentally incapable of vulgarity in thought or deed. He was fastidious and distinguished in all he did, unable, in showing a pupil how not to phrase, even of imitating bad taste. When he played jazz to amuse his friends or shock the seriousness out of some too-earnest guest, he could not avoid giving the most trivial tune the lustre of his magical sound and delicate sensibility. He approached music with a composer's mind and his love for his favourite masters was blended with reverence. When I first knew him he had never played Beethoven: he felt that he was not yet worthy. That he played the *Waldstein* Sonata in the last two years of his life was due to the encouragement of Artur Schnabel who, as a wise and paternal admirer, persuaded him to take the plunge.

Lipatti's sense of responsibility to the public came out of his reverence for music. In the five years we worked together I was able to offer him a repertoire for recording for which many another pianist would have sacrificed his wife and family. Lipatti was not to be deflected from his devoted approach. To prepare the *Emperor* Concerto he would need four years, even for the Tchaikovsky he needed three. Nothing in his work was unprepared or left to chance. He had his schedule of works to be studied and practised carefully mapped out for five years in advance. He never played a note in public that was not meticulously prepared: his miraculous playing was the result of a mastery of the physical-technical part of his art, so complete that his mind and spirit were free to express themselves in music.

The softness of his sound came through strength. He had enormous and powerful hands – the 'little' finger as long as its neighbour – and the shoulders of a wrestler, quite disproportionate to his frail build. As he played each finger had a life and personality of its own, independent of its neighbours, of his wrists and arms: each finger seemed prehensile and the ten of them, when he played contrapuntal music, looked like a fantastic ballet danced by ten elephants' trunks each obeying the orders of its own mahout. This visual impression of each finger having its own life is evident in the sound of his playing. Every note he played had a life of its own. To his pupils and to himself he preached giving every phrase and every note in every phrase 'character'. Every note in every part must live and contribute its meaning to the whole. He aimed at presenting the music of other periods in such a way that it would have for us today the vitality and significance it had had for the composer and his contemporaries. He did not seek in Bach to imitate the sound of a cembalo or clavier, he set out to play it as he believed Bach would have done if he had had a modern concert grand at his disposal. For this reason he occasionally and discreetly added octaves or transposed the lower voice down an octave. In certain works of Liszt he used the modern resources of pedalling to obtain effects implicit in the character of the music, but beyond the resources of Liszt's instruments. These were the only liberties he allowed himself or his pupils, who adored him.

Half an hour before he died he was listening to the Schneiderhan Quartet's records of Beethoven's F minor Quartet. To his wife he said, 'You see, it is not enough to be a great composer. To write music like that you must be a chosen instrument of God'. By the same light we may say that it is not enough to be a great pianist: to play as Lipatti played you must be a chosen instrument of God.

God lent the world His chosen instrument whom we called Dinu Lipatti for too brief a space.

III. THE MAHARAJA OF MYSORE

A bright prospect was opened when a young, wealthy and music-loving Indian prince, the Maharaja of Mysore, offered in 1947 to finance some recordings of music by Medtner. Walter Legge made two visits to India in order to discuss the project, and as a result not only were recordings of Medtner's music made under the auspices of The Maharaja of Mysore's Musical Foundation, but the Medtner Society volumes were followed in 1949/50 by first recordings of music by other composers, including Balakirev, Roussel and Bartók. Financial support for Legge's Philharmonia Concert Society was also made available. But alas property belonging to the Maharaja was soon seized by the new independent Indian régime, and as a result he was forced to halve the original subsidy of £10,000 per annum after one year, and to abandon the scheme altogether after just three years.

Walter Legge had recorded Egon Petri in London between 1935 and 1938.

31 March 1949.

My dear Egon,

Through the sort of miracle that happens only once in a lifetime an Indian Prince has interested himself in neglected European music, and commissioned us to record certain works. Among his suggestions was the Busoni *Indian Fantasie*. I naturally had only one answer as to the right soloist for this work – your good self – and His Highness proposes a fee of £600, to include your travel expenses to London to make this recording. This would be quite apart from any existing recording contract you have. I feel confident that Columbia would make no difficulties about this. As conductor I have engaged Herbert von Karajan, who is probably known to you by name, a musician after our own hearts. Can you manage to do this sometime between September and November this year? I need to know because of fitting in the dates with Karajan, and His Highness, being both a Prince and a young man, is impatient for the realisation of his dreams of a first-class recording of this work.

If you will let me know how much time you can spare, and when, I will immediately get in touch with your old agents and ask them to arrange other things for you. It is high time that you came back to Europe and reminded us first-hand of the grand manner. How are you otherwise? I saw a good deal of your youngest son during the war when he was with the Dutch Squadron in England, and we met several times in Paris after that.

I do hope most sincerely that you will feel disposed to come over and make this recording, both on artistic and personal grounds. My kindest regards to your wife, and take this first sign of life from me for many years as irrefutable evidence that you have been in these ten years constantly and most affectionately in my thoughts.

Yours always,
[Walter Legge]

14 April 1949.
4684 Reinhardt Drive
Oakland 19, California

My dear Walter:

Your letter came as a great surprise, first by bringing us a sign of life from you and second by its contents which reminded me of the 'thousand and one nights'. I am very honoured and flattered that you suggested me to His Highness and I want you to thank him most warmly for his most generous offer. I wish I could accept it but the days for these adventurous undertakings are unfortunately over for me.

The first reason for my having to decline is my health. I don't know whether anybody has told you that three years ago I had what the doctors called a coronary thrombosis. I was put to bed for three months and told to give up all thoughts of ever concertising again. So, I cancelled about 40 concerts in this country and decided to settle in California and to limit my activities only to teaching. In 1947, I had another 'attack' during the recording of the *Hammerklavier* Sonata in New York. I was quite sure it was not my heart but my familiar old gall bladder complaint which I contracted during my early Russian tours through injudicious living. But, I was taken by force to the hospital and after all the usual tests the doctors decided to cut out my gall bladder. As it was just a month before my summer master class at Mills College, I politely refused and decided to go on a diet. Lately a doctor in Oakland diagnosed all my troubles as an excess of gas (how undignified) – due to a sluggish gall bladder. Whether I ever had a heart ailment will be one of those unsolved mysteries. Anyhow, here I am teaching at Mills, playing occasionally in San Francisco and the immediate neighbourhood, watching my diet (more or less) and feeling as they used to say in Germany 'like God in France'. Even my doctor here has warned me against all over-exertion and excitement, so I have to lead a quiet and regular life whether I want to or not.

The second reason is that I am absolutely fed up with travelling, living in hotels, playing in public, going to receptions, being interviewed and photographed, and generally speaking 'taken notice of '. I have, at last, my own house, a lovely garden and beautiful view. I have enough money to live comfortably and don't see any reason why I should be tempted to exchange this paradisiacal life for the strenuous one of a travelling Montebank and you can figure out yourself how wonderful it is for me to be told by the doctors to lead the life I really prefer.

Please do not think that I am just lazy and heartless. I know very well that I have certain obligations to the world of music, but then I can fulfil those by teaching and playing in a limited area. And, I certainly would love to see my friends, not only in England, but in Poland, Russia, Germany, Italy and Switzerland and so on.

It is easy to see that under the present circumstances such things are impossible of fulfilment, so I shall be content to sit in my little arbor in the sunshine where I dictate this letter and wait for the third act of the world war.

187

Someone suggested that the recording of the *Indian Fantasie* might be done in Hollywood, but I am perfectly convinced that you and the Prince would not be interested in that.

I really am sorry that I have to take this attitude, but I hope you will understand my position and sympathise with me.

Many thanks again and kindest regards and best wishes from

> Your old friend,
> Egon

14 June 1949.

My dear Egon,

Your enchanting letter was marred only by two factors; the one that you are not to be tempted to Europe, the other that you have been ailing. I understand all too well how you feel about the parade of the life of [a] fêted artist; how any man of the sensibility being an artist calls for can long endure is beyond my comprehension. And the men who travel the world for two years playing only a couple of concertos and almost interminably repeating the same couple of recital programmes are intellectually beyond the range of my comprehension.

I wish I could say 'yes' to recording in Hollywood, but my Maharaja insists on London recording – and mine not to reason why! He is also out for the *Fantasia Contrapuntistica*. Do you recommend the first (I believe) solo version, or the two piano? The latter seems clearer to me. Is the two piano version all his own work? An afterthought, matter of convenience, or what?

I have, owing to deeply regretted defection, got a young Rumanian pianist to learn the *Fantasy*; Dinu Lipatti by name, and a player after our own hearts. He is musical to the nth degree, with formidable dexterity and a magical and resourcefully varied range of sonority. If he is not the supreme pianist in the world of those men under your present age, I am the *Fliegende Holländer*. Ask our good friends at Columbia to make you a present of his records of the Chopin B minor Sonata and Ravel's *Alborada*, and I think you'll find extreme pleasure. He is only 30, and suffers at the moment bad health; his red and white corpuscles have not worked out a mutually agreeable balance of power. I would be grateful for your frank views on his playing on the evidence of those records, or of his performance of the cadenza of Grieg's regrettable essay in concerto form.

I still do not despair that some bait may be found to tempt you back to Europe, if only to break up the theory which has grown up since the war that America has speeded up, desensitized and chromium plated the distinguished artists she has over from Europe.

My kindest regards and best wishes.

> Yours always,
> Walter Legge.
> International Artists Department

188

III. *The Maharaja Of Mysore*

14 October 1950.
THE PALACE,
MYSORE.

My dear Legge,

I have had several chances of listening to Schnabel's *Rhapsody*. Believe me Walter, I have listened to nothing so boring for a very, very long time. I cannot believe it can be called music. I may be one of those incorrigible purists (but as you know my tastes are most Catholic), I find it very difficult to swallow this. I have the deepest regard and respect for Schnabel the pianist, but this music is no surprise to me as I have few things Schnabel wrote for the piano, which bear the same stamp of unoriginality or lack of tunes or inspirations. I feel guilty of writing this letter but as you know, I am an utterly frank and sometimes unwelcome friend. Nevertheless, you know I am genuinely sincere in whatever views I hold. So I thought I should let you know personally. Last and not least, I have so much regard for Schnabel and your good self that I would very strongly advise the non-issue of these records – if not ever, at least for some considerable time. For the public and even layman like myself must have time and repeated hearings to convince us personally. Twenty-five hearings have not convinced me, my dear friend, so I would suggest deferring any action about issue of the records.

About Schumann – can you not arrange to record soon the following:

a) Carnaval, Op. 9
b) Etudes après Paganini, Op. 10
c) Sonata, Op. 11
d) Sonata, Op. 22
e) Intermezzos, Op. 4
f) Blumenstück, Op. 19
g) Faschingsschwank, Op. 26
h) Etudes symphoniques, Op. 13 (with posthumous variations)
i) Abegg Variationen, Op. 1
j) Novelletten, Op. 21
k) Nachtstücke, Op. 23
l) Sonata, Op. 14

Can you not divide these between Solomon, Lipatti, Gieseking and Moiseiwitch ? These can be recorded and issued by you as and when you think fit. Any other final adjustment of artists you are at liberty to make as you deem fit.

Once more may I repeat that you will not misunderstand my remarks about Schnabel. I did my best to please you and to see if I liked it but – I really and honestly cannot.

One last word. I am very anxious we should do in our recordings the Janáček Mass and the Roussel Piano Concerto. Will you keep that in mind when you finally submit lists for me to approve of.

The Dasara is on and I am very busy. More in my next.

With love and every good wish.

> Yours sincerely,
> [personal signature]
> [The Maharaja of Mysore]

PS: If we record any Schumann, let us plan to have all the repeats done.

Schnabel's *Rhapsody for Orchestra*, in the recording conducted by Paul Kletzki, was finally issued by Columbia in January 1952.

> 13 December 1950.

May it please Your Highness,

I have been puzzling my brains to think of some gift which would give you pleasure; some token of my gratitude and, if I may say so, love for your Highness, which would particularly please you. I have not been able to think of anything better than these very private records. They are things which are unlikely ever to be published, for one reason or another. The Fischer Bach Concerto, for example, because although neither he nor I noticed it during the sessions, the piano is not in tune with the orchestra. The Lipatti Sonatina for Left Hand only, because I made it as a private joke to please and tease Lipatti.

The history of the piece is this. He was asked some years ago to write a sonata for a pianist who had lost his left leg in an accident. Poor Lipatti, who had a charming sense of humour, wrote a sonata for left hand only to re-establish as he said, the balance of power. The pianist, Béla Siki, is a young Hungarian pupil of his, who has the manuscript and who played the work to me. I recorded it one afternoon and sent the pressings of it to Lipatti, all of them labelled 'Jesu, Joy of Man's Desiring, Pianist Dinu Lipatti'. He died before he could hear it.

When I next have the privilege of seeing you I will give you the history of the other fragments in this assortment which, on the face of it, may appear only chips from the sculptor's workshop, but are really unique documents which will never see the light of day. It is in the latter light that I venture to send them to you in reverence and devotion, hoping that they may give you a private and personal pleasure.

I thought the little Princess would like these new records of *Peter and the Wolf* as a small token of my affection.

With all good wishes for a very happy Christmas, peace and prosperity in your land, and the health and freedom to realise your noble dreams and wishes.

> Your devoted
> Walter Legge

The recording of Lipatti's Sonatina was issued on the Parlophone label. *Peter and the Wolf* must have been the Markevitch recording, with Wilfrid Pickles as narrator.

III. The Maharaja Of Mysore

30 December 1950.
THE PALACE,
MYSORE.

My dear Walter,

Many thanks for your letter with information of to be released recordings [*sic*]. It is indeed kind of you to do so. I am a little disappointed that most of them are things already in the catalogue. But nevertheless, I am glad to know them.

As regards your suggestion that I should mark the records of my personal selection, I would suggest that you would be a better judge of them than any personal choice I might make. As a matter of fact my choices keep varying daily according to my moods, so it is a bit of a job to select a final list. I must confess that the Galliera Seventh Beethoven a little disappointing. I thought Karajan would do it. He would have been wonderful. His Fifth Symphony is a shock because one hears it as Beethoven wished it to be – not as we have become used to it. So I thought No. 7 by Karajan would have been wonderful. Speaking of Beethoven symphonies, how delightful it is to have Furtwängler's Fourth. I have not for long time been so thrilled, though the critics mauled it by saying Furtwängler's idiosyncrasies marred the rhythmic flow. How wrong they are? I for one would not have Toscanini's correctness in place of Furtwängler's idiosyncrasies. Pray give me more Furtwängler and Beethoven. It is such a tonic after Toscanini's highly strung, vicious performances. You must have heard Toscanini's efforts on records. It is abominable. The speed and energy are those of a Demon – not an angel or superman as one would ardently hope for. I have begun to loathe all the things Toscanini is recording. They are so abominable. Take the *Leonora* No. 3, Tchaikovsky Sixth, Ravel *Daphnis and Chloë* No. 2 to mention a few or even the *Jupiter* and *Haffner* symphonies – they are unbearable. At least it is my view. I do not know what you think.

So coming to the point of Beethoven symphonies may I hope that Furtwängler will do his complete Beethoven symphony cycle. I hope his Seventh which you were to do last January is soon coming out.

I am very pleased Cherkassky is on HMV. He is a fine artist. We are badly in need of the Chopin B flat minor Sonata without cuts as well as the *Preludes*. The Moiseiwitsch was a disappointment.

Speaking of pianists Rubinstein has become an abominable player. I have his recent Op. 31 No. 3 Beethoven. It is so bad – wrong notes, fast speed, no consideration for dynamics. Equally abominable were the Decca Backhaus releases of Beethoven Sonatas Ops. 26, 53 and 109.

You will I trust have given consideration for the recording. I propose we do. I am here to do what I can though you will realise that it is not possible to take on big works like Bruckner or Bach for the time being at any rate. So I want to make the best we can of a difficult job. The others can be considered later on. This is mere suggestion which can be fitted in or cut out as need be.

191

Thank you so much for your Christmas gift which I shall look forward to when it arrives.

I was shocked to hear of Lipatti's death. It is very sad to have lost so great an artist. Nevertheless, and thanks to you, we are fortunate in having been left a legacy of his great art through the wonderful recordings of the Bach Partita and the Chopin *Waltzes*. Let me hope the Mozart Sonata will soon be available to complete the list. It is a great pity. Lipatti was a real genius. But it is a cruel world we live in.

I am very busy now with conferences and what not. So I shall look forward to hearing from you in the near future when you have a little time.

I do not know if I shall be able to come in 1951. It is so difficult to say these days. But I hope for the best.

With good wishes for your happiness and prosperity in 1951 and grateful thanks for your selfless work in the cause of music.

> I am,
> Yours very sincerely,
> [personal signature]
> [The Maharaja of Mysore]

IV. ALBERT SCHWEITZER

Between 1935 and 1937 Walter Legge supervised recordings by Albert Schweitzer of Bach's organ music as part of the Society series which he had instigated. After the war Schweitzer, heavily involved in his medical and missionary work in Africa, was approached by American Columbia to re-record some of the Bach and also repertoire by other composers. There were some misunderstandings, as the following correspondence reveals.

[translated from German]   9 March 1952.
                                              Lambarene
                                              Via Port Gentil
                                    French Equatorial Africa.

Dear Friend,

I am trying not to imagine what you must be thinking about my long silence. But you must bear with me. You were able to observe even when I was in London the terrible state of fatigue I was in. It became worse afterwards. I have had to allow my correspondence to deteriorate into chaos. On the boat, on the journey to Lambarene, I tried to deal with the chaos of more than 500 unanswered and partly unread letters, but fatigue made this impossible. Here in Lambarene I found an awful lot of work waiting for me. Unfortunately I had to do some reconstruction work which really exhausted me and took up a lot of my time. My correspondence has become even more chaotic. I remember vaguely having had a telegram and a letter from you, in the chaos. I replied to your telegram, asking you not to carry out your intention of visiting me in Strasbourg in the days before my departure. I had to make my final purchases and to organise the paperwork for 125 crates which I brought with me. You cannot imagine what a job that is, because your homeland protects you from dealing with such considerations, and filling in the many abnormal papers required for customs clearance. The chaos as regards matters to be dealt with by letter has increased still further. There is no question of my thinking of searching for your letter in the sacks which contain the correspondence. My time, work and fatigue prevent me from doing this. However, I can discuss the matter with you even without the letter. I can remember it clearly. I just did not have the energy (or the time) to write this letter. Just like many other letters from publishers lie unfinished amongst my affairs since the autumn. No human being should be given such a hectic working life as I have been given. So please be kind and forgive my silence. I should have loved to write to you long before now.

PS.   10th March 52.
In the meantime a nurse has delved into the chaos of letters and brought to light all the Columbia letters, including yours. I would not have thought it possible for her to do so.

> Yours sincerely,
> Albert Schweitzer

[translated from German]   10 March 1952.
                                                                                     Lambarene.
Here is a resumé of the whole business.

For my 1950 stay in Europe I undertook to re-record on modern recording apparatus as many as possible of the records which I had made in 1936 for English Columbia, and in addition, some new works (Sixth Organ Symphony in G minor of Widor; last organ sonata of Mendelssohn-Bartholdy, on 'Vater unser im Himmelreich', Chorale No. 3 by César Franck in A major, Fantasia and Fugue in G minor J.S. Bach, Prelude in D major Bach (IV Vol. Peters).

I made a start with these records with apparatus belonging to my son-in-law, Mr Echat, on the big new organ in St Moritz Abbey in Switzerland. I stopped doing this recording, however, after completing some of it, because the organ was only available to me for a few hours each day with interruptions, which tired me too much. I was considering abandoning the recording, especially as I had much more work to do in Europe than I had thought I would have for the relatively short stay.

I should interject here that when I was with Mr Goddard [Lieberson] in New York in 1949 I promised him to make records for the American Columbia Company as well. I simply imagined this to involve my making part of the records for the American Columbia Company and another part for the English Columbia Company and that the two associate companies would each supply their records to the other. My American friends also demanded that I should make records directly for America.

I had therefore almost given up the plan to make the number of records which I had envisaged playing, when Mr Hill came to Günsbach in the autumn with his recording van to record a short piece of me on the organ in picture and sound. In this short recording it turned out unexpectedly that the organ built and tuned according to my instructions, although it is only of medium size, was splendid on the film strip. Whereupon Mr Hill suggested making the equipment available to me for two weeks for recording, in which case the metal tapes would not be company-owned, but would be my own property which I could offer to whomever I chose (in return for recording expenses to Mr Hill). I was then able to make recordings at my ease on an organ and in a church which were at my disposal 'day and night'. I also re-recorded on the Günsbach organ the pieces which I had recorded in St Moritz, thinking that the recordings made in St Moritz would be suitable for the English Columbia Company and the recordings made in Günsbach for the Americans. As regards the recordings which were only made in Günsbach, not in St Moritz as well, I assumed that the American Columbia Company would also make them available to the English associate company, just as the Americans purchased the records of the English Company in 1936.

I thought everything was then settled when Mr Lieberson informed me latterly that it was not at all customary for me to make available to English Columbia different recordings than those used by the American Company of the same pieces. As I could not refuse to have the Günsbach records produced via the American Company, I was obliged to agree with a heavy heart not to make the St Moritz recordings available to the English Company.

I am therefore now left hoping that the American Company will do their utmost to give the English associate company access to the recordings by the best means possible. By the same post I shall be writing to Mr Lieberson to explain the situation to him and to ask him to show the utmost cooperation towards the English company with regard to my records, as I did these recordings thinking they were for them as well. I had imagined them to be closely linked associated companies, bearing the same name and jointly owning the records.

I want the management of the English Columbia Company to know that I am extremely grateful to this company for the fact that they recorded records by me when I was not very well known and that the proceeds from these records have helped me to earn my living in the last few years. With this feeling of gratitude I owe loyalty to the English Columbia Company. Because I did not have a full picture of the situation (I have so little time to deal with my own affairs) I was not able to make available to them in 1951 any recordings specifically for them. But I still intend making recordings and making some of them available to them.

I am very upset that I have been unsuccessful so far. But I hope that in the meantime the Günsbach recordings which the American Columbia

Company will place at your disposal will give you some degree of satisfaction.

Here are the details of the Günsbach recordings which the American Columbia Company is producing.

1) *Pieces which I played in 1936 in St Aurelia, Strasbourg and of which I made new recordings in Günsbach.*
a) César Franck Chorale No. 1 in E major
b) Bach Fugue in A major
c) Toccata and Fugue in C major
d) Canzona in D minor
e) Chorale prelude: O Mensch, bewein dein' Sünde gross (Peters Vol. V)
f) " " Wenn wir in höchsten Nöten sein (Peters Vol. VII)
g) " " Nun komm' der Heiden Heiland (Peters Vol. VII)
h) " " Herzlich tut mich verlangen

2) *Pieces which were not recorded previously, but for the first time in Günsbach.*
a) Symphony No. 6 (G minor) Ch. M. Widor
b) César Franck Chorale No. 3 A minor
c) Felix Mendelssohn-Bartholdy Sixth Organ Sonata on 'Vater unser im Himmelreich' (Lord's Prayer)
d) J.S.B. Fantasia and Fugue in G minor
e) J.S. Bach : Little Prelude in C major (Peters Vol. IV)
f) Prelude in D major – J.S. Bach (Peters Vol. IV)
g) J.S. Bach – Chorale Prelude, 'Ich ruf zu dir Herr Jesu Christ' (Peters Vol. V)
h) J.S.B. – Chorale Prelude 'Gelobet du, Jesu Christ' (Peters Vol. V)

Thus I have given you a resumé of matters as they occurred because I did not see the situation clearly from the outset. But the English Columbia Company should not have any doubts about my grateful affection for it and should have confidence in my setting things right by means of new recordings and not lose faith in my friendship. It is you whom I have to thank for the fact that I was able to make the recordings in St Aurelia's in Strasbourg in 1936. I shall never forget it.

Now I have a request for you: please write and tell me precisely from which recordings from St Aurelia's you made records. I have no notes of this. My first endeavour will be to make new recordings of these records for you with modern equipment. Do not forget to write and tell me this soon.

Please forgive my writing everything by hand and expecting you to read it. But I cannot do otherwise. I am working very late at night and the airmail post leaves tomorrow morning.

Yours sincerely,
Albert Schweitzer

[translated from German] 8 July 1952.

On *Foucauld* near the mouth of the Niger.

Dear Friend,

In the winter I wrote you a long letter. I told you that I had thought, when I promised the American Columbia Company records, that the two Columbia companies belonged together and that the records which I made for the one would also be available to the other and that I only learned that this was not completely the case when I was signing the contract. I also told you how much this had upset me because I have a great affection for the English Columbia Company and feel great gratitude towards them because they asked me to make records when I was not at all well known and the proceeds from these records have formed a major part of my means of support in the past few years. I also told you that I wanted to do all that was possible to ensure that the modern microgroove records which I made for America would also be available to English Columbia Company and that in future I would also make records for English Columbia. You did not reply to this letter in which I poured out my heart to you, which upset me in view of the close nature of our mutual relationship.

In the process of discussions which I have had with the American company I have finally made them understand how very upset I was at appearing to be ungrateful towards the English company, and persuaded them that all the records made for the American company for all times, whatever the relationship between the two companies may be, will also be available to the English company. They made this concession to me because they appreciated my unhappiness at appearing ungrateful towards the English company. In consequence it is now possible for the English company also to own Bach coupled with César Franck on modern microgroove records. I think that what I have achieved in lengthy negotiations will give you some consolation. In addition, I will also make records (new ones) for you on metal tape, if I can make these available to you in a few months' time, if you are interested in having new records recorded for you.

Please tell the directors of English Columbia what I have managed to do and write and tell me what you think – whether you are pleased about the concessions which I have obtained and the prospect of new records made for you. It would give me great satisfaction if this were the case, for I have been very upset to have landed in the position of appearing ungrateful towards you, which I certainly am not. I am going to Europe for a fairly long visit. I shall be coming to London in October and hope then to find time for a relaxed meeting with you. I really regretted so much that this was not possible during my last rushed visit. But then the whole of my excessively busy life is always in a rush. I find this difficult to tolerate.

Please give the directors of Columbia my best regards and write to me at Günsbach, just to let me know at least whether my letter has arrived. For when one posts letters in transit through an African port, it is not at all certain that they will get there. I have lived through some terribly difficult months. I dragged myself to the daily round of excessive work, as best I could, always had to work far into the night only to have to be on my feet again the next morning at 6.15, which led to a chronic lack of sleep. Only now on the boat, where I can sleep as long as I wish, have I become half human again.

> With best wishes,
> [Albert Schweitzer]

[translated from German] 19 November 1952.
Günsbach/Alsace
France.

Dear Friend,

Let me tell you first of all what a pleasure it was for me that we were able to meet again and discuss at leisure everything which had to be discussed. It was a great comfort to me that everything is now cleared up. I must also thank you for the many really valuable records which you had sent to me. This gave me such great pleasure.

Now I am in the middle of preparations for the return to Lambarene, and am completely preoccupied with material things. Only in the quiet of Africa will I find time for myself.

> With best wishes to you and your wife,
> Yours sincerely,
> Albert Schweitzer

V. EMI COLLEAGUES

It was not to be expected that Walter Legge's relations with his company chiefs and associates would always be smooth – he was too outspoken and definite in his ideas about what should be done and what he wanted to be done for that to be the case. If his actions sometimes aroused resentment and suspicion he often got his way, and there was recognition, albeit sometimes grudgingly given, that he had vision and flair. Legge's chief was Brenchley Mittell, a somewhat remote figure who had become head of the International Artists' Department in 1946 (he was also head of record production) after a successful career in the technical side of the company. Mittell retired in 1957.

Inter-departmental MEMORANDUM Date: 3 July 1951.
To: Mr Mittell
Re: OTTO KLEMPERER

Did you hear either of Klemperer's concerts last week with the Philharmonia? Or see the *Times* criticism?

I missed the first concert but heard the second and endorse all *The Times* said in his favour. Denis Matthews, whose attitude to conductors has previously been 'Only Toscanini – the rest are makeshifts', tells me that he has never heard such a superb Beethoven Fifth as Klemperer's, or comparable performances of the two Beethoven concertos. The Philharmonia players are unanimous in ranking him with Karajan; several even prefer Klemperer.

I have engaged him for some concerts in January and February next year and feel that we should do some recording with him. He is not a man for the modern repertoire except Mahler and Strauss. His field is Bach, Mozart, Beethoven and Brahms and I feel that we must record him. How would you feel about the popular classical symphonies and overtures for HMV plum? I hesitate to suggest red or light blue because of collisions with Furtwängler or Karajan. But we must have him.

I doubt if he will give us exclusivity because he is doing a lot with Westminster Vox and Remington.

I suggest we select the repertoire from:

Beethoven *Egmont*   2 sides.
Fidelio   2 sides.
Coriolan   2 sides.
Leonora III   4 sides.
Symphony No. 5   9 sides.
   "   No. 7   10 sides.
Mozart Symphony No. 39   6 sides.
   "   "   "   40   6 sides.
   "   "   "   41   8 sides.
Brahms Symphony No. 1   10 sides.

WALTER LEGGE
International Artists Department.

Klemperer was only in fact recording for Vox at this time.

Inter-departmental MEMORANDUM   Date: 16 January 1952.
To: Mr Mittell
Re: *Fidelio*

The opera of which a complete recording is most necessary is Beethoven's *Fidelio*. When we first contracted Furtwängler after the war we promised him either *Tristan* or *Fidelio*. We have got the means and the cast for *Tristan* but he has already postponed it from the summer of 1951 to 1952 and now he is trying – I hear – to put it off to September 1952. Karajan has just done a splendid *Fidelio* in Milan with a cast which – with a few minor alterations – would be ideal.

I consider *Fidelio* a number one priority and I would like your sanction to negotiate the recording of it thus:

Offer Karajan at once to record it in London before the end of September under his present contract. Explain to him the urgency and the necessity of imposing the time limit. If he declines offer it to Furtwängler on the same basis. If he declines get the best available conductor – it must be a German or Austrian – and do it. The best cast would be:

Leonora Martha Mödl or Inge Borkh
Florestan Wolfgang Windgassen
Marcellina Elisabeth Schwarzkopf
Pizarro Hans Hotter
Ministro Hermann Uhde
Rocco Ludwig Weber
Jacquino Gerhard Unger
First Prisoner "   "
Second Prisoner Hermann Uhde
Philharmonia Orchestra and Covent Garden Chorus

It is clear from the reviews discussions and sales that for LP operas the public wants, in operas where there are recitatives or dialogue, enough of this connecting material to give cohesion and continuity to the action and this is vital in *Fidelio*.

I estimate with the dialogue shorn of its inessentials we should get the complete opera on to six or at the most seven LP sides – 12 to 14 orchestral sessions, two with male chorus, two with mixed chorus. By doing the whole job on tape we could save the otherwise wasted orchestral time in recording the dialogue.

To let Decca be first in the field with *Fidelio* would be as unwise as it was to let them get away with *Fledermaus*.

Walter Legge

To: Mr Mittell, copy to Mr Fowler   4 March 1953.
Sir William Walton's Coronation March

Walton will record his new March *Orb and Sceptre* for the Coronation of H.M. Queen Elizabeth II on 18th March. This will be one 12-inch Double Sided Columbia. It will also be part of a DS LP which will contain:-

Crown Imperial March
Portsmouth Point
and
'Sheep may safely graze'

in short, a popular Walton LP. We have given an undertaking that these will be published on 3rd June – not before because the first performance has been commissioned. Will you please give the necessary instructions to give this recording the highest priority for it to be through and well transferred in ample time.

It is also well that you should be warned that I am arranging to record the ten unaccompanied madrigals which have been written for the Coronation and which are being first performed on Coronation Eve. I cannot yet promise to get these recorded well in advance but efforts are being made. They will together make one LP 12-inch.

Vaughan Williams is performing his *Fantasia on a Theme of Thomas Tallis* on June 1 with the Philharmonia. We have just done it for HMV with Sargent and the BBC but it seems to me that we should be commercially obtuse not to take the opportunity of recording the authentic performance under the composer's direction for the new mark. The Americans will almost certainly like it and we could record a few days after the public performance.

Walter Legge

The chance to record Vaughan Williams's performance of his *Tallis Fantasia* was alas missed.

Inter-departmental MEMORANDUM   Date: 9 March 1953.
To: Mr Mittell

Far be it from me to question the mysterious ways in which God works to perform his wonders but, as a commercially-minded practical person, I am surprised to see that on Friday morning we recorded for HMV the Brahms Violin Concerto in [EMI Studio] No. 1 with Ida Haendel and in the afternoon the Brahms Violin Concerto (the same one – there is only one) in the Kingsway Hall with Gioconda de Vito, also for HMV.

No doubt there is a good reason for this but it escapes my poor brain. Will you enlighten me?

Walter Legge

If Walter Legge sometimes showed little respect for some of his senior colleagues, he valued the work of his more immediate associates, as the following two letters demonstrate clearly. Albert Deering was a cutting engineer, and Douglas Larter a balance engineer.

23 July 1970.

Dear Mrs Deering,

Please accept my and my wife's heartfelt condolences on your dear husband's death. No man had better deserved a long, healthy and happy retirement. I do wish he or you had let me know sooner that he was ill; I would have made a special journey to see him again.

He had worked for the Company many more years than I had. Unlike me, he had made many friends among his colleagues. Of all the people I came into contact with in the Company, he was personally the closest to me. I have never known a man so reliable, so selflessly helpful as he was. In the last 15 years of my time in EMI he made my work a delight. He was the only man with the patience to put up with my incurable perfectionism and the only man who conspired with me to make our work together a matter of historical interest which, you will live to see, will be the case.

200

From the early days of tape recording he was the man who produced out of the tapes I had made, the artistic results I knew were there but no one but Albert could get on to record.

Many of the greatest artists I worked with – Karajan, Gieseking, Callas, Gobbi – owed to him much of the fame they gained through records. Most of all my wife, who was deeply attached to him, treasured the work he did which helped to make her fame – not only in gratitude but in admiration. He knew her voice to the last overtone and conveyed it to records as no one else could have done or has done since. He gave her records the life of her own radiant personality and helped it reach the homes of millions of music lovers.

And he made us both laugh – an invaluable and treasured gift that made work with him not work but a delightful and happy adventure.

The passion we shared for gardens was for him, I believe, as for me a strong link. When the factory drove us nearly mad by ruining some work we had been proud of, we forgot our fury by talking about roses.

If at any time I can be of help to you, do not hesitate to write to me. I owe it to Albert to express as well as I can the debt of friendship and collaboration I shall always owe him. Our association was one of the great joys of my career.

Now try to remember the happy years you had together. It is better that he should have died as he did with his poor suffering body rather than have lived on to suffer longer.

Forgive the length of this letter but it helps me to ease my own sadness at the loss of a dear friend.

> Yours very sincerely,
> [Walter Legge]

> 15 August 1970.

Dear Mrs Larter,

A few days ago I heard to my grieved surprise that your husband had died recently. Please accept my and my wife's heartfelt condolences in your sad loss.

Duggie was one of the best colleagues I ever had. Only those who worked closely with him for many years know how greatly he contributed to the fame and success of artists who were unknown when he first recorded them, and who became famous owing much to Duggie's skill, patience and his wonderful ear.

You must have cursed me many a time for insisting that he came with me on long trips to Vienna and worked hundreds of evenings at Kingsway Hall: but I know that, particularly until your son married, he was happy both at home and in his work.

> Yours very sincerely,
> [Walter Legge]

VI. Two Composers: Sibelius and Britten

In post-war years there were a few more brief communications between Sibelius and Legge.

18 December 1950.
Järvenpää.

Dear Mr Legge,

Please accept my most cordial thanks for your kind congratulations on the occasion of my eighty-fifth birthday.

With kindest regards,
Yours sincerely,
Jean Sibelius

23 March 1953.

My dear Friend,

I have received your kind letter of February 27th and was very pleased to learn that you are contemplating to record Shakespeare's *The Tempest*, with my music.

The music for *The Tempest* was ordered by Det Kongelige Teater in Copenhagen and was composed to Danish words. The music, of course, will not suit the English original text but the Danish text would have to be translated by a very competent man. The copyright to the work is with Messrs Wilh. Hansen, Musik Forlag, Copenhagen. The two published suites I have composed freely from the incidental music which of course is much wider than the suites.

With my kindest regards and all best wishes,

Yours very sincerely,
Jean Sibelius

8 December 1953.

SIBELIUS JARVENPAA FINLAND

WE SALUTE YOU ON YOUR BIRTHDAY IN DEEPEST ADMIRATION AND AFFECTION STOP IN CELEBRATION WE ARE LISTENING TO RECORDS WE HAVE JUST MADE OF YOUR FOURTH SYMPHONY AND TAPIOLA WHICH WE ARE SENDING AND WHICH WE HOPE WILL PLEASE YOU

WALTER LEGGE
HERBERT VON KARAJAN

15 September 1954.

Dear Friend,

Thanking you cordially for your letter. I am glad to express my enthusiasm about the recordings. As you know, I have always been a great admirer of Mr v. Karajan and his magnificent rendering of my works has given me the keenest satisfaction. Especially in the Fourth Symphony, his great artistic line and the inner beauty of his interpretation have deeply impressed me. I beg you to present my grateful greetings to him.

> With all best wishes,
> Very sincerely yours,
> Jean Sibelius

> 11 May 1955.
> Helsinki.

Dear Friend,

You have perhaps wondered why I have not written to you before and thanked you for the excellent recordings of my Fourth and Fifth Symphony. I have now heard them many times and can only say that I am happy. Karajan is a great master. His interpretation is superb, technically and musically.

In the presentation by John Amis on the cover I have noticed a sentence reading: 'God opens his door etc.'. In my correspondence I have often been used to repeat expressions which the addressee has used previously and that was the case this time too. I am surprised that my words have been taken seriously.

The Sibelius Festivals are approaching and whole Finland is waiting for Elisabeth Schwarzkopf, not least I myself. I know her great Art from recordings and I am indeed happy that she will sing here in June. Please tell her my admiring greetings.

With kindest regards and all good wishes,

> Yours always sincerely,
> Jean Sibelius

In September 1952 Walter Legge recorded Britten's *Young Person's Guide to the Orchestra*, with Igor Markevitch conducting the Philharmonia Orcheatra. Legge hit upon the idea of asking the composer to record the commentary which accompanies the work, but as the letter below indicates, Britten felt obliged to decline. His suggestion of Peter Pears as a substitute was accepted by Legge, but it was not until June 1954 that the speech part of the recording was completed. The record was issued by Columbia in early 1955.

> 3 October 1952.
> 4 Crabbe Street,
> Aldeburgh, Suffolk.

Dear Walter Legge,

I am sorry that this reply to your letter about the *Young Person's Guide* is so late, but I've been terribly busy, & actually unable to get some information about the matter – necessary to answer your note.

First of all, I am afraid that my writing keeps me chained to Aldeburgh for this winter & so I can't do the talk, commentary, for the Markevitch records – much as I'd have liked to have been associated with him or them. But I thought you were in touch with Peter Pears about this – wouldn't it be better to stick to that? He has done it, in America, I know, & would do it well.

About the various versions, which seems to me to be an excellent idea, the copyright of the commentary belongs to Boosey & Hawkes, & so I think you'd better send them along to them – to Erwin Stein – for approval. They are, I believe, writing to you direct about this. Anyhow it wouldn't be much use sending them to me, because (apart from the French & German) I wouldn't understand sufficiently. I would suggest by the way, that the translations are quite free & colloquial.

I shall be here always if you want to ask anything –

> in haste,
> Yours sincerely
> Benjamin Britten

VII. NICOLAI GEDDA

In July 1952 Nicolai Gedda made his recording début with Walter Legge, singing the part of Grigory in a complete recording of *Boris Godunov*. Many years later Legge was prompted by a magazine article into telling the story of how he had 'discovered' the young Swedish tenor.

7 March 1973.

The Editor
High Fidelity Magazine

Dear Sir,

May I add a rider or two to Edward Greenfield's excellent piece on Nicolai Gedda.

The reason I went to Stockholm was to see for myself if Issay Dobrowen who was then musical director of the Stockholm Opera had sufficiently recovered from a major operation to carry through the heavy task of our planned recording of *Boris Godunov* with an almost entirely non-Russian cast in Paris.

On my arrival at the airport I was asked by a swarm of journalists if I were not interested in hearing their excellent young Swedish voices. Naturally I was interested, but I did not expect either the front page stories that appeared next morning or the mass of letters and almost incessant telephone calls asking to be heard. I had to ask the Director of the Opera for a room for a couple of days to hear about 100 young aspirants. The first to sing to me (at 9.30 in the morning) was Gedda who had I believe sung only once in public. He sang the *Carmen* Flower Song so tenderly yet passionately that I was moved almost to tears. He delivered the difficult rising scale ending with a clear and brilliant B flat. Almost

VIII. *Two Operatic Recordings*

apologetically I asked him to try to sing it as written – *pianissimo, rallentando* and *diminuendo*. Without turning a hair he achieved the near-miracle, incredibly beautifully and without effort. I asked him to come back at 8 that evening and sent word to my wife that a great singer had fallen into my lap and to Dobrowen that, believe it or not, this 23-year-old Gedda was the heaven-sent Dmitri for our *Boris*. Among the others I auditioned and asked to sign their names were Elisabeth Söderström, Kerstin Meyer and others who are still making distinguished careers. That evening Gedda sang both the *Carmen* aria and the two *Don Giovanni* arias to Dobrowen, Schwarzkopf and me. I engaged him immediately for Dmitri and telegraphed both Karajan and Dr Ghiringhelli, then Sovrintendente of La Scala, that I had found the ideal Don Ottavio. Ghiringhelli at once telegraphed Gedda to fly at La Scala's expenses for an audition. That autumn Ghiringhelli told me that in all the years he had been Director of La Scala no non-Italian singer had auditioned with such exquisitely clear and flawless Italian. He was immediately engaged for La Scala.

I am surprised that Gedda prefers his recent *Wiener Blut* recording to the old one. It is extremely unlikely that he will find again in his life a conductor for operetta to equal the late Otto Ackermann or Lovro von Matačić. Great conductors of Johann Strauss or the best of Lehár are rare.

Yours very truly,
[Walter Legge]

VIII. TWO OPERATIC RECORDINGS

In the early 1960s EMI produced a regular monthly publicity journal called *Record Times*. Walter Legge was persuded to make two contributions, one on Leoncavallo's *Pagliacci*, recorded in July 1960 and released in September 1961, and another on the second Callas recording of Bellini's *Norma*, made in September 1960 and released in November 1961.

Columbia's new *Pagliacci* – A new milestone in operatic recording

Pagliacci is one of the most popular operas because it has the right mixture of all the ingredients essential to make an Italian opera appeal to the widest public. It is a sordid yet moving *News of the World*-type story of love, lust, infidelity and treachery culminating in a double murder in full view of the audience. What more can they want?

The story and the music were written by the same man, and they fit like a glove. There is no padding, no time wasted. The extended lyrical parts are devised and spaced to delight the senses and by their prettiness intensify the heartbreak and horror of the dramatic climaxes.

As conductor I chose Lovro von Matačić who had recently directed the new production of *Pagliacci* at the Vienna State Opera and who has just been appointed Director of the Frankfurt Opera. He is a Yugoslav, a giant

205

of a man who has spent the greatest part of his life in the theatre. He, more than any other conductor today, has as one side of his nature the earthy, primitive gusto to play this music as if every note were a drop of his own blood.

For Canio, the part in which Caruso made his greatest fame, we had Franco Corelli, a young Italian tenor discovered by Toscanini, and principal tenor of both La Scala and New York's Metropolitan Opera. He is the only great young heroic tenor in the world. He has the authentic exciting ring of the pure tenor voice and the instinct to express without restraint the jealousy, passion, despair and rage of the part.

Three years ago I had seen in New York a performance of *Pagliacci* when the soprano was Lucine Amara, a young American of Armenian origin, who obviously sensed that Nedda is a slut, sharp-tongued, capricious and sensual. She was the best Nedda I had seen for years and in the recording she has more than fulfilled expectations.

Tonio is one of the many parts Tito Gobbi has made his own, and his famous interpretation of the part made him the inevitable choice. But the medium of stereophonic recording stimulated this great singing-actor's imagination to new and more powerful dramatic accents. His hunch-back's wooing of Nedda is a terrifying blend of lust and the pathetic dignity of a soul malformed by the ugly frame it must inhabit, and his corny fooling in the Comedy played on the stage within a stage puts before our minds' eyes the sordid little troupe of small-time performers unwillingly kept together only by their mutual need to earn the bare necessities of existence by entertaining simple peasants.

As Silvio, the villager whose passing infatuation for Nedda precipitates her death and his own we have Mario Zanasi, a young Italian baritone. An admirable and sensitive singer with an enviable future.

The recording was made in the traditional home of Italian opera – La Scala, Milan. The orchestral pit was covered as it is for orchestral concerts in this theatre, and the orchestra was seated on this cover and the front part of the stage, where it sounds best in La Scala. The theory that operatic recordings should be made with the orchestra 'in the pit' is a fallacy. In practice it does not work. Operatic orchestras are boxed in a sunken pit only because they would otherwise obscure the audience's view of the stage. Operatic orchestras must be heard but not seen. No conductor has ever given an orchestral concert with the orchestra seated in the pit: it always sounds better on the stage.

We made our 'stage' on the stage of La Scala by raising the bridges – those parts of the stage which can be raised and lowered at will – to their fullest height. Together they gave us a far larger stage area than the majority of theatres can offer, and the ideal separation between singers and orchestra.

Our stage was covered with a canvas cloth divided into sections each one metre square. Several months before the recording took place, the conductor and I worked out and agreed in detail the 'production' of the opera – the movements and position of all the singers – chorus as well as soloists – to convey to every listener the dramatic situations and action.

In recorded opera words and the inflections of voice are much more important than in the theatre: they have to communicate all that the singer in theatre expresses by gesture and facial expression. Together with the invaluable Maestro Tonini (the best operatic coach in Italy and now a conductor in his own right) I worked with the singers in relay 12 hours a day for seven days to put the drama of the words and music into the colour of their voices. In the meantime Lovro von Matačić rehearsed the orchestra and Maestro Mola prepared the chorus.

All the carefully prepared elements of our *Pagliacci* came together for their first time at a general rehearsal at which the whole opera was recorded as if it had been a performance. We spent a long day studying what we had achieved and what we had still to achieve to make the recording of *Pagliacci* which on the one hand would shun all the gimmickry which will make so many recent operatic recordings old-fashioned in a year or two but at the same time use to the utmost the vast resources of EMI's technical superiority for purely musical, dramatic and artistic needs. The actual recording took us only four days.

I believe that our new *Pagliacci* starts off as one of the great recordings of the century.

Norma

Norma is one of the great 'old fashioned' operas which has been given a new lease of life by the genius of Maria Callas. If she had done nothing else but recreate for our generation the nobility, pathos and overwhelming dramatic power that lies dormant in this opera she would still have secured her permanent place in the history of operatic art.

The Italians have an affectionately derisive term for an operatic bass who just stands and sings; they call him a *basso in toga* [the dress on a Roman statue]. It would not be an exaggeration to say that all the characters in *Norma* are *cantati in toga*, they just have to stand and sing. The drama is all in the music and the text: it is not dependent on where the characters stand. But what they have to sing!

Norma is a static opera, and not one that lends itself to trick exploitation of stereophonic recording. The real value of stereophonic recording is the improvement in the actual quality and naturalness of sound which is magnificently evident in this recording made on the very stage where Norma was first performed on December 26th, 1831.

An opera must have great qualities to hold its place in the repertoire for 130 years. What are the particular qualities that have given *Norma* such a long lease of life?

In the first place it is a challenge to the abilities of great dramatic sopranos. The music is terrifyingly difficult to sing: it needs the power of a heavy dramatic soprano combined with the agility of a trapeze coloratura. It needs super-human staying power and, above all, fierce and telling dramatic instinct; the ability to charge Bellini's recitatives with the drama and suffering implied in the words. Callas has met the challenge of this part as no other singer of our time.

The composer does not always help her. Bellini's supreme quality was his ability to write noble melodies of length and classic serenity that no Italian composer since has been able to match. It is not without significance that he was born in Catania, the last important Greek settlement in the Mediterranean. The qualities we most admire in Greek plastic art – its great span and timelessness seem to have seeped through the blood of centuries and become the heart of Bellini's slow tunes.

His quick music is less inspired and often so curiously short-breathed that an irreverent mind occasionally thinks of the fortune Bellini could have made had he been alive today, as a composer of jingles for television advertising. The quick sections of the two duets for the two sopranos would be ideal fodder in a revue for the two Hermiones (Baddeley and Gingold) or Beatrice Lillie and a comparable partner strutting out – in black silk tights and spangled corsages. But popular Italian opera is not a highbrow art. It was written for 'the general public' – men and women who are moved by direct emotional stimulus, who can easily remember a good tune, and are not ashamed of themselves for doing so.

Norma is a story of two priestesses, Norma and Adalgisa, who have fallen in love with the same man, Pollione, inconveniently as he is the Roman proconsul occupying their country. As priestesses they are sworn to chastity. Norma, the daughter of the high priest has taken so liberal a view of her vows that she has had two children by Pollione: Adalgisa is preparing to elope with him to Rome. Adalgisa confides to Norma that she has fallen in love and Norma, deeply conscious of her own problems, is about to release her from her vows when she learns that Pollione is also Adalgisa's lover. She decides to kill both Pollione and their children but the sight of her innocent victims moves her to spare their lives, and she decides to expiate her sins by the traditional druidic punishment – the funeral pyre, but first entreats Adalgisa to take Pollione and care for her children.

Adalgisa unsuccessfully tries to induce Pollione to return to Norma and his children and Norma exhorts her tribe to overthrow the Roman occupiers. When Pollione is discovered among her own people she claims the right to kill him herself, but in the last moment she cannot kill the father of her children. Pollione still refuses to give up Adalgisa. Norma confesses to the assembled priests and claims the right to purge her sins in the sacrificial fire. Moved by her nobility Pollione asks and is allowed to share her fate.

The cast Columbia has assembled for this recording cannot be equalled by any other team of contemporary singers. Norma is one of Callas's supreme achievements. With her uncanny instinct for conveying emotion through the colouring of a word – even a syllable – she reveals new and unsuspected dramatic lights, and gives Bellini, whom the German poet Heine described as 'a sigh in pumps and silk stockings' with a majesty and nervous fibre that would have electrified and probably terrified that rosy-cheeked and golden-haired fop.

The Pollione is Franco Corelli, the great dramatic tenor, who has been her partner in the most notable recent revivals of the opera. The part is not a favourite with tenors: Pollione is as much a cad as the aptly initialled B. F. Pinkerton, and the music calls for the staying power of a young Siegfried. Bellini described Adalgisa as 'soprano' but by tradition the part is sung by a mezzo-soprano, even though it calls for agility and range to match Norma's. Since Ebe Stignani retired there has been no great Adalgisa. I found her in Christa Ludwig, the young German mezzo-soprano. When the recording was completed Tullio Serafin said, 'I have heard and worked with all the great Adalgisas of the last 70 years. This girl Ludwig is to be compared only with Stignani.' The Oroveso (Norma's father), Nicola Zaccaria is, like Callas, Greek. He pours out a noble flood of tone.

The directing hand in this superb recording is Maestro Tullio Serafin, the last of the senior generation of Italian conductors. He has been earning his living by music for 75 years. At the age of seven he began to pay for his lessons by playing violin and viola in café orchestras. He played in the orchestral pit of La Scala under Toscanini and Faccio who had known Verdi intimately, and he has been conducting in the great opera houses for more than 60 years. With his vast knowledge of style and tradition in Italian singing Serafin has been the guide and fatherly friend of four generations of singers in Italy and America. It was from Serafin that Callas learned the refinements and subtleties of her art and he was the only possible choice for the conductor to show Bellini's masterpiece in all its glory.

It gladdened the heart to see this bright-eyed, tubby little man, with his black sombrero stuck rakishly on his head, working with an enthusiasm and untiring alertness unknown in men half his age. He was always the first to arrive in La Scala and the last to leave it, happy as a child to recreate anew a masterpiece he has cherished for a long lifetime.

IX. OTTO KLEMPERER

Walter Legge brought Otto Klemperer out of comparative obscurity to the Columbia label and the Philharmonia Orchestra and caused him to enjoy a glorious artistic Indian summer. Legge and Klemperer worked together for a decade, but their association came to a dramatic end in March 1964. Tension between the two men had already been created as a result of Legge's intentions to disband the Philharmonia, and a disagreement then arose as to whether Legge should or should not attend a piano rehearsal for a recording of Mozart's *Die Zauberflöte*.

[translated from German]   27 February [sic]* 1964.
                                                        Hotel Hyde Park, London SW1.

Dear Mr Legge,

In the telephone conversation which we have just had you concluded by saying that you would think over what we had discussed and call me tomorrow.

However I feel I must now inform you without delay that, as I see it, there is nothing to think over. I intend to hold the piano rehearsals for *The Magic Flute* on my own with the singers. This stands to reason and in no way exceeds my authority since it concerns purely musical and interpretive matters. For recordings just as much as for concerts I alone am always responsible for both.

Please confirm your receipt of this letter by this evening.

                                              I remain, yours truly,
                                              Otto Klemperer

Sent by messenger

* Actually March.

                                                             27 March 1964.

Dear Dr Klemperer,

It is evident to me that you completely misunderstand the reasons why it is essential for me to be at all pianoforte rehearsals of *Zauberflöte* – or any operatic recording. You have made so few recordings of opera that you cannot possibly know the intricacies of this type of work. I understand your preoccupation with the purely musical aspects of the work. But a modern stereophonic recording of an opera (and this will be the *first* stereophonic recording of *Zauberflöte*) needs the closest cooperation and mutual help of the conductor (which *you* are) and the producer – which I am. If it is a success – and that is what I strive for – *you* will get the profit, the glory and the fame: the complaints, the blame for any deficiencies are my reward.

The reason I need to be present at your piano rehearsals is to know the tempi, dynamics, pauses and expression that you wish to make. Only in this way can I translate these effectively into stage movement, microphone placing etc. There are myriad technical details which must be prepared well beforehand. You must realise too that every minute of such sessions as these costs EMI more than ten pounds: *more than ten pounds a minute*. Besides this, we have a very tight schedule – to which you have agreed from the outset.

It is world-wide practice for the above-mentioned reasons that conductor and producer, and through him the technicians, know well beforehand what is necessary to achieve the best results. For that reason it is essential that I attend all your piano rehearsals.

210

One further reason. Not one singer in the whole cast was known to you until I had found them and placed them, at one time or another, at your disposal.

Yours sincerely,
Walter Legge

CITY TELEGRAMME – DIRECT   28 MARCH 1964
MR WALTER LEGGE 3 OAKHILL AVENUE HAMPSTEAD NW3

YOUR LETTER UNACCEPTABLE YOUR REASONS DO NOT CONVINCE ME STOP THEREFORE I HAVE ASKED EMI TO INFORM ME IN WRITING BY TOMORROW SUNDAY EVENING WHETHER MY CONTRACTUAL DUTIES AS CONDUCTOR OBLIGE ME TO HOLD PURELY MUSICAL PIANO REHEARSALS IN PRESENCE OF PRODUCER STOP WILL ADHERE TO THEIR DECISION STOP REGRET NECESSITY OF THIS STEP SINCERELY OTTO KLEMPERER

CITY TELEGRAMME – DIRECT   28 MARCH 1964
MR PETER ANDRY 951 FINCHLEY ROAD NW11

AFTER MUCH CONSIDERATION MUST HEREWITH ASK EMI TO INFORM ME IN WRITING BY TOMORROW SUNDAY EVENING WHETHER MY CONTRACTUAL DUTIES AS CONDUCTOR OBLIGE ME TO HOLD PURELY MUSICAL PIANO REHEARSALS IN PRESENCE OF PRODUCER STOP WILL ADHERE TO EMIS DECISION AND HAVE INFORMED MR LEGGE OF THIS TELEGRAMME STOP REGRET NECESSITY OF THIS STEP SINCERELY OTTO KLEMPERER

29 MARCH 1964
KLEMPERER HYDE PARK HOTEL KNIGHTSBRIDGE SW1

I HAVE ALREADY INFORMED EMI THAT IRRESPECTIVE OF THEIR WISHES I WILL NOT ATTEND REHEARSALS OR RECORDINGS OF ZAUBERFLOTE OR ANY OTHER WORK AT WHICH YOU ARE PRESENT YOURS VERY SINCERELY LEGGE

X. CARLO MARIA GIULINI

Another recording artist who became caught up in the aftermath of Walter Legge's decision to leave EMI and disband his orchestra was the conductor Carlo Maria Giulini.

[translated from Italian]   24 January 1964.
Tel Aviv.

My very dear Walter,

Thank you for your telegram. The concert of the 30th of July is fine but the one for the 7th of September is not possible. This means that I shall only do one. For the programme, the *Four Sacred Pieces* are all right, but in place of Mozart's Requiem you will need to think of something else because I have never done it and I cannot possibly prepare it by then. What would you say to Haydn's *Nelson* Mass or a symphony, or Fauré's Requiem? Here the *Don Giovanni* has had an enthusiastic and successful reception. Just think – we will be doing 15 repeat performances of which 12 have been sold out even before the first night. The orchestra plays very well, with a genuine and committed love of music. Of the company I will speak to you personally in more detail; the design and decoration are very effective. The work has been crazy but, thank God, everything has turned out very well.

I have received a sort af contract from EMI to conclude *El Amor Brujo* and to record *Don Carlos*. I just don't understand it! Isn't this what was already planned with you? I have not given them an answer and will not do so until you have explained the situation to me. Please give me some information. In any case the problem will have to be sorted out when I come to London in February.

Stephen Gray has written to tell me that the BBC wants to offer me the job of conducting Elgar's *Falstaff* this year. When you get the chance to see him would you mind telling him that I would like him to telephone Mr Osland to thank him on my behalf for the invitation, and to inform him immediately that it is not possible for me to accept it. Thank you.

I hope that you and your good lady are in splendid physical, mental and artistic form. My most affectionate thoughts go to both of you.

> I embrace you.
> Yours,
> Carlo Maria

Stephen Gray was General Manager of the Philharmonia Orchestra and General Manager and Secretary of the Philharmonia Concert Society from 1959 to 1964. He was responsible initially to Jane Withers, the orchestra's Managing Director.

[translated from Italian]   21 October 1964.
                                                   Via Jacopo da Ponte
                                                   49 Rome.

Dear Walter,

As I mentioned to you, I have been to Amsterdam to receive the 1964 Edison Prize for the recording of the *Four Sacred Pieces*. I am well aware of how much I owe you for this success, both for the artistic and technical help you have given me in placing your amazing orchestra at my disposal. The same goes, of course, for everything to do with my work since I began my collaboration with you. You know what my estimation is of your profound ability and quality. From my contact with you I have amassed a priceless wealth of experience for my musical life. I shall always be grateful to you for this. Unfortunately, something has happened to our personal relationship, and it is a thing that I have always deeply feared all these years, namely, that if, for whatever reason, we had a difference of opinion, this would seriously affect your feeling of friendship. You know, Walter, that I was wholehearted in my support of you during the difficult time you went through last spring, as I perfectly understood your point of view and shared it fully when you told me one evening at your house that you were no longer in a position to support the financial burden of the orchestra, and that consequently you were in the painful position of having to disband it. A few days later, as we were leaving the Festival Hall together after a concert, you told me that you were hanging fire on your decision as Mr Bean had assured you that the entire English musical world would come to your aid in order to avert the winding up of an orchestra that was now synonymous with quality and style. Afterwards, you left for France and I for Florence. I had been there a few days when the press published the news of the disbanding of the Philharmonia. When I had finished my engagement in Florence I returned to London, and at the airport I found [Bernard] Walton who had come especially to talk to me and who confirmed the news of the break up, adding that all the members of the orchestra and particularly those, like himself, who had always been with you right from the beginning, were very saddened and surprised, not only because of the fact itself but also from reading in one of your statements to the press, set out under five headings, that the chief reasons for the disbanding were artistic, and that if you wanted to or could reform the orchestra, you would ask every member to re-audition. Walton told me that, following a meeting, the members of the orchestra, faced with the necessity of personal and artistic survival, had decided to stay together and trust in the solidarity of the artists who had worked with them for years with complete mutual contentment. He asked me if I also would be willing to come to their aid and I agreed without the slightest hesitation. That same evening, after recording, I came to dinner at your house, and in the presence of your good lady and Jane [Withers], I reported all this to you, and I said that I would still conduct the orchestra. After some bewilderment, you, your wife and Jane eventually acknowledged that I could not do otherwise and that you were all in agreement with me.

This was the last normal conversation that you and I have had. We have seen each other a few times for work and I have tried everything in order to re-open and deepen the discussion, but without success. I have not seen anything of you since. I have lost count of the number of times I have telephoned you at home to give you news of the rehearsals I have been having, above all because I wanted you to have peace of mind and freedom from other thoughts that might plague you, but your wife told me that you were not well and that it was better not to disturb you, something I perfectly understood and found logical, far from suspecting that in this attitude of yours there lay resentment towards me. After this I lost contact with you. When I saw that you were not present at the performance of the

Requiem I realised that something was wrong. I talked to Jane about it and told her of my intention to write to you. She, however, begged me not to, saying that you should be left in peace, and that calm would return after the storm. This is what I did. Now all this is understandable, explicable and acceptable, but there is one thing that I can neither understand, explain or accept. I discovered that you said that I went behind your back. Is it true that you said this? If it is true you must tell me when, where and how, and if you can show me that you are right, first, I shall be surprised at myself because, although I have my faults, hypocrisy and falseness are not among them, and second, I would apologise to you with the deepest and sincerest regret. You can be sure of this. I must tell you, however, that I know for sure that nobody, much less you, Walter, can accuse me of duplicity.

I have written you this long letter because I know that it is always wrong to say nothing. Even when it comes to saying unpleasant things, one must still speak out, otherwise one founders in a quagmire of misunderstandings and one can never get out of it.

I wish you and Elisabeth all the very best, first for your health, then for your life and work: please believe that I truly and deeply desire your well-being.

Carlo Maria

XI. GEORGE SZELL

After his departure from EMI Walter Legge continued to supervise recordings by his wife Elisabeth Schwarzkopf. In almost all of those involving an orchestra the conductor was George Szell. In September 1965 Schwarzkopf and Szell made their famous recording of Strauss's *Vier letzte Lieder*, coupled with five of Strauss's songs with orchestral accompaniments.

21 December 1965.

Dear George,

Happy Christmas and a wonderful New Year.

My New Year will be miserable unless you can bulldoze EMI into repeating *Zueignung*. It's their own damned fault fobbing us off with old Bobby Heger's home-knitted version when there exists a splendid orchestration by Strauss himself, done in Garmisch on June 19th, 1940 for Ursuleac and published by Hawkeye & Booze.

I thought Wechsberg's piece in the New Yorker was absolutely splendid.

My obeisances to your enchanting wife and kindest regards from your

Devoted admirer,
[Walter Legge]

27 December 1965.
THE CLEVELAND ORCHESTRA
GEORGE SZELL, Musical Director
Severance Hall – Cleveland 6, Ohio

Dear Walter,

Many thanks for your charming note and most cordial reciprocation of your New Year's wishes from both to both.

Needless to say, I should be glad to remake *Zueignung* in the proper orchestration with Elisabeth whenever possible, but I fail to see how I could 'bulldoze' EMI into this. It is not really their fault that we got the Heger orchestration at the time when we searched for orchestrations. Neither you, the unbeatable polyhistor and inexhaustible fount of information, nor the most knowledgeable gentlemen at Jecklin's in Zürich, let alone my poor self, knew that an orchestration by Strauss himself existed. Where did you dig up in the meantime this valuable bit of information?

Fondest greetings from your
Devoted admirer,
[George Szell]

29 November 1966.

Dear George,

John Coveney of Angel Records has sent me the last batch of reviews of our Strauss record. The letter arrived three hours ago and the pleased purring has not yet abated! So two grateful collaborators feel obliged to thank you and say that we should all be damned fools if we didn't do a lot more work together while we are all in possession of our faculties! It need not be in Berlin where you have shown us all the best restaurants – you choose time, place and repertoire.

But frivolities apart! I think we all owe it to ourselves! I have ordered for examination the scores of the Schubert operas and the incidental music he wrote for plays because there are fine things hidden among them – for example, the two arias in *Claudine von Villabella* and the 'Romanze' from *Rosamunde* – which are in his happiest vein. We might get a whole side from that source. I have also ordered all Wolf's orchestrations of songs suitable for a woman's voice. Since he heard so little of his own scoring they might need some discreet surgical aid but that we can provide. It is easier to thicken-up Wolf's inexpert pointillism than to make anything but a home-knitted minestrone of Heger's *Zueignung*. We also found some more Strauss orchestrations which are the purest magic of the musician's craft. Look at *Meinem Kinde* and *Ruhe meine Seele* – they couldn't have been done by anyone but the magician whose instinct was so certain that he launched you when you were still a teenager. And with that sentence the term 'teenager' becomes a *Lobeshymnus*.

Mit freundlichen Grüssen von Haus zu Haus,

[Walter Legge]

215

13 January 1969.
THE CLEVELAND ORCHESTRA
GEORGE SZELL, Musical Director
Severance Hall, Cleveland, Ohio 44106

Dear Walter,

Miss Chapman just writes me about the project of a Lieder recital record with Elisabeth about which I have heard nothing before this date. Of course it is a very exciting idea. The only trouble is that I don't see any time in the near future to practise the piano.

But I would like to follow up the matter with you and if you should be in Geneva in late February, I would call you around the 22nd or 23rd when I shall be somewhere in Switzerland for a few days of rest before going on to London to struggle with the NPO, etc.

What composers do you have in mind? I would be most keen to do Schubert and Schumann, *but please no Hugo Wolf.*

It is a long time since I have heard from you. I hope you are well and we both wish you and Elisabeth all good things for the New Year.

Cordially,
[George Szell]

Diana Chapman was an executive in EMI's International Classical Division.

27 January 1969.

Dear George,

EMI, emulating God, works in a mysterious way its wonders to perform! But the most important thing is that you are interested in the prospect of a Lieder Platte by George Szell (at the Stimmbänder Elisabeth Schwarzkopf). The joke on EMI is that they wrote that you particularly wanted to do Wolf whereas you, in fact, are most keen to do Schubert and Schumann (and not Wolf): Elisabeth would do even Schuman (William) if it were with you!

I hope to be in New York before this letter reaches you. We fly tomorrow and stay at first at Hampshire House, then I shall probably move over to Essex House as soon as they have room. Elisabeth in the meantime will be on tour.

Are you in New York during the first three weeks of February? If not, I will try to make the journey to Cleveland to hear you and your fabulous and fabled orchestra. Have you any particularly luscious programmes in that period?

Now that Elisabeth has recovered from a series of three virus infections we are – so zu sagen – well. Keep you ears open for a young Italian conductor called Aldo Ceccato. I have heard him at work with two seventh rate orchestras – Paris Radio and Milan Radio – both of which he made play as if they were fourth-rate bands!

All good wishes from house to house

Yours ever,
[Walter Legge]

PS: On September 11th the Grand Prix Mondial of Montreux is bestowing on me a special award as 'the man who has made the greatest contribution to the art and science of recording'. Will you be on a golf course nearby to be their guest for the occasion? I should be most honoured!

8

Artists and Friends

I. Fritz Kreisler

Walter Legge knew Kreisler and admired his art almost unreservedly – as some of the reviews in Chapter 1 make clear – but he was never given the opportunity to work with the great violinist in the recording studio. Shortly after Kreisler's death in 1962 he wrote the following tribute.

An Appreciation of Fritz Kreisler

Fritz Kreisler had three qualities which distinguished him both from his contemporaries and from his successors – the deep humanity and spiritual elevation of his interpretations, the warmth and dark golden radiance of his tone, and the crispness, elegance and fire of his rhythms.

The sound of his playing has haunted my ears and memory since my childhood when I first heard him play. In contrast to Ysaÿe, whose brilliance suggested that he had four E strings, Kreisler gave the impression of having four G strings. It was a tone that filled the vast spaces of the Albert Hall with an enveloping and generous warmth, yet he always seemed to have vast resources of sonority and power in reserve. It was a tone that seemed to speak. John McCormack often told me that he had really learned how to sing, how to phrase, how to convey the meaning of words in song from Fritz Kreisler's tone and articulation.

I cannot convey the spiritual qualities of his playing in words. They were the audible projection of the nature of the man who was modest, noble and utterly sincere. As I write dozens of felicities of phrasing, of matchless jewels of Kreisler's art pass through my memory. I think of him not as I last saw him, hard of hearing and nearly blind. I think of the tall, sad, distinguished, military-looking man on the platform of the old Queen's Hall playing slow movements – the slow movement of the Elgar concerto which was dedicated to him and which he made famous: the timeless flow of the slow movements of the Beethoven and Brahms concertos and the spells of magic he wove in the few bars after the cadenzas of the Beethoven and Brahms concertos.

For more than two generations of musicians and music lovers Fritz Kreisler was the noblest violinist and the supreme master of the fiddler's art. For the greater part of his long life he was a legend, and the object of veneration both of his fellow musicians and the general musical public.

II. David Oistrakh

The last time David Oistrakh was in London he showed me with reverent pride a copy of Kreisler's cadenza for the Beethoven Concerto which Kreisler had autographed for him.

Kreisler was a Viennese – the son of a famous Austrian surgeon. Like every great violinist he was a child prodigy, and his world fame was established long before the turn of the century. But unlike most virtuosi he was never his instrument's slave. At one period in his early manhood he put the violin aside to study medicine: at another time to study art in Rome and Paris. Instead of regarding his period of compulsory military service as an odious interruption in his musical career he devoted himself to his military studies with such energy that he became an officer in a crack regiment of Austrian cavalry.

Fritz Kreisler probably enjoyed greater fame and popularity than any other violinist has ever achieved. By the serious musical public he was acknowledged as the greatest interpreter of the classical repertoire from Bach to Elgar. But he also had a quality amounting almost to genius for composing short pieces in the best tradition and style of popular Viennese music and playing them with a charm, elegance, tenderness and grace that I have never heard matched by any other instrumentalist.

II. DAVID OISTRAKH

For Walter Legge there was only one violinist who matched Kreisler's genius and that was David Oistrakh. In this case there was both a close professional relationship and also a warm personal friendship between the two men. The following appreciation was written after Oistrakh's death in 1974.

David Oistrakh
1908 – 1974

A great and glorious sun set with the death of David Oistrakh and those who were privileged to know him have suffered irreparable loss. Our hearts go out to his beloved widow Tamara and his son Igor around whom his life revolved.

He had suffered cardiac trouble for some years, serious trouble, but making music was more necessary to his spirit than physical well-being and he continued playing, conducting and teaching with his quiet, undemonstrative but tireless energy against all medical advice and the pleas of his family and friends to relax and take life easier.

I am firmly convinced that David Oistrakh's matchless art, his modesty, his gentle friendliness and the warm humanity he radiated were an important and vital factor in improving the Western world's opinion and understanding of the Russian people. Many a country in today's chaotic world would benefit by having had David as its ambassador.

Oistrakh's development and his career's course were different from and, I believe, healthier than those of other string players in his and older

generations. He had only one teacher, Pyotr Stoliarsky. David was predes-
tined to be a musician from earliest childhood, probably prenatally,
specifically a violinist. Stoliarsky sensed his extraordinary talents when
the boy was only five, his inborn musicianship, super-humanly sensitive
ear for intonation and colour, his rare rhythmic sense, his passion for
beauty, his sense of form, his musical memory, his implacable diligence
and his instinctive taste.

He escaped the exploitation as a child prodigy which often ruins the
character, trivializes the repertoire and exaggerates the sense of their own
importance through excessive praise for quick passage-work in these
hot-house plants. Many such *Wunderkinder* soon come to regard praise
and uncritical adulation as their right, and develop into vain egocentrics
or nervous wrecks. David avoided all this. His development was concentrated on music and the mastery of his chosen instrument, but his life
otherwise was that of a normal, often poor child, a healthy youth and
grown man. When Stoliarsky considered him ready he entered the important Russian and international competitions and took the first prize
everywhere except only in Warsaw where he was placed second to Ginette
Neveu.

When he won the Ysaÿe Competition he was already 28, an age at which
most instrumentalists with great futures have established at least their
names in a dozen countries. In normal circumstances he would have been
world-famous at 30 but the Second World War and its aftermath delayed
his first concert in the Western world until 1954. He was already 46 when
he first played in Sweden and nearly 50 before he made his débuts in the
world's most important cities.

I first heard him at the Russian Embassy in London in 1937 when, as
Neville Cardus's London deputy on the *Manchester Guardian*, I was sent
to cover a private concert at the Russian Embassy where, with justified
pride, the USSR displayed their young violinists who had won five of the
first six prizes at the Ysaÿe Competition in Brussels (Oistrakh had taken
first prize). Even before writing my criticism I sent a letter to the Russian
Ambassador asking him to let me make a test recording with a view to a
long recording contract with David Oistrakh whom I considered the best
violinist since Fritz Kreisler in his prime. I had no reply, but one day 25
years later Oistrakh took my letter out of his wallet and said: 'Do you
remember this? To be compared with Kreisler who, through his records,
has been my idol since childhood was more than I had ever dared to hope.'

We met for the first time in Prague in 1946 where, to my delight and
surprise Oistrakh and Oborin were giving a series of concerts in the first
Prague Spring Festival. They immediately agreed to record in all their
spare hours during their stay in Prague. Rafael Kubelík freed a suitable
hall and I telephoned my company in London to send immediately by air
my own favourite technicians and waxes galore (this was in the days
before tape recording). There was no need for recording gear – I had found
some that our German company had deposited there for emergencies. The

technicians and the waxes arrived but, alas, no permission from the Russians to record unless I signed a contract guaranteeing to provide Moscow with matrices of all recordings made by their artists for publication and exploitation throughout the Communist sphere of influence without payment of royalties or pressing fees. For this I had no authority and the spectre of creating such a precedent made me doubly cautious. My second attempt to record David Oistrakh had failed: but in those few days, in spite of having no common language except David's then limited German vocabulary, we had sown the seeds of a friendship which was to last until his death.

For eight years I heard nothing from Oistrakh, only a few 78rpm records which I found in East Berlin including the Khachaturian Concerto. Karajan was staying with us when I took these treasures home and that evening we played the Concerto through twice hardly daring to believe that violin-playing of such incredible perfection in sound, brilliance, rhythm and vitality was possible. From that day to this it is an infallible sign that my wife is in a particularly good mood when she whistles the last movement of that Concerto in Oistrakh's tempo – although the top notes are a bit above her range!

The next approach came out of the blue from Oistrakh's agent in Scandinavia in the spring of 1954. I was in New York at the time when one of my staff telephoned me to say that Oistrakh was in Stockholm and wanted to record for me immediately. I telephoned his agent, fixed terms and repertoire and asked him to engage the best available orchestra and conductor. Unfortunately I could not escape from my New York commitments but I induced EMI's senior technician, Edward Fowler, to fly at once to Stockholm taking his best microphones with him and to make the recordings himself. Fowler was the man whose technical skill and patience more than 20 years earlier had finally broken down Schnabel's reluctance to record.

A year later Oistrakh was in London, now speaking German fairly fluently and our serious though inevitably sporadic recording collaboration began. In those days it was not all caviar and vodka or even beer and skittles recording Oistrakh. Not because he made any difficulties but because the Russian bodyguards who attended him were very suspicious, posted themselves in the control room, and repeatedly checked every cable leading from every microphone to the recording equipment. I believe they felt that I and my staff were determined to discredit Oistrakh by having him drowned by the orchestra. Their insistence in this way actually worked to Oistrakh's disadvantage because several critics had the impression from his first recordings that he was a loud player, insistent on being in the tonal limelight – the very opposite of his nature. By the end of our first day's recording we had mutually discovered each other musically and found complete faith in each other's judgement and taste.

Most of the recordings made between 1954 and 1964 were hastily improvised because Oistrakh could never be certain far in advance that he would get the necessary visas. The Beethoven Concerto with Cluytens and the Brahms with Klemperer had to be done in Paris in the Salle Wagram (a vast and grubby venue for boxing matches which I had never liked) because for some reason which neither David nor I could ever fathom he had visa trouble and could not get permission to come to London.

At the time Paris had attractions more magnetic for Klemperer than Brahms: he refused to listen to playbacks and resented to the verge of physical violence my insistence that several passages must be repeated. While Oistrakh and I were listening to playbacks in another room a friend of his asked Klemperer where Oistrakh was – Klemperer, who could be very ungracious answered: 'In Moscow, I hope.'

For my Philharmonia Orchestra's New York début with Karajan I tried to get Oistrakh as soloist – he was due there a week or so later for his own recital début – but that proved impossible. By the purest luck it happened that David and his wife were put in the apartment next to ours, a fact my wife discovered within ten minutes of the Oistrakh's arrival because she heard through the wall David's unmistakable, glorious tone. He had already started practising!

We opened the separating doors and for ten days the Oistrakhs and the Legges were living together as one family. David, blue-chinned, dressed in pyjamas and a dressing-gown started practising as soon as he woke, walking up and down the large communal living-room we had opened up. We realised in those days why he was such a flawless artist, the sort of artist I have always preferred – nothing left to chance, every note, every colour, every nuance so prepared that nothing could go wrong in public performance, yet be illuminated by the impulse and fantasy of the moment. I have never known any interpretative artist of such obsessed diligence. Carl Flesch used to say that a violinist needs two hundred per cent accomplishment because nerves may take away a hundred per cent at the concert. David had a thousand per cent accomplishment because he worked unceasingly and listened with absolute concentration to every note he played.

A couple of days before his New York début it suddenly occurred to me to ask where Fritz Kreisler and his wife were sitting at the recital. To my horror and disgust the promoters of the concert had not even thought of inviting Kreisler, David's idol. It did not take long for me to raise such Hell that within a couple of hours I had tickets for two extra seats in the middle of the front row of Carnegie Hall, telephoned Kreisler and taken the tickets to him. Over a glass of sherry he talked of his own boundless admiration for David whose playing he knew only from records. He surprisingly remarked: 'I am particularly interested to hear Oistrakh: he is the last of the great violinists to have escaped the influence of Auer.'

Before he left New York David, with the modest reverence of a schoolboy before his idol, asked Kreisler to autograph his well-thumbed copies of his cadenzas to the Beethoven and Brahms concertos.

Carnegie Hall was bedeviled the day of Oistrakh's US début. At 2.30

that afternoon Mischa Elman had a recital including Tartini's *Devil's Trill* Sonata in his performance. At 5.30 Oistrakh's programme included the same work and at 8.30 that same evening Milstein played the *Devil's Trill*. David was prepared to change his programme but we induced him to let the others take their self-brewed medicine.

When we arrived at Carnegie Hall quarter of an hour before his concert David was effusively greeted by Elman. At the interval his adored and adoring wife Tamara, my wife and I went up the stairs to the artists' room passing Elman who had been congratulating David. When we were out of earshot Elman, notorious for his jealousy of all colleagues, was heard to remark, 'Well if dat's Oistrakh vy even Heifetz plays better!' No mean feat to disparage two vastly superior colleagues in nine words!

Next day Oistrakh lunched alone with Elman at the latter's apartment, reluctantly, because he feared that his host might start talking politics, a subject David never discussed. Oistrakh remarked how fortunate Elman was to live in a country so rich in great colleagues. 'Heifetz, Menuhin, Stern, Milstein, Francescatti ...' Elman interrupted him: 'If you call dose fellows my colleagues you haven't heard my play,' fetched his violin and proceeded to give Oistrakh an hour's unaccompanied recital. As Oistrakh recounted the episode it was entirely without malice. He was the best of colleagues, generous in his praise, long-suffering without murmur against many of the less-gifted conductors he had to play with. Like many other European musicians the great joy of his American tours was playing concertos with George Szell.

Oistrakh's technical prowess was limitless but he avoided displaying it for any but purely musical purposes. His first encore at his New York début was Wagner's *Albumblatt*, a slow piece calling for nothing but the noblest *legato* and sincere musical expression. As he finished I looked at the next box where Isaac Stern was sitting and saw that his eyes, like mine and no doubt hundreds of others in the hall, were full of tears.

Oistrakh's consideration for his pupils was extraordinary. He once telephoned me to go to Paris to help him choose a fine violin particularly suitable for Kogan. One year he called me to say that he might be able to record in Brussels so I flew over to find a suitable hall. He was in Brussels to coach his pupils for the Ysaÿe Competition. The Russians nurse their competitors carefully. That year they had been sent nearly two weeks before the first round to acclimatize themselves, get used to Belgian food and work under Oistrakh's fatherly but rigorous guidance. Every morning starting at seven he made the rounds (I was privileged to go with him) of the various hotels where the young musicians were living, went to their rooms and worked with each of them, sometimes for a couple of hours, each day. His patience and gentleness were moving: in his saintly devotion to music he reminded me of my Rumanian pianist-friend, Dinu Lipatti. And it was not only his young people he helped; both Shostakovitch and Khachaturian and no doubt other Russian composers sought his advice on the solo parts of their concertos. An obsessed record collector, he found time

– goodness knows how – to listen to the thousands of records he collected on his tours and discuss the performances in detail. He seemed to collect cameras and recording equipment too and even Steinway concert grands, although there was not room for them in his Moscow apartment. I believe he sent them to the Moscow Conservatoire for the use of students. His son's (Igor's) career meant more to him than his own and the last time I heard him a couple of years ago in Vienna they played Mozart's *Sinfonia concertante* together – Igor the violin, David viola and conductor. His tone was as noble and pure, his style as impeccable as ever and he crowned the concert conducting an inspired, unaffected performance of the *Jupiter* Symphony.

One of the essential characteristics of a great musical artist and a *sine qua non* for world-wide fame and appreciation is a personal and immediately recognisable tone. This is equally true of string players and singers. David had this quality in the highest degree. His tone was immediately recognisable by its golden beauty but also by its incredible variety of colours. His tone, like his extraordinarily subtle rhythmic finesse changed from composer to composer. In a purely musical sense he was not a recognisably Russian violinist. He played Bach and Beethoven and Brahms with the mind and rhythm, the colours and style of a super-human German violinist – though none of them could ever have rivalled him. He played Vivaldi and Corelli as if he had been an Italian of their time. In the Franck Sonata he was as essentially a Belgian violinist as Ysaÿe for whom the work was written. And in the works of Shostakovitch and Prokofiev, Tchaikovsky and Khachaturian every non-Russian knew instinctively that Oistrakh's interpretations were the Russian spirit made manifest. He was in sensibility and imagination and penetration into each composer's mind the completely protean artist.

I believe I was responsible for giving David his first taste of conducting. It happened in this way, in 1958. We had successfully recorded the Prokofiev Second Concerto with a distinguished Italian conductor. When it came to a Mozart concerto the Italian's views on tempi and texture were so diametrically opposed to David's and my convictions on Mozart style that I feared we could never convert him to our way of thinking. Over lunch I told David that I wanted him to play and conduct. When he protested that he had never held a baton in his life I succeeded in convincing him that every man in my orchestra, the Philharmonia, would play his or her best out of their admiration for him and to show him how well they could play. At heart every first-class orchestral musician is a conductor *manqué*. We recorded the Mozart G major Concerto in three hours! The results and the taste of conducting-blood were much to David's liking – I did not know at the time that he had secret ambitions to conduct, but from then on conducting became an increasingly important part of his activities. In later years he often said to me, 'Conducting is so much easier than playing an instrument. If I put one finger wrong on the violin someone will notice it – perhaps the whole audience: if I give half a dozen wrong beats in a symphony, even in an overture, the orchestra will either helpfully cover my mistake or have their eyes on their music and play what is printed without noticing my blunder.'

In rehearsal and in teaching his gentleness imposed extraordinary discipline, his soft speaking voice and deliberate choice of kind words for his admonitions commanded awesome respect but always encouraged. I never heard him raise his voice. His ear and memory for every note he played were phenomenal. Listening to playbacks of recordings, often of a whole concerto movement, we sat together, score and solo part in front of us, pencils in hand, and half a bar or so before a single note which had not pleased him as he or the orchestra had played it, he would raise the index finger of his left hand as a warning 'listen carefully to this!'

In all the years I knew him I tried to get photographs of David which showed his loveable humanity – I needed them particularly for the covers of his records. No professional photographer in London or Paris caught the image as I knew him – the nearest and quite unsuitable for commercial purposes was a snapshot taken in our London home when he, Tamara and my wife Elisabeth Schwarzkopf were playing on the floor with Siamese cats. I gave him up as camera-shy or simply unphotogenic. Recently I bought a marvellous book of photos by Evelyn Richter with over 100 incredibly natural pictures of David as I knew him. Suddenly as I turned the pages of this treasure-book I realised why all other photographers had failed to capture the living image, the heart, the seriousness and the essence of my friend – in all moods, in all activities, playing, conducting, teaching, rehearsing; he was listening with superhuman concentration and his face was the mirror of what he heard and his utterly unselfconscious reaction to it.

His left hand and his right arm and wrist were the natural, obedient, instinctive prolongations of his musical will and they were controlled by one of the most completely musical minds and perfect pairs of ears I have ever experienced. He gave himself no airs, he considered himself and was in fact music's most obedient servant.

David's recorded legacy is vast. It could have been wider and better if his other professional commitments and circumstances beyond his control had not limited his availability. In the last two years before I resigned from EMI I had been working on a plan which David fully supported, if time and place could be found, to record the great masterpieces of chamber music with the quartet David Oistrakh (first violin), Igor Oistrakh (second violin), Rudolf Barshai (viola), Mstislav Rostropovitch (cello) and, for the works with pianoforte, Sviatoslav Richter. The rehearsals according to my scheme were to be simultaneously master classes for advanced students followed by concerts, and the recordings would be made immediately afterwards. A dream that was never and now never can be realised. But what a monument it would have been to the musical history of our times!

A few days after David's death I met Sviatoslav Richter. He said, 'Although I grew up with David and we were close friends all our lives I do not feel that he is dead. Such art and such a spirit will live with us all our lives. I feel as if he were here with us now.'

I have heard all the celebrated violinists in the last 55 years. For me none has been comparable with Fritz Kreisler and David Oistrakh either in natural musicianship or in radiant humanity. Of these Oistrakh was the greater.

III. DE SABATA AND CANTELLI

The careers of both these eminent Italian conductors were cut short; in Victor de Sabata's case by illness and disillusionment in the mid-1950s, and in Guido Cantelli's case by the fact of his death in an air crash at the age of 36. Walter Legge knew Cantelli but did not work with him, but he did have the opportunity to produce two major recordings by De Sabata shortly before the latter's retirement – Puccini's *Tosca* in 1953 and Verdi's *Messa da Requiem* in 1954.

> 3 April 1963.
> Teatro alla Scala
> Ente Autonomo
> L'Alto Consulente Artistico.

Dear Walter,

Many thanks for your exquisitely kind letter of March 31st.

Vaguely as I can remember the 'menu' of the luncheon we had in Ste Margherita (to which you refer) – but not your presence! For a lot of solid musical and literary reasons, every 'bodily' appearance of Walter holds firmly in the landscape of my memory and my affection! – the wine we drank was a rather plain Sicilian red wine of, at the best, fortunate vintage, but by its very self-effacing conspicuity, of a nature to be easily forgotten, proves to have slipped out of the attention of spellbound – by your unparalleled conversation – Victor.

To survive both you and I, this heartbreaking reality I suggest the following: So come here, dear Walter: let's have a leisure meal encompassing a few hours of stern toiling through sampling all kinds of red Corvo and fix that tragically hamletic problem.

About your forceful hint concerning my conducting the wonderful, dear to my heart Philharmonia in 1964: a thousand facts, my present composing activity included, make that matter momentarily uncertain; so ascribe, please this contradictory statement and 'saut d'humeur' to a blasted whimsical attitude of cantankerously spoilt and lazy child! Your smiling, understanding philosophy, as far as I know Walter, is broad and generous enough to suggest a catastrophe of such a magnitude, and, if necessary, worse ones.

Awaiting a word of yours about all above I am, Dear Walter, yours and Elisabeth's most affectionately,

> Victor

2 August 1967.

Carissimo Victor,

You have probably been wondering why so many months passed since I talked to you. The reason is simple, I had a heart attack in Zürich in January and probably another in London in February. Only very recently did I learn from Felicitas – to my utter astonishment – that you too had suffered the same unpleasant illness. I want at the earliest opportunity to come and see you to learn – as I always can from you, no matter what the subject – how to live with this rather frightful inconvenience. Every other illness one can fight with will and determination: apparently these are the two characteristics or exercise of the human spirit which are harmful with this illness. At the moment I am in a clinic in Hamburg and I'll get away with normal luck by the end of the week.

Now I have a new idea. I don't know how you feel about the Alfano (Toscanini?) finale of *Turandot*. I HATE IT ... If I am wrong, prove it to me: it'll be difficult. You know Puccini's style of melody, of melodic construction, of modulation, of vocal writing and instrumentation better than any other man in the world. Why don't you take up your pen where Puccini put his down and write a finale absolutely in the very heart of the style of Puccini? The idea is full of virtues. First of all it will keep you intellectually occupied and release the incredible flood of music that is inside you. You and you alone could achieve for *Turandot* what it has never achieved with its weak ending, permanent acceptance in the international repertoire. Ricordi, not to mention Valcarenghi and La Wallman, would most certainly pay you a fortune in anticipation of royalties, because the copyright in *Turandot* will be extended for another 40 years if they withdraw the Alfano finale. Everybody would be happy, especially your devoted

[Walter Legge]

Who would feel on the way to good health if he'd inspired you to some form of musical activity. Elisabeth is in Australia. She telephoned this afternoon and I told her about this idea with which she wholeheartedly agrees. She sends her devoted and most affectionate regards.

Felicitas Keller was an agent based in Madrid.

Guido Cantelli: a tribute
born Novara 27 April 1920 – died Orly 24 November 1956

Guido Cantelli was only 36 when he was killed in an aeroplane crash outside Paris. Thirty-six is no age in a conductor's career: no other conductor in the history of the art has established, so early in life, so wide a fame as Cantelli.

His musical talent showed itself early; first as a pianist and organist, later as choral conductor in his native town. The unusual clarity of his beat he attributed to the lessons he had learned working with local amateur choruses. When the Second World War started he was studying at the Milan Conservatoire: before it ended he had been conscripted into the Italian Army and interned in a German labour camp; later he escaped and worked in a bank in Milan under an assumed name.

When Toscanini returned to Italy after the war, Cantelli had already begun to establish his reputation as a conductor, and he had the talent and good fortune to impress Toscanini, who, after a few meetings, put the protecting arm of his endorsing patronage around the shoulders of his young countryman. From the summer of 1946 onwards, Cantelli had the unique and inestimable privilege of Toscanini's guidance and advice, and the heavy responsibility of the nominated heir to a great throne. Only those who have observed the deep father-and-son relationship that warmed ten of Toscanini's later years can imagine how deeply he suffers the loss of his chosen successor.

Cantelli first came to this country in 1950 with the La Scala Orchestra, when he conducted both at the Edinburgh Festival and in London. Less than a year later he gave a series of concerts in the Royal Festival Hall with the Philharmonia Orchestra – the beginning of a happy and mutually stimulating association which lasted until his death. At his last two concerts with the Philharmonia he gave unforgettable performances of Verdi's Requiem.

Cantelli was one of the four great conductors who, through close association, rehearsals and recordings, have contributed to the present quality and style of the Philharmonia Orchestra. Like every Italian conductor of quality he favoured a brilliant, translucent sonority, Mediterranean intensity of expressive playing, and soloistic virtuosity in the execution of quick passages. In preparation he left nothing to chance. He was not, I believe, a quick learner and he habitually prepared every work months, if not years, ahead, so that from his first rehearsal of a work he was conducting for the first time he was so prepared that he could, as he usually did, rehearse without a score. Even the rehearsal letters or numbers he knew by heart.

His orchestral rehearsals were used from first moment to last with a burning intensity that made it physically impossible for him to rehearse more than once a day. He was self-critical to the point of self-torture, and his incandescent will to re-create in each work he played the glow it had had in the crucible of the composer's imagination at the moment of creation left him soaked through with perspiration, breathless and physically exhausted after every rehearsal and every concert.

A week before his death Cantelli had been appointed Principal Conductor of La Scala, a just appointment but to the outsider surprising, because – for an Italian – he had, comparatively speaking, little experience of opera. The history of the art of conducting shows that the only real school is the hard routine of the opera house – from coaching small-part singers, through conducting off-stage bands and choruses, to taking over performances without rehearsal. The only considerable exceptions to this are

Koussevitzky (who started as a double-bass player) and Cantelli. He had done some performances in the Italian provinces, but he was reticent about them. In the summer of 1955 he accepted the invitation to conduct *Così fan tutte* in February 1956 at the Piccola Scala, the exquisite 'little' theatre that Dr Ghiringhelli has built behind La Scala itself. I have rarely known an artist of Cantelli's acknowledged status so preoccupied with a sense of responsibility. Even before he began to discuss the choice of scenic designer or cast he compared all known editions of the score, and so identified himself with the work that months before the first rehearsal every detail of the performance he intended to give was clear in his mind's ear and eye. After the first orchestral rehearsal he had the very structure of the orchestral pit altered until it gave him the sonority he wanted. It is said that he had 30 orchestral rehearsals. He took every solo rehearsal, every ensemble rehearsal, and after the first stage rehearsal, produced the work himself, because he felt that only under a one-man direction can opera really be the *Gesamtkunstwerk* that it should be. After the dress rehearsal he invited the whole cast to a dinner party at which I was the privileged outsider. He was relaxed as I have rarely seen him because he knew he had done all that he or any other man could do to ensure a worthy presentation of the work in hand. Neither that, nor the success of the first performance prevented him from calling rehearsals for any member of the cast who had erred by a demi-semiquaver in any of the subsequent performances. That is the stuff of which great opera directors are made.

Guido Cantelli's tragic death leaves a void which time itself will hardly replace. For Italy the loss is irreparable: for the world too. If Cantelli had lived another 50 years he would still have been no older than Toscanini was when he last conducted the Philharmonia in London. And what he would have contributed to music in those 50 years!

Ave atque Vale!

In 1970 the BBC's Julian Herbage invited Walter Legge to broadcast a tribute to Cantelli.

23 March 1970.

Dear Julian,

Although I would be delighted to pay tribute to Guido Cantelli in *Music Magazine*, I am not certain that I am the right man to do it.

I knew him well and although he repeatedly begged me to supervise his recordings, some Hayes-located Machiavelli successfully made this impossible. I still don't know who or why! And since Gorlinsky was Cantelli's agent for the United Kingdom and always engaged the Philharmonia Orchestra for Cantelli's concerts, he never gave a concert under the Legge-Philharmonia auspices. I would like you to reconsider your invitation in the light of these facts.

As far as I know his operatic conducting was confined to *Così fan tutte* at La Piccola Scala. The evening after the first orchestral rehearsal he telephoned me from Milan begging me to fly at once and help him: the orchestral sound was horrible and he couldn't improve it. I arrived at the theatre the next day half an hour after the rehearsal was due to start. I found the theatre empty except for Cantelli who had dismissed the orchestra and who, in the pit, was savagely kicking orchestral stands and clutching and reclutching his right arm muttering 'this cursed arm'. I am sure he blamed himself for the sound that displeased him!

Think it over again – but if you would still like me to pay the tribute, I could do it between April 17th and 21st here. You would have to make his records available to me here.

But please do not take these doubts of mine as declining your offer. I would love to broadcast in your programme if and whenever you have a subject I can do justice to. I hate retirement.

> Kindest regards to you both,
> Yours sincerely,
> [Walter Legge]

IV. FOUR SINGERS

Walter Legge and Hilde Konetzni were close friends before the Second World War: their relationship was bought to an end in September 1939 when Britain declared war on Germany.

[translated from German]

15th February 1967.

Dearest Hilde,

You will be amazed to hear from me again, but I was so pleased to hear from Gertrud Wagner how enthusiastic she is about you, that I thought you would also be pleased to hear it from me as well. She describes your performance in such glowing terms that I wanted to come to your première. I am unfortunately not a very well man and am only truanting from the hospital for a farewell concert in honour of our lifelong accompanist Gerald Moore. It is a quite charming programme and the soloists are: Elisabeth, Fischer-Dieskau and Los Angeles. But I will certainly hear a repeat of the *Dutchman* with you. Perhaps at the end of March after the crucifixion, burial and resurrection comedy of St Herbert at Salzburg.

From Gertrud Wagner's description you are looking marvellous which pleases me greatly and I hope your Moni is in fine form also. I have lost nine kilos in less than four weeks and am now only a touch stouter than I was 30 years ago when we first got to know each other, but not much shrewder.

> Sincere best wishes,
> Your old friend,
> Walter Legge

IV. Four Singers

The soprano Rosa Ponselle was an artist whose singing Walter Legge had much admired in pre-war days. Joanna Simon was a young singer who had visited Ponselle in order to study with her.

1 March 1973.

Carissima Rosa,

The record of your Christmas party arrived safely and at once we sat down like two determined detectives not only to enjoy it but to analyse the secret of Rosa's legato. And that of course sent us to the other Rosa records and we had an orgy of bathing our ears and hearts with the magical vintage port and double-cream richness of your incredible beauty of voice, your skill and art in the management of it.

To produce your incredible *legato* did you think subconsciously of moving from note to note with an inaudible *portamento*? I ask because the perfect unbroken *legato* dare not be interrupted – Casals once told me that anybody can learn to produce a beautiful sound on one note, but that it had taken him 50 years to learn how to move from one note to the next. We can hear, see and feel how your m-m-m Romani-Ruffo technique helped to bring the consonants forward so that they were projected beyond the lips into the theatre or hall. It is curious by the way that most of the Tuscan singers have this natural quality to word projection: Napolitani too – you, Caruso, Scotti. I won't bore you by thinking aloud like this on the problems of the art of singing in general and your unique magic.

I had a letter yesterday from Joanna Simon who says to my delight that you are in better health and have been very kind to her. Kindness is an essential part of your nature.

Elisabeth has been in Seoul (!) for a couple of recitals, packed houses (the theatre has 4,500 seats), temperature minus six centigrade! Today she has the first of two recitals in the Hong Kong Festival (temperature plus 28) and should be back here early next week and there will be more happy hours of enjoying and studying your art.

> Our fondest love to you,
> Your devoted,
> [Walter Legge]

The tenor Lauritz Melchior was another artist who had impressed Walter Legge in the opera house, and whose records he much admired.

9 September 1967.

Dear Lauritz,

I have spent the last hour listening to some Wagner records you made long before the war. In the hope that it will give you the pleasure you deserve, I want you to know that in the incomparable voices of the twentieth century and the miraculous ability to move to tears your generation, my generation, the next generation and the generations to come, your unique art will take its rightful place among the incomparables.

8. Artists and Friends

As long as gramophone records exist, the glory of your voice and the strange magic you had to move one to tears will, with Frida Leider's, Lotte Lehmann's and, I hope, my wife's, make the name Lauritz Melchior a dream, a myth and a glory as vivid for the future generations as it is for me and those young people to whom I can with your records prove that Wagner is not difficult and God sends us once in a generation or two a Lauritz Melchior.

[Walter Legge]

5 October 1967.

Dear Walter,

I must say that you nearly made me blush with your charming and flattering letter. I am glad and proud over your sentiment and your kind words and I hope that I have filled a place in the musical worlds to satisfaction.

Don't you think that there are some of the old recordings which could be reprinted? I am often asked about my Scandinavian songs. You know that I had two different albums of these. There was also one called 'The Lighter Side of Lauritz Melchior'. This could perhaps also be reprinted together with other things of mine which have not been reissued. There is a very fine recording of *The Holy City* and *The Last Chord* which has never been printed for sale. I think MGM made it when they started. But it doesn't exist any more, except for private copies, and it is really good.

When you receive this letter, I am in Mozambique on a safari. I will stay there until around November 9 and then go for a short visit to Denmark before I return to New York for the 125 years anniversary of the New York Philharmonic who have invited me as their guest. Any letter written to me here in California will reach me where I am, through my secretary.

I hope that you and your wife are fine and that everything is well. I would like very much to meet both of you again in life, somewhere, sometime.

Until then, my best wishes and greetings,

Your old friend,
[Lauritz Melchior]

In early 1953 Walter Legge persuaded Maria Callas to become an EMI contract artist, and he produced a sequence of classic recordings by her until May 1963.

[undated letter]
Via Michelangelo Buonarroti 40
Milano.

Dear Walter

Finally I find a little time to write. I'm sorry that you couldn't come to Naples because I even sang better than Berlin. Unfortunately Karajan was not directing and I simply can't hear the opera without him. Tell him I miss him and it is a shame we don't work more together – don't you think?

Here things go on as usual. I'm most comfortable at home even if every performance is a real bull fight! They all find my voice improving – I feel it too!

[Tullio] Serafin is furious because you don't use him and his son-in-law, that I didn't know – by the way – and the trouble is [Mario] Rossi thinks it's me that contributed to not having his contract renewed – and I'm sorry that he thinks that because it's not true so far as he's concerned – no?

As you've probably heard, the Maggio Musicale is opening with *Traviata* – [Renata] Tebaldi and Serafin – How do you like that?

As for our work we will try to do all we can also *Vestale* and *Sonnambula* in February. Walter, I must be very particular on recording because I can't have excuses for anything – not with the fame I have – try to understand that.

Please write details and all news. By the way *Parsifal* is postponed to later on next year – no decent conductor free. When I see you I'll tell you all. It's rather amusing to get with Parafin-!

My dear friend, give my love to Elisabeth – and best regards to Karajan and a big hug to yourself and when are you coming here – ? We are doing another six *Traviatas* imagine and a bit earlier *Fedora*.

Webster is begging that I do *Traviata* in June – of course I said no because I have to rest after Vienna.

Yours
Maria

PS. Battista sends you all his love.

The reference to Naples dates this letter at a point shortly after Callas had sung three performances of Lucia in Donizetti's *Lucia di Lammermoor* at the San Carlo Opera House on 22, 24 and 27 March 1956. The conductor was Francesco Molinari-Pradelli: she had recently sung the part in a La Scala production of the work under Karajan in Berlin, and the reference to Vienna is to three more performances of *Lucia* there in June, again with the La Scala company under Karajan. There were recording sessions in London in February 1957 but the work recorded was Rossini's *Il barbiere di Siviglia*. Though she had sung Kundry in Wagner's *Parsifal* at an earlier stage of her career she did not in fact perform in the work again. Sir David Webster was the artistic director of the Royal Opera House, Covent Garden between 1945 and 1970. Giovanni Battista Meneghini was Callas's husband from 1949 to 1959.

*

After a 1963 recital recording of French opera arias Callas and Legge parted company, but nearly six years later Legge sought to heal the breach.

233

8. *Artists and Friends*

20 January 1969.

Dear Maria,

I played our *Tosca* recording with De Sabata a couple of days ago and it came forcibly home to me how ridiculous it is that two highly intelligent people – you and me – who have together made immortal contributions through records to the artistic history of our time, should have broken off all communications and relations. Don't you feel the same? I was on the point of writing or telephoning dozens of times during your emotional crisis but I refrained only because you were certainly too preoccupied to hear from me 'out of the blue'.

Now that you have that behind you, I hope it would amuse and please you to have dinner with me next time I am in Paris. Naturally I would come specially to Paris for the sheer pleasure of seeing you, but not until the end of February because I am going to New York at the end of next week for two or three weeks.

Do let me hear from you.

My love to you as always,
[Walter Legge]

18 March 1969.
36 Avenue Georges Mandel
Paris 16e.

Dear Walter,

Did you have to hear the *Tosca* recording with De Sabata to understand that it is and was ridiculous that two highly intelligent people (as you say you and me) who have together made immortal contribution through records to the artistic history of our time, should have broken off all communications and relations.

Pity you did not write or call the dozens of times during my emotional crisis, as you say, but it was really then that friends are to be approached. Life is very long and complicated, I know you have been through a lot, so have I.

Of course, I will never forget what we have done together as I will never forget the odd things also. Nevertheless I was pleased to receive your letter.

I am in Paris, and you can call whenever you wish. My number is KLEber 25.89 and please, give my favourite singer, Elisabeth your wife, all my most affectionate love.

As always, yours
Maria Callas

12 April 1969.

[Dear Maria]

I was in Florence when your letter arrived here, then in Salzburg for Karajan's wonderful Easter Egg Festival, so I have only just received it.

It was so good to hear from you again!

234

The reason for my visit to Florence was to hear a really excellent young Italian conductor who was recommended to me by De Sabata shortly before he died. Ceccato is now married – as I suppose you know – to Eliana [née De Sabata]. Keep your eyes and ears on this boy, he has great talent.

We are leaving today for Budapest where Elisabeth has two recitals and since my only serious occupation now is rehearsing and travelling with her I shall not be near Paris until mid-May. Will you have lunch with me on May 12th or 14th at any restaurant you care to name? If these dates are impossible for you, I would make a special journey to Paris for lunch with you on April 28th. Just drop me a line to say which of these dates would best suit you.

I expect that with your superhuman resistance you have overcome your sorrows.

> With all good wishes,
> Yours always,
> [Walter Legge]

29 May 1969.

Dear Maria,

How was it in Turkey? Presumably strenuous and hot? I was disappointed not to have had a call from you chez Chaplin. Tomorrow I leave for Milano and Firenze to see Strehler's production of *Fidelio*. I don't know who is singing or conducting, but he started rehearsals a month before the première and I have never yet known him to put a foot wrong as a producer.

Where are you on September 11th? A feature of the Montreux Festival is the Grand Prix Mondial du Disque, and this year they are making a special award to me as the man who has made the greatest contributions to the art and science of recording. It would be a great honour to me if you would consent to be present. So much of our best work has been done together that I regard your presence as essential to the occasion.

You have no idea how your television programme has altered your public image. It has given you a personal kudos as a great woman greater even than you had as La Divina. No one now believes the stories spread by your mother because they have seen you as the *grande dame* – beautiful, wise, human, humorous and modest. And all that unrehearsed!!!

> My love to you.
> Yours always,
> [Walter Legge]

30 August 1971.

Dear Maria,

Our telephone chat was the happiest event in my life for a very long time: it was wonderful to hear you full of energy as ever, full of plans and wise penetrating observation. And I was deeply touched that you had telephoned to enquire into my state of health. I suppose I am improving but as you know, I have never had much faith in doctors – except Ivor Griffith! – and nothing that has happened in these last months has changed my opinion of them. They are like conductors: few of them are any good anyway and it is a matter of luck whether one finds the right one for the right job.

Salzburg was interesting – and disappointing. The public has fallen off both in quality and numbers. The only things really sold out were Karajan's two concerts and his *Otello*, Böhm's two concerts and his *Nozze di Figaro* and a beautiful production by Herbert Graf of Cavalli's *Rappresentatione di Anima e di Corpo* which is not really an opera (it was written circa 1550) but it was admirably done apart from the singing.

I heard Riccardo Muti's *Don Pasquale*. He is enormously talented with the sort of fire that Serafin had on his best nights. I talked with him about working with you and his bright eyes became three times as bright. He tends to accompany loudly but we could easily cure that. Considering the cast he had – Emilia Ravaglia a wisp of a soprano whose only virtue was clean *staccati*; a *tenore di disgrazia* Pietro Bottazzo who sang everything over F *mezzo castrato* and bellowed everything below it; Corena who never amused me and Panerai singing and acting very well.

I am sorry you are already in America; I had made up my mind to cut Salzburg short and fly to Paris for the joy of seeing you. The idea of working with you breeding a sense of style into young American singers excites me enormously and Elisabeth is all in favour of my doing it; she also believes it would be the best way of getting me completely well again.

Now we have bridged the gap of eight wasted years, let us get together again as soon and as often as possible.

My love to you,
[Walter Legge]

Dr Ivor Griffith was a London ear nose and throat specialist who treated many singers, including Callas.

19 April 1973.
Milano.

Dear Walter,

Thank you for your wishes and your letter, and I am sorry to hear that you cannot find peace and quiet. I know, I imagine how you are bored with yourself, and I do agree that you should not have stopped working. But, as everything is destiny, you should not feel so restless, as you have done the most beautiful work during your lifetime. Also remember that the artistic level was much higher than now.

I hope to see you soon. Give my love to Elisabeth, and all my love to you as always.

Maria

12 July 1973.

[Dear Maria]

It must have been you in that smart Mini Cooper who hooted and waved in Via Manzoni. Why didn't you stop ? We should have loved to chat, even though it would have meant keeping Alain waiting. You're a *monstre*, but *sacré*.

We are delighted that you are both getting down, or rather up, to singing again at long last. If you need me or I can be of any help in programme planning, hand-holding, sitting on accompanist's head, encouraging or nursing (artistically speaking) I am completely at your disposal as you know always.

[Walter Legge]

Alain was Callas's dressmaker, who lived in the Via Manzoni, Milan.

V. MORE ENGLISH FRIENDS AND COLLEAGUES

The writer and critic Ernest Newman (1868-1959) was the most important of Walter Legge's musical mentors (see Chapter 1), and the two men remained friends until Newman's death.

2 December 1939.
Polperro
Epsom Lane South
Tadworth, Surrey.

Dear Walter,

Unique One!

I call you this in tribute not only to your intellectual qualities but also – and even more – to your amazing memory. How on earth did you know that the 30th was my birthday? Among human beings you were the only one to achieve that feat, apart from Cook, in whose ancestry I suspect an elephant, for she never forgets. [Granville] Bantock also remembered. The rest is silence.

I feel better than I have done for a long time, though I am anxious that this incessant work is knocking my eyes to pieces.

When am I to feast them on the sight of you? Vera [Mrs Newman] said that when you did come here you would bring with you the *Manon* records. Can you get them with automatic copulation? I'm getting too lazy to keep changing the records.

What a world! Still, what remains of civilisation will probably last your time. With luck, it may even run to mine, though I don't give it more than another 30 years or so.

Yours always,
Ernest

8. Artists and Friends

Following Beecham's suggestion that he should conduct a recording of Delius's opera *A Village Romeo and Juliet* (see Chapter 4), Legge sought to canvas support for the venture on a subscription basis. The project came to nothing in wartime Britain, and it was not until 1948 that Beecham recorded the opera with a different producer.

24 April 1941.

Dear Walter,

It goes without saying that I shall be one of those who will want the Delius records; but if I hesitate to sign the postcard at the moment it is for a reason which, I fancy, will occur to more than one potential subscriber. Two reasons, perhaps. One is that no price is stated; and I don't think you will get many people to sign what is the equivalent of a blank cheque, especially in these days, with the income tax what it is. Then again, no singers are mentioned in the circular.

Wouldn't it have been as well to have cleared up these two little points in the appeal to the public? It may be, of course, that there is something in the articles of association of the Delius Society that regulates the price of the records to be issued; but if so, I don't know of it, and I fancy most other people will be in the same difficulty.

When are you coming here? There are various things I want to talk about – your friend and Nietzsche, for instance. I simply can't write long letters about matters of that kind. I'm working up to the extreme limit of my time and my strength and more than the irreducible minimum of letter-writing is a pure impossibility for me. Even the letters that simply have to be written make a grievous hole in my working day sometimes.

Choose a day for your visit to Tadworth when Jerry isn't proposing to call. It's no fun here when the bombs start dropping all round us.

Yours always,
Ernest

6 June 1945.

Dear Walter,

We shall see you tomorrow at *Peter Grimes*, I hope; but if we don't, this is to ask you to see if you can find for me a copy in Germany of Marius Schneider's *Geschichte der Mehrstimmigkeit*. It was published in 1934 and 1935, I think in two volumes, but possibly in three. (Don't mix him up with *Max* Schneider, another Johnny altogether.) Pay any price to get it. I suppose it's permissible to buy books in Germany and bring them away?

The other book I mentioned – if it was ever published, in which case it must have been after 1932 – is by Friedrich Suhtsheck, and will probably bear some title referring to the Persian origin of the Parsifal-Grail legend.

I hope that one of these days we shall be able to offer you a decent dinner here – not so Lucullan a feast, of course, as that of the other evening, but something better than war-time fare in Tadworth. I'd forgotten that

238

asparagus existed, and had to ransack my memory to discover where I'd heard the word.

> Yours always,
> Ernest

> 22 December 1948.

Dear Walter,

I ought to have written to you long ago, but you can guess how it has been with me lately. Ever since some misguided people started this public hue-and-cry against the old fox for the sin of being eighty he hasn't been able to call his soul his own. Why couldn't they have left him in the peaceful seclusion of his lair, with his vixen and his cub, who are all he needs for his happiness? I wore myself out letter-writing for a fortnight and my work went all to pieces. Never again! Being eighty once is more than enough for this child!

About your letter I will only say it was one of the three or four things that brought me pleasure. We've had an unbroken friendship now for nearly 20 years, I suppose, and there's no reason why it shouldn't continue for another 20. I profoundly hope it will.

We leave tomorrow. I shall be glad to get away, partly because I am in sore need of a rest, even more for Vera's sake. I am very worried about her: the strain of the last few months has told terribly on her. I can only hope that Monte-Carlo will pump a bit of strength into her. It's happiness that she needs most of all.

> Yours always,
> Ernest

If you will look after the Calm Sea I have no doubt the Devil, when he sees us in the Casino, will make it a Prosperous Voyage.

> 3 December 1956.

Dear Walter,

It's kind of you and Elisabeth to remember the birthday of so useless an old ruffian as myself, and more than kind to remember the whisky that we received today. But you shouldn't encourage me to go on living. It's nothing more than a bad habit I've acquired, and in a really rational world I would be punished for indulging myself in it. When I think of poor young Cantelli!

I hope you are both well and not taking this crazy world too seriously. It appears to be going to hell as fast as it can. Perhaps this time in 100 years we shall all be looking back nostalgically to the golden days of 1956.

Well, well! Take care of yourselves and be as happy as you can.

> Love to you both.
> Yours always,
> Ernest

239

8. Artists and Friends

In February 1953 Karajan conducted an Italian radio performance of Tippett's *A Child of our Time*. Before this performance there were consultations with the composer: the tape Tippett refers to is of a radio recording of a performance he conducted at Monte Ceresio, near Lugano, probably in 1951.

> 2 December 1952.
> Tidebrook Manor
> Wadhurst, Sussex.

Dear Walter,

I was glad to see you last night because I've wanted to see you for some time. And if you can recall your suggestion to meet again when you are back from America I'd welcome that – in a more personal and leisured manner. I want to take your advice – or at any rate ask it! On the whole matter of my strange opera. You cheered me up a bit over the *Observer* articles, which some folk have attacked me for, as being too near self-advertisement. But they are the moralists rather than the professionals – who have in general taken them for what they're worth in themselves.

Look – I'm going to make a fresh set of metronomes of *Child* for Karajan. But remind him that he *can* hear a kind of performance on the Monte Ceresio tape.

Hoping to see you again soon. Just write me or ring me. The address card is for your secretary.

Michael Tippett

In June 1969 news reached Walter Legge and Elisabeth Schwarzkopf that the two-year-old Maltings concert hall at Snape, Suffolk had been destroyed in a fire just before the beginning of that year's Aldeburgh Festival. Benjamin Britten and others who had been initially concerned with providing a suitable venue for Festival and other local events now faced the task of having to start again almost from the beginning. The rebuilt hall was opened in June 1970.

> 8 June 1969.

BENJAMIN BRITTEN THE RED HOUSE ALDEBURGH SUFFOLK.

DEEPLY SHOCKED BY NEWS OF YOUR LOSS STOP IF IT WOULD HELP MY WIFE WOULD BE DELIGHTED TO GIVE A RECITAL IN ANY ALDEBURGH HALL OF YOUR CHOICE IN 1970 TOWARDS YOUR REBUILDING FUND.

WALTER LEGGE

> 25 July 1969.
> The Red House
> Aldeburgh, Suffolk.

My dear Walter,

Your very kind telegram helped us all at a very low moment! Thank you very much for sending it. We were overjoyed at your suggestion that your wife would possibly help us with a concert – what a most handsome & welcome suggestion! We haven't yet had time to work out exactly how we are going to plan our raising of the enormous sum which has got to be found. Certainly, until the Maltings is rebuilt there is no hall here which would make her visit worthwhile. If she would consider coming *after* that re-opening (which we hope will be next summer), or a small very special concert in London – if she can find the time – it would help us all practically and spiritually, I know! May I write later?

I am sorry not to have answered before but I think you can guess what a labour it was to re-arrange 3 weeks of Festival, after a short break, now we have to replan the next year, & our own lives into the bargain!

Warm greetings & the warmest thanks to your wife,

from both Peter
and
Ben

6 August 1969.

Dear Ben,

I hope you realise that you are the first composer since Wagner (there were none before him) to have the energy and foresight to build your own opera house!

I feel certain that you will collect the money for rebuilding fairly easily, but it is terrifying to think of the additional effort and time it will cost you personally to see that the new building is as good (and perhaps more capacious?) than the one it replaces.

As soon as you know when and where you would like Elisabeth to sing for the building fund, write to me again.

Our kindest regards to you and Peter.

Yours always,
[Walter Legge]

Elisabeth Schwarzkopf gave the promised fund-raising recital after the new Maltings had been re-constructed, when there was still a need to raise funds to pay for work which had taken place.

5 May 1972.

My dear Walter,

Thank you so much for bringing Elisabeth down here last week. It was good to see you again after so many years. I am sure you felt, as everybody did, that it was a splendid success; she sang most beautifully, & everyone enjoyed it hugely, & it made a mountain of money for the Maltings!

I am so glad that you both seemed to like the building, & that Elisabeth enjoyed singing there. If she ever has time, she must come back for us!

241

Do give her our love & warmest thanks – I hope the drive back wasn't too awful for you but I fear you were terribly late.

> With every good wish
> Yours ever
> Ben

10 May 1972.

Dear Ben, Benissimo!

We are delighted that the recital was such a success and that we could make some contribution to the rebuilding.

We have fallen completely in love with the Maltings, its acoustics (which we should like to take round with us) – now we know why you and Peter refuse to give recitals in the concrete horrors of the South Bank – and your lovely house.

The journey back would have been pretty unpleasant if we had not had the great pleasure of seeing you again.

> Our love to you both,
> Yours always,
> [Walter Legge]

Walter Legge's 1942 tribute to Gerald Moore is reproduced in Chapter 3. In 1967 Moore decided to retire from the concert platform, and Legge had the idea of presenting another tribute in the shape of a farewell concert involving three of the great accompanist's most admired singer colleagues – Victoria de los Angeles, Dietrich Fischer-Dieskau and Elisabeth Schwarzkopf. The event was held at the Royal Festival Hall in London on 20 February, and was a great success. However, Walter Legge, who had been treated for a heart condition in hospital, and who had discharged himself in order to travel to London and oversee arrangements for the concert, suffered a further heart attack in the night after the concert as a result of over-exertion.

23 February 1967.
Beechwood Cottage
Penn Bottom
Penn, Bucks.

My dear Walter,

My first letter since I have come down to earth after 'The Homage' is to you, my old friend. I did not get downstairs till now and immediately telephoned you to learn, to my sorrow, that you have had a relapse and that Elisabeth has had to cancel some of her concerts. All this is my fault!! Without Monday night's little affair your condition would be better than it is and Elisabeth would still be in good voice. Nevertheless we five made history on Monday night (is it selfish of me to recall it?) – and Elisabeth's stage management of my entry was enough to bring tears to my eyes. It was the Accompanist's Apotheosis: and all devised and engineered by you.

The letters I have had have been quite overwhelming (the highlight to

242

many was the Wolf group) and in nearly all of then I read of the 'listener's debt of gratitude to Walter Legge – not only those in the hall – but those who listened on the air – and those who are going to buy the record'.

So Walter, do not be bitter about the odd letter which has upset you and accept from me my love and gratitude for the genius of conception and the labour you put in to the most memorable concert of my life.

> Your old friend,
> Gerald

In 1969 EMI produced an LP involving a number of artists in recordings with Moore in honour of his seventieth birthday. Legge and Schwarzkopf chose a hitherto unpublished recording of 'Träume' from Wagner's *Wesendonk Lieder*, as their contribution.

7 August 1969.

Dear Gerald,

In the rush of getting Elisabeth off for her annual tour of American summer festivals, we overlooked – to our regret – to send you a telegram on your birthday. Thank you for so graciously reminding us!

EMI have not yet had the grace to send us a copy of your birthday record. I hope 'Träume' sounds as well as I believe it does. The reason I chose it was that your playing down to the entry of the voice has the dreamy, sensual, almost drugged effect which Wagner certainly wanted, and which is so fiendishly difficult to play.

Our love to Enid and you, dear septuagenarian.

> Yours always,
> [Walter Legge]

23 June 1973.

Dear Walter,

Thank you for your two letters.

Taking them in order of appearance I find you make a slight mistake when you say we left the battlefield too soon. You did indeed, and your absence has left a void that cannot be filled. But I? No. After my wonderful farewell concert (all due to your vision, energy and regard for me – plus my three beloveds) which made history, I have no wish whatever to make a come-back and since that day in February 1967 I have not played one single accompaniment in public.

This Schwarzkopf recital for Lord Boyle (if it takes place) will be a private affair and when the proposition was put to me I couldn't resist the temptation of playing for Elisabeth once again. The period Oct 24 to Nov 12 will be, I fancy, the one Boyle will choose but all this will be in Emmie Tillett's hands.

But, coming to your second letter. I was asked by Yehudi [Menuhin] last May to represent England in a UNESCO concert in Paris (Conseil International de la Musique) to play the *Vier ernste Gesänge* for Fi-Di [Fischer-Dieskau] on January 9th. Although the prospect is not pleasing (appearing again in public) I consented only on condition that I play this one group of songs only. I do not feel up to doing an entire recital (or even half a recital) in public. You do not know what it is to be 74! The private concert with Elisabeth is another thing, and although I am rusty, the thought of being associated with that great woman urges me to do it just once more (always with the proviso she chooses a programme I can manage! But Wolf especially *Italienisches* I hope she will do with me!)

I have not heard about this EMI concert – you see I am in blessed retirement.

So, dear Walter, with my profound apologies to Elisabeth, no EMI 75th birthday celebrations for me!

Regarding David Willison, I hardly know him personally, but he has done some brilliant work with Benjamin Luxon; to swell his slender resources he has to teach and do proof-reading for Lengnick. I imagine he speaks German.

You may remember years ago I strongly recommended George Reeves as an ideal partner for Elisabeth in America – I feel that Willison could be a second Reeves.

Please embrace Elisabeth for me and we send our love to you both,

> Yours ever,
> Gerald

In 1973 *Grove's Dictionary of Music and Musicians* asked Walter Legge to write an entry on Clifford Curzon for their new edition. As a result Legge contacted the great pianist, and from this contact there grew a friendship between the two men.

2 July 1973.

[Dear Mr Curzon]

Your warm letter has given me much pleasure. I too regret that we did not have the opportunity of working together but although the Philharmonia Orchestra and the Concert Society were my own private property, out of a mistaken sense of loyalty to EMI I concentrated on engaging artists who were not under contract to their competition – the only form of nepotism to my discredit. But it may not be too late – I am so wearied by the boredom of retirement that if anyone should want to make use of what I know and can do I should jump at the opportunity like a shot!

Before sending copy to the Grove people I shall get your approval of the facts, but don't be impatient: I'm a slow worker in such matters. I don't expect to be in England this month – we are looking for a house where the climate is more clement than here and the artistic life less arid: perhaps Cap Ferrat which has the advantage of the Mediterranean air and light without the invasion of tourists. And the Monte Carlo Orchestra is not worse than the Suisse Romande! However we shall be in Salzburg at the Fondachhof between August 11th and 23rd and not committed to performances on the 18th and 21st. May we invade you in Attersee on one of these days? We should both be enchanted to do so. Do at least, send me a postcard here giving your Austrian telephone number. And if you are in London on October 16th and 17th may we accept your invitation to Highgate ?

Another little job for you! Do let me know:

1) your most favoured composers – Mozart, Beethoven, Schubert, Brahms – I presume. Any others?
2) your concerto repertoire
3) have you played in public all Beethoven and/or Schubert Sonatas?

[Walter Legge]

16 November 1973.
The White House
Millfield Place
Highgate
London N6.

Dear Walter,

How could you think for even one moment that I wouldn't like it? My difficulty is going to be to try to thank you adequately for this splendid article. All I can say is that if I had permitted myself to imagine how it might be if done ideally (which is not to be confused with deservedly) this is how your Grove article would have been. It reaches far beyond the merely laudatory to that which, as you well know, is most gratifying of all to an artist – an appreciation of the things he aims for but which are usually overlooked by others. I shall try hard to justify so splendid and encouraging, so stabilising a milestone in my career – and this will perhaps be my best way of trying to thank you, dear Walter, for all the precious time you must have taken over this entry, all the thought you have given it. Although you insist that writing comes hard to you, I must tell you that when I read it over the breakfast table it lived up beautifully to the proverbial 'easy reading'. And Lucille's reaction to it was so spontaneous: 'How perceptive that is! How far, too, from the usual routine observations. Walter Legge really does say something.' So who am I to quarrel with her views of a writer who has given me so much pleasure?

The two cuttings I am enclosing in case you may not have seen them when you were on the move and out of touch with English papers. I thought you might find them interesting, being interviews with other self-expatriated artists, among whom you and Elisabeth are going to shine in France like kohinoors.

I have thought so much of your removal since your letter came (it must have crossed with one of mine to Geneva) and in some inexplicable way felt happy about your being in France rather than in Switzerland. But I know how utterly wearying it all must have been. So many daunting decisions to be made, not the least being the consideration of which articles to let fall gladly from the back of the van in the hope of never having to see them again!

Please let me pick you both up at Brown's (petrol still being available) when you have got all your other appointments settled and you feel you can spare us the time to come here for a quiet luncheon (although the house and garden were designed for summer living, nature's bare bones visible through the windows in late autumn have their own attraction); the day could be of your choosing, and I would of course return you to your afternoon appointment. We really would love to see you both. Meanwhile, we are eagerly anticipating hearing Madame on the 24th.

My heartfelt gratitude again. How lucky for me the day that I fell to you in the great Grove gamble!

> Yours always,
> Clifford

VI. WIELAND WAGNER

Walter Legge came into contact with Wieland Wagner when making preparations for recordings at the 1951 Bayreuth Festival. Over a period of years the acquaintance ripened into close friendship, and Wagner frequently sought Legge's advice on artistic matters.

[translated from German]   3 March 1954.
> Bayreuther Festspiel
> Bayreuth.

Dear Mr Legge,

How kind of you to send me right out of the blue as it were your new *Hänsel und Gretel* records, and without my having any inkling of their coming. The recordings are brilliant, the orchestra is distinguished and I thank you most sincerely.

In spite of it being a gift horse I nonetheless looked it in the mouth: I find it awful and the whole work exceedingly phoney. With your star cast of Schwarzkopf, Grümmer and von Karajan you have multiplied the discrepancy between form and content in this work and treated me to a terrible evening. What sort of times must they have been which acclaimed this impudent mixture of *Meistersinger*, Tchaikovsky, operetta and *Moldau*? Who is actually going to buy these records?

> With sincere best wishes,
> Wieland Wagner

[translated from German]

30 March 1963.

Dear Wieland,

After the evening we spent together in Munich you promised me some well-deserved praise for the *Merry Widow* and *Così fan tutte* recordings. I am no Ochs, but 'I would be glad of a small recommendation'. And I need it urgently because I want to launch these two de luxe recordings with your recommendation. So please get moving.

Your SOS regarding Giulini came just at the right time as he had visited me and already planned how he could get out of your invitation in the most polite way. As he said himself, I pushed him into it and now he is full of enthusiasm to collaborate with you.

Now a few practical matters: he is very anxious that all the soloists should arrive five days before his first orchestral rehearsal in order to work with them and with you in the same way as we prepared our two Mozart operas: textual expression, freedom in the recitative-like passages but still with some intensity.

I telephoned Schmidt and he is waiting for your invitation, especially for *Tannhäuser* with Giulini; I think it would also be easy to get him for *Meistersinger*.

When we spoke about *Tannhäuser* you said that this opera must be a battle between singers. Please come to Milan on 9th or 10th April with a list of the finest men's voices so that we can decide definitively on the cast.

Then, as regards the two women: do you know of a better Elisabeth than Janowitz? Do you think it would be possible to get Price for Venus instead of Bunbury [*sic*]? I do not know of any more sensual voice with effortless high notes than Price's.

I have now listened to Ghiaurov for ten days. It is not a Hagen voice, but a heaven-sent Gurnemanz, Landgraf and Könige: also Mark.

That should give you enough to think about until our next meeting.

Awaiting your letter of recommendation,

> Yours sincerely,
> [Walter Legge]

PS. Do not tell anyone that Giulini is conducting *Tannhäuser*, otherwise all the 'dogs in the manger' will lock away the singers we need.

[translated from German]

1st April 1963.

Dear Sir Walter [*sic*],

Please jot down, without obligation, your ideas for the 1964 *Tannhäuser* on the enclosed piece of paper. They, that is the cast, should be the best obtainable and because of this they would have to be engaged straight after consultations between Giulini and Wagner. With the exception of Ludwig any of the names are suitable.

> Kindest regards,
> WW

8. Artists and Friends

[translated from German]

22 February 1964.

Dear Walter,

Mr Hotter recommends Mrs Gwyneth Jones to me who is contracted to Covent Garden. Do you know her? Would it be worthwhile, in considering Rhinemaiden or some other role, to get her to Bayreuth at the expense of the impecunious festival? I have meanwhile enquired through Coast [an agent], Edinburgh etc. about the lady by the name of Neal whom you recommended, but in vain. Everywhere I ask they maintain that such a person of that name does not exist.

Do you perhaps know of an address for this phantom?

Kindest regards,
W.W.

[translated from German]   25th December 1964.

Walther [sic] Legge in Ascona

Dear Sir Walther,

It was just as well that you stayed away from the *Tristan* performance which was not very good. It is said to have been quite a success however. Maazel stole the show from Nilsson ... How did you find the *Traviata*?

Best regards from WW, who would like to thank you again for so much.

VI. Wieland Wagner

[translated from German]   [undated]
                                                                              Casa Ortensia
                                                                              Via Lido, Ascona.
Dear Wieland,

The white lilies and bright pink carnations at Easter were a very joyous surprise for Elisabeth and me. Our grateful thanks for them. We tried everywhere to reach you by phone, just to express our thanks personally and second to let myself be inoculated with a squirt of artistic geniality. But in vain. Lhasa, ladies' toilets and even Brünnhilde (*Siegfried,* Act 3, Scene 2) are easier to penetrate than the secret of where you can be contacted by phone.

Gertrud and Nike [WW's wife and daughter] were here and we all enjoyed ourselves enormously together. With a keen sense of observation, charm and a viper's tongue (as well as a rare capacity for self-ridicule) Nike already demonstrates the immortal streak of Wielandblood. I think your people felt just as much at home as we did.

Now to a small but not insignificant request:

William Mann who is the leading critic of the London *Times* and who has written a very positive article on the basis of his interview with you, is coming to Bayreuth on the day preceding the first *Rheingold*. He has asked me if he, together with his wife and three daughters (Nike knows them all) might attend all your rehearsals. They are all young, intelligent and house-trained (for an auditorium).

A visit from you would considerably brighten life for us or, if I am alone, for me. Otherwise with whom am I going to discuss the important things of life? Have pity on me.

[Walter Legge]

[translated from German]   8 May 1965.
                                                                              Vienna.
Dear Sir Walter,

I was delighted to get the kind words from your voluntary exile in Ascona but I must emphatically contradict the first paragraph. Both Gabriele Taut and the House Manager of the famous Bayreuth Festival always have my telephone number.

Of course Mr William Mann with his wife and three daughters can attend the rehearsals if you vouch for them. Can I now still count on you for some sort of contribution to the programme notes? You are assured complete freedom to write what you want.

We have made progress here up to the main piano rehearsal. Böhm is again quite outstanding. With him one completely forgets the numerous four quarter beats, moreover the strings are better by some margin than in Bayreuth. Every evening the grand ladies of European Opera from Della Casa to Güden, sing here. Unfortunately there has again been no new voice for me to discover.

With best regards,
Yours always,
Wieland Wagner

[translated from German]   16 December 1965.
                                                            Bayreuther Festspiele
                                                            8580 Bayreuth.
Dear Sir Walter,
    I would really like to know after your experiences in Munich what you
think of my suggestion that you write me a really original contribution
about Knappertsbusch.
    Can I count on one?
    It is a pity that you have not seen either *Salome* or *Elektra*. You must
certainly have read about the two conductors that I have acquired. Boulez
for *Parsifal* and Melles for *Tannhäuser*. Better further experiments than
German general music directors.

                            With kindest regards,
                            Wieland Wagner

[translated from German]

                                                            18 December 1965.
Dear Wieland,
    To write a really original contribution about Knappertsbusch is much
more difficult than I had thought.
    When I was in Munich Frau Knappertsbusch was not to be seen and
your impeccable Frl. Taut did everything possible to bore me a hole in the
iron curtain which surrounds Kna. But with meagre results. A questionnaire to Frau Knappertsbusch came back with all the probing questions
unanswered. It seems to me that behind his Bavarian façade and Wieland-
like loquacity there hides an over-sensitive and tender being.
    Despite all this I will try to put down something decent on paper: but
not before the end of February,
    I have strutted around in Munich for two evenings with your lovely Iris.
When I told her how irritated to death I was by Hartmann's *Così* performance she reproached me that I was no music and theatre lover but a dirty
old masochist.
    Boulez and Melles will certainly entice me to Bayreuth. Both in 1966?
1 would like to urge you to consider the possibility of bringing in a new
young conductor alongside these two leading authorities. If talented young
conductors exist at all they will be glad and grateful to learn their art and
craft under such outstanding personalities. It can only be in Bayreuth's
favour that Karajan brings such nonentities as Conz and Pritchard to
Salzburg.
    Best Christmas and New Year greetings from our household to yours.

                        [Walter Legge]

PS. May I use the following (from the questionnaire to Frau Knappertsbusch): 'Did he agree with Wieland's production and stage design?' Answer: 'As regards *Parsifal*, yes!' Or could this cost me your highly valued friendship?

VII. WOLFGANG SAWALLISCH

Walter Legge produced Wolfgang Sawallisch's earliest EMI recordings between 1954 and 1958. In 1972 Sawallisch entered into discussions with VEB Deutsche Schallplatten regarding a plan that he should record all the Mozart symphonies with the Staatskapelle Dresden. This was to be a joint venture between the East German state record company and Philips.

[translated from German]

6 February 1972.

Mr Walter Legge
For reference

VEB Deutsche Schallplatte
Herrn Direktor Költsch
Berlin, Reichstagsufer 4/5

Dear Herr Költsch,

Heartfelt thanks for your letter of 31 January. I have read your comments very carefully and I am, of course, prepared to respect your decisions as I am moreover convinced that they have been taken after thorough consideration. So that we have no misunderstandings, I have not the slightest resentment whatever, or anything of the kind towards Herr Bluth and his team. Furthermore, I do not in the least doubt his artistic and technical capacity to carry out such a project.

However, it is possible that I have still not expressed quite clearly and unequivocally my understanding of what constitutes an above-average success. In such a case, it is indeed not solely a question of the artistic suitability of the recording manager but also that of a far-reaching consensus within a long-standing personal and musical relationship, which must exist between the conductor and – in the case of a record production – his immediate collaborator. I beg you to realise that it has nothing to do with Herr Bluth personally if I have expressed a request in my first letter to you to work with Herr Worm, being at the same time convinced that the recording team suggested by you meets the highest demands. Moreover, the restricted session time allowed for the complete Mozart recordings does not permit an artistic censensus to be reached perhaps until after a few days later, or under certain circumstances, not even until after the complete first recording period. If this were in fact the case, we would have already lost too much time, or, in other words, everything.

I have no intention of wishing in this letter to influence the decisions you have taken or to make another request about Herr Worm being allowed to participate. I have, of course, been thinking about how we can come jointly to a solution which is satisfactory to me artistically and thereby to you and your company, and one which is acceptable to all sides. I would make the suggestion that I will only too happily work with Herr Bluth on a one-off recording which could quite certainly be offered at a later date, not only in order to get to know him but also to establish a contact for possible future collaboration. I set such great store by the realisation of the recording of the complete Mozart symphonies with the Staatskapelle Dresden, if I may mention this fact again, but at the same time a guarantee must be given for optimum success from the very outset of the recording, so I would like you to agree that Mr Walter Legge should act as recording manager. You may remember that I wrote about him in my previous letter, and indicated that he was the first recording manager to enjoy my complete confidence, and with whom I was always of one mind in our many discussions about all sorts of detailed musical questions. Perhaps such a collaboration can be realised and I am sure that this solution would be the best. To this end, I have just spoken on the telephone to Mr Walter Legge in order to sound out his true opinion. To my great delight he has agreed, since he also thinks that the Staatskapelle Dresden is a first-rate orchestra, and in addition he has produced all the Mozart symphonies during his involvement as recording manager in London, and is therefore best equipped from the very beginning to deal with any problems which may arise in the course of recording.

Once more, be assured that I understand your decisions and for now accept my greetings and best wishes.

> Yours,
> W. Sawallisch

[translated from German]
6 February 1972.
8211 Grassau.

My dear Walter,

Just before setting off again for the Opera in Munich a brief greeting with my grateful thanks for showing your ready agreement. At the same time I am sending you for your information a carbon copy of my letter to the VEB Deutsche Schallplatten. I think we can discuss this personally in the near future. I would be very happy if this Mozart undertaking were to come off.

Meanwhile, my best wishes likewise to Elisabeth, and also from Mechthild.

> Yours always,
> Wolfgang Sawallisch

[translated from German]

3 April 1972

My dear Walter,

Once again two people – who understand each other – i.e. the two of us, had come up with an idea and the others have not played along. I have

252

cancelled the whole Mozart project because VEB Deutsche Schallplatte and also the co-producers – Philips – could not be prevailed upon to accept a record producer of my choice. So I have drawn the only possible conclusions and said 'no' for my part. Your commitment would be concerned with further expenses (that is quite logical!) and this would have been the case even if Herr Bluth had been able to make the recordings. It should be said, moreover, that I do not know Herr Bluth at all, I do not know what his work is like and I think that such a unique offer which will certainly not be repeated for me, i.e. the recording of all the Mozart symphonies, should only be carried out under first-class conditions. And this includes familiarity with a record producer and unlimited confidence in his personal, artistic and technical capabilities. The recording times set were also very short, which is, however, quite understandable, so that I had to have a guarantee from the first moment of recording that the right man was sitting behind the control booth window. As that is not the case, or I cannot tell whether it is, I think I have done the right thing.

We shall have to come up with some other idea. It did not work out this time. I would like to thank you, however, very much once again for your spontaneous agreement and I am quite certain that the future will bring us together in some form or other, as I hope and pray it will.

Best wishes from Mechthild, also to your dear wife; I hope that you have got over your visit to Japan. In two days time we are flying to Tokyo for five weeks.

> All the best from your ever grateful
> Wolfgang

> 5 February 1979.

Lieber Wolfgang,

You cannot know how delighted I was to receive the Strauss Bayreuth correspondence, and particularly because it came from you. My warmest thanks.

I have not yet had time to read it properly but have pushed my nose into the places where I might get confirmation of my surmise that Strauss conducted in Bayreuth for Paulina's advantage, and that Cosima was trying to nail Strauss down as the husband of those dreary daughters. What amuses me is the friendly tone of the letters between Richard the Second and Siegfried the less-than-second.

I've been trying to wring out of my Muse a piece for Beecham's Centenary, which has sent me hunting through the repertoires of the contemporaries of his youth, that it is to say Nikisch and Strauss, comparing them to Beecham naturally, and seeing how much better a judge Strauss was of the music he conducted, contemporary and otherwise. Of course he preferred to conduct his own works because he got performing fees, and others played for him as well as they knew how because he was Richard Strauss.

I am going to revenge myself on you by sending what I consider an absolutely first-class book on Toscanini written by a young American conductor, with all his repertoire in it. Strange that Toscanini who nailed himself to the cross of Wagnerian virtue did the last three *Ring* evenings innumerable times but never played a note of 'Rheingold'.

God knows I don't wish you ill but I do wish you were old enough to have heard Strauss's *Così* which surpassed all imagining, and I am still hoping that Szell's widow will send me the notes, or at least some of the sheets on which Szell jotted down what Strauss actually played in the recitatives, never twice the same, but witty references not only to other Mozart operas but to his own as well.

May I talk about Prey? The sort of singing and acting he did in *Fledermaus* in London has impressed me so much that I think he is beyond doubt the best possible Figaro, Comte, Guglielmo and could be made into the best Don Giovanni but I am sure that with your guidance he could be as good an Amfortas and Wolfram as one could find anywhere today. If you have in your repertoire, or intend to do any of the lighter Donizetti (not, for God's sake, *Lucia*) I feel confident that Prey has the right light touch. Have you ever looked at *Comte Ory*, which I find the best of the Rossini operas after *Barbiere*?

I don't know whether either Elisabeth or I have told you of the extraordinary young bass we had in our classes at Bloomington. His name is Kevin Langan and from the moment he opened his mouth, it was evident that he has a voice of the most exceptional beauty and size. In seven or eight years' time, a Gurnemanz. He sang Handel *coloratura* with the speed, accuracy and elegance that made my hair stand on end and we couldn't believe our own ears. He is still at Bloomington studying with a ferocious old battle-axe called Harshaw, but after half an hour's crucifixion with *Doppelgänger* we couldn't believe that any youngster, or in fact any bass known to us, could get so into the heart of the text and music.

I am putting on a recital for him in London on May 19, and if it is convenient to you, I'll bring him to Munich, or wherever nearer you are, to sing to you. Actually the voice is like the young Weber in the days I first heard him singing Wozzeck and even *Walküre* Wotans, but if you like him, don't let this fine-looking young fellow push his voice upwards.

All this, by the way, has Elisabeth's complete endorsement. If you can induce your theatre to start building up an ensemble, nothing would be better for the young man, nor if I may say so, for you, that he should fall into your hands. In Bloomington, he has already done Daland, in American I presume, but he's very intelligent and it took Elisabeth astonishingly little time to get good German punctuation out of him.

I won't waste any more of your time, but hope that we shall meet soon. Letter-writing is too slow. It'll be so good to have a really long talk about things that matter. Kindly arrange with the meteorological authorities that Föhn will be suspended from one day before I come to bring that young man for you to hear.

9

Sir William Walton

Walter Legge first met William Walton in the early 1930s. He produced most of Walton's EMI recordings as conductor, and the two men remained close friends until Legge's death in 1979.

> 5 January 1944.
> Ashby St Ledgers
> Rugby.

Dear Walter,

The parts of the Sin. Con. [Sinfonia concertante] only turned up this morn. having been mislaid by the RAF in their move. The score has not yet been found!

The rehearsal and performance of the Vl. Con. [Violin Concerto] is on Jan 17th at 2.30pm at the Civic Hall, Wolverhampton. There is another at Birmingham on the 18th – and the other at Liverpool on the 19th. I hope you will be able to get to one of these, preferably the one at Wolverhampton when I'll be there. On the other hand if you can't manage any of those dates there is another perf. with Eda Kersey on an as yet unspecified date sometime in March.

Will you be kind and forward the enclosed Pfte copy of the Sin. Con. to Cyril Smith as I don't know his address. He has no need to memorise it – in fact – I'd sooner he didn't so as to try and emphasise the point that the Pfte is not really any more important than any other instrument in the orch. However, he can please himself about that. If he has any alterations to make as regards the way it is laid out, I hope he'll make them. The perf. is on Feb 9th at Liverpool and I hope you'll be able to come.

> As ever,
> [William Walton]

In 1949 Walton and his wife Susana left London, and rented a house on the Island of Ischia.

> 14 December 1949.
> Convento San Francesco
> Forio d'Ischia
> Prov di Napoli, Italia.

My dear Walter,

... We've had no papers at all since being here so are completely out of contact with the horrors without. Each time I've seen a Con. Dai. Mail [*Continental Daily Mail*] it is just too much first Neveu – how ghastly then heaven knows what.

As for my opera – the less said the better – I'm having a hell of a time with the libretto and with the post being what it is it takes ages to get anything altered. As it stands no-one has anything to sing at all except a sentence of some three or four bars at a time. However C.H. [Christopher Hassall] is very amenable and I hope to get straightened out soon. But I've got something down – not a vast amount and am now waiting for C.H.'s latest effort.

Otherwise it is pleasant here – the house fairly tolerable likewise the food and wine – the weather variable, not cold and one can swim about one day in four.

I'm sorry that the Philharmonia Con was such a financial disaster – but I imagine no concerts are doing too well – but they ought to pick up once it is realised how good they are.

I hope this will reach you before you leave for India. Enjoy yourself.

This brings you all good wishes for Xmas and the New Year from us both.

Sue wants to know if you're married yet? When and where? So do I.

as ever,
William

PS. Keep an eye on the Hungarians for recording the quartet also on Yehudi [Menuhin] for the sonatas that is if you come back.

16 January 1950.

My dear Walter,

... I've heard further from Parry Jones about the state of things at Cov. Gar. [Covent Garden]. He actually does mention that Christoff was very rude, but it is the other things/questions – lack of discipline and co-ordination etc. Waste – 19 rehearsals for *Salome*, 18 I ask you, for *Lohengrin*, and typically enough for *Boris* and you mention two for *Butterfly*. P.J. has been asked to be a more or less permanent member of the Co. So keep all this under your hat as I don't want to get him into trouble.

Thank you for the welcome news about *Scap* [*Scapino*] and B's F [*Belshazzar's Feast*]. I'll certainly join the artistic directorate as soon as they are out of the way.

I'm sorry about Kubelík – it would have been a help to have one decent conductor permanently in the country.

We went to Naples last week ostensibly to see *Wozzeck*. But it turned out that it had been such a flop, though Gui told me the performance was good with Gobbi and Böhm conducting, that it was changed and we were let in for *Zazà* instead. The Zs are the only things in common I fear.

Goossens was there – incidentally he might do for the BBC as he has to decide in June whether to renew or not his contract in Australia.

There's to be a performance in Rome of the original *Façade* in March with K[eith]. Falkner reciting. He might be good, but we shan't go because of the expense and the impossibility of getting a room being Anno Santo.

The opera is beginning to move and I hope to finish Sc. 1 of Act II by the middle of next month. I shall then set to on Act I.

I started on Act II as I felt that if I couldn't do that it was no use bothering to try with the rest.

However, having got at least the libretto for this Sc. more or less right, things have not gone too badly.

There is quite a good concerted Sc. to open with – the chess game and the song for attending maids (lifted from *Hamlet* – film I mean) a recit. and aria for Elisabeth about three and a half mins. with a nice top C at the end – a bit sailing near the wind, slightly neo-Puccini, but what can one do with a very neo-Novello poem. A 'Jealousy' aria for Pandoras followed by a love duet which ends the Sc. and leads to the pornographic Interlude.

So I contemplate having two-thirds of Acts 1 and 2 done before I return. When I say done, I mean a very sketchy sketch.

Our love to you and Elisabeth and let us know the happy day.

> As ever,
> [William Walton]

A house near to the Convento San Francisco was the Waltons' second home on Ischia.

> 3 March 1952.
> Casa Cirillo
> Forio d'Ischia
> Italy.

My dear Walter,

I am sorry to have neglected writing you for so long, but my news of the op[era] was so depressing that I did not feel like writing anyone. Libretto trouble as usual, at last I think more or less satisfactorily ironed out and the end of Act II is at last in sight. I now understand why no-one has attempted an opera with love interest since Puccini. Scyllas and Charybdes surround one at every bar. Give me Buddery every time – or even plain rape. Anyhow most of Act III is now scored as well.

I now aim to have it ready for the Coronation Season. Also I've got my eye on another Coronation March which as yet has only got as far as the title *Orb and Sceptre*.

I'm sorry you couldn't get to see us and also, as Sue will have told you, we missed Elisabeth.

It's good news that Karajan is doing the Symph and I shall try to listen in. Only hope it is not the 'Terza programa' which is on micro-waves and impossible to get on the battery set.

About the Co's agreement regarding T & C [*Troilus and Cressida*], I cannot grant the score and parts as the OUP [Oxford University Press] are part owners so I will send the copy to Alan Frank to see what he thinks.

Why not try to get Unesco to help over the Philharmonia tour? They are apparently paying for Buddery [Britten's opera *Billy Budd*] in Paris, so I see no reason why they shouldn't help with this 'goodwill' tour. But who to get hold of I don't quite know. Perhaps David W[ebster] could put you on to somebody. On the other hand you could get on to Chris Hassall's secretary who is also mine and ask him, as he has been dealing with an invitation to me to attend a Unesco Conference in Venice in September, so he would at least know someone who might put you on the track of someone else.

I hope K is conducting *Scap* on the tour some time.

The only things of interest we've heard at the San Carlo were *L'assedio di Corinto*, which is the only Rossini opera-seria I've heard, very interesting and full of lovely things divinely sung by Tebaldi and *Padmâvâti* Roussel, which is quite interesting to hear if not an absolute masterpiece. Both well sung but its production – Cov Gar is heaven to the San Carlo.

I'm delighted you've got Harry Blech to do one of the Mysore concerts. I'm sure he'll do well – I'm glad Karajan is taking on the other concerts. It is time he got going properly in London.

We don't return till the end of June. By which time, pray heaven, the end of the op will be either accomplished or in sight.

As ever,
[William Walton]

PS. When do the Symph records appear ... for March 29th my 50th birthday?

12 November 1952.

My dear Walter,

I hear from the Brit. Con. [British Consulate] in Rome that the Symph. is not included in Herbert von K programmes. Can this be so? You might ask him if he is going to do it (and I shall be very disappointed if he's not) if he would be so kind as to let me know when and where.

Not much news – if any. Lord Waverly wrote me and asked if I wouldn't like to resign from Cov. Gar. so I said I would. I shall be asked to rejoin next Nov. when I'm back for a long time. I don't think it portends anything.

Is there any chance of seeing you and Liz in these parts?

Our love to you both and Herbert.

Yours ever,
William

9. Sir William Walton

21 October 1956.

Dear Walter,

If you are now back, I hope you [had] an agreeably busy time in the US.

About the Jo'burg Fest. Ov. 1956 (otherwise known as the IDB). A. Frank is asking about recording. It was, by the way, a 'wow' in Jo'burg, not that [that] means much (except for 400 smackers 'tax free') and Malcolm S[argent] cabled 'Overture complete triumph repeating by request next concert, and in Pretoria'.

Kurtz, who is doing the first English perf. on Nov 13th would like to record, so doubtless would Malcolm – so doubtless would I; as I haven't a bean except 'blocked' ones in England (of those I've quite an amount) a fee paid on the nail would probably [be] more than welcome when we return in Jan for the first London perf. of the Ov. Jan 23rd and the Vlc. Con. [Cello Concerto] Feb 13th after which we return here for me to complete a work for Cleveland and Sue to carry on her building operations on our new acquisition which it is high time you visited.

I shall finish the Vlc. Con. in a couple of days or so and it is on the whole fairly satisfactory, which from me is saying a lot. It is in fact the best of the three concerti.

The island is very quiet all the great (Herbert, Callas, Ghiringhelli) etc. etc. having departed and is divine with wonderful weather.

I suppose there is no hope of persuading Herbert to think about putting on T and C in Vienna. It is to be revived at CG [Covent Garden] in '58 for the centenary. Could Elisabeth be persuaded to sing provided DW [Sir David Webster] asks her in time?

Let us hear from you some time.

> With our love
> as ever,
> [William Walton]

19 July 1962.

Dear William,

First of all thank you for having written that wonderful cycle of songs which Elisabeth had the privilege of baptising yesterday.

We have read the critics and decided that it would be unfair of Elisabeth to retain the exclusive rights of performance or indeed to sing them in New York.

It is the same old story as with Toscanini and the *Enigma*: He performed it in London for the pleasure of doing a great English work and all the thanks he had were insults from the press.

> Our love to you both.
> Yours always,
> [Walter Legge]

9. Sir William Walton

By now the Waltons had settled in the house on Ischia which had been specially built for them.

1 April 1963.
La Mortella
Forio d'Ischia
Italy.

My dear Walter,

Thank you for the cable and for your success in inveigling the Karajans to attend the first night of *Troilus*. I have written at once to Sir DW asking for a box, which I am sure will be forthcoming.

Peccato! that Szell is unable to accept the invitation for next year, but I am sure he would accept for the following season. He has written saying how sorry he was that he couldn't accept and saying almost embarrassingly laudatory things about the H[indemith] variations which he does on the 8th.

I hope we can induce you to return here with us about May 8th.

> With our best love to you both,
> as ever,
> [William Walton]

6 May 1965.

Dear William,

I don't know whether it's by accident or malicious intent but the English papers which I buy every day have – with the exception of a feature article in the *Daily Mail* or *Daily Express*, I forget which – overlooked your English appearances. I hope they have gone well.

Have you seen *The Mines of Sulphur*? Siciliani and Herbert were so enthusiastic that I got hold of the piano score. It's a damned good libretto and as far as I can make out looks like a very good opera where the tenor part is so high and awkward that it may stand in the way of the work's success. When you feel like writing another opera I think it would be worth considering the librettist.

> Our love to you both.
> Yours always,
> [Walter Legge]

The Mines of Sulphur is an opera composed by Richard Rodney Bennett.

In December 1965 Walton was found to be suffering from lung cancer, and he had an immediate operation. This was followed by treatment with cobalt rays.

23 May 1966.

Dear Walter,

How nice to hear from you.

According to the latest X-rays I am keeping very well with no sign (as yet) of a recurrence. The doctors don't seem to expect one which is encouraging – but one never knows. Anyhow I shall continue with the X-rays every 3 months.

I'm hardly doing anything – even listening to music, let alone composing. There's a sort of delayed shock and one will have to start all over again I feel, which I think may be a good thing. I was actually in the middle of an opera on Chekhov's the *Bear* for Aldeburgh. It's for next year and could be quite funny. Do you know the play? Very short – about 40 mins.

I think you are right about Ascona – Salzburg will be far more congenial I suspect.

> With our best love to you both,
> As ever,
> [William Walton]

27 June 1966.

Dear Walter,

I am delighted to hear that your check-ups have been so satisfactory. I returned from London about three weeks ago after having had also a satisfactory check. It's all a bit nerve-wracking, I find and I think I'm becoming a hypochondriac.

The press for the *Mines of Sulphur* was not at all good and I've not come across anyone who thought really well of it. It seems to have had the same kind of reception at La Scala as did T & C.

Are you going to Salzburg to hear Hans H[enze]'s *The Bassarids*? I saw the libretto – quite incomprehensible I thought – but I know I'm exceptionally stupid. If you hear it let me know what it is like.

Paul Dehn is doing the libretto for the *Bear* – on the whole very well if just a bit too witty here and there.

> With best love from us both,
> [William Walton]

8 September 1966.

Dear William:

Since I see you announced to conduct the New Philharmonia in works by Mozart and Walton I happily assume you are completely well again.

Do you feel like writing a two or three minute trio for two sopranos and baritone unaccompanied. I can promise you a distinguished cast for the première – Schwarzkopf, Los Angeles and Fischer-Dieskau! The occasion is Gerald's Farewell Concert at the Royal Festival Hall on February 20th 1967. Make it a canon on *For he's a jolly good fellow* if you can't find an apt and suitable short poem. Neither of the ladies wants to go above G and no one can expect a baritone to either. And since it is unacc. no highly personal difficulties of intonation!

> My love to you both,

Yours always,
[Walter Legge]

19 September 1966.

Dear Walter,

I don't [know] where you saw that I was to conduct the NPO [New Philharmonia Orchestra] but it's off. There was talk of my doing *Façade* but they could find no reciters, luckily as I feel unfit to conduct anything even with one finger. I'm having a good deal of pain from the operational area and my left arm. The doctor here says it's rheumatism!

Well, I go to London next week for a check-up. I don't think I'd better undertake the little piece for Gerald. I've only just begun to resume work on the *Bear* and I assure you I'm not at all in form. Sir Michael T[ippett] I think is the answer and very appropriate too.

Our best love to you both,
As ever,
[William Walton]

28 November 1966.

Dear Walter,

... We go back to London mid-Feb next year, I for a check-up – and incidentally to hear Mr André Previn do Symph. No. 1 at an LSO concert. (He's at Houston.)

There's a mad situation. Without warning – suddenly EMI & Decca have decided to record Symph 1, EMI with Sir M.S. [Malcolm Sargent] and the NPO Decca, with Previn & the LSO. Both records come out in Feb. and I've had to write 'blurbs' for them both!

Both recordings are very good, naturally in parts one is better than the other, but on the whole Decca is the best. But what a 'pasticcio' after all those years to bring out both at the same time.

The *Bear* gets more difficult as it goes on. In fact the end is the end in all senses of the word and I do[n't] quite know how it will turn out.

With our best love to you both – bless you.

As ever,
[William Walton]

Come and see us.

Previn's recording of Walton's First Symphony was in fact made for RCA.

14 December 1966.

Dear William,

From your last letter what interests me most to hear was that you are definitely better. I hope we shall meet in London in February. We shall be

262

there from the 17th to the 21st – probably at the Savoy – and I hope you will be in London at the same time.

The ways of the gramophone world get madder and madder. It would have been so much wiser for EMI to contribute what they paid [Ernest] Fleischmann of the New Philharmonia to Epic for them to do the different version with George Szell – though I hear quite good reports of Previn. Anyhow, simultaneous publication insures you plenty of publicity and space. 1966 seems to have been a bad year for British composers. I have just heard from Tippett that he too had a major operation this year.

All good wishes for Christmas and the New Year,

Yours always,
[Walter Legge]

4 March 1967.

Dear William,

It was not discourtesy that I did not call you after the 20th., merely that I had a relapse which has incapacitated me or rather imbedded me for a fortnight. Subject to an ECG I shall be released on Wednesday next to live a sane solid life and 'remember my age'. With luck I shall be back in Ascona by next weekend and after a few days I am going house-hunting in the South of France preferably near Nice airport.

I attribute my malady to having done so little in the last two years, that is to say, nothing but licking my wounds.

Have you finally put *The Bear* to bed?

I have a theory which I will expound to you as soon as we meet, that atonality and twelve-tonery are on the way out. The public has rejected almost everything except *Wozzeck* which is, after all, only a sentimental and distorted afterbirth of *Tristan*. If you read the English papers as I do, not to mention the German, Scandinavian and Italian you will see that any collection of amateurs who put on forgotten Donizetti, Bellini or Verdi operas pack the houses and are praised by the critics of both sexes. At Gerald's farewell concert I put on 19 pieces unknown to the press and public, from Haydn trios to Rossini, Schumann and Mendelssohn duets: not only did the public roar with delight but the critics are talking about it as the Concert of the Century and even to me that it was one of the great experiences of their lives. Quite simply the public has made up its mind that it wants to enjoy what it hears: you won't believe it but Elgar on records at last is becoming a best-seller. So when the mood takes you, don't be ashamed to indulge in a 20-minute piece of Pomp and Circumcision.

My regards to you both,
Yours always,
[Walter Legge]

9. Sir William Walton

9 March 1967.

Dear Walter,

Sorry to hear about your relapse and hope you are now fully recovered. In about ten days' time I shall have finished the *Bear*. Your theory that twelve-tonery is on the way out pleases me, especially as the *Bear* gets more tonal frivolous and vulgar as it progresses.

Though I would like to think you are right I was slightly horrified by the enthusiastic reception given to the NPO concert of atonal music, but it was I like to think more for Mr Downes who conducted extremely ably.

Incidentally, Previn is a splendid conductor and did Symph. 1 proud and it and I got a huge ovation. Sylvia Male's sec. told me some time ago that his version had already topped 5,000 and Mr Angle told me that Decca were outselling HMV five to one. I wonder.

I hope EMI will bring out a record of Gerald's last concert with those 19 lollipops. I read I thought strangely enthusiastic notices about Walter Legge? So it must have been super.

> Look after yourself.
> As ever,
> [William Walton]

16 March 1967.

Dear William,

... At the moment the London public seems to applaud anything. Six years ago I put on a concert of Mahler 1 and 9 conducted by Horenstein. The audience was smaller than the orchestra; two or three months ago with the same orchestra conductor and programme, the place was sold out ten days beforehand. I can understand the Festival Hall being sold out when Boulez does Berg or even his own music. No doubt there will be a wave of enthusiasm for Charles Ives which you looked at I believe when Cecil Gray was doing his book on contemporary music in the late 1920s, but it won't last.

Did you perchance see Picasso's recent utterance on Stravinsky – quote 'now he's making bird cages'.

I will try to find out exactly how Malcolm's version of Symph. 1 has sold. Frankly I doubt 5,000 in so short a time. The only European conductors who get into those figures on European sales are Karajan and now to a lesser extent Klemperer and that only with late eighteenth and nineteenth century music. There is so much music reasonably well performed and recorded on cheap labels now that so-called classical sales are not nearly what they were except for a few opera singers who happen to be in vogue.

> My regards to you both.
> Yours always,
> [Walter Legge]

9. Sir William Walton

12 August 1967.

Dear Walter,

I was about to write to you and tell you how much I missed you during the recording (EMI) of the *Bear*. I hope it will turn out better than I fear. Hard luck on the singers, etc, for there didn't seem to be any time for any play-backs during the recording – only during the interval or after the session. However, it is too late to start bothering about it now.

I'm much interested by the *Frogs* idea. I will re-read it and have a talk with Paul Dehn. He is I think, one of the better, if not the best of the librettists about at the moment – especially if there is a sound structural basis there already as in the *Bear* where he had only to cut and adorn the text with his (more often than not) witty, amusing and to-the-point lyrics, and I've got him in control! I don't think I want a commission as yet from Cov. Gar. It may sound a bit conceited, but I've got or could have so many commissions that I don't know where to begin – in fact I'm giving them all up and when I write another piece I'll put it up for auction!

With our best love to Elisabeth when she gets back.

As ever,
[William Walton]

2 October 1967.

My dear Walter,

I've only just returned from Montreal where the *Bear* was being performed at 'Expo'. We had previously been three weeks in Greece which will explain why I have not answered you before.

I will certainly look at *Baruffe chiozotte* and the other Goldoni plays. It was done with *Acis and Galatea* in Montreal – much too long for another opera in the same programme. However, it was quite a successful evening in spite of competition from the Vienna State Op, the first rain (heavy) for about a month and an extensive bus strike, so the audience was rather meagre – but not noticeably more than for *Midsummer Night's Dream* when things were normal!

I've heard the record. Not too bad, but lacking in brilliance in parts. However, I'll send it to you when it's out in December.

Our love to you both,
[William Walton]

9 January 1968.

Carissimo Guglielmo,
A happy New Year to you both!

The Bear has obviously justified all the blood, sweat and tears that its composition involved. Already in the first six months, it must have had more performances than *Troilus and Cressida* in ten years. Looking at the concert programmes for the present season you and Elgar have obviously pushed all your British contemporains in the shade. Even men as good as

Hindemith – a damned good composer until his wife started meddling in his choice of subjects – are lying in the shadow of the maestro d'Ischia. I am more than delighted.

How is the health? Why not write a Requiem (Brevis) 'dedicated to the memory of Sir M– S– without whose performances my works would have been internationally acknowledged 30 years earlier'?

> My love to you both.
> Yours always,
> [Walter Legge]

13 January 1968.

My dear Walter,

Delighted to receive your letter and get your new address.

Actually the *Bear* hasn't had so many perfs as all that. It is awkward being a one act to find something to go with it. But with the record out – have you got it – I'll have it sent to you if you haven't – and coming out in the US in March I hope it may get some perfs from those opera workshops of which there are so many or get on to the TV.

I should have thought it was made for TV – three voices, one scene, small orch and 45 mins in length – but so far not a bite. The record is not bad on the whole but it is (my fault or P. Dehn's) about three or four mins too long and of course I have seen, too late, where to cut it. Anyhow I shall be most interested to know what you think.

I'm delighted to hear your doctor is pleased with you – mine is also pleased with me, but I keep a careful look out.

We should be delighted if you come to stay any time you like. It is difficult to say what the weather will be like in Feb – probably wet, as it is now being freezing but dry – but till the end of April it is a toss-up. Anyhow the house is nice and warm and we have a lift!

The gramophone cos are off their rocker again – or perhaps they aren't – as they are now bringing out the Viola Conc RCA with Trampler and Previn. EMI with Downes and Doktor.

I'm not too keen about either, but I suppose the two versions of Symph 1 must have gone well – at least well enough to gamble on this. I've always found it impossible to discover how many records have sold. Anyhow, it is quite pleasing – especially as devaluation is no joke. I had more PRS [royalties from the Performing Rights Society] than ever this year but with devaluation it amounts to less than last year!

Best love to you both and looking forward to seeing you.

> As ever,
> [William Walton]

Karl Doktor's recording of Walton's Viola Concerto was in fact on CBS. The Trampler version was not released.

9. Sir William Walton

6 March 1968.

Dear Walter,

I hope that you are both back safely and well after your sojourn in the US. I'm well, in fact we both are, but I get terribly tired, especially if I have to force myself to look at a piece of mss paper. I'm consequently well very well behind with my overture for the NY Phil. which is unfortunate as they are paying very handsomely and it will be quite a wrench if I have to forego it.

We are thinking and are almost certainly going to the Scala on the 26th for the first night of Hans H's *Bassarids*. Is there any chance that you might be going too? I hope so – it would be so nice to see you again at long last.

I found two easy and excellent 'cuts' in the *Bear* and have done as you suggest in the printed score which should be out soon. A pity I couldn't do them before it was recorded – but one is so stupid about 'cuts'. I never see how to do them till too late. But now it will be some eight minutes shorter. Rather necessary.

Hoping to see you in Milan.

Our best love to you both,
[William Walton]

14 October 1968.

Dear Walter,

It was very nice seeing you again and thank you for having us to stay. I hope that your cold is better by now.

I bullied the OUP and the EMI about the *Bear* so I hope that by now both the score and the record have arrived.

The recording with Yehudi went well. I really think he plays the viola better than the violin. He is going to record the Vl. Con next year so that there will be one on each side.

Best love from us both.
[William Walton]

16 January 1969.

Carissimo Guglielmo,

Please accept my warmest thanks for the record and v + p score of your *Bear*. I have played it three times at intervals of roughly a week and enjoyed it more each time.

I think you are wise to make all the cuts as printed except the third one i.e. 8 after 63 to 8 after 65, which, I feel, should be kept in to have an episode of sufficient length at that juncture. I don't think you will have made yourself more popular at Aldeburgh by your magical exploitation of a tiny orchestral group. Can't you find a Grand-Guignol shocker to go with it as a double-bill?

9. Sir William Walton

Elisabeth is in Schruns taking skiing lessons and recovering from three consecutive virus attacks.

This is Geneva's worst season: I admire snow only at a great distance and even though the lake is beautiful to look at, a succession of sunless weeks gets me down. Old age no doubt!

Make a note of the period May 10th to 19th. A young conductor in whose abilities and future I believe is doing *Il Conte d'Ory* at the San Carlo – first performance May 14th. I shall arrive there about the 10th and stay probably until after the second performance. Perhaps you'll both feel like invading the mainland?

> Our love to you both.
> Yours always,
> [Walter Legge]

21 December 1969.

Dear Walter,

Delighted to hear from you. I would have written sooner but I've been up to the eyes with music for Larry's [Sir Laurence Olivier's] film of the *Three Sisters*. Not much music but very difficult to do.

Presumably you refer to the *Capriccio burlesco* – the Kensington Symph must be a bit out of touch as it was first played in London in January and several times since, and twice recorded. The BB [Benjamin Britten] variations are to be given in San Francisco on Jan 14th. Not very happy about it – but we'll see.

All seasonal greetings and our love to you both.

> As ever,
> [William Walton]

Walton's *Improvisations on an Impromptu of Benjamin Britten* was completed in 1969.

1 April 1972.

My dear Elisabeth & Walter,

Thank you so much for your greetings telegram.

The birthday celebrations could not have gone better. 'Sold out' everywhere (at the Fest. H. within two days much to everyone's surprise – & irritation?). Previn did B's F really wonderfully and recorded it the next day.

The culmination was a marvellous party given by the PM at Downing Street with the Queen Mum. Most enjoyable and non-pompous.

We shall probably be calling in on you at the end of the month as we are motoring out with all the loot! Will let you know later.

> Our love to you both.
> [William Walton]

We go to Oxford the 15th.

9. Sir William Walton

13 April 1972.

Dear William,

We were deeply touched and happy as we followed in the English papers the crescendo of interest and enthusiasm that built up into Il trionfo di Ser Guglielmo. Naturally some were more than irritated. From where we were the gnashing of teeth and howls from the bowels of Aldeburgh were hardly audible.

I think Herbert ought even in belated celebration to do *Belshazzar's Feast* in Berlin or at one of his Salzburg Festivals. He ought not to forget that his great fame was first established with Philharmonia in London and on records there.

For your 75th you ought to get a life peerage, something no British musician has ever had. Try boating with Ted [Edward Heath]!

> Our love to you.
> Yours always,
> [Walter Legge]

24 July 1974.

Dear Walter,

1976 is the 25th Anniversary of the opening of the Festival Hall. In order to celebrate the occasion the GLC [Greater London Council] have invited several orchs. including the Berlin Phil with Herbert, and the idea is that I shall write a piece for the occasion with Herbert conducting the B Phil. I'm not at all sure it is a good idea. It is all very hazy and even if I do write a piece I'd bet anything that HK would get out of it, just as he has avoided ever doing *Belshazzar* ever since that marvellous perf. in Vienna – it was unforgettable, but alas, not to be repeated. Every time it has been scheduled he got out of it at the last min – leaving someone call[ed] Abravanel (a Mormon) to do it the last time it was announced in Berlin. So I'm not inclined to get excited about writing a new piece for him – someone else can do it – Malcolm Arnold, or Lennox B[erkeley], or even Sir Michael T[ippett], and I hope he enjoys it.

> Our best love to you both.
> As ever,
> [William Walton]

3 August 1975.

Dear Walter,

... Yes T & C is being revived – in fact I've re-written and cut it quite a lot and now believe it may be OK. Janet Baker is Cress[ida] (necessitating a lot of re-writing) Remedios Tro[ilus] Colin Graham producing an entirely new production. So I have hopes. The *Bear* seems to have got off the ground in Germany, first at Kassel, a month or two ago. Next season it is being repeated there and at Wiesbaden, Munich and two or three other places. And B's F is being done twice in Munich next Nov.

9. Sir William Walton

I'm busy on a piece for the 25th Anniversary of the RFH – not a very inspiring idea.

Our best love to you both,
[William Walton]

15 September 1975.

Dear Walter,

I have been meaning to reply every day to your letter and on the receipt of your justly reproachful card I'm now at last doing so. The barest excuse I have to offer is that I have been trying to get going (I fear vainly) on this work I've stupidly accepted to do for the 'Consecration of the 25th Anniversary of the RFH'. The only thing to be said for it is that the sum offered is quite acceptable for these days. But it's a difficult type of piece to get going on – for one thing, the length 10-15 mins is a good deal to cope with, even if inspired and there's not much inspiration in the RFH or in one John Denison CBE. But somehow I must finish by Xmas – good, bad or indifferent.

… Thank you for your excellent suggestions about T and C. Alas the cast is all set, I fear unchangeable. It is on the whole, about as good as Cov. Gar. can find or afford. But I think the recording is the really important thing. *Midsummer Marriage*'s success to me is one of the mysteries of life. But Philips and Schotts mounted a really devastating PR act, especially in the US and it paid off very nicely, with extraordinary sales. So I feel if the record of T & C is what it should be it should at least equal MM in sales. What with Janet and André. I've not heard Remedios except on record of MM. Not at all bad and I'm told he's improving considerably and if he can overcome the difficulties of MM he ought to find T & C more sympathetic. Of course T & C's sex-appeal is nowadays of the wrong sort. And I'm sure EMI and OUP won't afford the necessary PR. *The Bear* is doing well. It's had a lot of perfs. all over the place and now it is being repeated in Kassel and being done in Wiesbaden and Munich next season. Also the Munich Philharmonic opens its season with B's F.

The new version of T & C should be and is at least twice as good. All the awkward bits of Hassalese and Walton having been eliminated. As soon as it is in print I'll send you a copy. A great help has been Colin Graham who is producing at CG. He's excellent.

Our love to you both,
[William Walton]

Give HK my regards and tell him to go and [xxxx] himself. He's refused to record B's F. Blast him! He's probably getting too old for such a strenuous piece, tho' Adrian Boult is doing Sinf 1 shortly and he's 86!

270

9. Sir William Walton

17 December 1975.

Dear Walter,

Thank you enormously for your kind and helpful letter. It was awaiting us on our return from Munich where we attended the extremely enthusiastic and successful perf. of B's binge [Belshazzar's Feast] with the Munich State Orch and Chorus, conducted very well by James Loughran. It may lead to a lot in one way and another, as with perfs of the *Bear* in Kassel, Wiesbaden and Munich next season, the name of WW will begin to be known in Germany and I hope his music played.

Now about T & C, the only way to get it recorded is by recording every performance and making a choice from them. It is the only way open for it to be done, I know it may not be entirely satisfactory but as things are, we'd have to wait till 1978 at the earliest, and heaven knows what inflation will be by then. Also, none of us is getting any younger and Janet is agreeable to recording the work that way. The great question at the moment is for a tenor who can speak English well enough to get by and of course be able to sing! Solti has collared our tenor for at least six months (in spite of his contract to Cov. Gar.) to learn the *Ring*. I say I am devastated by the news, but it, at the moment, leaves a hole which has to be filled and filled very well. Colin Graham (the producer of T & C) has got two names of tenors whose English is perfect – but no-one has heard them yet. They are Josef Köstlinger (Tamino in Ingmar Bergman's film – an Austrian) and Jonny Blank – a Swede who is too grand to give an audition. Both are said to be excellent. Do you know of either or have you any further suggestions? It would be a marvellous help if you knew someone, as I know you are to be trusted about singers!

I've been trying – vainly – to trace you in Berlin and hope you are back by now and will get this letter safely and will be the help you have always been.

With our best love and seasonal greetings to you both,

As ever,
[William Walton]

10 January 1976.

Dear Walter,

We are just back from Taormina where we went for some days to avoid the holidays. Marvellous weather, as it is here and I'm pretty certain that it is with you at Cap Ferrat at the moment.

Firstly, a thousand thanks for your help and ideas about T & C. I will write to Lord G[oodman] to see if he can help to put them over to Tooley. Meanwhile the die is cast, in that I've accepted to have the actual performances recorded. There seems to be no other way of doing it. I made Christopher Morris OUP tell Andry, so I've had no direct touch with him. If I can get them all to agree about the points of your suggestion, I think all will be well – but the thing is to persuade them to do so will be the difficulty.

271

Everyone is so busy doing something else. And, of course, we are still undecided about the tenor and nothing can get going till that key chap has been decided upon, and there's not so much time left for him to be found. I've no personal suggestions to make not having heard any singers except Italians, but I'll write Tooley about the people you mention, especially Gedda, who would be my first choice and James King and the young Finn. Remedios is still under contract for it and I don't think that Solti has as yet got him to give up Troi in favour of the *Ring*, but I should think it very unlikely that he will succeed. But the position, as you can see, is v. unsatisfactory.

The production rehearsals on Oct 11th and a new 'Dame' Janet Baker joins on the 22nd and Previn on the 25th (he's in Pittsburgh till then). The stage and pfte. rehearsals start on Nov 2nd. Stage orch Nov 5th – Act I, Nov 8th – Act II, Nov 9th – Act III, Nov 10th final dress rehearsal. It doesn't seem to me to be very adequate, but what can one do? Well with many many thanks again for your help.

Give our best love to Elisabeth. I'm delighted at her resuscitating *The Song of L.M's T*. [*the Lord Mayor's Table*].

> Blessings,
> [William Walton]

Peter Andry was head of EMI's International Classical Division.

> 18 February 1976.

Dear Walter,

I can't tell you how grateful I am to you for all the trouble you have taken to find a Troilus. Gedda, alas, feels he's too old to start learning a new role, and I suppose he knows best. A Swedish tenor by name of Gösta Winbergh – he's apparently very good – so good, in fact that the Intendant of the Stockholm Opera is loath to let him go. Colin Graham has seen but not heard him, but says he'd suit the part admirably. Then there's an American Jack Trussel who CG heard in Santa Fé. Quite good and would be possible if no-one better is found. Richard Lewis told Alan Frank who kept it to himself, that he'd like to do Pandarus. I'm sure he'd be a splendid P. and a tower of strength as he knows the whole opera v. well. But there it is.

We go to London the 29th till March 7th for the Italian week at CG. The Ambassador in London is a great pal of ours so we are going to help out, so to speak. No chance of your being there I suppose?

> With our best love to you both,
> [William Walton]

> 25 February 1976.

Dear Walter,

Do you know anything about a tenor called Richard Cassidy? or it is Cassilly? He's not even a name to me, but he's been chosen to sing Troi, and everyone is happy about him, except Colin Graham. Who I gather isn't worried about his voice, but says he's too tall for Janet, or at least that is what I understand. But anyhow, that's settled, and we've now got to get down to the performance whether we like it or not.

We go to London (The Ritz) on the 29th and stay there till March 6th. We shall be much occupied with the Scala set-up, as the Italian Ambassador in London is a good friend of ours and has asked me to dine with HM the Queen!

Let us know when you'd like to come and stay. I think life will go along at my rate for the moment, I hope not too unpleasantly.

Love to both,
As ever,
[William Walton]

23 February 1978.

Dear Walter,

How kind of you to write. Health is on the whole fairly good, but I get very depressed about my work. I don't seem to be able to get anything worthwhile down on paper – otherwise I'm still doing well enough to allow Sue to follow her ideas out, her latest being to have a trout stream in a new bit of land we bought a few weeks ago. Not quite so balmy [sic] as it seems to be at first glance.

I can hardly believe that the Vl. Con. is having such success. I must look more carefully at my next PRS returns.

The *Bear* has been having quite a success in Germany, in Kassel, Munich, Köln, Passau etc and on the Hungarian TV. Quite a help. And now OUP tells me that Russia has bought the rights! I wish I could find a subject for a companion piece for it. It is being done here as well.

I've been wondering if it would be an idea to write to Karajan suggesting that not he, but Solti and the LPO came over to Salzburg and did a perf. of the old 'binge'. After all it did have a huge success in Vienna when he did it and he helped with German text etc. and I don't believe its been done since. Though it was very well done in Munich about a year ago by an excellent chorus in English conducted by Loughran, not much came of it regarding further perfs. But the effect of a success with it in Salzburg could be far-reaching both for Solti and the work. He's done an excellent record of it. It and the *Te Deum*, which has had a renewed span of life, were both recorded three times last year. Enough about my goings-on. Now that there are distinct signs of spring why don't you both come here for a bit?

With our best love to you both.
as ever,
[William Walton]

9. Sir William Walton

18 April 1978.

Dear Walter,

I'm in gross defect in not writing you before, but both your P.C. and your letter arrived virtually at the same time, though the P.C. is dated 1.3.78 and the letter 8.3.78, but it is surprising that they've arrived at all considering the state of everything here. I'm delighted at the Viennese perfs. of B's Binge, better with an outside chorus and conductor than anything sent by the Brit. Con. I know nothing about Miltiades Caridis.

Odd you mentioning Rostropovich. I'm not on the best terms with him! You may remember that he gave a few years ago, a series of progs. of V/C Cons. [Cello Concertos] including idiotic ones like Sauguet – but not a mention of W.W. On reproaching him a year or two ago about this, he said he knew it very well, in fact taught it to his pupils. Then said 'You write me a new concerto and I play both' and I didn't feel terribly enthusiastic about the idea. However, thinking about it again, it has struck me that a *Poème* à la Chausson, might be an idea to do instead. You'll doubtless remember Ginette Neveu playing. What an artist! It's a pity there's no recording of it. Or is there? Talking of recordings, have you heard Kyung-Wha Chung's recording of mine. Superb! As good as Heifetz or Frances-catti. Perlman has said (but so far no signs) that he wants to record both the Vla and Violin.

With our best love to you both,
[William Walton]

7th October 1978.

Dear Walter,

What the post is like – an Express letter – 16 days! However, your letter is very welcome. It's no use going in for 'star' names for reciting *Façade*, like Gielgud, Larry, etc., much better to stick to people like Tear or P.P. [Peter Pears] who can follow the music. Anyhow they all, I suspect, think Noel C[oward] much better than Edith Sitwell! I don't know quite what to do about *Façade* II. Cathy Berberian has taken up both I and II and is excellent and she does them quite often here, at Florence, Reggio Emilia, etc. Now P.P. wants it for the next Aldeburgh Fest. but it seems a long time to wait till the end of June next year. It would I think be better to follow your advice and get in touch with Humphrey Burton, who I know quite well and would possibly fall for the idea and do it on the TV.

Much better proposition from all points of view if he will take it on.

I'm all for a longish piece from you on myself, with no holds barred! At least not too many. I've just written you a week or two ago about Beecham and Symph. I, so I won't say more.

I imagine you are having the same fantastic autumn as we are having here. Quite incredible – sun all and every day!

With our best love to you both,
[William Walton]

9. Sir William Walton

14 October 1978.

Dear Walter,

We came back three days [ago] and found your very welcome letter.

Your hard work on C.G. seems to have borne fruit up to a point, that being that the F. ballet is being revived. But I'm all for the *Façade* entertainment being linked with *Carmina Burana* which I liked very much when you played me a recording years and years ago – (more than I like to think of!). I must get another recording as I've not heard it since then.

We were invited to Siena for the 50th anniversary of the perf. there. It went very well, especially considering the implications of the Int. Soc. of Con. Mus. with which it was associated in 1928. Now it was done by Cathy Berberian, your telepathic suggestion. She has done it a number of times now, with Jack Buckley of the Brit. Con. in Rome helping out – quite a good combination. She has quite taken the piece to heart and is doing it a lot, all over the place, so C.G. would have no difficulty in getting her if the dates are all right. In fact I've just finished re-hashing eight old pieces from the original 30 odd, which I've had lying about, for her. They are quite up to standard now.

Apart from that, I've been my usual non-productive self. I think I shall do the brass band piece. The B.B.s are tremendously popular and if one wrote the right kind of piece, it would produce the PRS very vast and fast, so I'm told.

I am back on Sibelius due to Herbert's recordings of 4, 5, 6 & 7. Wonderful.

> With our best love to you both,
> [William Walton]

Received a record of Ida Haendel playing Vl. Conc. coupled with B. Britten – a really splendid early piece – if he had only continued in that vein.

1 February 1979.

Dear William,

You complain about the post: your letter of October 7 has just reached me.

Façade never was and never will be a piece for actors. It's for people who have rhythm and can play with words (incidentally, Elisabeth will probably do it well one of these days if she removes the last traces of Teutonic accent – you haven't heard her speak English for a long while, but in New York the critics were astonished that she was so eloquent in flawless English). Berberian is probably excellent by any standards, but does she do it in Italian, English or Barbarian?

I don't think it's a very good idea that it be done in Aldeburgh. I'll get in touch with Burton too, but am not quite at rest in my mind that he who loves to be seen on the screen, is quite musical and speaks clearly won't want to speak it himself.

I've crucified myself doing an article on Beecham and he'll probably rise from his grave (or Delius's) to persecute me for the rest of my living days. It's high time we met because we can exchange more in a ten minute chat than in two hours of correspondence.

Elisabeth joins me in sending love to you both.

[Walter Legge]

P.S. If only Angela Rippon [the BBC Television news reader] were musical – she's done *Peter and the Wolf* but that needs less and a different sort of skill – Sue would be able to build at least two more houses.

Postscript

Elisabeth Legge-Schwarzkopf

Walter Legge died on 22 March 1979, shortly before his seventy-third birthday. He had retired sixteen years before and was no longer with EMI or running the Philharmonia Orchestra, but confined his activities to producing my late recordings and master-minding my concert appearances during those same years. He did however insist on my joining him in giving master-classes, starting with Juilliard.

After the launch of Compact Disc in 1983, many older recordings were reissued in the new format, and an astonishingly large proportion of my husband's recorded legacy has now been made available on CD, covering the whole of his career in the studios, from 1932 until 1979. As I understand it, this activity has not been confined to EMI and their affiliated companies. It seems that since the earlier material has fallen out of copyright, much of it has been reissued by independent companies who specialise in vintage material – some of the older recordings are even available in competing editions.

As each year passes, Walter Legge's posthumous reputation as a towering figure in the world of music continues to grow. One can now clearly judge his achievements as the inspirer and conjuring producer of many and various great recordings. We can also now recognise the true perspective of his consistency in achieving the highest musical and technical standards. Today many more listeners than ever before are probably converted by his great 'classics', which will continue to provide illumination and pleasure for countless music lovers in the years to come.

I came to know most of the giant figures he worked with, and even to perform with some of them. I particularly want to remember Wilhelm Furtwängler, who for all his greatness proved to be a kind and fatherly friend.

After his last two performances of Beethoven's Ninth Symphony in Luzern (1954) we met next morning in the train to Zürich, when he smilingly said to me something like, 'Frau Schwarzkopf, I would like you to cross the Ninth off your list soon. All leading Ninth sopranos arrive after some years at the same decision, since they possess the kind of voices which can still grow into more dramatic possibilities.'

Recently I heard a broadcast of the Ninth and I thank Furtwängler for having saved me from further disaster by helping a younger artist round a dangerous corner.

Index of Names

Abravanel, Maurice, 269
Ackermann, Otto, 121, 205
Albanese, Licia, 52
Amara, Lucine, 206
Amis, John, 203
Ammermann, Liselotte, 39
Anda, Géza, 164
Andrésen, Ivar, 39
Andreva, Stella, 34, 35
Andrew, Helga [née Legge], 16
Andry, Peter, 211, 271, 272
Angeles, Victoria de los, 230, 242, 261
Ansermet, Ernest, 180, 184
Aranyi, Jelly d', 61, 62
Arnold, [Sir] Malcolm, 269
Ashton, [Sir] Frederick, 106, 171
Ayrton, Michael, 109

Backhaus, Wilhelm, 18, 191
Baddeley, Hermione, 208
Baillie, [Dame] Isobel, 113
Baker, [Dame] Janet, 269, 270, 271, 272, 273
Bantock, [Sir] Granville, 73, 74, 237
Baracchi, Aristide, 27
Barbirolli, [Sir] John, 50, 111, 114
Barrell, W.S., 181
Barshai, Rudolf, 225
Bartók, Béla, 46
Battistini, Mattia, 7
Bax, [Sir] Arnold, 70, 92, 93, 114
Bean, T.E., 213
Beard, Paul, 18, 19
Beecham, [Sir] Thomas, 12-14, 18, 19, 21, 22, 24-9, 31, 44, 48, 49, 52, 53, 60, 66-9, 70, 71, 74-83, 89, 90, 92, 94-9, 102, 112, 123, 238, 253, 274, 276
Beer, Sidney, 96, 123
Benda, Hans von, 184
Bennett, Richard Rodney, 260
Berberian, Cathy, 274, 275
Berger, Erna, 146
Berkeley, [Sir] Lennox, 269
Bernac, Pierre, 177
Bettoni, Vincenzo, 27
Bicknell, David, 142, 143
Bispham, David, 117
Blank, Jonny, 271

Blech, Harry, 258
Blech Quartet, 96
Bliss, [Sir] Arthur, 67
Bluth, Reimar, 251-3
Bockelmann, Rudolf, 39
Böhm, Karl, 43, 142, 146, 178, 236, 256
Borkh, Inge, 199
Bos, Conraad, 11
Bottazzo, Pietro, 236
Bottermund, Hans, 31
Boulanger, Nadia, 180
Boulez, Pierre, 250, 264
Boult, [Sir] Adrian, 27, 42, 45, 59, 63, 81, 82, 96, 111, 113, 270
Boyle, [Lord] Edward, 243
Brain, Aubrey, 122, 125
Brain, Dennis, 121-5
Britten, [Lord] Benjamin, 203, 204, 240-2
Brodsky, Adolf, 101
Brooke, Gwydion, 127
Bruckner, Anton, 72
Buckley, Jack, 275
Bülow, Hans von, 165
Bumbry, Grace, 247
Burg, Robert, 39
Burton, Humphrey, 274, 275
Busch, Adolf, 17, 45, 63
Busch, Fritz, 52
Busch, Hermann, 45
Busoni, Ferruccio, 73
Bustabo, Gyula, 177

Callas, Maria, 201, 205, 207, 208, 232-7, 259
Cameron, Basil, 96, 111
Caniglia, Maria, 52, 53
Cantacuzene [Lipatti], Madeleine, 180, 183-5
Cantelli, Guido, 226-30, 239
Cardus, [Sir] Neville, 12, 220
Caridis, Miltiades, 274
Caruso, Enrico, 6, 206, 231
Casals, Pablo [Pau], 9, 127, 128, 182, 231
Cassilly, Richard, 272
Cave, Alfred, 15
Cebotari, Maria, 175, 176
Ceccato, Aldo, 216, 235
Chaliapin, Feodor, 6, 7

Chamberlain, Neville, 13
Chapman, Diana, 216
Chemet, Renée, 117
Cherkassky, Shura, 191
Christoff, Boris, 256
Chung, Kyung-Wha, 274
Ciana, Fernanda, 49
Cigna, Gina, 51
Cinquevalli, Paul, 40, 41
Clark, Alfred, 97
Cluytens, André, 222
Coast, John, 248
Coates, John, 117
Cohen, Harriet, 70, 92, 93
Collingwood, Lawrance, 143
Collins, Anthony, 57
Conz, Bernhard, 250
Corbett, Geoffrey, 110
Corelli, Franco, 206, 209
Corena, Franco, 236
Cortot, Alfred, 9, 179
Coveney, John, 215
Coward, [Sir] Noël, 274
Curzon, [Sir] Clifford, 67, 244-6
Curzon, Lucille, 245
Cutner, Solomon, *see* Solomon

Dawson, Peter, 6, 117
Dean, Basil, 14
Deering, Albert, 200, 201
Dehn, Paul, 261, 265, 266
Denison, John, 270
Desmond, Astra, 34
Desormière, Roger, 109
Dobrowen, Issay, 175, 204, 205
Doktor, Karl, 266
Donalda, Pauline, 117
Douglas, Keith, 96
Downes, [Sir] Edward, 264, 266
Dua, Octave, 27
Dubois-Ferrière, Dr, 181
Dukas, Paul, 180

Eckersley, P.P., 9
Elgar, [Sir] Edward, 8, 10
Elman, Mischa, 6, 7, 223
Elwes, Gervase, 34
Emanuel, Phillip, 96, 97
Enescu, George, 179
Erb, Karl, 119
Evans, Nancy, 15, 16, 106

Faccio, Franco, 209
Fagan, Gideon, 96
Falkner, [Sir] Keith, 257
Feuermann, Emanuel, 30
Fischer, Edwin, 134, 139, 148, 164, 178
Fischer-Dieskau, Dietrich, 143, 152, 154-7, 230, 242, 244, 261
Flagstad, Kirsten, 41, 61, 131, 134, 137, 138, 140-3, 152, 166
Fleischer, Hans, 26

Fleischman, Ernest, 263
Flesch, Carl, 28, 177, 179, 222
Fonteyn, [Dame] Margot, 171
Formichi, Cesare, 49, 53
Fournier, Pierre, 177
Fowler, Edward, 199, 221
Francescatti, Zino, 223, 274
Frank, Alan, 258, 259, 272
Franklin, David, 51
Fuchs, Marta, 39, 119
Furtwängler, Wilhelm, 18, 31, 32, 38, 39, 56, 59, 131-67, 191, 198, 277, 278

Gaisberg, Frederick [Fred], 10, 11, 14, 78, 79, 86
Galli-Curci, Amelita, 6, 7, 17
Galliera, Alceo, 180, 181, 191
Gaubert, Philippe, 50
Gedda, Nicolai, 204, 205, 272
Geissmar, [Dr] Berta, 89, 131, 132, 133
Gerhardt, Elena, 11
Ghiaurov, Nicolai, 247
Ghiringhelli, [Dr] Antonio, 205, 229, 259
Gielgud, [Sir] John, 274
Gieseking, Walter, 189, 201
Gigli, Beniamino, 7, 18
Gingold, Hermione, 208
Giulini, Carlo Maria, 211, 213, 214, 247
Gluck, Alma, 6
Gobbi, Tito, 201, 206, 256
Goldberg, Szymon, 31
Goodare, Laureen, 104
Goodman, [Lord] Arnold, 271
Goossens, [Sir] Eugene, 111, 257
Goossens, Léon, 64
Gordon, Gavin, 109, 110
Gorlinsky, S.A., 173, 174, 229
Graf, Herbert, 236
Graham, Colin, 270-3
Gray, Cecil, 70
Gray, Stephen, 212
Greenfield, Edward, 204
Griffith, [Dr] Ivor, 236
Grinke, Frederick, 114
Grinke Quartet, 96
Gripenberg, Georg, 29
Grumiaux, Arthur, 109
Grümmer, Elisabeth, 146, 246
Gui, Vittorio, 256

Habich, Eduard, 26
Haendel, Ida, 200, 275
Hallé, [Sir] Charles, 101
Hambourg, Charles, 96
Hambourg, Mark, 116, 117
Hambourg, Michael, 116
Hammond, [Dame] Joan, 113
Harty, [Sir] Hamilton, 19, 32, 54, 112, 120
Hassall, Christopher, 256, 258
Heath, [Sir] Edward, 269
Heger, Robert, 214

Heifetz, Jascha, 21, 22, 28, 47, 81, 82, 83, 109, 223, 274
Hempel, Frieda, 8
Henderson, Roy, 51
Herbage, Julian, 229
Hess, [Dame] Myra, 58, 59, 96, 137, 139-42, 181
Heward, Leslie, 55, 96, 106, 110-14
Hilbert, [Dr] Egon, 133, 169
Hindemith, Paul, 124
Hofmann, Josef, 45
Holt, Harold, 95
Horenstein, Jascha, 264
Horowitz, Vladimir, 37, 40, 45, 171, 172
Hotter, Hans, 162, 199, 248
Huberman, Bronislaw, 28, 29
Hughes, John, 142
Hüsch, Gerhard, 11, 12, 84-6, 119
Hylton, Jack, 95

Inghilleri, Giovanni, 25
Ingpen, Joan, 133, 169
Ireland, John, 105, 113, 114
Iturbi, José, 40

Janowitz, Gundula, 247
Janssen, Erna, 90
Janssen, Herbert, 11, 25, 26, 39, 64, 65, 84, 86-92, 118, 119
Jecklin, Paul, 142, 181
Joachim, Joseph, 62
Jones, [Dame] Gwyneth, 248
Jones, Parry, 256
Joyce, Eileen, 106, 113, 114

Kabasta, Oswald, 42
Kajanus, Robert, 24, 68, 74
Karajan, Herbert von, 124, 126, 131, 133, 135, 142-4, 151, 167, 174, 180, 181, 186, 191, 198, 201-3, 205, 221, 232-4, 236, 240, 246, 250, 257-60, 264, 269, 270, 273, 275
Kautsky, Robert, 37, 74
Kell, Reginald, 126
Keller, Felicitas, 227
Kentner, Louis, 15, 104-6
Kersey, Eda, 255
Khachaturian, Aram, 223
King, James, 272
Kipnis, Alexander, 11, 26
Klemperer, Otto, 36, 124, 197, 198, 209-11, 222, 264
Kletzki, Paul, 190
Klose, Margarete, 39
Knappertsbusch, Hans, 250
Kobiger, Hugo, 31
Köchert, Ilse, 37
Kogan, Leonid, 223
Költsch, Harry, 251
Konetzni, Anny, 43
Konetzni, Hilde, 230
Köstlinger, Josef, 271

Koussevitzky, Serge, 23, 24, 44, 68, 74, 80, 81, 229
Krauss, Clemens, 162, 169
Kreisler, Fritz, 6, 7, 20-2, 28, 66, 218-20, 222, 226
Krips, Josef, 163
Kubelík, Rafael, 220, 256
Kulenkampf, Georg, 18, 62
Kullman, Charles, 26, 37
Kurtz, Efrem, 173, 174, 259

Labbette, Dora, 27
Lambert, Christopher [Kit], 107
Lambert, Constant, 103-10
Landowska, Wanda, 57
Langan, Kevin, 254
Larter, Douglas, 143, 200
Lefébure, Yvonne, 54
Legge, Harry, 5-8
Legge, Florence, 6, 7
Lehmann, Lotte, 34, 35, 37, 232
Leider, Frida, 38, 232
Lemnitz, Tiana, 12, 35
Leon, Mischa, 117
Lewis, Richard, 272
Lhévinne, Josef, 44, 45
Licette, Miriam, 15
Lieberson, Goddard, 193, 194
Lillie, Beatrice, 208
Lipatti, Dinu, 169, 179-85, 188-90, 192, 223
Lipatti, Madeleine, *see* Cantacuzene
Lissitschkina, Sinaida, 52
List, Emanuel, 35, 36
Liukkonen, Helmi, 69
Ljungberg, Göta, 69
Londonderry, Lord, 19
Lorenz, Max, 39
Loughran, James, 271, 273
Loveridge, Iris, 115
Lubin, Germaine, 49, 50
Ludwig, Christa, 209, 247
Luxon, Benjamin, 244

Maazel, Lorin, 248
McCormack, John, 120, 218
McCulloch, Derek, 100
McInnes, Campbell, 117
McLeod, John, 173, 174
Mahler, Gustav, 72
Malko, Nicolai, 47
Markevitch, Igor, 162, 190, 203, 204
Martinelli, Giovanni, 6, 7, 48, 51,
Matačić, Lovro von, 205, 207
Mathias, Gwen, 144
Matthews, Denis, 123, 197
Mayr, Richard, 34, 35
Melchior, Lauritz, 61, 231, 232
Melles, Carl, 250
Meneghini, Giovanni Battista, 233
Mengelberg, Willem, 17, 55
Menges, Herbert, 65

Menuhin, [Lord] Yehudi, 10, 62, 63, 64, 139, 179, 223, 243, 256, 267
Meyer, Kerstin, 205
Michel, E.A., 117
Milstein, Nathan, 223
Mittell, Brenchley, 142, 143, 197-200
Mödl, Martha, 199
Moeran, E.J., [Jack], 115
Moiseiwitsch, Benno, 6, 7, 15, 96, 113, 123, 189, 191
Mola, Norberto, 207
Molinari-Pradelli, Francesco, 233
Moore, Enid, 243
Moore, Gerald, 115-20, 230, 242-4, 262-4
Morris, Christopher, 271
Morris, Gareth, 126, 130
Mossel, Max, 117
Mottl, Felix, 165
Müller, Hans Udo, 84-6
Müller, Maria, 39
Munch, Charles, 179, 180
Musicescu, Floria, 179
Muti, Riccardo, 236
Mysore, Maharaja of, 180, 186-92

Nash, Heddle, 25, 27, 34
Neveu, Ginette, 177, 178, 256, 274
Newman, Ernest, 10, 11, 69, 70, 78, 118, 143, 237-9
Newman, Vera, 237, 239
Newton, Ivor, 15
Nicholson, Sydney, 110
Nikisch, Arthur, 165, 253
Nilsson, Birgit, 248
Nissen, Hans Hermann, 37
Noble, Dennis, 15

Oborin, Lev, 220
O'Connell, Charles, 96
O'Donnell, [Wing-Commander] R.P. 122
Oistrakh, David, 219-26
Oistrakh, Igor, 219, 224, 225
Oistrakh, Tamara, 219, 223, 225
Olczewska, Maria, 8
Olivier [Lord] Lawrence, 268, 274
Orff, Carl, 171
Osborn, Franz, 105

Pachmann, Vladimir de, 6, 7
Paderewski, Ignace [Ignaz] Jan, 6, 7,
Palmstierna, [Baron] Erik, 61
Panerai, Rolando, 236
Paray, Paul, 53
Parikian, Manoug, 148, 162
Parker, D.C., 32
Pears, [Sir] Peter, 123, 203, 204, 241, 242, 274
Perli, Lisa [Dora Labbette], 26, 27, 95
Perlman, Itzhak, 274
Petri, Egon, 45, 105, 112, 186-8
Pettitt, Stephen, 121
Piatigorsky, Gregor, 31

Pickles, Wilfred, 190
Pinza, Ezio, 25
Pölzer, Julius, 43
Pons, Lily, 25
Ponselle, Rosa, 35, 231
Ponzio, Léon, 27
Poulenc, Francis, 109, 177, 180
Preetorius, Emil, 38, 39, 172
Previn, André, 262, 263, 264, 266, 268, 270, 272
Prey, Hermann, 254
Price, Leontyne, 247
Pritchard, [Sir] John, 250
Prohaska, Jaro, 39
Prokofiev, Sergey [Serge], 57

Rachmaninov, Sergey [Serge], 17, 45, 65, 66
Rankl, Karl, 181
Rautawaara, Aulikki, 52
Ravaglia, Emilia, 236
Rawsthorne, Alan, 109, 110
Raybould, Clarence, 96
Reeves, George, 244
Reiner, Fritz, 34, 36
Reinhardt, Delia, 34
Reinking, Wilhelm, 172
Remedios, Alberto, 269, 270, 272
Reményi, Eduard, 29
Reszke, Jean de, 66
Rethberg, Elisabeth, 26, 34, 35
Richter, Evelyn, 225
Richter, Hans, 66, 101
Richter, Sviatoslav, 225
Rippon, Angela, 276
Ronald, [Sir] Landon, 30, 31, 117, 120
Rosenthal, Mauriz, 117
Rossi, Mario, 233
Rostropovitch, Mstislav, 225, 274
Roswaenge, Helge, 12, 39, 119
Rubinstein, Artur, 191
Ruffo, Titta, 7, 51, 231
Russell, Thomas, 131, 132, 133
Ryan, Pat, 112

Sabata, Eliana de, 235
Sabata, Victor de, 226, 227, 234, 235
Sala, Antoni, 114
Sarasate, Pablo de, 179
Sargent, [Sir] Malcolm, 34, 66, 96, 259, 262, 264, 266
Sawallisch, Mechthild, 252, 253
Sawallisch, Wolfgang, 124, 251-5
Schmidt, Heinrich, 247
Schnabel, Artur, 8, 185, 189, 221
Schnéevoigt, Georg, 69, 75, 78, 79
Schöffler, Paul, 26
Schorr, Friedrich, 11, 37, 128
Schulthess, Walter, 127, 128, 161, 167-9
Schum, Alexander, 43
Schumann, Clara, 62
Schumann, Elisabeth, 8, 34
Schwarzkopf, [Dame] Elisabeth, 12, 121,

123, 133, 139, 143-8, 150-2, 154-8, 171,
199, 201, 203, 205, 213, 214, 216, 221,
223, 225, 227, 230-3, 236, 239-44, 246,
252-4, 257, 259, 261, 265, 268, 272,
275-8
Schweitzer, Albert, 192-7
Scotti, Antonio, 231
Seefried, Irmgard, 134, 139
Serafin, Tullio, 117, 209, 233, 236
Shadwick, Joseph, 105
Shostakovitch, Dmitry, 223
Sibelius, Jean, 29, 68, 70-84, 202, 203
Siciliani, Francesco, 260
Siki, Béla, 190
Simon, Joanna, 231
Simonds, Bruce, 59
Sitwell, [Dame] Edith, 274
Smith, Cyril, 255
Smith, Leonard, 144
Söderström, Elisabeth, 205
Solomon [Solomon Cutner], 15, 189
Solti, [Sir] Georg, 272, 273
Somigli, Franca, 37
Soria, Dario, 173
Soria, Dorle, 173
Speiser, Elisabeth, 151
Stabile, Mariano, 37
Stein, Erwin, 204
Stern, Isaac, 223
Stiedry, Fritz, 162
Stignani, Ebe, 209
Stokowski, Leopold, 101-3, 123
Stoliarsky, Pyotr, 220
Storm, Erika, 90
Strauss, Richard, 44, 169, 175, 253, 254
Strehler, Giorgio, 235
Strobach, Hans, 43
Strobel, Heinrich, 157, 158
Supervia, Conchita, 8, 21
Susskind, Walter, 143, 177
Sutcliffe, Sidney [Jock], 126
Sutherland, Graham, 109
Szecheni, Countess, 6
Székely, Zoltán, 46
Szell, George, 63, 214-16, 254, 260, 263
Szigeti, Joseph, 22

Tamagno, Francesco, 48
Tauber, Richard, 18
Tear, Robert, 274
Tebaldi, Renata, 233, 258
Tetrazzini, Luisa, 6, 7,
Teyte, [Dame] Maggie, 113, 119, 120
Thibaud, Jacques, 9, 53, 177
Thurston, Frederick, 125, 126, 128

Tibbett, Lawrence, 50
Tietjen, Heinz, 38, 39
Tillett, Emmie, 243
Tippett, [Sir] Michael, 240, 262, 263, 269
Tobin, Marie, [née Legge], 5, 17, 86, 89, 90
Tonini, Antonino, 207
Tooley, [Sir] John, 271, 272
Toscanini, Arturo, 36, 37, 44, 60, 73, 90,
112, 117, 123, 125, 129, 143, 191, 197,
209, 228, 229, 254, 259
Trampler, Walter, 266
Tregurtha, C. Maxwell, 8, 9

Trussel, Jack, 272

Uhde, Hermann, 199
Unger, Gerhard, 199

Valois, [Dame] Ninette de, 106
Vaughan Williams, Ralph, 200
Vedder, Rudolf, 172
Villiers, Vera de, 60
Vito, Gioconda de, 200
Völker, Franz, 39

Wagner, Gertrud, 230
Wagner, Wieland, 246-50
Walter, Bruno, 8, 34
Walton, Bernard, 125, 126, 213
Walton, [Lady] Susana, 255, 257, 259, 273,
276
Walton, [Sir] William, 109, 199, 255-76
Waverly, Lord, 258
Weber, Ludwig, 199
Webster, [Sir] David, 102, 233, 258-60
Weingartner, Felix, 14, 22, 23, 41, 42, 59, 60
Weldon, George, 123
Widdop, Walter, 15
Wiedemann, Hermann, 37
Willison, David, 244
Winbergh, Gösta, 272
Windgassen, Wolfgang, 199
Withers, Jane, 129, 148, 152, 153, 159-61,
212-14
Wolf, Hugo, 72
Wolff, Fritz, 39
Wood, [Sir] Henry, 61, 73, 74, 99-101, 105,
113
Worm, Dieter, 251

Ysaÿe, Eugène, 53, 218, 224

Zaccaria, Nicola, 209
Zanasi, Mario, 206